Birds from Hell

History of the B-29

Wilbur H. Morrison

CENTRAL POINT, OREGON

Birds from Hell: History of the B-29

© 2001 Wilbur H. Morrison
Published by Hellgate Press

HELLGATE PRESS
P.O. Box 3727
Central Point, Oregon 97502-0032

(541) 245-6502
(541) 245-6505 fax
info@psi-research.com *e-mail*

Book designer: Constance C. Dickinson
Compositor: Jan O. Olsson
Cover designer: J. C. Young

Library of Congress Cataloging-in-Publication Data

Morrison, Wilbur H., 1915–
    Birds from hell : history of the B-29 / Wilbur H. Morrison.— 1st ed.
       p. cm.
    Includes bibliographical references.
    ISBN 1-55571-550-8 (cloth : alk. paper)
    1. World War, 1939–1945—Aerial operations, American. 2. World War, 1939–1945—Campaigns—Japan. 3. Morrison, Wilbur H., 1915– 4. World War, 1939–1945—Personal narratives, American. 5. B-29 bomber. 6. Bombardiers—United States—Biography. I. Title.

D790 .M6189 2001   2001016709

Hellgate Press is an imprint of Publishing Services, Inc., an Oregon corporation doing business as PSI Research.

Printed and bound in the United States of America
First Edition 10 9 8 7 6 5 4 3 2 1

 Printed on recycled paper when available.

Dedicated to
Pamela Rice

Table of Contents

Acknowledgments

I am particularly indebted to the late General Curtis E. LeMay, Major General (Ret.) John B. Montgomery and the late Major General Haywood S. Hansell, Jr., for their revelations about events involving themselves during World War II. They were explicit with personal details and placed no restrictions on their use although some of them were painful to recall. They gave no other writer this same privilege because I fought with them from the inception of the 20th Air Force in 1943 to the end of the war.

Many people contributed to this book but those whom I would expressly like to acknowledge include: retired Colonel Victor N. Agather, Guido J. Bianchi, the late Eldridge Beck, Ted P. Banks, Albert I. Carmona, Edwin A. Loberg, Denny D. Pidhayny, Allan Parker, Bobby Roth, Frank Rosenberger, Colonel (Ret.) Roscoe Norman, Thomas R. Vaucher, and Leroy J. Wieschaus.

Preface

There have been few books published about the 20th Air Force in addition to my personal memoir for young adults in 1960, *Hellbirds: The Story of the B-29s in Combat* and *Point of No Return: The Story of the Twentieth Air Force* in 1979. The latter is a historical work that primarily involves world figures and behind-the-scenes events dealing with this unique air force. Each book explores different aspects of the 20th Air Force. When I considered writing a new book, two objectives were foremost in my mind. First, I had acquired a vast amount of new material that was unavailable to me earlier, and secondly, I hoped to convey to a new generation of readers — as well as those of my generation — the truth about the air war in the Pacific during World War II.

Most Americans still believe that the two atomic bombs won the war against Japan. In truth, as this book will seek to prove, the war was won by August 1, 1945, before those bombs were dropped. It is not my intention to discount the effectiveness of nuclear weapons. As a former bombardier I am too knowledgeable about such weapons of destruction, and the dire threat they pose to mankind. But Japan's destruction by conventional weapons can now be duplicated on a massive nuclear scale all over the world. Modern warfare, even without nuclear weapons, has become so deadly that fear of nuclear weapons obscures the fact that powerful nations have the capability of destroying one another. Therefore, it behooves all of us to understand the true facts about Japan's defeat in 1945.

This book relies upon personal accounts to a large extent, including some of my own, because I was assigned to the 20th Air Force a month after its formation on April 10, 1944 until the 58th Wing was returned to the United States in October, 1945. These 18 months with the same organization gave me a unique opportunity to get to know the principals involved in its combat operations, and an unmatched opportunity to learn at first-hand the 20th Air Force's history.

Prior to World War II, I had been a radio newsman for six years, two of them with the National Broadcasting Company at WGY in Schenectady, New York. Later I was able to put my interviewing expertise to effective use in person-to-person interviews with hundreds of former comrades. There is no fictional dialogue because all of the principals were tape recorded as were most of the combat and ground personnel whose stories appear in this book.

After the war I spent hours with General Curtis E. LeMay, taping his recollections. Each time I was amazed by his total recall of events. My last meeting with him was at his home in Newport Beach, California, about a year before he died. He had long suffered from angina and his body was bloated with fluid that his heart could no longer eliminate in a normal manner. During the interview he constantly banged his pipe on an ashtray as he smoked incessantly. Then, he stopped after an hour, filled his pipe one more time, and lit it. He had answered all my questions forthrightly, and I had no more. I sat quietly, hoping some after-thought would occur to him. He turned as if to speak and I waited expectantly. But he said nothing, blowing a wreath of smoke around his head. When he did speak, there was a depth of bitterness in his voice that I had never heard before. "And to think that all I'll be remembered for is that comment I made about bombing the North Vietnamese into the stone age!"

"General, did you really say that?" I had heard it reported several times.

"It was in the Mac Kanter book about me. I didn't mean it the way it sounded, but I spoke in sheer exasperation about the way the Vietnam war was being fought."

I nodded. "I've made similar comments in private. For a man in your position, those words sounded cruel and heartless."

He looked at me pleadingly, making no effort to hide the tears. "Can't you do something, Wilbur?"

"I can and I will, but it won't be easy and it won't produce quick results. In my books about you I've tried to be objective, and I think I've succeeded. In the long run I believe my views will prevail." (His concern proved accurate. I read a half dozen obituaries after his death and most began with something like this: "The man who said we should bomb the North Vietnamese into the stone age died today." There were just casual references to his service in World War II and as head of the Strategic Air Command.)

I prepared to leave. "Curt, promise me one thing." He looked up and his eyes were dry. "Let's have no more talk about bombing anyone into the stone age. Okay?"

He grinned sheepishly, and nodded.

During World War II the Japanese called our B-29 Superfortresses the "birds from hell." They learned to fear and hate those who flew them. Hopefully, *Birds from Hell: History of the B-29,* will provide greater knowledge about a bomber command, superbly led by Curtis E. LeMay that achieved a phenomenal victory. I believe such a book is important because there is still an incredible misunderstanding about LeMay and the results he achieved against an implacable enemy.

Part I

The Superfortress Is Born

Introduction

"Board up!" Loberg yelled after he completed his visual inspection of our new B-29 Superfortress, assuring himself there were no hydraulic or fuel leaks, or obstructions to the control surfaces. We had flown in a B-17 Flying Fortress to the Boeing Airplane Company's plant at Wichita, Kansas, from our base at Walker Field in Victoria, Kansas, in early August, 1943, to pick up our group's first production airplane.

We had started to taxi out the previous day but our "Follow Me" had misjudged the span of our 141-foot wing and the right tip had collided with a brick wall, much to Loberg's disgust. We had to remain another night in Wichita while the tip was replaced.

I scrambled up the short ladder that led to the flight deck and squeezed myself past Major Edwin A. Loberg in the pilot's seat and Captain B. K. Thurston in the co-pilot's seat. They were the only members of our crew with extensive combat experience, having flown 87 missions together in the South Pacific as members of the 11th Bombardment Group during World War II's earliest months. Our navigator, Lieutenant Richard G. W. Renz, had served a year flying combat patrols with the 6th Air Force guarding the approaches to the Panama Canal, and I had spent four-and-a-half months in a similar capacity as a bombardier. Dick and I had come out of the entertainment world. He had been a singer in stage shows and on radio while I had been an NBC radio announcer for WGY in Schenectady, New York. Our flight engineer, Lieutenant Robert C. Albert, was a graduate engineer in civilian life. Now we had been brought together to form a crew for the United States Air Forces' newest bomber.

As the B-29's bombardier, I sat in the nose of the plane, with curving panes of Plexiglas surrounding me on all sides except the rear, providing me with unobstructed forward vision. There was no extra room for my six-foot body, with the Norden bombsight in front of me and the control panel on my left, and a stowed gunsight on my right. I adjusted my headset to listen to Loberg and Thurston as they went through the checklist prior to take-off as a similarly equipped mechanic listened outside.

"Start one," Loberg called.

Number one engine's 16½ foot four-bladed propeller, the largest ever installed on a production airplane, moved jerkily at first. Then the engine belched smoke and the propeller began to spin, becoming just a blur as Loberg slowly advanced the throttle. He repeated the sequence with the other three engines, running them to full power to assure himself that these Wright Cyclone 3350 engines were performing properly. Designed with two rows of 18 cylinders to develop 2,200 horsepower for take-off, they had revealed an unpleasant characteristic. They were so compact, with front and rear rows of cylinders, that there was an insufficient flow of air around the cylinders to properly cool them. Several B-29s had been lost due to uncontrollable engine fires.

The B-29 had two superchargers for each engine, the first time more than one had ever been used, to provide each engine with air at sea-level density to permit it to "breathe" better at high altitudes.

Prior to boarding up, most of the crew had helped to "pull through" each propeller while another crew member listened at each turbo exhaust for the telltale "swish" indicating an exhaust valve was unseated. In time, it was learned; a bad exhaust valve could cause the engine to "swallow the valve." When this happened an engine failure resulted and the cylinder had to be replaced. If this condition was not noted, during combustion the unseated valve would cause a "blowtorch effect" on the valve's stem that would warp it and break it off. Once this happened, the engine rapidly broke up and a fire could be expected.

Several "fixes" were in the design stage to resolve these basic problems that led to over-heating. Boeing engineers, working with their counterparts at Wright, later designed a system to increase the oil flow to the exhaust valves, and the engine cowl flaps were re-designed to bring in more cooling air through the nacelle, while baffles were installed to direct a stream of air on the exhaust valves to keep them cooler. Cuffs were also added to the propeller blades near the hub to act as fans to drive more air into the engine's cowling. But all of these refinements were not included in the early airplanes, and it would be months before they were, resulting in increased anxiety for crews during take-offs when engines were running as maximum power.

While I listened to the sequence of starting the engines, I recalled with a shudder Loberg's description of a Boeing's Chief of Flight Test, Edmund T. Allen's last flight in the second XB-29 on February 18, 1943. Engine fires had been occurring on an almost weekly basis since Allen flew the first B-29 on September 21, 1942. But the high priority B-29 was desperately needed on the world's war fronts and test flights continued while remedies were sought to resolve the engine's cooling problems. The most intense portion of an engine fire was caused by the magnesium accessory housing because this material burns at an extremely hot temperature. Once a fire started, if the extinguishers failed to contain it in the forward section of the engine, it was impossible to stop. After the housing ignited, the fire usually burned through the engine's firewall in to the wing, causing it to break off. From the time the housing caught fire, a crew had one-and-a-half minute to bail out. The few survivors said the gyrational forces of the spinning airplane pinned them to a given spot and they were unable to move. They had managed to escape only when their airplane broke apart and they were hurled free of the wreckage. Magnesium was designated because it was one-third lighter than steel. Design goals for this new engine specified that it develop one horsepower for each pound of weight. Therefore, weight control was of paramount importance and magnesium was chosen because of its relative lightness for the housing and crankcase.

But magnesium also has the unfortunate characteristic of breaking up under certain vibration conditions, and it burns at an extraordinarily high temperature. During ground tests the usual defects did not appear as serious drawbacks, but in flight crank cases lasted only a few hours before the engine tore itself apart. Later crankcases were made of aluminum, which partially solved the engine's problems.

The XB-29 with veteran test pilot Allen at the controls, took off normally at 12:16 P.M. but then a fire started in the number one engine's nacelle. They were flying at 5,000 feet so Allen had some maneuvering room. He threw the propeller feathering switch, closed the throttle and told the flight engineer, Fritz Moh, to close the cowl flaps and discharge the carbon dioxide fire extinguisher to smother the flames.

Seattle tower operators listened anxiously as Allen called, "Fire in number one engine. Coming in. Had fire in engine and used CO_2 bottle and think we have it under control."

"Tell us if at any time you think you need fire equipment," the tower operator replied.

Allen remained silent as he maneuvered the airplane in a gentle right hand turn, heading north in the vicinity of Sumner, a community south of Seattle.

Five minutes later Allen called again. "Renton, 2,400 feet descending, request immediate landing clearance. Number one engine on fire, propeller feathered and trouble not serious. Order crash equipment to stand by."

"Roger," the tower operator replied. "Cleared to land, wind south ten, runway thirteen."

Fire engine sirens alerted everyone that a plane was in trouble, and anxious eyes peered skyward although few could see the B-29.

In the tower there was a state of breathless suspense as they prayed silently that the veteran pilot would bring the plane in safely. He had done so many times in the past during similar emergencies and he seemed almost invulnerable. One of the world's most experienced test pilots, Allen didn't look the part. Thin, small-framed, and mostly bald, he was a philosopher and a psychologist. A vegetarian, the esthetic Allen had long been a Yoga practitioner.

Allen called the tower two minutes later. "Lake Washington Bridge, 2,500 feet; correction 1,500 feet."

Those in the tower watched the plane as it continued its descent, everything seemingly normal except for the smoke pouring from the number one engine as the B-29 flew over Seattle's business district at 1,200 feet. But now bits of metal began falling from the airplane, and the smoke increased in volume.

In the same voice he had used all along, Allen called the tower again. "Have fire equipment ready. Am coming in with wing on fire."

The airplane continued on its southerly heading towards Boeing Field but it was steadily losing altitude, and the plane was now burning brightly. Pieces of the de-icer system and nose clamps fell from the wing. Flaming gasoline ate into the plane's wing and fuselage as flames traveled along the wing's leading edge as the gasoline exploded.

Control tower operators listened with horror as they heard an interphone conversation from the bomber. "Allen, better get this thing down in a hurry! The wing spar is burning badly."

It was obvious that Allen was using all the skill of his long years as a test pilot but the propellers were just windmilling as the remaining engines lost power. The B-29 gradually lost altitude while the pilots remained in their seats to keep it in a level altitude.

Radio Operator Relation bailed out just as the plane's propellers struck the top of high-tension wires. His body struck the last wire, his parachute ballooning after him, as it snagged across the wires. There was a blinding flash as the wires short-circuited.

Allen tried to gain a few feet of altitude, forcing the B-29 into a left turn at building level.

Observers on the ground noted with tear-filled eyes that flames enveloped the cockpit. The huge plane smashed into a cattle chute at a meatpacking plant but incredibly continued on course in a steep bank until it crashed into the fifth floor of a brick building. The plane exploded, killing all on board.

"Pilot to bombardier."

Loberg interrupted my reverie, and I quickly acknowledged.

"Close bomb-bay doors."

"Roger." I closed the doors as our B-29 started to move towards the end of the runway. I listened anxiously to the engines but they were positioned so far behind me on the wing that all I could hear was a deep throbbing of leashed power. When Loberg released the brakes, the engines broke into a full-throated roar and the B-29 headed down the long runway, rocking gently on its tri-cycle landing gear until it reached flying speed and its 120,000 pounds lifted cleanly from the runway and we were airborne. This was not my first B-29 take-off, but I only had a few hours in the air in the Superfortress. Our 462nd Group's first three camouflaged-painted airplanes, instead of our normal complement of 40 B-29s, had spent most of their time in hangars undergoing repairs instead of flying its crews. Our new airplane was bare aluminum instead of olive drab like all previous Air Force airplanes. Officials used to think that camouflage colors were needed for concealment from enemy aircraft. Experience in the early days of the war proved that the paint job was worthless. Air Force headquarters gave orders that all new airplanes would have bare aluminum surfaces. Without paint they weighed several hundred pounds less which increased their range.

I had no duties on our flight to Walker Air Force Base so I tried to relax in my bombardier's seat. I had returned in May from Talara, Peru, in South America where I had flown patrol missions with a crew back and forth to the Galapagos Islands. Our flights were part of a tight perimeter defense on the southern approaches to the Panama Canal. Our leaders in Washington had feared since the Japanese bombed Pearl Harbor on December 7, 1941, that they would send a task force of carriers to bomb the canal, or use submarines to attack Allied shipping. I had been commissioned September 5, 1942, and assigned to a B-17 provisional group headed for England later that fall. In our final phase my pilot had taken ill and we were kept behind while the others went to England and later to North Africa. Along with a squadron trained at Gowen Field in Idaho, our crew had been sent to Panama first and then to Peru. In May, six bombardiers in the squadron received orders to return to the States with the 40th Bombardier Group then stationed at Salinas, Ecuador. Our squadron commander sought to retain us but he was sharply rebuked by orders out of Washington. Years later I learned the reason for our sudden departure. General Henry H. Arnold, chief of staff of the United States Army Air Forces, was establishing the first wing for the new B-29 Superfortress and he sought the AAF's most experienced people to man it. At this stage, such men were few in number. Only a small percentage of officers had command experience and those who did had already served more than their fair share in combat theaters. But Arnold was rapidly building the Air Forces to a strength of 2.5 million men from a pre-war total of slightly more than 11,000 personnel, including 1,200 regular and reserve officers. The fact that he eventually achieved his goal is one of the miracles of World War II.

My thoughts were abruptly brought back to reality when Loberg directed our B-29 into Walker's flight pattern and announced over the intercom, "We've got a reception committee waiting for us."

I looked down and sure enough the ramp was filled with hundreds of cheering men as we flew the down-wind leg and prepared to land. Our mission in life, wherever it led us, had reached a minor milestone with our delivery of the first production B-29 to our group. After landing Loberg taxied up to our hangar and parked. He was first out of the airplane as Colonel Richard H. Carmichael hurried over. "Where have you guys been? I expected you yesterday."

Loberg grinned broadly as he saluted our group commander. He knew Carmichael's query was rhetorical because he had wired him following the incident with the wing tip.

"How does she fly?" Carmichael said.

"Fine," Loberg said. "We've got a great airplane — the best in the whole damn Air Force."

In the months ahead Loberg often regretted his overly optimistic assessment of the B-29 Superfortress. But we all knew that it was being rushed into combat at least a year before it was fully developed due to the urgency of the war situation in the Pacific theater. Fortunately none of us realized the price we would pay for being guinea pigs.

Chapter 1

Hangar Queens

General Arnold had been obsessed by the growth of Germany's Luftwaffe all through the 1930s, and he had fought to build up America's bomber fleet despite strong opposition due to the Isolationist sentiment throughout most of the United States.

Boeing's prototype for the B-17 Flying Fortress made its first flight in 1935. Despite its crash in October, Arnold and other bombardment pioneers retained their faith in strategic warfare and later persuaded the War Department to order 13 more.

Even as late as the 1939 Congress, responding to the nation's anti-war feelings, still refused to appropriate funds for long-range bombers because they were considered offensive weapons that might draw the United States in to the war in Europe.

General George C. Marshall, who assumed command of the Army as chief of staff on September 1, 1939, had the courage and vision to accept the recommendations of the Army Air Corp's chief, "Hap" Arnold, the day after Adolf Hitler's armies invaded Poland. He quickly realized the validity of Arnold's plans for a strategic air force and endorsed them, saying, "This establishes for the first time a special mission for the Air Corps."

Arnold was appalled later to receive orders from the War Department to cancel the B-17 Flying Fortress program. He told intimates that strategic air warfare had received its worst setback in years. To his relief, the program was later reinstated.

The growing war in Europe made a more rapid buildup of America's defenses imperative and Congress specifically set aside $4.7 million to procure five experimental bombers. Arnold used part of these funds to order a new very long-range bomber. Several companies made proposals in the spring of 1940 after Nazi Germany had conquered Denmark and Norway and Hitler had sent his armies in a blitzkrieg attack through Holland into Belgium and then to the outskirts of Paris.

President Franklin D. Roosevelt reacted by sending a message to Congress asking for production of 50,000 airplanes a year.

Boeing had earlier used its own funds to develop a new bomber and it had gone through several design stages until the XB-29 was approved by the Army Air Corps September 6, 1940. Boeing was ordered to build two prototypes, later increased to three, plus a static-test article for ground testing. The Consolidated-Vultee Aircraft Company received a similar contract for parallel development of the XB-32 but its many problems prevented its use in combat until almost the end of the war. But the B-29 had now developed into a 120,000-pound airplane with a wing raised to the mid-fuselage position and with a nose wheel instead of the traditional tail wheel.

At first engineers believed it would be necessary to use powered "boosts" on the flight controls because the ailerons, rudder and elevator were the largest ever placed on a practical aircraft. By testing models in wind tunnels it was determined that aerodynamically balanced control surfaces would give pilots easy direct control of the airplane and the important "pilot feel" was thus achieved. The B-29's four Wright Duplex 3350 Cyclone engines, largest ever hung on an airplane, developed 8,800 horsepower for take-off. The B-29 program was expected to be the greatest single industrial undertaking ever underwritten by the War Department.

Arnold had to defend the airplane because critics in the War Department resented the huge allocation of funds and resources needed for this one project. He wrote Robert A. Lovett, Assistant Secretary of Air, that the B-29 was the only weapon that the United States could use against Japan in the event of war without costly preliminary operations.

Anti-war activists were joined by, noted flier and national hero, Charles A. Lindbergh, who spoke out strongly against American involvement in Europe. Millions of Americans applauded his isolationist views. As the star of "America First," he asked whether America should join corrupt nations in an absurd war or would it remain true to its ideals. The nation was seriously divided and Lindbergh's comments only aggravated the situation.

Boeing completed the XB-29's engineering design in the spring of 1941, but it was obvious that the normal five year span for designing and flight testing a new aircraft would have to be reduced by at least a year if the bomber was to meet General Arnold's schedule.

Models of the XB-29 were tested during the spring of 1941 in wind tunnels at the University of California's Institute of Technology, and the National Advisory Committee for Aeronautics. Meanwhile, at Boeing's Seattle plant a full-scale plywood mock-up had been built in secrecy and engineers completed their aerodynamic research for the B-29's detailed design in order to start producing the first airplane. Army Air Corps officials from Wright Field inspected the mock-up and were so impressed that on May 17 they placed an order for 14-service test XB-29s and 250 production airplanes. Never before had such a revolutionary airplane been ordered in quantity prior to extensive flight tests. Boeing officials were in a state of shock, reminding Air Corps officials that tooling would have to begin at the factory long before the XB-29 made its first flight.

This was a dangerous precedent, fraught with endless problems, because all new airplanes were redesigned in part after deficiencies were noted during flight tests. Everyone agreed that there were risks, but the desperate need for a new long-range bomber outweighed the risks. Boeing and Army officials agreed that changes would not be made in production in order to keep the lines moving, but later at modification centers.

While these decisions wee being made in the fall of 1940 and early the following year the War Department became concerned whether Great Britain, fighting the Nazis alone in Europe, could hold out. Arnold readily agreed that the B-29 would be inadequate to perform its strategic mission if bases in England were denied the United States. He told his staff that an entirely different long-range bomber would be needed: one with a 10,000-mile range and a five-ton bomb load capable of hitting targets in Germany from American bases. By now Boeing had had the B-29 under development for two years, but its maximum range was about 4,000 miles and not with a 10-ton bomb load.

But the war in Europe had changed its character after the Royal Air Force defeated Hitler's Luftwaffe in the fall of 1940 in its attempts to bomb England into submission prior to an invasion across the English Channel. The war situation improved even more for England and the United States on June 22, 1941, when Hitler's armies invaded the Soviet Union and the U.S.S.R. became an ally with England in its fight to defeat Nazi Germany.

Boeing President P. G. Johnson was in Dayton, Ohio, May 7, 1941, with company treasurer Harold Bowman, Attorney William Allen and sales Manager F. B. Collins. They had returned to their hotel suite after meeting with Air Force procurement officials to discuss the cost of 14 pre-production B-29s for an accelerated flight-test program. They had barely settled down when the phone rang. It was General Arnold calling from Washington. "I would like," he said, "for you to recommend how American can build the greatest number of bombers in the shortest time."

"That's a pretty big order," Johnson replied. "I'll have to think it over."

"Call me back in the morning," Arnold said and he hung up.

Johnson explained to his staff what Arnold had requested and shook his head in disbelief.

The next morning while Johnson was shaving, Collins called to him. "P. G., don't forget to call General Arnold."

Johnson sat down and began to scribble notes to establish the framework for the most ambitious aircraft production program in the history of the United States. When he called Arnold he read his scribbled recommendations: 1. Establish the principle of one or two proven production models of heavy bombardment airplanes, 2. Arrange for the models selected to be built in factories having facilities now used for other purposes, 3. Give first priorities to such factories for materials and machine tools, and 4. Continue the development of replacement types for the models selected so that in time they can become the production model.

Arnold liked the plan and ordered it to be put into effect. The plan was followed precisely and proved to be one of the key decisions that contributed to America's ultimate victory.

After the United States War Department gained more confidence in Great Britain's survival, the B-29 program received a new lease on life. Boeing's May letter of intent for 250 airplanes wasn't signed until September 1941, and plans were initiated to build the bomber in the new government-owned facilities at Boeing's Wichita plant. The contract was increased to 500 airplanes in January 1942. This decision to go into mass production was taken a full year before the first airplane took to the air!

During the development phase it became apparent that manually operated guns, such as those used on the B-17 and B-24, would not work satisfactorily in the pressurized cabin proposed for the B-29. But incorporation of General Electric's fire-control system added more than 200,000 engineering hours in structural changes to the airframe. This was approved to permit the bomber to fly unescorted missions and to enable gunners to concentrate firepower from one or more gunners' stations at an attacking fighter. Pressurization was limited to crew positions fore and aft of the wing, connected by an overhead tunnel over the two bomb bays. The tail gunner had his own pressurized section.

Fortunately the B-29 went through most of its basic changes on the drawing boards before it went into production. The bomb load was set at 20,000 pounds, but range and speed had to be reduced from the original specifications to keep the airplane's maximum weight at 135,000 pounds. (Later, on some missions, the gross weight exceeded 140,000 pounds.) The British experience against the Luftwaffe mandated more guns and ammunition, armor plate and radar antenna than originally anticipated.

Despite these additions the airplane remained a sleek and aerodynamically "clean" airplane because the original lines were incredibly good for that era. But Boeing engineers were forced to increase the wing loading to 70 pounds per square foot — twice the B-17's wing loading — that caused Air Corps officials increasing concern because of higher take-off and landing speeds.

After the Army Air Force came into being March 9, 1942, replacing the old Army Air Corps designation, Arnold called for development of a new master plan on which to base future aircraft procurement. The old plan had called for deployment of 24 B-29 groups to be used against Axis Europe but the new plan specified that all B-29s be used against Japan because they would not become available in time to make a significant impact on the war in Europe. The plan stated that the B-17s and B-24s already in use in Europe were adequate to do the job because their shorter range was not a drawback, whereas longer-range B-29s were essential to reach targets in the Far East. A vital section of the new plan stated, "Considering the great distances involved, it is apparent that the majority of the bombing effort against Japan must be carried out by long-range bombers of the B-29 type. And these will not be available in quantity until late in 1944."

Just as the carefully laid plans were set for B-29 deployment, the plane itself became immersed in problems. The cabin pressurization system alone had innumerable failures because of production defects in riveting the cabin, and blisters began to blow out at the gunners' stations. All new airplanes develop problems but the B-29 was so revolutionary in concept that everything had to be developed from scratch. One-by-one the problems were eliminated. Even the pressurization system later became so effective that this same basic system was still in use in jetliners decades later. The air-position indicator, although crude by later standards, became the forerunner of the inertial navigation system that helped to put astronauts on the moon. The B-29 system was developed to navigate over vast distances, under conditions of radio blackout and overcast skies, when celestial navigation was impossible. Many electronic, radar, fuel and safety systems in common use decades later were developed, at high cost and with great ingenuity, by Boeing for the B-29.

At the Casablanca Conference in January 1943, President Roosevelt told Allied leaders that China must be given sufficient support to keep her in the war. Japan's armies in Burma had isolated China except for aerial supply from Assam, India, over the Hump to Yunnan. He reminded the Combined Chiefs of Staff that China's plight would become desperate by summer.

Roosevelt's strong stand on China moved the Combined Chiefs to agree to re-establish land communications with China and find a way to increase the flow of supplies to Chiang Kai-shek's armies. Churchill reminded the president that such action might impact on the North African campaign then underway, and American air leaders like General Spaatz were concerned because diversion of heavy bombers to the African campaign had already weakened the strategic effort against Nazi Germany from England. But a Combined Bomber Offensive against Germany was approved at the meeting. The Combined Chiefs sought assignment of B-29 groups to England, but General Arnold reminded them that Superfortresses would not be available for any theater prior to the spring of 1944.

Although the Combined Chiefs, Roosevelt, and Churchill had discussed the Combined Bomber Offensive against Germany in depth, this was the first meeting where Allied leaders discussed the bombing of Japan in similar detail. General Marshall said that it was the Army Air Force view that Japan's industries were vulnerable to air attacks, and that heavy, sustained attacks would drastically reduce Japan's war effort.

Roosevelt replied that he viewed even limited bombing of Japan as having a great uplifting impact on the Chinese people. He suggested that 200 to 300 bombers be sent to China, not necessarily B-29s, because he knew they were not available. The president said he realized such a force would create a supply problem but that they could operate out of bases in India, refuel in China, and fly to and from Japanese targets. Such attacks, he said, would prove useful to the war effort.

Marshall expressed his doubts about the feasibility of the president's plan, reminding him that supplying these bombers would be terribly expensive and a drain on transport aircraft needed elsewhere.

Roosevelt refused to accept Marshall's arguments. At the close of the conference, Roosevelt wired Chiang Kai-shek that General Arnold would come to Chunking as his personal representative to discuss further American aid. He said he was determined that Major General Claire L. Chennault's newly designated 14th Air Force would be increased so it could take the offensive against the Japanese who occupied most of China, including its principal cities.

The president later compounded General Arnold's and General Marshall's problems when he met in Washington with Chennault who presented Roosevelt with his personal plan for taking the offensive in China. Roosevelt was receptive but he failed to realize that the demands of the European theater were straining the ability of the Army Air Forces to fight in several of the world's war theaters simultaneously at a time when the Air Forces were just beginning to build up a war footing. Roosevelt's desire to help China overruled the commonsense realities of the world situation. Roosevelt made unrealistic promises to Chennault and Chiang Kai-shek that the Air Forces couldn't possibly meet. The situation was compounded by quarrels between Lieutenant General Joseph W. Stilwell, American theater commander, Chiang's chief of staff, and General Chennault. They could not agree on a realistic overall strategy although they were unanimous in agreeing that China was necessary if Japan was to be defeated. "If we are going to bomb Japan we will have to have China bases," each said in a rare moment of agreement. Later events proved them wrong.

Chennault's 14th Air Force increased its attacks on the Japanese after more transport aircraft, authorized at the Casablanca conference, were assigned to Hump operations. The serial route began to carry 10,000 tons of supplies a month, and an offensive was approved to oust the Japanese from Burma after the fall monsoon. Although two Chinese divisions were sent to the new front in Burma to join British troops, the fighting became intense and more prolonged than anyone could have foreseen at the time. Despite savage fighting in a series of bloody battles that started in the fall of 1943 under intolerable jungle conditions, Japanese units were not driven out of Burma until January 1945.

Some of the uncertainties about prospects for ultimate victory were dissipated after Germany's 6th Army surrendered in 1943 at Stalingrad. This major defeat proved to be the turning point of the war in Russia. The ending of the war in North Africa on May 12, the ouster of Premier Mussolini on July 25, and the Allied landings in Italy after Sicily was overrun all pointed to the fact that the Germans were not invincible. The war against Japan had shown a sharp improvement after the United States Army and Marines drove the Japanese out of most of the South Pacific following the decisive defeat of the Japanese Navy in 1942 at the Battle of Midway. The successful defense by American forces of Guadalcanal and its evacuation by Japanese forces in early 1943 was another critical Allied victory. Although it wasn't realized at the time, the Japanese had achieved their maximum penetration of the American-Australian lifeline. It was all downhill for Japan's armed forces after 1943, yet the war still raged on more fiercely than ever.

Brigadier General Kenneth B. Wolfe, who had been assigned by General Arnold to take charge of the B-29 program as a special project, had a reputation as a soft-spoken, but hard-hitting leader who achieved results. Short, bald, with prominent ears, Wolfe was a man of action without an ounce of fat on his lean 165-pound frame. One of his first steps was to take over the flight test program from Boeing. He assigned Colonel Leonard "Jake" Harman as flight test officer. In June 1943 Wolfe was named commanding general of the 59th Wing and charged with preparing it for combat operations the following year. Harman, conducting flight tests at Wright Field, and 2d Lieutenant Colonel Abram Olson, flew the third B-29 for the first time on June 6, 1943. Then on the 25th they flew it to Wichita. He wired Wolfe that the B-29 was the greatest airplane he had ever flown.

Brigadier General LaVerne "Blondie" Saunders, former commander of the 11th Bombardment Group, and air advisor to Admiral Halsey during the Solomons campaign, joined Wolfe's command to provide some much-needed combat experience. Wolfe was basically a production man and knew little or nothing about combat operations.

I had originally been assigned to the 40th Group (Very Heavy Special) when I returned from South America. I had actually joined the group in Salinas, Ecuador, and returned to the States with it. The group's commander, Colonel Lewis R. Parker, had extensive patrol experience but no real combat experience against the Germans or the Japanese. We were intrigued to learn one day that he had mysteriously disappeared and rumors were prevalent that he had been fired. The truth was not revealed until after the war. Parker was sent to England to fly several missions over Germany to gain combat experience but was shot down and became a prisoner of war. Out of fear that the Germans would know of his B-29 background with the 58th Wing — he was privy to some of its top secrets — he became a non-person and fortunately survived the war in a German prison camp.

With so much experienced personnel in the 40th Group, it was decided by Wolfe's headquarters that the group would be split with half of the crews and ground personnel sent to the 462nd Group at Walker Air Force Base, Victoria, Kansas.

I was one of those who was transferred and assigned to a crew. Shortly thereafter I was appointed the 769th Squadron's bombardier and designated for Major Loberg's crew. I was pleased because Loberg was friendly and easy going, matching his Norwegian ancestry. We were both the same age and at 28, two of the oldest men in the squadron.

After Loberg returned from the South Pacific in March 1943, he was assigned to a B-17 group in Pendleton, Oregon, where he helped train raw crews for England. He then received a message to report to Marietta, Georgia, to join a group of former members of his 11th Group and the 19th Group. While on a brief visit to his home in Wisconsin in May, Loberg received a wire to report to Pratt, Kansas, instead of Marietta.

In mid-July he became one of the first Army pilots to check out in the B-29. Such was his skill in flying four engine bombers that he completed his qualification as a B-29 airplane commander in one afternoon. That morning he had checked out in the B-26 Marauder, an older bomber that had been assigned to Pratt because its only B-29 was almost constantly out of commission. The 40th Group had been given 35 B-26s supposedly because they resembled the B-29's flight characteristics. Actually the only similarity was that both used a nose wheel. It was a "hot" aircraft and the earlier pre-war models had a six-foot shorter wingspan than the ones now assigned to the 58th Wing. The B-26 had been nicknamed "The Flying Prostitute" because she had no visible means of support, and "The Baltimore Whore" due to the fact that the Glenn L. Martin Company of Baltimore produced the airplane.

James H. Doolittle, a veteran pilot dating back to World Ward I, and a phenomenal racing pilot between the great wars, applied for return to active duty in 1940 and his request was gratefully accepted by General Arnold. His first assignment as a major was to fly the new Martin B-26 and make a private report to Arnold. The Air Corps chief had authorized the plane's production but pilots had become leery of flying it because quite a number had crashed. In particular, most crashes occurred on take-off after one engine failed. Martin engineers insisted that the airplane could take off on one engine, and demonstrated this capability. Air Corps pilots remained skeptical, and reports kept coming to Arnold that they were afraid to fly it even though it admittedly had speed and maneuverability characteristics that no other American bomber of that period could match.

Doolittle, one of the greatest pilots of the century, flew the B-26 a number of times, found it an excellent flying machine but with a tendency to be unforgiving in the hands of anyone but a skilled pilot. He filed a report with Arnold and recommended that production of the aircraft be continued, with the intensive flying program to convince pilots that when the B-26 was properly flown, it was safe as any other airplane. Pilots remained skittish about the B-26, pointing out that few had Doolittle's skill — which was true — and that it was just too "hot" for the average pilot.

Later, Doolittle made a recommendation that Arnold heartily approved. Jacqueline Cochran, famed aviatrix during the 1930s, had become a service pilot for the Army Air Corps and would later serve as director of the Women's Air Force Service Pilots in 1943. She was one of a growing number of women and the smallest and most feminine of the service pilots who would put on a demonstration while their male counterparts stood on the ground with their mouths open, literally shamed the doubters by not only performing every maneuver in the book, but deliberately shutting down one engine just before the airplane was ready to leave the ground and completing the take-off on one engine! Opposition to flying the airplane largely disappeared, although some fear remained, and the B-26 continued to have a high loss rate. This was particularly true at Pratt.

Captain J. S. Slack, who had been a B-26 instructor at Barksdale Field in Louisiana, had accumulated about 2,500 flying hours before he joined the 40th at Pratt and later transferred to Walker. He described some of his experiences in checking out Russian pilots in the B-26. Under Lend-Lease the B-26 was sent to Russia in large quantities and Russian pilots came to the United States to check out in them, and then fly them home through Alaska.

Slack related how he had taken one pilot up to 10,000 feet to demonstrate the various controls and flying attitudes of the aircraft. By voice and gestures he told the Russian pilot to take over the controls. The pilot pushed the nose down into a steep slide to treetop level, put the plane through slow rolls and pulled out just above the trees. Slack was in a state of shock, with both hands clutching the armrests. The Russian pilot was amused. "Vats the matter, are you afraid to die?"

When Loberg was transferred to the 462nd Group at Walker Air Force Base he reported to Colonel Richard H. Carmichael, commander of the 462nd Group. He briefed Carmichael about the B-29 and described its flight characteristics. "It's a big, beautiful machine, but it has to be handled carefully. It's cumbersome on take-off because it's a big lumbering beast. I'm disturbed about cockpit visibility," Loberg said. "Those curved panes of glass prevent a pilot from seeing the runway properly."

Carmichael listened carefully because he had not flown the airplane yet. They discussed the early days of the war in the South Pacific, and compared notes about experiences. They had been in separate locations so this was the first time they had met.

Carmichael had been observing Loberg carefully throughout their conversation. He reached a decision. "The 769th Squadron needs a CO. You've got the job, starting immediately," he said.

Loberg was pleased because he had long sought a command, and he knew he couldn't do better than with and up-and-coming outfit destined to do great things.

Carmichael stood up. "I want you to check me out in the B-29, and all of our top people," he told Loberg.

"Whenever you say."

"First, we've got to get one of our two hangar queens in a flyable condition," he said ruefully.

They both looked up when someone at the door spoke. "Can I come in?"

"Come in, Kal," Carmichael said. "I want you to meet my deputy, Lieutenant Colonel Alfred F. Kalberer. Kal was on the Halvorsen raid against the Ploesti oil fields in 1942, and flew quite a few missions in the Mediterranean."

Kalberer chuckled. "I'm afraid we didn't do much damage to the oilfields. We had only 13 bombers, and landed in neutral countries when we ran short of fuel. We did better against the Italian fleet at Taranto."

"Kal has about 18,000 flying hours," Carmichael said. "He flew with KLM royal Dutch Airlines before the war."

Loberg looked at Kalberer with new respect, but Kalberer merely shrugged. "We flew from Holland, through the Middle East and across India to French Indo-China and on to Japan on our regular routes," Kal said. "I know the area intimately."

Loberg was unaware of the group's ultimate destination and his eyebrows lifted. He wanted to ask the question uppermost in his mind, but Carmichael and Kalberer ended the discussion.

On his way out, he thought of those two men who, more than anyone else, would determine the groups' fate in the months and years ahead. He instinctively liked Kalberer, a man only 10 years older, but those graying sideburns and thick set body radiated authority. Like most men in the group, Kalberer's out-going personality and self-assurance were almost overwhelming to those younger and less experienced. They were in awe of him but they learned to admire Kalberer's undoubted abilities. Loberg was not so sure about Carmichael. He didn't have Kalberer's command presence — he seemed stiff and had a forced smile that appeared condescending.

After Loberg got to know Carmichael better he realized that, despite his extensive combat experience, Carmichael's relative youth — he was 28, Loberg's age — made him uncomfortable with command responsibilities. There was a basic insecurity in Carmichael that he tried to hide. Actually, he was better on the social level in his dealings with men than as the group's top boss.

As soon as a B-29 became available Loberg began training flights for Carmichael, Kalberer and Group Operations Officer Major Donald A. Roush. Loberg became exasperated with Carmichael's tendency to drag the B-29's tailskid on take-off and Loberg adamantly refused to check him out until he overcame this tendency. Kalberer breezed through the checkout procedure and Loberg approved him first. Carmichael was bitter, and he spoke harshly to Loberg, insisting that he be checked out first. Loberg refused until Carmichael's flying improved. Roush later easily qualified.

Chapter 2

A B-29 Program in Shambles

Although they concerned our fate, none of us was aware of the high-level decisions reached at the Quadrant Conference in Quebec that met in late August of 1943. General Arnold submitted a plan to Allied leaders that called for air operations against Japan from advanced bases in eastern China. He told conferees that these operations could be supplied by air from the vicinity of Calcutta, India. The previous March, Arnold had requested his Committee of Operations Analysts to identify strategic Japanese targets that B-29s could reach from bases in China. Major General Laurence S. Kuter's group drew up a proposed plan, later called "Setting Sun," that called for a sustained bombing campaign against Japanese war-making industries such as aircraft and engine plants, naval and merchant-shipping bases, aluminum factories, iron and steel mills, and oil and chemical installations. His plan specified that Chinese bases within 1,500 miles of these targets, could be used to send B-29s to bomb the majority of them with a 10-ton bomb load. Kuter's plan did not consider Japanese electric-power systems and Japan's transportation system, because they were considered more suited to Navy aircraft operations. This was a strategic oversight that was later corrected.

The plan was rejected by the Combined Logistics Committee.

Kuter's plan called for use of B-29s to help carry fuel in bomb-bay tanks from rear bases in India to China and using Calcutta as the port of entry.

Arnold felt so strongly about Kuter's plan, and with Roosevelt's backing, that he insisted it be referred directly to the Combined Chiefs of Staff, despite rejection by the logistics committee. These top decision-makers liked the plan for two reasons: the fact that it called for the start of operations by October 1944 and that it would be self-contained without the need for a port of entry on the China Sea that could prove costly to acquire.

The plan had one basic weakness. It assumed that the Chinese Army, and Major General Claire L. Chennault's 14th Air Force, could protect these proposed B-29 bases in the Kweilin area. After the Japanese suspected that the United States planned to use bases around Kweilin, their army occupied the entire area without much difficulty.

The plan later proved accurate in predicting the effectiveness of future B-29 operations by estimating that 780 B-29s, flying five missions a month, would destroy Japan in six months. Kuter claimed that if his plan were followed, Japan could be occupied by the end of August, 1945.

The Combined Chiefs ordered an in-depth review of the plan and sought comments from General Chennault and Lieutenant General Joseph W. Stilwell. The latter called the plan overly optimistic because of the difficulties of supplying air bases north and south of Changsha. The American theatre commander had experienced logistical difficulties in getting acceptable quantities into China from India and he reminded the Combined Chiefs of the limited port facilities at Calcutta.

Stilwell proposed an alternate plan that recommended advance bases along the Kweilin-Changsha railroad with rear bases in the Calcutta area. He recommended that much of the B-29's fuel be carried to China by the bombers themselves, aided by cargo planes over the Hump. He recommended that operations start in April 1945, with 10 B-29 groups flying an average of 500 sorties a month. His plan was rejected because it was predicated on the establishment of 50 American-trained-and-equipped Chinese divisions to protect the airfields, and a great number of fighters for defense.

At the Quadrant Conference the Combined Chiefs reorganized the Far East Command to assure maximum use of limited resources. A Southeast Asia command was established under Vice Admiral, the Lord Louis Mountbatten. Stilwell was appointed his deputy, and was given command of all United States Army forces, ground and air, in the China-Burma theater. Royal Air Force units in India and Burma and the Army Air Forces, including the 10th Air Force operating over the Burma front, were formed into the Eastern Air Command under Major General George E. Stratemeyer.

These commands were charged with taking the offensive in north Burma and extending the Ledo Road from Calcutta to Assam. It was also proposed that a pipeline be built form Calcutta to Assam, with another alongside the Ledo Road to increase the flow of fuel to China.

The Combined Chiefs ordered Lord Mountbatten to double the capacity of the Hump airlift to 20,000 tons a month. Another 85,000 tons of supplies were expected to be delivered by ground and air routes. It was anticipated that 53,000 tons of petroleum products could be sent through the pipelines.

There was only a single railroad line from Calcutta to Assam and its tracks changed from broad to meter gauge en route, and trains had to be ferried across the Brahmaputra River because no bridge had ever been able to withstand monsoon floods.

In regard to direct operations against Japan, the Combined Chiefs reminded field commanders that it would handle all resources. Pacific operations would remain under the American Joint Chiefs of Staff, which directed General Douglas MacArthur to continue operations along the New Guinea coast and to land in the Philippines by the fall of 1944. Admiral Chester W. Nimitz, commander-in-chief-Pacific, was directed to initiate an independent Central Pacific drive against the Gilberts, Marshalls, and the Marianas. He was charged with responsibility for obtaining bases near Japan in the Ryukyus by the spring of 1945. At the meeting, Admiral Ernest J. King, American chief of naval operations, said he was confident that a decisive battle would be fought between the United States and Japanese fleets sometime during Nimitz's Central Pacific drive, and eliminate the Japanese Navy as a threat to future operations.

General Arnold recommended in September that plans for the capture of the Marianas, set at the Quadrant Conference for early 1946, be moved up to the middle of 1944. He recommended the earlier time period to permit eight B-29 groups to be stationed in the Marshalls or Carolines and staged through the Marianas for strikes against the Japanese mainland by March 1945 or sooner. The air staff said such operations were feasible but only if other Pacific islands were bypassed.

Arnold established a special review board to consider the latest proposals for using B-29's in combat and on September 20 a modified plan was proposed by board members. The earlier decision to concentrate Allied military strength against Japan only after Germany was defeated was re-affirmed. The board recommended that another appeal be made to the Soviet Union to permit American B-29 bases in Siberia. The United States had sought air bases there the day after Pearl Harbor but the Russians were afraid such a move would draw the Japanese into the conflict against them. The plan that Arnold approved was much like the one that President Roosevelt had suggested at the Casablanca Conference. It recommended bases in Calcutta with groups operating in and out of forward bases in China. The board claimed that the use of rear bases would assure earlier maintenance of the airplanes and provide for better ground security.

Arnold ordered Brigadier General Kenneth B. Wolfe to draw up an operations plan to bomb Japan with the maximum number of available B-29s at the earliest possible time. Wolfe had earlier organized the first B-29 wing — the 58th.

After Wolfe studied the plan he was concerned about the vulnerability of advanced air bases in China and the long supply line. He submitted his own plan to Arnold on October 11, 1943, and it included portions of the plan the Air Force chief of staff had sent to him. He committed his new command to earlier operations by saying he would be ready to fly the first mission by June 1, 1944, instead of March 1945. Wolfe's plan specified that by March of 1944 he would have 150 B-29s and 300 crews at bases north of Calcutta, with twice that many planes and 450 crews by September 1. He said he planned to establish a bomber command, with two wings of four groups each. Stilwell's insistence that the earlier recommended bases around Kweilin must be guarded by 50 Chinese divisions before they could become effective, was considered by Wolfe as unrealistic. Instead he recommended that the Chinese bases be moved further inland to the Chant area where additional ground and air defenses would not be needed.

On October 12, 1943, General Arnold approved Wolfe's plan in principle, and plans were immediately implemented to construct bases in India and China. Arnold was still primarily interested in operating B-29s out of the Marianas, once they were occupied by the Pacific Fleet, but he accepted Wolfe's plan to put B-29s in action against Japan by using the India/China bases for a year. Actually he had no choice. There were no other Pacific bases available within reach of Japanese mainland targets.

Stilwell didn't like Wolfe's plan, and had no faith that airpower could defeat Japan without an invasion. But he agreed to approve the plan although he had no illusions the B-29 operations out of China would be successful in seriously hurting the Japanese. In this regard, Arnold also had no such illusions.

Arnold had earlier promised Army Chief of Staff General George C. Marshall that B-29's would go to China by January 1, 1944. He now had the unpleasant task of informing President Roosevelt through Marshall that the B-29s would not be going overseas until March or April of 1944.

Marshall forwarded Arnold's letter to the president and Roosevelt replied on October 15 that he was upset by Arnold's letter. The president expressed what he called his disgust with the India-China situation, and Arnold in particular. "The worst thing is that we are falling down on our promises to China every single time," the president said. "We have not fulfilled one of them yet. I do not see why we have to use B-29s. We have several other types of bombing planes."

Arnold replied in a letter to the president, in which he made it clear that there were always unforeseen problems in getting a new airplane like the B-29 into combat. "This time," he wrote, "our problems have been aggravated by labor difficulties in the Wright engine factory." For earlier operations Arnold recommended the use of B-24s instead of B-29s, although he admitted that they could not hit targets on the Japanese mainland.

Roosevelt decided against the use of B-24s, much to Arnold's relief, and reluctantly agreed to the later date for B-29 overseas deployment.

Arnold endorsed Wolfe's operational plan in his own handwriting. "I have told the President that this will be started on March 1. (1944) See that it is done. H.H.A."

The president wired Prime Minister Winston Churchill on November 10 while they both prepared to meet in Cairo, this time with Generalissimo Chiang Kai-shek. "We have under development a project whereby we can strike a heavy blow at our enemy in the Pacific early next year with our new heavy bombers. Japanese military, naval and shipping strength is dependent upon the steel industry, which is strained to the limit. Half of the coke for that steel can be reached and destroyed by long-range bombers operating from the Chengtu area of China. The bombers can supply themselves by air from bases to be constructed near Calcutta without disturbing airlift commitments. In order to expedite the project I ask you to arrange for the Government of India to render every possible assistance to the construction of these four air bases for long-range bombers. This is a bold but entirely feasible project. Together, by this operation, we can partially cripple the Japanese naval and military power and hasten the victory of our forces in Asia."

Roosevelt wired the Chinese leader the same day to request construction of five bomber bases in the Chengtu area for use by the end of March 1944. He told Chiang Kai-shek that the United States would supply the engineering advisors but that the Chinese Government must furnish labor and materials.

In conclusion, he said, "I am personally convinced we can deal the Jap a truly crippling blow."

Churchill and Chiang Kai-shek approved the president's request and movement orders were issued on November 14 to aviation engineer battalions by the War Department. These units were instructed to proceed to India to start construction of the fields. The first contingent arrived 10 days later.

At the Cairo Conference, attended by Roosevelt, Stalin, Churchill, and Chiang Kai-shek between November 22 and 25, Roosevelt promised the Chinese leader that B-29s would be in combat by June 1944. Chiang Kai-shek promised Roosevelt that runways would be built at advance bases in China, ready for arrival of the first bombers by April 15. It was publicly announced for the first time that an invasion of Japan's home islands was under consideration, but at an unspecified date. It was not announced, although it had been agreed to at a meeting in November at Tehran, that Russia would enter the war in the Far East after Germany's surrender.

Brigadier General Hayward S. Hansell, Jr., who had been assigned to the 8th Air Force in England as commander of the 1st Air Division, was ordered by Arnold to return to Washington to become the air member of the Joint Plans commission. A VMI (Virginia Military Institute) graduate, and son of an Army surgeon, he was one of Arnold's special favorites. Hansell told committee members that the B-29 would be extremely vulnerable to head-on attacks with only two .50-caliber guns in the top forward turret. He recommended that the number be doubled; and the committee acted upon his recommendation despite the increased weight and the cramped crew conditions that would become worse with the addition of a larger ammunition drum.

The 58th Wing's four group commanders viewed Wolfe's plan in early November 1943, as totally unrealistic. Their organizations still didn't have the airplanes they had been promised, and the few that had been delivered were constantly being repaired and modified. Wolfe was not sympathetic to their complaints. He had his own problems. He had committed his 20th Bomber Command to a date set by the chief of staff of the Army Air Force and he advised them that come hell or high water he would meet the schedule.

Now that production planes were coming off the lines at the Boeing plant in Wichita, it appeared that the 58th Wing's problems were behind it. Crews were soon disillusioned. Meanwhile, they continued to fly in B-17s although such training was a far cry from training in B-29s that they were expected to take into combat in less than six months.

All groups were in bad shape, including the 462nd at Victoria, the 40th at Pratt under Colonel Leonard F. Harman, the 444th under Colonel Alva Harvey at Great Bend, and the 468th under Colonel Howard Engler at Salina.

Among the more fortunate personnel were the mechanics who were attending the Special Emergency B-29 School at the Boeing plant in Wichita.

General Wolfe reversed his earlier decision to assume responsibility for Boeing's flight test operations by turning this phase of operations back to the company. Boeing's analytical flight test engineer, N. D. Showalter, proved to Wolfe during August and September that his organization was better equipped to do the job despite previous shortcomings in running flight-test operations. He had worked closely with Colonel Howell S. Estes and Lieutenant Louis Sibilsky at the Wright Field Test Section and developed accurate data on the B-29's flight characteristics. Wolfe realized that his command, as well as Boeing critically needed this new data, and high gross weight take-offs were completed on the extra-long runways at Salinas.

During the five months after the airplane made its first flight in September 1942, the first B-29 had flown only 27 hours although other planes were now in production. During that period there had been 16 engine changes on the first airplane. Then, the second airplane, with many changes incorporated in the Wright Cyclone engines, was lost due to an uncontrollable engine fire.

I met Lieutenant Leroy J. Wieschaus, a flight engineer in the 770th Squadron, one October night over a beer at the officers club. "How's it going?" I asked.

"Our damn B-29 is on the ground three days for every hour it flies," he said with disgust. "After working like fools for four solid days and nights, it flew about seven hours yesterday and it's grounded again today."

"It's a great airplane, despite its problems," I said.

"When you can get it off the ground," Lee said grudgingly.

Two more B-29s arrived at the end of October and Wieschaus was the only officer in the hangar when they arrived so he signed for them. In other words, he accepted full responsibility for $2 million worth of airplanes. He told me afterwards that he didn't sleep very well trying to calculate how long it would take for him to serve in the Army as a 2d lieutenant to repay the cost of the airplanes if anything happened to them.

Despite continuing modifications to resolve the Wright engine's cooling problems, a B-29 had an engine fire on November 16 at 30,000 feet. When the pilot tried to feather the propeller (turn its blades so the propeller blades wouldn't offer resistance to the air after the engine was turned off) the engine refused to shut down. Instead, the propeller's governor failed and one of the tips exceeded the speed of sound. The propeller spun off the engine and cut through the wing. The B-29 went out of control, began to spin towards the earth, and then broke into four pieces. Some crewmembers escaped. We were stunned by the tragedy, reminded once again that flying the B-29 was a dangerous occupation.

During the flight in October, one of the side blisters of a B-29 blew out at high altitude while the bomber's cabin was pressurized and a gunner was sucked out. Unfortunately he wasn't wearing a parachute and was killed. After that episode no one had to be reminded to wear his parachute.

By November 1 each of the 462nd Group's four squadrons had only three B-29s instead of the seven called for in the table of organization, and seven crews instead of 14.

Bombardiers and navigators received a shock when word came from Bomber Command that they had to be dual rated. This meant that the four groups would be stripped of their bombardiers and navigators after months of grueling training as crews. Group commanders tried to get the order changed, but to no avail. Bombardiers had to be navigators, and vice versa, and that was that. In as much as navigation training took 15 months, and bombardier training nine months, sending bombardiers and navigators to regular schools was out of the question. Many of us had grown attached to the group and, despite the horrendous problems with the B-29, we still believed in it. When someone suggested that those who wished to remain — some chose to transfer out — could be trained by group personnel it seemed to offer the ideal solution. But the command had set a date for the new order to be put into effect and that date was slightly more than three weeks away. Captain Edward A. Perry, the 462nd Group's navigator, and a pre-war navigator for Pan American World Airways, took over responsibility for training the bombardiers. The group's navigators were likewise assigned to classrooms to be trained as bombardiers. And thus began one of the most intensive periods in my life. I had shuddered at the thought of overcoming my lifelong aversion to mathematics but I wanted to remain with the group so badly that for three weeks, we worked night and day to qualify as dead reckoning and celestial navigators. In a classic case of overcoming difficulties, I graduated at the top of the class due not so much to my ability but to a stubborn insistence that I would master the intricacies of navigation. It was a proud achievement for each of us, but Perry made the difference. He was a great navigator and a superb teacher.

In the midst of all our troubles, a winsome, petite blonde waitress in the officers mess belied her wholesome appearance as one of Kansas's local beauties. I had been attracted to her demure smile but so had dozens of other lieutenants. One day she disappeared and never returned to her job. Curious, I asked the club's office in charge what had happened to her.

He looked at me sharply. "Did you go out with her?" He asked

I admitted that I had not, although I had admired her.

"It's a good thing you didn't."

"Oh?"

"She gave more than 20 lieutenants as bad a dose of clap (gonorrhea) as our flight surgeons have ever seen. If she hadn't been stopped she would have incapacitated most of the group."

He walked away and I stood there with my mouth open. Granted his comments were exaggerated for my benefit, but they shocked me. It was a strong reminder that appearances can be deceiving.

Now that Boeing's flight test staff had resumed responsibility for the B-29 program, accurate test data began to accumulate. One crew simulated a high altitude flight at high gross weight to determine the aircraft's range. Its take-off weight was set at 130,000 pounds, or 10,000 pounds over the originally specified weight of the airplane. After burning off 3,000 pounds of fuel the airplane climbed to 30,000 feet. Although the flight was completed successfully it was learned that the engines were still in need of fundamental improvements. It was obvious that lubrication of the rocker arms was insufficient and exhaust collector rings were still failing.

On one such high altitude flight a blister blew out at 30,000 feet and the pressurized sections were suddenly exposing the crewmembers to sharply lowered pressures that could have killed them without their oxygen masks. All were wearing parachutes and side gunners now had restraining harnesses so this time no one was sucked out of the airplane. The cabin was designed to withstand such sudden depressurization, and once crewmembers put on their oxygen masks they suffered no ill effects. It had been feared that a crew might suffer the "bends."

Meanwhile, to correct deficiencies, production airplanes from Boeing's Wichita plant were sent first to a modification center at Marietta, Georgia, or to Wright Field, before they were assigned to groups.

Engine failures were still occurring with annoying regularity, forcing crews to train in B-17s and on ground trainers. Late in December the average crew had flown only 18 hours in a B-29. Little of this time was flown in formation above 20,000 feet, and only one B-29 had flown a long-range mission. At this time, with less than four months before General Arnold had promised to have the B-29s in India and China, only 67 men had been checked out as B-29 first pilots in the whole 20th Bomber Command! Each B-29 was averaging only two flight hours during each 24-hour period.

Crews kept flying, but in B-17s, making simulated bombing runs on cities throughout the mid-west. P-47 and P-51 fighters made simulated passes at their airplanes to get them acquainted with real attacks in combat. But the B-17s did not have the B-29's central fire control system, and firing mostly hand-held guns provided little training for the B-29's revolutionary gunfire control system, where computing gun sights automatically corrected for wind and plane velocity while maintaining the gun sight on the attacking fighter. We had studied the system, and knew its capabilities, but as yet we had not had a chance to use it in the air against a target sleeve that could duplicate the actions of an enemy fighter. We knew that its "brain," or computer, did the work of a gunner who had to guess at the speed and distance of an attacking fighter. In effect, the computer took the guesswork out of sighting and firing. The concept intrigued us. We hoped our first use of the system would not be against an attacking enemy fighter.

By now six Superfortresses had been involved in training accidents throughout the command, and after one B-29 had exploded at altitude in November, all flights were restricted to an altitude of 20,000 feet.

On December 22, Colonel Carmichael and his crew flew one of the group's first three YB-29s to Washington to permit General Arnold and other top officials to see one of the new bombers. The visit was made secretly, but 155 officials, including Arnold and the Secretary of Treasury Henry Morgenthau, Jr., inspected the airplane. For Arnold, this was an emotional moment to see the airplane that he had fought for so long to get produced.

The day before Christmas we were a dispirited group. None of us was permitted to take home leave and most of us were working 12 and 14-hour days. Walker Field was probably the bleakest part of Kansas. Officially at Victoria, which had only a few hundred people, Hayes and Russel were 15 miles to the west and east of the base. Although they were pretty towns with less than 4,000 people, there was not much for a couple of thousand servicemen to do. Kansas was a dry state, so those of us who savored a drink, found it almost impossible to get one. Earlier in the war the governor insisted that all bases honor Kansas' laws against selling alcoholic beverages. In 1942 the base commander at Topeka, a final phase training base for crews bound for England, stood up to the governor when he said he would send the National Guard to uphold the laws of his state. The commander told him to come ahead, but he warned that the Guard would be met with armed Air Force men with orders to shoot first and answer questions later. The governor backed down, but getting liquor for the bases depended upon bootleggers (you could get all the rotgut whiskey you wanted for $15.00 a bottle at a time when the best scotch was selling in other states for less than $3.00). As a result, planes were routinely sent to Nebraska to pick up beer and liquor. But to get a bottle of good bourbon you normally had to buy a half dozen bottles of gin or vodka, which were not then popular with most drinkers.

When Colonel Carmichael was advised that the liquor supply for Christmas and New Years would be almost non-existent, he called Loberg and directed him to send a B-17 to Chicago and bring back 40 cases of good liquor. "No more of that rum or vodka crap," he said. "Give the pilot enough money to get good stuff."

Loberg agreed and assigned Major Cecil Durbin to the flight. Durbin was eager to go and he promised to be back before Christmas Eve.

Durbin flew a B-17 to Chicago, filled its bomb bay with 40 cases of choice liquor, and prepared to return to Walker the day before Christmas. He glanced up at the lowering sky with misgivings. Fog was rolling in and, when he called the tower for permission to take off, he was advised that the field was closed.

Durbin was in a quandary but he hoped that the air would clear and he could take off. Hours went by but the conditions worsened. He went over to operations to get the latest weather report, and he was advised that no change was expected until Christmas Day, if then. He put in a call to Loberg and explained the situation.

"I understand the problem," Loberg said. "But Carmichael has been on my ass all day as to when you were getting back. You'd better talk to him. Hang on. I'll transfer you."

Once Carmichael was on the line Durbin explained the situation, saying he had been forbidden to take off.

"Durbin," Carmichael said, "I'm not interested in your problems. But if you don't get that booze back here by Christmas Eve, you'll be a second lieutenant on Monday."

Durbin, a normally mild-mannered individual, had hoped for greater understanding. But one didn't argue with a full colonel so all he said was "Yes sir."

He returned to his B-17, noting that the visibility was still limited to a few hundred feet, and explained to his crew that they had been ordered to get back.

One member started to protest, but Durbin shushed him. "I have no choice."

Crewmembers helped to guide Durbin along the taxiways to the main runway, and he went slowly. Fortunately he was familiar with the airport's layout and without incident he arrived at the end of the runway. He aligned his compass heading to match the runway's precise heading, knowing he would have to make an instrument takeoff. Just as he started to roll, the tower called. "The field is closed. I repeat the field is closed."

Durbin ignored the warning and pushed all four throttles to the stops. He was lightly loaded and he wanted to get into the air and, hopefully, above the fog and clouds as soon as possible. As the fog swept by the cockpit windows Durbin kept his eyes on the compass and maintained the runway's precise heading until he reached flying speed. Then he pulled back on the column with a sign of relief that he had not wandered off the runway where the grass was soft and would have flipped the airplane over on its back. He headed upwards in a rapid climb to the cheers of all on board. It had been foolish and possibly dangerous for Carmichael to order him to ignore normal safety precautions, but Durbin's outstanding skill as a pilot under all possible weather conditions in the South Pacific was brought to bear and the B-17 and its cargo arrived at Walker Field just before dinnertime. Durbin and his crew, once they were on the ground, were first to pronounce that the liquor was just what they all needed.

That night it did not take much of Chicago's finest liquor to make us forget our cares and relax. At the officers club Colonel Carmichael arrived with his wife and it was soon apparent that he had imbibed too freely. His wife tried to get him to return to their quarters, but he refused, although he could barely stand. Colonel Kalberer came in and Carmichael's wife turned to him. "Kal, I can't do anything with him. Get him to leave."

Kalberer talked to him quietly, but Carmichael briefly argued against his suggestions that he return to his quarters. Finally, after he almost fell down, he agreed to be led away.

Carmichael's condition momentarily put a damper on our spirits and we all eased off the drinking. At first our commander's condition shocked us. We had never seen him like this before, and the sight of his abject drunkenness disgusted us.

When someone made a disparaging remark, Kalberer whipped around and faced the lieutenant. "If you'd been through what he has endured, you'd have been a basket case long ago. Carmichael spent a year flying airplanes that should never have been in combat in some of the most miserable islands in the South Pacific. He had done more than his fair share, and he should have been given a cushiony job in the States. He's earned it. But he volunteered to go out again with us. A man can take so much, and Dick Carmichael has taken more than any human being should be expected to take."

Kalberer's words sobered us. We knew he was right, and we felt ashamed of our disparaging remarks. It made us think, how would we stand up to a year of combat? We knew that before many months passed we would probably find out and that our manhood would be tested to its utmost limits.

New Year's Eve found most of us in a deep sense of gloom. We knew it would be the last New Year's Eve we would spend in the United States and for untold hundreds of us it might possibly be the last such occasion in our lives. For those who tried to blot out the future with alcohol, the morning after brought the inevitable expressions of "never again." The reality of a B-29 program in shambles had done more than the fear of death to reduce our morale almost to the breaking point.

Our crew was assigned to fly to Wichita on January 19, 1944, to pick up the B-29 we would take overseas. Loberg couldn't leave his squadron duties so Major Durbin was assigned as aircraft commander. After we picked up our new airplane at the Boeing plant, Durbin flew it to Birmingham, Alabama. There, for the next three days, and working around the clock, hundreds of modifications were made to the airplane; many of them wire installations that had recently been changed. The de-icer boots were removed from the wing because they reduced the B-29's range. We viewed this change with misgivings because a high-altitude plane such as the B-29 could easily accumulate ice on the wing and make it unmanageable. We were told that ice would not form because of the speed at which we would fly, but we had our doubts. But Boeing engineers were found later to be correct in their assumption.

When we went to check the airplane on the final day in the cavernous assembly building, our reception by the predominately feminine work force was boisterous as many of them whistled and waved. I was impressed at the time by the tremendous job women were doing to build our nation's airplanes and other war materials. Prior to the war, women had been restricted to jobs such as teachers, nurses, and secretaries. Without fully realizing the significance of the changes underway in American life, it only became apparent years later that the ability of America's women to take on previously male jobs of all types — some requiring physical strength as well as routine skills — would forever change masculine views of women. These women — young, middle-aged, and some in their retirement years — performed magnificently regardless of the demands made upon them. Two years earlier most of them had never been in a factory, but they learned quickly how to fabricate parts and assemble airplanes. They established an unmatched record for building airplanes on a tight schedule, on time and below estimated costs. They were in all defense plants, freeing men for the nation's armed forces in a collaborative effort such as the world has never seen, and quite possible will never see again. Their enthusiasm was contagious and lifted our spirits. Our morale was badly in need of a lift because our training had been held up by the horrendous maintenance problems with the few B-29s assigned to us, including the first production airplanes we had obtained at Wichita. But as we stared at our new airplane on the end of the line, with workers swarming over it, we all hoped that the modifications that had been made on the engine would be the answer to the B-29's major problems.

Upon our return to Walker we learned that Captain Raymond K. Childress, flying the first B-29 the group had received and known as "Irene the Hangar Queen" by members of the 770th Squadron, had gotten into trouble during a night mission and ordered his crew to bail out. He remained with the airplane, hoping to land it safely, but he had to make a belly landing in rough country 10 miles from the field. Fortunately no one was injured.

Air Force tradition dictated that any flyer that bailed out successfully had to furnish a case of beer to the rigger who packed his chute. One rigger had packed five of the chutes for Childress's crew. The parachute department was literally stocked with beer by those who had bailed out.

This action was followed a week later by one in which a 768th Squadron's B-29 — a brand new, fully-modified airplane — broke her back in front of its hangar when someone mistakenly retracted the nose gear.

One of the nagging problems that caused several accidents was the pilot's inability to "feather" an engine when it overheated and was in danger of catching fire. If a leak occurred in the oil system, it all drained out, leaving no reserve to "feather" the propeller. A temporary fix alleviated this problem when a "hopper" tank was placed inside the regular tank to provide a 10-gallon oil reserve. Hydraulic systems resolved this problem in later aircraft.

By now, all pilots had qualified to fly the B-29. Aircraft commanders, or first pilots, had 60 hours at most, which was the barest minimum even for experienced four-engine pilots, while crews averaged 12 hours.

Our group's Captain Thomas R. Vaucher was assigned to fly a modified B-29 to check out the latest changes. He had become an aircraft commander at Pratt in a three-and-a-half hour flight, but he had accumulated more than 1,000 hours in other four-engine bombers, which was far above the average. Although in his mid-twenties, Vaucher was selected as the pilot to pick up the first B-29 accepted by the Air Force for the 40th Group at Wichita, and fly it to Pratt. Later he became the first B-29 pilot to log 1,000 miles in the airplane.

On what Vaucher considered a routine flight, he flew his B-29 to 38,000 feet, made a bombing run and noted with satisfaction that the engines maintained their cylinder-head temperatures and that the new pneumatic bomb bay doors snapped open properly.

When he returned to operations he was informed that General Arnold was on the telephone and that he wanted to speak to him.

"I've just heard about your successful flight at 38,000 feet. Were you able to hold your airspeed on the run?"

Vaucher assured him that the flight had been normal in every respect.

"Did the cabin pressurization hold?" Arnold asked.

"Yes sir," Vaucher replied. "There were no problems with it whatsoever."

But problems continued to multiply and combat crews were unable to attain sufficient airtime to complete their training. The first air-to-ground gunnery missions were not flown until late December. Such missions at 500 feet were of little use to us because in combat we would be flying at high altitudes. Most gunners were skeptical of the General Electric Central Fire Control System because almost all gunnery missions in late December and in January had to be cancelled after the guns jammed.

Lieutenant Frank Rosenberger joined our group on December 19, 1943, and he was assigned to the 768th Squadron as armament officer. Three days later he was ordered to check out gunners in the air although he knew very little about the General Electric system. The pressure to check out gunners had reached the critical stage so he joined crews at dawn to fly to a desolate area in Wyoming for air-to-ground gunnery practice. At the time he was unaware of the B-29's many problems, particularly the tendency of its engines to catch fire, so he was ignorant of the dangers to be faced flying at 500 feet where it was impossible to survive a parachute jump in the event the B-29 developed problems. In the event an emergency occurred in flight, Rosenberger was to "stay with the ship" and not try to bail out. These gunnery missions gave crews little practical experience of firing at live targets in the air. Rosenberger was frustrated, as were the gunners, because during these missions the guns frequently jammed. On the ground, working to free them after a mission in the frigid weather, their already limited patience was taxed to the utmost.

Our 462nd Group was based in one of the bleakest parts of Kansas, where severe winter storms were common. This winter was no exception. Our flimsy barracks, with their tarpaper roofs, permitted cold and snow to penetrate them. They were heated by coal-burning potbellied stoves in the halls that used soft coal so full of impurities that clinkers would form and the fires would go out. We had protested in vain about maintenance of these stoves. One morning the officers of my 769th Squadron, including Loberg, refused to get out of bed for an early flight. During the night a blizzard had almost buried our prefabricated, one-story barracks and all the stoves had gone out. Inside, the air was as cold as the sub-zero temperature outside, and we burrowed under our blankets and refused to get up. Loberg was so irate about the situation that he called Colonel Carmichael and objected to such treatment in no uncertain words.

Shortly afterwards, Carmichael and the base commander arrived and they were both appalled by the conditions under which we had been living. We grudgingly dressed for the day after they promised that this would never happen again. And it didn't.

Then we were all informed that our ground crews would leave for an undisclosed location overseas on February 12. Now each airplane's crew was expected to maintain its airplane under the capable hands of an experienced crew chief. In this respect, the enlisted crewmembers were well trained before they came to Walker, and many of them had gone to Boeing's B-29 schools.

We thought conditions in December and January would not get worse, but we soon realized how wrong we were after the ground crews departed. Only half of the crews were sent across the Pacific by ship to assure that some of those highly experienced men would survive the submarine infested waters between the United States and India.

Normally the service testing of a new airplane, and training crews to fly them, takes two years to complete. The 20th Bomber Command was given six months! The decision to expedite our departure by going directly into production before the first B-29 was test flown then making modifications at designated centers to bring each airplane up to the latest specifications, may have looked good on paper. In reality, it resulted in chaos. Due to material shortages, lack of skills at the modification centers and on the combat bases to make mandatory changes, and failure to coordinate all activities at widely separated modification centers finally brought the B-29 program to a resounding halt, although production of the new airplanes continued. Airplanes off the lines at modification centers emerged almost unflyable, filled with non-standard equipment, and modifications that were so poorly made they did more harm than good. In some cases airplanes were delivered to bases without thorough inspections.

Colonel Carmichael, and other group commanders, refused to accept any more airplanes because they considered them unsafe. Instead they demanded that all future deliveries be completely modified or remain in the factory until the job was done properly.

Their forthright actions created a verbal storm, and soon all hell broke loose that galvanized General Arnold into personal action to resolve the situation.

Chapter 3

The Battle of Kansas

Although combat crews did valiant work in maintaining their airplanes, the many problems associated with inadequate modification work defeated their efforts to keep the airplanes in the air for an appreciable number of training hours.

Meanwhile, the ground personnel were on their way, with no knowledge of their ultimate destination. Eventually they would travel by ship for three months halfway around the world constantly in danger of attacks by enemy submarines. The decision to divide the personnel into two groups on routes diametrically opposed to one another was indicative of the high priority command headquarters gave to their safe arrival at their destination. The 1,000 westward bound men under Major Roscoe Norman embarked from California with a brief stopover at Melbourne, Australia, after 35 days at sea without touching land. General MacArthur refused to let them off their ship after their long journey. Instead they went on to Bombay, India, and then took a train to their base at Piardoba. The entire trip was completed in 45 days.

Lieutenant Frank Rosenberger, the 768th Squadron's armament officer, boarded a Liberty ship at Norfolk News, Virginia, for the eastward crossing of a similar group to Oran in North Africa.

This contingent became part of an 80-ship Atlantic convoy with six destroyer escorts. In Mid-Atlantic they encountered a bad storm and their ship had to reduce its speed to three knots instead of its normal 12 knots. As the ship healed over 30 degrees to the left, and another equal tilt to the right, they all became seasick. Rosenberger kept thinking, "How long can I take this?" His friend, John O'Donnell joined him on deck, exclaiming, "You've got to eat, Rosie," as he peeled oranges and fed him. Nothing helped and Rosenberger got to the point where he didn't care whether he slid down the deck into the churning ocean.

One night while Rosenberger slept fitfully in his bunk he had a dream that he was on his farm in Ohio. He seemed to be caught between the house and the barn. Just as he was about to smack into the barn the wind would reverse itself and blow him violently back toward the house, but before he slammed into his brick house, the wind would reverse again, and the cycle repeated over and over. This went on in a seemingly endless fashion. Finally, he awoke and found that he was rolling from one side of his bunk to the other as the ship rolled. He was so exhausted that he could barely get out of his bunk.

On the night of their 19th day at sea, faint lights were spotted in the distance. Daylight revealed they had reached Gibraltar and the beautiful blue-green waters of the Mediterranean. The ship continued on and docked at Oran in North Africa; a port filled with the masts of French warships sticking out of the water. The ships had been sunk by British warships in 1940 when the French Command refused to surrender.

The crew spent two weeks at Oran, sleeping on cots on the ground despite the damp, cold, and dismal surroundings. When their new ship, a sleek little number about 250 feet long, arrived, they eagerly boarded it. It had been a French cruise ship before the war and was now operated by the Royal British Navy.

For the next two weeks they literally toured the Mediterranean with a stopover at Naples. There a Nazi bomber reminded them that the war was still on as it dropped a couple of bombs on the already demolished harbor. They departed the next morning, but before leaving, they were greeted by one of Mt. Vesuvius's periodic eruptions. B-26 bombers headed for Cassino to continue the pounding of that beleaguered city. It surrendered to the Allies shortly thereafter.

Still with no knowledge of their ultimate destination, Rosenberger and the other Americans found themselves going through the Suez Canal and entering the Red Sea. Their ship stopped for two days at Aden to take on fuel, water, and other supplies. When they left, traveling through the Arabian Sea and the Indian Ocean, two destroyers provided protection against lurking Japanese submarines.

The officers on board this former luxury liner were treated like royalty by the British crew, receiving three meals a day in the large lounge whose walls were made of inlaid wood paneling. The service was everything they could have desired, complete with tablecloths and cloth napkins. Tea was served each afternoon at 4 P.M. with cookies. They eagerly awaited the call each afternoon that "tea was now being served." The menu was typically British with two or three kinds of meat (one a cold fish) for breakfast, plus porridge. At dinner, mutton was a staple, but one most Americans did not relish although the rest of the menu was broad and varied. Such was life for the officers, but the enlisted men finally rebelled on their diets of two serving of porridge a day and little meat. A spokesman complained to the American officers about their poor fare, and brought evidence that even their porridge had bugs in it. Rosenberger, who grew up on a farm, inspected a dish of porridge and, although the bugs were so small you could barely see them, he identified them as members of the weevil family. Regardless, the American officers viewed such a situation as intolerable and brought the matter to the attention of the British captain. Thereafter the food for the enlisted men improved. Such discrimination shocked the American officers because at their own base's officers and men usually ate the same food albeit in different mess halls.

As their little ship headed east across the Indian Ocean they became convinced that they were headed for India, with the possibility of ending up in China. They had still not been told. The calm ocean, mild temperatures, and balmy sea breezes made them feel like tourists for the first time in the two months since they had left their frigid base in Kansas. As nomads of the sea for weeks they crowded the rail as land appeared and the outline of a large city emerged out of the mist. One impressive structure caught their attention because it dominated the scene as they entered the harbor. They learned later it was the famous "Gateway to India" monument dedicated to the honor of King George V and Queen Mary of Great Britain. They had arrived in Bombay, India's most attractive city, and a center of banking and textile industries with an unmatched reputation on the sub-continent for its cultural activities.

Officials of the 20th Bomber Command had known since it was formed June 1, 1943, at Smoky Hill Army Air Field in Salina, Kansas, that if the B-29 program was to operate smoothly there must be exceptional integration between the production of airplanes and spare parts and supplies, and between training and forwarding of ground personnel and supplies to bases. Due to the unique nature of the program, it was early realized that each group's ground and air personnel would need more information, knowledge, and skill than had ever been required by any comparable organization. After early operational training, the crew size for each airplane was set at 11. Flight engineers, in particular, were given special training. After 12 weeks in officer training they were given 16 weeks at aircraft mechanics schools, 12 weeks at the Boeing B-29 mechanics and electrical specialization school, and 10 weeks of flight engineer training.

The orders for crew training were explicit. All crews must be interchangeable. Each crewmember must be an expert in his field and know how to maintain his equipment.

At Eglin Field, Florida, Lieutenant Colonel Paul W. Tibbits was assigned to supervise gunnery tests on the Superfortress. At Gulfport, Mississippi, other B-29s made overwater flights to test the new gunnery system. Unfortunately, special crews made most of these flights, and only the information — and not the actual experience — became available to the combat crews.

Initially, another wing, in addition to the 58th, was established under the 20th Bomber Command with Colonel Thomas H. Chapman in charge. It was later transferred to the 21st Bomber Command assigned to the Marianas.

General Arnold became concerned about meeting his commitment to the president to get B-29s in action by spring, after a meeting on December 21, 1943, with General Wolfe. When he learned that there were only a small number of men assigned to the China-Burma-India theater, he told him, "Get over there yourself, with some of your staff."

Wolfe and a small staff arrived in China by early 1944 and became immediately upset when he noted the lack of progress in getting the bases ready for his crews. After he held a meeting with Lieutenant Waldo I. Kennerson, arrangements were made for extending the existing airstrips at Hsinching, Pengshan, and Kiunglai and to construct a new base at Kwanghang.

Work began at Hsinching on January 24, 1944 with Wolfe in attendance to assure himself that Kennerson understood the gravity of the problem. Thousands of blue clad men and women crushed rocks with hammers while others carried pails of sand and crushed rock suspended from shoulder poles.

Wolfe gazed at the high peaks to the west over the valley, and Kennerson appreciated his concern that they might prove an obstacle to B-29 operations. He told Wolfe, "General, Tibet is not too far beyond those mountains."

Wolfe nodded soberly. He was aware that this province of Szechuan was the biggest in all of China, 40 percent larger than the State of California with a population in the tens of millions of people. This mid-China province was subdivided by vast valleys whose rivers became torrents during the monsoon season, and whose mountains rose to 22,000 feet. Szechuan's western third included the 12,000-foot Tibetan plateau, which stretched to the Himalayas 750 miles away. There was only one way to get to Tibet, and that was over rough, dusty trails.

Wolfe found the situation in India equally bad. After he met Colonel L. E. Seeman, the officer responsible for base construction, Wolfe learned that Seeman's units had arrived without their heavy equipment for a job that required the movement of 1.7 million cubic yards of earth. Seeman told Wolfe that Indian cement was of such poor quality that he had to import American cement at enormous cost to surface the 10 inch thick runways.

Wolfe was upset by the lack of progress and his feelings were not alleviated by the chocking red dust, the heat that radiated from the parched ground in suffocating waves while thousands of Indians — most untouchables — tried to complete the job by hand. Women carried baskets of dirt balanced on their heads while they chewed betel nuts that stained their mouths red. Betel was used to deaden their hunger pains. Their once white garments were wrapped around their bodies, over their heads and across their faces. They too were stained a reddish hue. Wolfe shook his head in exasperation, wondering how these poor starving creatures could finish such a mammoth undertaking. He knew it was not humanly possible. He had heard that at least a million natives had died of starvation in Bengal the previous year, and more elsewhere.

Wolfe flew to General Stilwell's jungle headquarters and demanded that the theater commander temporarily assign several Army construction battalions to help build the bases. Stilwell reluctantly agreed, but he warned that work on the top-priority Ledo Road from Burma to China would suffer.

Once modern equipment became available, along with 6,000 United States Army construction engineers and 700,000 native laborers who worked around the clock in India and China, the bases were completed.

In China, rocks were broken by hand and then carried in pails and wicker baskets to pony carts with wheels removed from abandoned automobiles that no longer had precious fuel to run them.

Day after day the work went on as blue-smocked Chinese laborers carried thousands of tons of rock, gravel, and mud to fill the 8,500-foot runways to a depth of 19 inches. Mud was used to bind the rocks and gravel, and a black tar-like substance from the oil of the Chinese tung nut was spread on top.

Huge stone rollers, carved from sandstone hills and each weighing 10 tons, were pulled by hundreds of Chinese laborers to smooth the surface of the runways. Once these rollers were moving they could not easily be stopped. Therefore, when a worker stumbled and fell his body was pressed into the fabric of the runway. Those on the ropes roared with laughter, much to the astonishment of the American overseers who were appalled by such a calloused attitude toward violent death. Twenty-five Chinese rope handlers perished in this fashion, while another 25 died in other accidents.

In addition to the four bomber bases in China, additional strips were constructed for Chennault's 312 Fighter Wing that had been assigned to protect the bases.

The bases were completed in September 1944, months after the B-29s became operational out of them. Twenty-six American officers and enlisted men supervised the construction. In the process, 160,000 tons of rock and mud were used to build them.

China was ruled by warlords during these years and in this area they were strongly opposed to the Nationalist government. The Min River Valley in the Chengtu area for thousands of years had been one of the most fertile regions in the world. The Chinese had diverted the river into a series of canals to irrigate the land and prevent spring floods from devastating it. Thus was created a delta-type plain that was 70 miles long and 1,700 square miles in area at the foot of huge 20,000-foot plus mountain peaks to the north and west. Rice was the staple crop and it supported 2,200 people per square mile. The loss of thousands of small farms to build these airfields created an explosive political situation that fortunately never got out of control. This was due primarily to Colonel Kennerson's efforts in working closely with the governor of Szechuan who agreed on January 11, 1944, to draft men to build the bases. Two weeks later, 200,000 people were working, and another 60,000 were added in mid-February.

Generalissimo Chiang Kai-shek demanded $2 billion in Chinese currency for work on the bases and a personal guarantee from President Roosevelt that it be paid. Roosevelt agreed to pay this sum but at the rate of exchange of $100 Chinese to one American dollar, or $20 million in American money. Chiang Kai-shek countered with a 20 to 1 rate to help, he said, control inflation in his country.

American officials balked at paying $100,000 million American. The Generalissimo refused to back down, claiming the shortage of money in China was real although American officials insisted that there were $10 billion in Chinese funds available. Stilwell was forced to guarantee payment at a rate to be decided later; otherwise work would have stopped on the bases.

The Chinese government froze all funds in China so there was no way to pay for supplies or the wages of the Chinese workers. Stilwell was forced to allocate space on planes of the Air Transport Command to ferry $200 in small Chinese bills whose weight became a serious problem. Many vitally needed supplies had to be temporarily left in India until the money was delivered.

Stilwell advised the Joint Chiefs that Chiang's action was not due to a shortage of money — he had turned down a $1 billion loan at the Cairo Conference — but a matter of prestige. The issue wasn't settled until July 1944 when the United States paid China $210 million in American money to resolve a number of claims. Part of this money went to pay for the Chinese bases, but no one knows how much. There is no question but that Chinese Nationalist officials pocketed a good part of it because Chinese landowners were paid a pittance for their ancestral farms while Chinese laborers got $25 in Chinese money a day, which barely paid for their food. Inflation had pushed the exchange rate to $270 Chinese to one American dollar. They would have starved had their families not fed them. Their anger was justified. Many lost their farms and were paid starvation wages for backbreaking labor. Why they didn't revolt is a mystery, but the Americans at first were not greeted as liberators when they arrived. Once the bases became operational to bomb Japan, most Chinese took pride in their great contributions.

General Arnold's original request to the War Department the previous November had recommended that a minimum number of construction battalions be diverted from other projects. The Joint Chiefs cut his request in half. Even with this reduced number, shipping priorities became so tight that vitally needed supplies for Stilwell's army were reduced so drastically that they affected his operations.

The bases in India's southern Bengal at Dudhkundi, Piardoba, Kharagpur (command headquarters), Kalaikundi, and Chakulia were selected because of their direct air relationship with the forward bases in China, and because they were not too distant from Calcutta's port facilities.

At the B-29 bases in Kansas, the number of airplanes available for training was still critical. Ninety-seven had come off the production line by mid-January, but only 16 were in a flyable condition, reducing the number of first pilots checked out to 70.

General Wolfe's belief that the B-29 Superfortress could be "debugged" during the production and training phases to save at least six months proved to be in error. Now the entire program had reached a state of collapse as problems mushroomed out of control. There were more than 2,000 engineering changes to the Wright engine alone. The central fire control system and the APC-13 radar bombing system proved baffling to aircrews because they were so often out of commission. The cost of each airplane rose to $600,000 — an extremely high figure for World War II — but this was not the final price that eventually reached a million dollars per airplane.

Major Victor N. Agather, assigned to the B-29 project office at Wright Field to help resolve the engine fire problems, was aroused out of bed at 2 A.M. in early February by his boss, Colonel Erik Nelson. "Vic, get your tail in the saddle and get out to Salina immediately with a list of all serial numbers of B-29s and the modifications required. General Bradshaw's airplane is standing by at Operations to take you."

The confusion at Salina appalled Agather, and he learned the same condition prevailed at all bases. Nobody knew what modifications were needed for any given aircraft. He was shocked to find that all B-29s were grounded.

Agather next was ordered to Pratt to inspect the 40th Group's aircraft. For five days he and a special crew went without much sleep as they checked each airplane and made a complete list of modifications that were needed to get the airplanes flying. They set out to identify the kits that were needed to modify each aircraft and most importantly to locate them in the supply system.

They flew to the Boeing plant at Wichita and, with a company manager, walked down the line, identifying workers whom they needed at the bases to complete the modifications. Each worker was driven to the airport and placed on a plane for Pratt while a car was dispatched to his home to get necessary clothes and to advise his family where he had gone.

Most modification work had to be done in the open because hangars were unavailable at the bases despite bitter cold and frequent snowstorms. Often work crews could stand the cold for only 20 minutes, but the work went on. One hundred engines were changed at Pratt to replace outmoded engines.

In Washington, General Arnold felt confident that the emergency measures underway at the bases would permit the B-29s to depart for India on time. He wired Wolfe on March 1 that they would start to leave their Kansas bases on March 10.

Arnold and his assistant Major General B. E. Meyer went to Salina on March 9 to watch the B-29s depart. He was shocked to learn that not one airplane was ready to leave. The modification program was still a shambles. With thoughts of explaining another delay to President Roosevelt, Arnold vent his wrath on the Technical Service Command's Colonel I. W. Stephenson, the highest ranking officer present at the meeting. He accused him of failure to coordinate the work properly between the Boeing factories, the modification centers, and the bases. He demanded to see a list of shortages and his temper rose when he learned that no one knew where parts were or when they would be delivered.

"Who's running this show?" Arnold demanded. "I'll do it if no one else is!" he turned to Stephenson again. "I want a list of shortages of everything by tomorrow morning. I want to know where each item is, and if it's in the factory, when it will be delivered."

Arnold departed, leaving Stephenson and his aides in a state of shock. They worked all night to prepare a status sheet on each aircraft and forwarded them to Pratt the next morning where Arnold was staying.

Arnold perused the status sheets and turned to Meyer. "Remain behind as my special project coordinator. You have full authority to act on my behalf. I've got to return to Washington."

The "Battle of Kansas" was a period of frenzied activity as 150 B-29s were prepared to deploy by the middle of April at the latest.

But a week later, not one B-29 was ready for departure to India. General Orval Cook, production division chief for the Air Material command, flew to Wichita to meet with Boeing officials. He demanded five to six hundred Boeing mechanics to work on the planes at the bases.

Boeing officials acted promptly and the men were at the bases and working on the planes the next day.

One of the basic problems was identified by Colonel C. S. "Bill" Irvine who found that so many changes had been made to the wiring diagrams that they were totally out of date. With 15,000 feet of electrical wiring in each B-29, crucial to the operation of the airplane, this was a condition that had to be corrected first. Irvine ordered that each wire system be traced so accurate drawings could be made on the spot.

It soon became evident that even more Boeing workers were needed if the job was to be done on time. At the risk of slowing production, more experienced Boeing workers were sent to the bases. Sub-contractors were advised to concentrate on finding missing parts and temporarily forget about future production.

Now a raging snowstorm and bitterly cold weather struck the Kansas bases while men and women on the flight lines worked around the clock. Then Boeing workers from the southern states threatened to walk away from their jobs unless their wages were brought up to the level of their northern counterparts. After Meyer appealed to their patriotism, they returned to work.

After days of frantic activity, the B-29s of the 40th Group were ready to leave for overseas by Easter. The teams who had performed this miracle were transferred to Great Bend and then on to the other two bases.

Brigadier General LaVerne G. "Blondie" Saunders, 58th Wing commander took off in the first airplane late March and headed for India with stops at Gander, Newfoundland; across the route's longest over-water stretch of 2,700 miles to Marrakesh; then on to Cairo, Karachi, and its base at Chakulia.

Colonel Frank Cook earlier flew a B-29 to England in a misguided attempt to deceive the Germans and the Japanese. Generals Eisenhower and Doolittle, and top British officials, inspected it. It was hinted that these new Superfortresses would soon be operating out of England. But those long runways in India and China convinced the Japanese that the B-29s would soon be contesting their air spaces over the main islands.

After the command's eastern contingent of ground personnel disembarked at Bombay they were taken to a Royal Air Force rest camp to await the scheduling of the train that would take them across India to their new base, although they were not told that it was at Piardoba.

Four days after their arrival, Frank Rosenberger and Wayne Williams were shopping downtown for star sapphires. Suddenly a heavy explosion rocked the city. They rushed out of the gem dealer's store and looked toward the harbor where a column of smoke was rising from the dock areas. When several fiery objects arched through the sky they hailed a cab and returned to the RAF camp.

Volunteers were sought to help fight fires in the dock area. Rosenberger did not go the first day but signed up to help on the two days afterwards. There he found the destruction overwhelming and he spent two days fighting small fires in rice granaries along the dock for a quarter of a mile in each direction. They learned that an Indian built Liberty ship was being unloaded of scrap metal, lumber, cotton, $4,923 million in gold bullion, and 300 tons of TNT when a fire started in the cotton at about 4 P.M. Seven minutes later the TNT exploded and everything on the dock, including seven fire engines, was destroyed. A householder a mile away was rocked by the blast that blew out every window in his home. To his surprise, a 28-pound gold bar worth about

$16,000 landed on his veranda. An officer staggered into the Taj Mahal Hotel, blackened and bleeding, crying, "The air — full of arms and legs and heads — horrible — horrible!"

Thirty minutes after the first explosion another occurred. Fires sprang up everywhere along the docks and smoke turned day into night while police, firemen, and troops fought to control the fires that raged for five days from spreading throughout the city of 1.5 million people. Sappers demolished hundreds of buildings to check the fires.

While Rosenberger helped in the fire fighting on the third day, there were still dead Indians lying around, putrefying in the heat, their bodies unnaturally swollen, and the smell nauseating. Final estimates set the death toll at 4,500. Sabotage was ruled out and the cause of the fire was laid to spontaneous combustion. It was later listed as one of the worst catastrophes of all time.

While they waited impatiently to leave Bombay, the Americans spent considerable time in the central part of the city. Much of it was modern and attractive but street beggars were numerous. Frequently mothers offered to sell their small babies for three or four rupees (between $.90 and $1.20), to get money to keep from starving. In a section of one street, Rosenberger came upon an area called "The Cages." These were small sidewalk rooms where prostitutes plied their trade. He and his fellow Americans viewed with revulsion these women with their supplicating hands.

India had experienced a succession of drought years and rice crop failures, and there was widespread starvation. Mahatma Gandhi, India's spiritual leader and nationalist, had been jailed in nearby Poona in 1942 on a charge of "civil disobedience" for demanding British withdrawal from India. Now civil discontent against the British Rule and starvation rocked the nation just as small Japanese forces reached the Burma-India border in the east.

Rosenberger and his fellow officers enjoyed eating in Bombay's most elegant hotel, the Taj Mahal. They were fortunate in meeting a British officer who knew the city intimately. He identified some Parsees, whom, he said, dominated Bombay's financial world. He said they were generally called Persian Jews although they were Zoroastrians and not Hebrews. He described their burial practices in the "Tower of Silence"; an area they later visited. He said that after the Parsees died their naked bodies were placed on an open outdoor urn or slab where vultures soon devoured their flesh, leaving only the skeleton. They visited the "tower" and watched as vultures circled above the place located in a secluded area of Bombay.

The Americans soon tired of the strange and alien culture in Bombay, and were delighted when word came that their train was scheduled for departure. Although their ultimate destination was still unknown to them, they were anxious to get on their way.

Through the years the British had spent huge sums to equip India with a reliable transportation system as well as a mail and communications system as key parts of the colonization policy. When the Americans boarded their train, they found that their car was built sparsely, almost entirely of wood. They kept the windows open in the 110 degree heat as they began their 1,500-mile trip on a route that bisected the Indian continent at roughly its midpoint. They had been told to bring their own water and food because neither would be available during the five-day trip. The group's mess hall people, who were accompanying them, had brought along a minimum of cooking equipment and food supplies. When the train stopped twice each 24 hours, a fire was started outside the train and they ate meals at train side. They also had two large cans of boiling water to wash and rinse their mess kits so that no one got sick.

They finally arrived in Calcutta and were advised they had to change trains and continue for another 50 miles to their destination. During this part of their journey they talked with the train's engineer who described the terrible starvation in the nearby province of Bihar during 1943. He claimed that two, possibly two-and-a-half million people had starved to death. Many died along the railroad tracks, he said, or near small stations. They were deluded into believing that if they could get to Calcutta they could get food and survive. But Calcutta, he said, had its own starving people; a condition that continued throughout 1944.

After nearly three months of traveling by ship and train, Rosenberger and half of the 462nd's ground personnel arrived at the village of Piardoba and its huge nearby air base, which 2,500 men and 35 B-29s would soon call home. Their first look at the small railroad station, about all there was to the village, brought out their most intense misgivings. There didn't appear to be anything that would provide the necessities of life.

Although the base was primitive by American standards, most Indians would have considered it a country club. There was limited power for electric lights although the diesel generator was turned off from midnight to 6 A.M. Water had to be pumped from wells and it was not plentiful but sufficient for short showers. Due to the recent drought, adjacent ponds had been reduced to cattle and water buffalo mud holes. The new arrivals were assigned "bashes" with grass-thatched roofs that leaked during heavy rains and caught fire during the dry season. Side walls were made of bamboo and mortar, anchored to concrete floors. There were crude windows, but no screens, necessitating the use of mosquito netting over each bed. Each bed was laced with ropes that served as spring and mattress. But with an air mattress on top they were quite comfortable. Although the natives freely walked through the base to get to and from their own dwellings, thievery was almost unknown.

Now that both sections of the ground personnel had arrived, they eagerly awaited the flight crews with their B-29s. Little did the ground personnel realize the incredible problems the airmen were facing on their flights half-way around the world in an underdeveloped airplane whose problems seemed to multiply in direct relationship to the miles they traveled from Kansas.

March was a hectic time in Kansas as flight crews made a few test flights — their airplanes were still undergoing modifications — and finalized preparations to leave for their overseas bases. Their destination remained a closely guarded secret, but it was obvious that getting there would involve long flights. This was apparent because specially designed fuel tanks were installed in the bomb bays. These 600-gallon, self-sealing neoprene tanks were similar to those in the wing tanks. Their self-sealing characteristics prevented a non-incendiary bullet from causing a leak because a bullet hole would immediately reseal itself with only a minimum loss of fuel. (Connections proved troublesome, however, and gasoline fumes later proved to be a problem inside the cabin area.) The tanks were elliptical in cross section with a length somewhat less than that of the bomb bay. One was mounted on each side of the bay, secured to the bomb racks on that side so it could be jettisoned in an emergency. A third tank was hung from the bottom of both sets of racks and it also could be jettisoned by either the bombardier or the pilot.

The wing tanks carried 7,200 gallons of fuel so, with three bomb bay tanks, each B-29 could carry 9,000 gallons or 27 tons of 130-octane gasoline. The planes loaded for the journey overseas had only two bomb bay tanks in the forward bay with a large cargo platform underneath to carry a spare engine and provide room for personal gear. The rear bomb bay was also filled with spare parts on another cargo platform.

One regular army master sergeant in the maintenance department stowed a case of bonded bourbon that his father sent from Kentucky as a going away present. Unbeknownst to the group's officers, the sergeant's luggage contained a coil of copper tubing to permit him to set up his own still after he arrived overseas.

Those of us on Loberg's crew were anxious to depart, but our pilot was also squadron commander and his responsibilities went far beyond our crew. We finally received word that we would leave on April 7, and we hurriedly packed our things the night before. At the briefing, when we learned that we would fly approximately 11 hours across the United States and land in Newfoundland, we worried about our plane's engines, which already had about 10 hours on them. Although these were modified engines, earlier engines had an average life expectancy of 15 hours before they failed! There was very little experience with these modified engines to justify confidence in their greater longevity.

While the pressure to get the 58th Wing overseas between April 1 and April 15 accelerated, General Wolfe paced the floor of his office in the sweltering tropical heat of the 40th Group's base at Chakulia on the first of the month. Not one plane had arrived. Colonel Harman had flown out of Smoky Hill, Kansas, bound for Gander, Newfoundland, on March 26, but during his flight across North Africa between Marrakech and Cairo, his Wright engines had developed serious overheating problems. Harman managed to complete his journey to India April 6, but the rest of the command was not so fortunate. Wolfe had been assured that the problems with the engine had been resolved during the final modification phase. It was apparent, he told his staff, that the "Battle of Kansas" must still be fought, but this time thousands of miles away in North Africa.

Crew confidence in the B-29 suffered a sharp setback as word filtered back from those who had left earlier that overheating problems were continuing to cause engine failures. But we were anxious to be on our way after so many false starts.

Loberg's crew took off April 7 with mixed emotions, anxious ears tuned to the slightest whimper from our four Wright engines. They performed well until we started to fly over Detroit. Number 2 engine suddenly got rough and we could feel vibrations shuddering through the airplane. I glanced back nervously at Loberg, and his face was set in grim lines as he feathered the engine. We breathed a sigh of relief when the engine shut down normally and the propeller's blades turned vertically into the slipstream.

"We'll have to land," Loberg called.

The landing at Romulus Army Air Field was routine and Loberg left us to call Bomber Command headquarters. We had an extra engine in the rear bomb bay and a decision had to be made whether to use it. If we did, we'd be without a spare engine overseas, and we suspected that we still had a long way to go.

When Loberg returned, we gathered around him. "They're sending a new engine here and a crew to install it. We'll be here a few days."

Such an experience had been foreseen and crews were on standby at all bases to depart on short notice to any place in the continental United States. An inspection of the bad engine indicated that the old problem was still with us: A valve had been swallowed, resulting in loss of manifold pressure.

After a test hop on the 10th, we went on our way flying across the middle of New York state. I gazed with special longing at Schenectady, where I had lived and worked at WGY for three years prior to the war. When it was behind us, we headed across New England for Presque Isle, Maine. Originally, the B-29 operational plan called for a non-stop flight from Kansas to Gander, Newfoundland, in approximately 11 hours but all B-29s now were diverted to Presque Isle as an added safety precaution. This leg of the flight went smoothly and on April 15, we took off for Gander — a short flight of about three hours and 15 minutes.

Newfoundland was bleak and dreary with a lot of snow still on the ground. The thought of the long flight ahead flying diagonally across the Atlantic Ocean, skirting the Azores, until we reached the coast of Africa was unnerving when we remembered the B-29's engine problems. But we put it out of our minds during the three days we spent at Gander.

It was with a sense of relief that we took off from Gander about 4 P.M. on April 19 for our 12-hour flight to Marrakech in North Africa, relaxing only after wheels were up and our B-29 headed southeast. Before we left Kansas we had adopted a name for our airplane and she was now called "King Size." On the left side of the nose section one of the squadron's artists had painted a lovely woman with bare breasts whose size matched the plane's name. We listened anxiously to the engines but they were running with a smooth, even sound, evidently enjoying the colder temperatures. We were loaded in excess of 130,000 pounds at take-off. That was 10,000 pounds heavier than the B-29's original gross weight.

I looked down at the blue-green ocean, marveling at the white caps that ruffled the surface, and used them to determine our drift angle by sighting straight down through my bombsight's telescope. For the remainder of daylight I periodically gave the readings to Dick Renz, our navigator. As *King Size*'s engines continued to purr smoothly, I was awed by the sight of blue-green icebergs in the open Atlantic — wanderers from the far north.

After dark, Renz asked me to take some sightings with my sextant. I made several and gave him the readings. He looked at me with troubled eyes. "If you are right," he said, "we're way off course."

I tried again, getting substantially the same readings. It was a troubling thought for both of us, but we kept our findings to ourselves. Much later we learned that the curved Plexiglas in my bombardier's compartment gave an erroneous reading. Light from the stars and moon became so distorted that it was impossible to get a correct reading. At this stage of our flight we did not understand this problem and it caused a great deal of concern. I suspected that, through no fault of my own, the Plexiglas was giving me incorrect readings, but there was the nagging doubt that my crash course in navigation might also be part of the problem.

Renz was an excellent navigator, with considerable experience, so I recommended that he use his own shots from the astrodome on the top of the airplane to check our track over the ocean's surface and ignore mine. His own observations proved that we were right on track, so we skirted the Azores and headed for North Africa.

It was an incredible night, soothing to our jangled nerves as we rode above the ocean at 8,000 feet with a universe of thousands of stars for a ceiling. Some were so brilliant that they stood out in sharp relief against the dark sky. Away from the industrial haze from cities, the stars shone more brightly than I had ever seen them. Some seemed so close I felt I could reach up and touch them.

We were bleary eyed and exhausted as we approached the west coast of Africa and moved inland across barren desert country. Our destination was the French airfield at Marrakech and it was alive with activity as we approached. Loberg set *King Size* down without mishap. From the snowbound wastes of Newfoundland to the sand scarred deserts of Morocco, we had come with hope in our hearts and a prayer for old *King Size*. She was a good old girl. She had not let us down.

We quickly learned that the town was infested with Axis spies, so we were restricted to base. From what we had seen of Marrakech from the air, we agreed that the restriction would not be a deprivation. And, we hoped to head for Cairo in a day or two.

The air base was situated on a high plateau close to the Atlas Mountains. Hot and dry during the daytime, at night the temperature dropped as much as 60 degrees. The following day we learned that our stay would be prolonged, much to our disgust. Sandstorms became so intense that they blotted out the field at times, causing the B-29s to circle for three hours trying to get down. Aircraft service and maintenance became a hellish chore for the crews because there were no hangars large enough to house our B-29s. We were advised that all take-offs at high gross weights must be made at night because the hot rarified air necessitated longer take-off rolls than the runway could accommodate. After take-off each B-29 had to climb quickly to altitude to clear the peaks of the Atlas Mountains only 60 miles away.

But the basic problem with the B-29 remained the same. The Wright engines were not designed to operate at ground temperatures above 115 degree Fahrenheit, and the cylinder head temperatures reached their red-line stage before an engine was even turned on. This condition was bad enough at Marrakech but we suspected it would become worse at Cairo and beyond.

In taking off at Cairo in a sandstorm, one of our group's planes, with Major Walter S. "Scotty" Fellows at the controls, came close to disaster. Fellows couldn't see and his

B-29 struck a radio tower, the tip of which scraped one side of the fuselage and carried away his pilot controls. Five of the crew bailed out. Lieutenant J. T. Billings still had aileron and elevator controls on the co-pilot's side but no rudder control. He used the automatic pilot for rudder control to keep the plane in the air. They flew around to use up gasoline and reduce their gross weight, and Fellows made a safe landing.

Our most serious concerns were the persistent reports of engines overheating on B-29s flying out of Marrakech for Cairo, and particularly at Cairo.

When Wolfe received word that his B-29s were on the ground across Africa, he wired for kits to be rushed overseas to correct some of the worst overheating problems. Engine baffles were redesigned literally overnight while crossover tubes were hastily made and technicians were rushed from the States to retrofit airplanes wherever they happened to be. These tubes were designed to pump more oil to the rear cylinders, which were most susceptible to overheating. Engine cowl flaps were identified as culprits contributing to the overheating. They were shortened to permit more air to reach the outside of the engine.

Our crew spent 10 days at Marrakech; days of anxiety and misery due to concern about the future and compounded by heat and sand that made our days hellish nightmares. Each crew remained by its airplane to guard it.

Word was received that we would leave April 29. We took off just before dusk for Cairo, glancing anxiously at the 13,000-foot peaks of the Atlas Range as we soured above them and headed across Morocco and Algiers and then on to the flat desert lands of Libya along the Mediterranean. When night closed around us we saw no evidence of the wreckage left by the battles fought by General Montgomery's British forces and Field Marshal Erwin Rommel's panzer divisions. We passed over Tobruck and Benghazi where decisive battles had been fought just a few years earlier.

Dawn was breaking when we flew over the Nile Delta and across its many tributaries to our British base, catching quick glimpses of the Sphinx and some of the pyramids.

Loberg received word at Cairo that all Superfortresses had made the Atlantic crossing safely, but that one airplane had made the flight on three engines. The 58th Wing's B-29s had averaged 7,630 air miles since they left their bases in Kansas.

Although we were not aware of it at the time, Wing Commander Brigadier General LaVerne "Blondie" Saunders had flown the first Superfortress across the "Hump" from India to China on April 24. In a 1,200-mile trip over the "roof of the world" Saunders had encountered violent downdrafts, high winds, and sudden snowstorms over the Himalayas, with temperatures dropping to 20 degrees below zero. At times they could see Mt. Everest 150 miles away rearing its lofty crown to 29,028 feet.

As they crossed the "Hump" Saunders' plane flew directly over the Japanese lines near Kohima Road and Imphal Plain where some of the most savage fighting was then being waged. They were not fired upon despite that rare day over the Himalayas when there were no clouds. They viewed with awe the incredible mountain valleys over the "Hump" with their deep gorges and tiny villages. They were told that three peaks about 200 miles from their flight path had no known heights because no one had ever measured them.

As they let down into the Chengtu Valley thousands of cultivated rice paddies emerged beneath them. They spotted their air base at Kwanghan and noted with amazement that thousands of coolies lined each side of the runway.

After landing they were met by General Chennault and his staff, Chinese officials and American engineers. Around them the huge crowd of Chinese waved and shouted "Ding Hao" — "very best."

Meanwhile, at Cairo we attended a briefing for the flight to Karachi on May 3. Crews were shown the route they would travel, and pilots were strongly warned not to fly over Saudi Arabia, but to head north of that country because the tribes were considered unfriendly.

Our flight from Cairo took us across the northern Sinai Desert as we overflew many of the storied Biblical lands, including Jerusalem. It surprised us with its lush greenness. Skirting Saudi Arabia, we headed toward the Persian Gulf, using the long promontory into the Gulf of Oman as a navigation checkpoint. Soon the Arabian Sea was beneath us as we continued our eastern heading for Karachi. We landed there May 3 after a trip that lasted six hours and 55 minutes.

Two days later we took wing for Piardoba on the opposite side of India. Our final leg offered only difficult problems in navigation. At first we flew over arid countryside with almost a total absence of human habitation, which was surprising in this land of more than 400 million people. After two hours of rolling desert land, the sight of vegetation and homes was most welcome, although the ground seemed dry and unproductive. It was difficult to understand how anyone, let alone millions, could survive in this arid land.

A sight of the Taj Mahal at Agra thrilled us. The brilliant marble mausoleum, erected in memory of Mogul Emperor Shah Jahan's favorite wife, shone brightly in the hot sun. It was surrounded by beautiful gardens and pools while the Jumna River mirrored its magnificence from its dark surface.

The land unfolding beneath us gained in diversity the farther we penetrated Bengal. *King Size* made a steep turn and Loberg pointed to our left.

"That's Piardoba," he said. "Your new home."

As we circled into the landing pattern our dangerous journey halfway around the world was near its end, May 7, 1944, just a month since we left Walker Field, Kansas, on a long and anxious trip to India.

Looking back from my bombardier's position in the nose of *King Size,* I studied Loberg's face while he prepared to land. There was a wide friendly grin on it that reassured me. He had that young-old look that was becoming so much a mark of my generation.

Beside him, Major Cecil Durbin gazed nervously at the 8,000-foot runway beneath us.

"Flaps," Loberg called.

Durbin flipped a switch and the huge craft slowed down as the wing flaps reduced our flying speed for landing.

Perspiration oozing from every pore of my body, I peered at the scene before me.

Clouds of dust swirled about the runway as giant bulldozers rushed the field to completion. The field was 80 miles northwest of Calcutta and the Bay of Bengal. Countless buildings were in evidence with thickly thatched roofs. The entire base was nestled in a land of scrub trees and brush with native villages scattered throughout the area. The excitement of going overseas was gone and only the stark reality of fighting in one of the world's worst battlefronts remained. It was a thought that chilled me despite the oppressive heat.

The screech of tires on hot concrete interrupted my thoughts as we rolled down the broad runway.

After *King Size* was parked in a revetment, swarms of group personnel, most of who had come to India by ship came running to greet us.

I jumped out of my sweltering seat and headed for the hatch to get a breath of fresh air. The full force on India's 120 degree heat hit me and set my head reeling.

When Lieutenant Fessler, our regular co-pilot, who had come by ship, slapped me on the back with the full force of his 200-pound lanky frame, I almost collapsed.

"Welcome to Piardoba," he shouted.

"Is it always this hot?" I asked, while shaking his hand heartily.

"This isn't hot," he said. "It isn't even summer yet."

I groaned inwardly. "I suppose one can get used to anything."

After we had removed our baggage, we were driven by truck to one of the long barracks set aside for officers of the 769th Squadron. Its bare walls and cord-laced beds were not inviting, but I felt better now that we were all together again and at last had a permanent home after our travels.

Part II

CBI Operations

Chapter 4

All Alone Over Enemy Territory

Shortly after our crew arrived at Piardoba "Tokyo Rose" sent her radio greeting to Loberg and our group commander. "Colonel Carmichael, welcome back." Then she singled out Loberg, saying, "You, the one who shot down one of our big flying boats. You, we'll get you."

Despite all the secrecy and the diversion of a B-29 to England, the Japanese knew all along of our intended activities.

With our arrival the number of B-29s in India reached 130 of the 150 that had started out from Kansas. Five Superforts were lost due to engine failure, and four were seriously damaged. One take-off accident was attributed to pilot failure and he was assigned to ground duties in China for the rest of the war. Another pilot, a major, refused to fly any more after he arrived in Karachi and he was sent home for a court martial. After all engines were modified, out of the next wave of 275 B-29s sent to India, only three B-29s were lost.

Before our crew had arrived in India a B-29 piloted by Major Charles H. Hansen had encountered 12 Nakajima KI-43 fighters, or "Oscars." The Japanese fighters appeared near the border of India 2,000 feet below them as the crew prepared to fly the Hump. Half of them climbed to the bomber's altitude, but remained beyond the range of its guns. When the Japanese pilots finally made passes they were only tentative and obviously done to test the B-29's defensive armament.

Hansen's gunners fired at the fighters as they swept in, and three of the B-29's turrets promptly jammed. One Oscar pilot, braver than the others, came in from the rear. Tail gunner Harold Lanham fired and thought he made a hit because the fighter began to smoke as it disappeared. The Superfortress was struck by enemy bullets in several places, but not in critical areas, and it proceeded to China as the Oscars disappeared.

Our crew attended ground school for 20 days, flew training missions, and oriented ourselves to life in India. Our original quarters were near a native well and one of our favorite pastimes was to observe the parade of young girls carrying jars of water from the well carefully balanced on their heads. Small, erect, and very dark skinned, they seemed bright-eyed and intelligent. They glanced shyly at us, usually with one breast peaking out from the weathered wraps — a cross between a sarong and swaddling clothes — that they wore. I'm sure that they were as curious about us as we were about them. Although their once white clothes were stained with the ever-present red dust, they kept themselves as clean and neat as was possible despite their miserable living conditions. Most of them bathed daily, but in pools whose waters had been muddied by water buffalo and were far from clean. But that is all that they had.

At night rustlings in our straw roof reminded us that rats were plentiful, and that cobras were known to crawl into the rice straw in search of them. Cobras were numerous, especially the king cobra, which can reach eight to 10 feet in length. They expanded their hoods when threatened, which increased their ferocious look. The American engineers who constructed our base told us some wild tales about their experiences with cobras that were routed out of their underground burrows by bulldozers. American promptly killed every cobra they found and almost created riots among the Indian workers for whom the cobra is sacred. They would reverently pick up a dead cobra's body, anoint its head with rancid butter and give it a solemn burial.

Cobras were bad enough, but the kraits really struck fear in our hearts. Long, thin and rainbow hued, their bite was considered invariably fatal. Their nocturnal habits made walking at night without a flashlight a risky adventure.

It was soon apparent that women did most of the manual, unskilled work, tilling the rice paddies, working on construction projects and building their huts alongside the men.

Starvation had taken such a toll the previous year that the natives were reduced to eating large termites. They first removed the wings, rinsed the bodies in a muddy pool of water, and then ate them with visible relish.

Although training flights at high altitudes were a pleasant experience and a chance to cool off from the ground's ever-present heat (often registering 115 degrees but 130 degrees inside the airplanes) we grumbled at all the classroom work and wanted to begin combat missions. We knew that until we had flown a certain number of missions, as yet undetermined, we had no chance of getting home.

The forward bases in China were officially opened on May 5 in the rich Chengtu Valley in Szechuan Provinces. Before missions could be flown of out China, however, gasoline and bombs had to be hauled over the Himalayas. Heavily loaded B-29s, with four bomb bay tanks full of gasoline, went out daily across the treacherous mountains with precious fuel and supplies. Bomber Command figured that six to eight flights across the Himalayas would be needed to stock fuel and supplies for each mission to Japan.

It was a heartbreaking task because all too often so much fuel was consumed that little gasoline was left. Twelve hundred gallons was considered a good off-load, with some leaving more, and some less. The exception to this rule was the time Captain Miles B. Thomas off-loaded 4,193 gallons. However, he was flying a stripped down B-29 that had been converted into a tanker. There were four in each group, and they did valiant service.

Each day one crew was placed on alert and when it came our turn *King Size* was taxied off the runway into a revetment. Shortly thereafter a nearby B-29 caught fire, and we ran for cover as bullets from exploding turrets whined overhead. It was an unsettling experience to watch another B-29 destroyed so suddenly, and it reduced our morale to near zero.

The crew of *King Size* had needled Loberg long and tirelessly to persuade him to take our crew on a gas-hauling mission. We were curious to see what China looked like and could hardly wait to get going. Loberg's many ground duties as squadron commander, however, prevented him from flying very often. The 27th of May we were told to get ready for an early morning take-off to China with a load of gasoline.

"Wilbur! Get up. It's three o'clock."

Our flight engineer, Bob Albert, stood over me as I slowly came to life. "Are you awake?" he asked doubtfully.

"Yeh," I said sleepily. "I'm getting up."

The full impact of the day's importance came to me and I jumped quickly out of bed. "This is more like it!" I said. "It's good to have something positive to do for a change."

Just as the first full rays of the morning sun cut through the murky atmosphere, *King Size* lifted her wheels off the runway, tucked them into their nacelles, and we were China bound. We wore money belts with gold and paper money of the countries we were to fly over just in case we had to bail out. Intelligence provided us with a packet of silk maps to aid us in the event we had to walk out of the mountains. The most important document that each of us carried was a "blood chit" with our personal serial number on the left margin under a message written in Chinese characters. This number was registered to the individual it was assigned to. We were warned never to change "chits" with anyone else. We were told that in the event of a bailout over China, the Chinese "underground" would rescue us and immediately check the serial number to see if agreed with the name on our other documents. Intelligence briefers made it clear that if the serial number didn't match, you probably would be beheaded on the spot. In our "money" belts there was a promissory note with a United States seal on it. We had been briefed that the Japanese and some of China's warlords worked together in a mutually advantageous scheme involving Americans. Those who were picked up by the underground were turned over to the side that offered the most money. Thus the promissory notes could be used to outbid the Japanese.

Briefers urged us to find someone in authority if we bailed out because in most inland areas of China the majority of the people couldn't read their own language, let alone English. The "pointy talkies" they also provided were of little use because the only reaction we got from our Chinese guards was "Ding Hao."

A B-29 take-off at this stage was always a sweat job. Time and time again pilots reported, "cylinder head temperature gauges are against the stops."

Three days prior to our flight Captain Robert W. Rosebush had headed for China and found it impossible to keep cylinder head temperatures at an acceptable level. Full power was needed to lift his heavily loaded B-29 to an altitude that would clear the mountains ahead of them. His problems was magnified by the fact that he had been ordered to fly north to Fort Hertz in the high mountains before turning due east to Chengtu in order to avoid Japanese fighters at their bases in northern Burma.

Lee Wieschaus nursed the engines along as they passed the Hump and arrived over China. Then he noticed a flicking of the manifold pressure needle on number four engine. He glanced at the other instruments, noting that their readings were normal. He got up and stood between the pilot and co-pilot. He asked Rosebush, "Do you feel anything unusual in the controls?"

Rosebush shook his head negatively. Just as Wieschaus began to speak, Rosebush held up a warning hand. His left hand pressed the microphone button on the wheel and Wieschaus watched the pilot's face freeze as he held up four fingers and his mouth formed the word "fire!"

Wieschaus dove back to his seat and looked out his window. He noticed that the two-foot square access panel on number four engine was gone and that a four-square foot square column of flame was coming out of the opening, following the contour of the wing, and trailing 10 to 15 feet beyond the wing's trailing edge. He quickly flipped the fuel switch off, turned the fire extinguisher selector switch to Number 4, and activated the discharge switch. His immediate reaction was, "Too soon!" He thought he should have waited a couple of seconds for the fuel to finish burning. Now he had only one more extinguisher. He turned off the ignition and feathered the prop. He noticed that the flames had greatly reduced in volume although there was still a lot of fire. He flipped the other extinguisher and silently prayed. All on board held their breaths as the fire died down. Their greatest fear was that the fire would start again. Rosebush considered the amount of damage the wing had sustained, and whether he should order his crew to abandon the B-29. He knew if the wing broke off that the B-29 would go immediately into a spin and no one would get out. Rosebush talked it over with the crew and they elected to remain with the airplane.

Rosebush adjusted the trim tabs and increased the power of the other three engines to maintain airspeed. They headed hopefully to A-5 in China.

The wing held and they made a smooth landing that put no additional strain on the damaged wind. Upon inspection, one cylinder had swallowed an exhaust valve and the fuel line — a one-inch diameter hose — was burned halfway through. The flickering of the manifold gauge's needle, that Wieschaus had noted, was caused by backfires that started a carburetor fire. If the fire had lasted any longer that column of gasoline squirting on the fire would have caused a catastrophic failure of the wing. The main wing spar, an I-beam that provided much of the wing's structural support had been burned almost half through.

Rosebush's crew had to spend 30 days in China before the plane could be flown out. Another B-29 had made a belly landing at one of the other bases but its right wing was undamaged. Its outboard wing and nacelle were used to make Rosebush's plane flyable.

We were all aware of what happened to Rosebush's plane, and it increased our anxiety as we headed for China. The country northeast of our base was more productive looking, as village after village passed beneath *King Size*'s wing. The country was liberally sprinkled with small lakes and rivers. The swirling, muddy Ganges passed beneath us and we flew into Assam, with the Shillong Hills, all green forested, adding relief to the water soaked countryside. I looked down at those forbidding hills and thought apprehensively of the fierce Naga warriors in them.

It was like looking at a travelogue as we flew across the Assam Valley, with the winding Brahmaputra River on our left and the mountains surround Imphal and Kohima on our right. The mountains were beautiful, and it was difficult to imagine that one of the bloodiest battles of the whole war was being fought in that rolling, hill country. The Japanese most feared the Gurkhas, similar to the Napalese who guarded our Indian bases. Small and dark, these proud, fierce looking warriors were open and friendly to us but they brooked no nonsense when you didn't know the password for the day. British officers who commanded Gurkha units had one grade higher than the rest of the British army for the same command size. Leading such men was considered extremely hazardous duty. Their heavy knives, sharpened to razor thinness, could remove a head with one full sweep of the arm. Japanese sentries dreaded them because they crept silently up to them in the dark and their comrades found their headless bodies in the morning.

"Watch out for Jap fighters," Loberg warned. "A crew was attacked near here."

This sobering advice brought us to attention and we started up our automatic gun computers and searched the sky with renewed vigilance.

After Chabua, the hills gave way to mountains, beautifully wooded and split down the middle by deep-rushing rivers. The Yangtze, the Mekong and many others fell tumbling down their rocky paths to the sea. There was little life visible but I spotted a temple on a mountain peak at 17,000 feet. We had been advised that the Buddhists had such remote monasteries. In the valleys below, villages began to appear in the center of rice paddies. These remote villages had no roads leading in or out of them. This was the land of the Lolos, we had been warned. Tall, tough, and handsome Mongolians, many of them practiced banditry as a normal way of life. A few intrepid Americans had made contact with the Lolos on the ground and informed them that fliers with "blood chits" should be protected and aided to get back to civilization. Rewards were promised to those who did so. Later, it was not unusual for Lolos to appear at a Chinese or American air base with part of an airplane but more often a rusty .45 automatic to claim the reward before releasing their prisoner. Automatics were worn by each crewmember, and proved to be an excellent guide to that person's identity because the gun's serial number could be matched to that individual. B-29s were identified by the Lolos as airplanes with five "heads": four engines and a nose.

Now we left the high mountains behind. The clouds were building up and obscuring our view so we started to climb. We had been flying at 20,000 feet and as the altimeter needle mounted, I turned to Loberg. "How high are we going?"

"I think I'll add a couple of thousand for the sake of our families back home," he said with a grin.

We had been warned by crews who had made the trip that the maps were not to be taken literally. The heights of the peaks were often false, and the mountains themselves were not where they were indicated on the maps. In the months to come, we were to make our own maps of the Hump, placing the mountains in our new maps where we actually found them.

We rode high above a sea of white clouds. Off to the right a peak thrust itself conspicuously through the blanket of whiteness. After four more hours of flying we entered China and turned west at a large lake.

The bright colors of China were a joy to see. Brilliant and pastel shades of green, red, and brown were everywhere. We were still in the mountains but they were receding as we flew along. The beautiful colors of the uplands gave way to the bright greens of thousands of rice paddies. It was evident the Chengtu Valley nourished crops of rice, corn, beans, hogs, chickens, and water buffalo. Unlike the rest of China it had never known floods or famine although most people were desperately poor. Centuries earlier the Chinese had built an ingenious system of irrigations starting with the rice paddies in the hills with their circular terraces down to the flat plains.

We flew straight to the base of the 40th Group and then headed for our own 462nd Group at Kiunglai just 10 minutes away. As we drew near, we could see the Himalayas, which half circled the valley, their snow capped peaks rearing majestically skyward — often to more than 25,000 feet — with a fluffy cloud touching each peak.

As we circled our China base — it was called A-5 — thousands of laborers blackened the runway, paying no heed to us. We thought if we circled they would clear the runway for us to land, but they blithely ignored us.

"I can't stay up here all day," Loberg said. "I'm going in and they'd better get out of the way."

Our plane entered the final approach and the multitude scattered and ran for the sides. One old man with a heavy basket ran almost to the side and then as suddenly retraced his steps and ran all the way across again in front of us.

"What's the crazy fool trying to do?" Loberg shouted. "He almost got it that time."

We learned later this was done purposely. The Chinese, or at least some of them, believe there are devils constantly following them. They believe that if they run in front of something moving fast, the devils won't be able to get out of the ways quickly enough and will be killed. This foolhardy stunt almost finished the old man as well as his devils.

We were greeted by a host of impassive Chinese and by a few of our maintenance men stationed in the forward area.

The invigorating air of China made us feel good after the sweltering heat we had undergone at our rear base. We dumped our belongings in the tent and hurried to the mess hall. Patient, hurrying Chinese brought dishes of rice, greens, and some kind of unappetizing meat they said was pork. We grabbed stools and went at it with ravenous appetites.

After dinner I met Lee Wieschaus and commiserated with him for the near loss of their B-29 due to an engine fire over the Hump. He told me that he had just returned from neighboring Chengtu, a city of half a million people who lived amazingly primitive lives. He described meat markets out in the open with cut-up sections of pigs and plucked fowls hanging from rafter beams while swarms of flies feasted on them. He described how small children, wearing one-piece garments, were held up by their mothers in a sitting position over a street gutter to answer a call of nature.

"The mothers weren't the least bit embarrassed," he said.

Wieschaus, whom I realized later had a rare opportunity that few others received, said most of Chengtu's buildings were old, showing the effects of centuries of use. Some, he said, were truly lovely with their unusual architecture and graceful sweeping eaves.

It was quickly evident to me that despite being poor, the Chinese had a great sense of humor — at time somewhat coarse and ribald — but their sense of pride and worth was evident although life was often held in low regard, particularly in their odd sense of humor when the huge runway rollers crushed a fellow worker. Many Indians in Bengal seemed cowed and servile — obsequious servants — but the Chinese were different. Mess hall attendants often reprimanded officers for leaving food uneaten on their plates. Such waste was anathema in a country with millions of starving peasants although this was not true in this region.

Chinese guards on the flight line were smartly military even though they were dressed in ragged uniforms. They were particularly rough on Chinese civilians who ventured near an airplane. One civilian talked back to a guard and the soldier tied him to one of the props and beat the hell out of him. Another time two guards jumped a civilian who happened to pass too close to suit them. They knocked him down and clubbed him insensible with their rifle butts. Then they picked him up and threw him into a nearby rice paddy.

We Americans made the mistake of judging them by western standards, but as Orientals they were accustomed to pain and death. To most Chinese human life was extremely cheap. But as we got to know them better we marveled how much the Chinese people resembled Americans. They were cocky, independent, and always appreciated a good joke, even when it was on them.

It was apparent, despite American political propaganda to the contrary, that Generalissimo Chiang Kai-shek was a dictator. He ran a one party government and boys from the age of six were trained to revere their leader and not their country. At the age of 18 they entered the army or government service. By then they were totally indoctrinated in the one party system of government. It was a totalitarian regime that had little respect for the Chinese people and demanded unquestioning obedience.

Chiang Kai-shek and his ranking army commanders were closely allied to the local warlords and were more interested in stock piling modern weapons for later use against Mao Tse-tung's communist army than in fighting the Japanese.

We were assigned a tent to spend the night. It was a cement platform and contained four beds made of small sawhorses at either end and a bamboo screen, like a door screen, on top. We checked out some verminous cotton padding from supply and spread this on top, forming not a bad pallet.

"I'm gong to take a walk over the countryside," I told Bob Albert the next morning. "Want to come along?"

"No thanks. I've seen all I want of China."

I walked out of the area and followed a rutted dirt road wide enough for carts or cars to pass if both drivers were careful. I crossed a small river on a one lane wooden bridge with no side rails, with the bed of the bridge under six inches of water.

I left the road and walked across fields of rice tended by stoop shouldered Chinese. They paid no attention to me as they waded in six inches of water. I walked along the ridge surrounding each plot of ground and headed away from the field toward a small village in the distance. En route I inspected a flourmill and watched, as the rice grains were ground into flour. A heavy wheel was pulled in a circle, its weight grinding the rice.

The village was deserted as I entered, but not for long. Soon hundreds and hundreds of blue-clad Chinese crowded around me and gazed solemnly. I was fearful because I was alone, miles from the airfield. On a sudden inspiration I held up the thumb of my right hand, grinned and said, "Ding Hao!"

They shouted, laughed, and hurled rapid Chinese at me, which I could not comprehend. They followed me everywhere, noting my interest in Chinese statues, and laughed uproariously at my attempt to make a shopkeeper understand by sign language.

It was impossible not to like these warmhearted people. The village was dirty, and a stench arose that was almost suffocating, but they made me welcome and I was grateful.

The poverty was overwhelming and gave me a sick feeling in the pit of my stomach. How little we knew of real poverty in America. I thought of the months to come, and the missions against Japan. Would my bombs be falling upon people like this, of another race, but still the poor suffering hordes of the Far East? I didn't like to think about it.

I retraced my steps and left the village behind me, and the crowd followed me to the gate. They gave me a tremendous shout as I left, and I waved to them.

Early the following morning *King Size* took off for the return trip to India, flying again over the lush Chengtu plain, and across the great rocks forming the Himalayas. It was an unreal world of treacherous beauty, spectacular, but appallingly deadly to the unwary.

The streams of tankers and combat planes flowed unceasingly across the Hump, bringing not only valuable supplies and gasoline to China, but also providing experience for the crews. Planes were lost and many men were killed, but the job had to be done and the men and planes equipped for the harder task of carrying bombs to Japan. It seemed as if we would never obtain enough gasoline for a mission out of A-5. The trickle of precious fuel piled up maddeningly slowly, but the flights went on.

"Did you see the notice on the bulletin boards?" Albert asked me as I lay on my bed.

"No. What's it about?"

"Our crew and some others have to report to the flight line tomorrow morning."

I was immediately excited. "Are we going on a mission?"

"The notice doesn't say. Sure looks like it."

The next morning we were on the line bright and early. We waited impatiently for Loberg to tell us what the score was.

We crowded around his jeep as he drove up. "*King Size* must be checked inside and out," he said. "I want each of you to go over your equipment thoroughly. Check it as if your life depended upon it, because it will. Are there any questions?"

"Are we going on a mission?" Staff Sergeant Norman C. McLeod, our tail gunner asked.

"That's what we came here for," Loberg said, with a wide grin on his face.

We spent the morning and late afternoon giving *King Size* a good working over, and went home that night with a tense feeling in the pits of our stomachs, as we thought about the morrow.

The 770th Squadron had seven planes assigned to the mission, but three of them were not considered in "flyable condition until after midnight." Rosenberger's armament men worked all night to prepare them for take-off. Shortly before dawn a 500-pound bomb fell from the rack of one plane and crushed one of the armorers. Sergeant Brown was rushed back to the States, and recovered after a prolonged hospitalization.

It was always hot during the summer months in India, but nothing compared to the briefing room the afternoon of June 4. The room was not large, and crews overflowed in every direction. There was an excited chattering from all and sundry. The briefing officers looked down upon us with the "know-it-all" smile that annoyed us to the extreme.

The group's intelligence officer, Major Joseph R. Fawcett, stepped up on the platform. "Our mission tomorrow is against the marshalling yards at Bangkok, Thailand."

I caught my breath with surprise, as Fawcett stood before us solemnly, aware of the tremendous significance of the announcement he had just made. We learned later that General Arnold had wanted a mission to Japan but that General Wolfe had insisted there was insufficient fuel to China for a mission on this date.

Fawcett explained the target, saying it was selected to help reduce supplies to the Japanese fighting in north Burma. He pointed out the aiming point and other details we had to know.

The mission was to be executed in flights of four planes and *King Size* was the lead of the 769th Squadron. I joined the bombardiers in a special study period to familiarize myself with the target.

"How high are we flying?" I asked Major Robert A. Mitchell, the group bombardier. He had been Loberg's bombardier during the war's first year in the South Pacific.

"Twenty thousand feet," he replied. "Think you can hit it from that altitude?"

"If I can see it, I can hit it," I said cockily, with more confidence than I really felt.

Take-off time was just after dawn on June 5, and as we rose from our beds the next morning, brushing the sleep from our eyes, we could hardly wait to get started to bring an end to the mounting suspense. We ate a hurried breakfast of toast and coffee in somewhat of a daze, and embarked for the line.

I checked our load of firebomb clusters and stood impatiently by the plane waiting for Loberg. When he arrived, we turned the four-bladed props over and boarded up. After the engines were warm, they were run up and checked, and we waited for time to taxi out.

We were loaded to a gross weight of 135,000 pounds. This was necessary because of the long, gas consuming flight and the heavy load of bombs.

The time came to taxi out, so slowly and carefully Loberg headed *King Size* to the end of the runway. We were not the first to take off and we waited our turn with the engines idling. The last plane ahead of us started to roll, and slowly and ponderously it lumbered down the mile and a half stretch of concrete. A vapor trail followed it as the B-29 cut through the hot, humid atmosphere.

One minute to go. Thirty seconds to go. Each second seemed an eternity. Fifteen, ten, five — and the green light from the tower flashed on. Our four engines broke into a loud road as *King Size* started on her way. She seemed reluctant to take to the air. The air-speed indicator wavered at 100, jumped to 105, 110, and then climbed to 130 miles an hour and *King Size* was no longer an earthbound monster but in her natural element. The ground flashed by underneath and then we were over the barracks area, still low, looking into the anxious faces of our squadron mates and then, they too, vanished behind us.

All was going well. We settled back to watch the scenery. Rendezvous with the rest of our formation was in the Bay of Bengal. As we approached the sea, several planes were visible flying in and out of the clouds.

"We're in luck," Navigator Dick Renz said to Loberg. "I was worried about finding the rest of our flight in this heavy cloud cover."

After a while the planes disappeared. We made one circle without anyone joining us.

"I'm going to the final rendezvous," Loberg said. "We don't have gas enough to circle any longer."

The sea was an oily, glassy mass extending beyond the horizon with the pale sky of blue overhead. Here and there a heavily laden merchant ship wearily plodded up the bay to Calcutta. The air was calm and we floated peacefully on our way to the final rendezvous, an island off the coast of Malay Peninsula, 200 miles from Bangkok.

After the first circle at the rendezvous, two planes from the milling throng turned to us. After the second circle we had one tucked under each wing, but there was no sign of the third.

"I can't wait any longer," Loberg said grimly. "I'm heading for Bangkok."

The weather had been in our favor, but the change was sudden as we arrived over the peninsula and found ourselves surrounded by an impenetrable screen of clouds. Our wing planes crept in closer and tried to stay with us. It was no use. When we broke into the clear, they were no longer with us.

The worried crease on my brow matched the misgivings I felt at being all alone over enemy territory.

"Are we going in alone, Major?" I asked.

"That's the only thing we can do," he replied.

"Didn't they say not to at the briefing?" Renz asked.

"Yes, but I'm not going to come all this distance without a try at the target," Loberg said emphatically.

"Radar to bombardier, over."

I pushed my microphone button to respond to Lieutenant James White. "Yes."

"Are you going to be able to bomb visually?"

"I don't believe so, Whizzer. We're in the clear but there's a cloud layer over the whole area as far as I can see."

"Okay," he said. "I'll make the turn on the IP. Take over any time you can see the target."

"Roger."

Our turning point to the target showed clearly on the radar set as Loberg alerted the gunners. "Keep a good lookout for enemy planes."

His warning wasn't necessary. Our eyes were tiny slits peering in every direction. We donned heavy flak suits and helmets. All alone, over enemy territory, with a possible 60 Japanese fighters in wait for us, made it a tense moment.

An infinitesimal speck dotted the sky ahead, now disappearing, and then as it gained in size, growing into the unmistakable outlines of an aircraft.

"Enemy plane closing in at 12 o'clock!" I yelled.

I nervously reached for the gun sight and took control of the two forward turrets. I tracked the tiny image in my sights and started to press the trigger.

"Don't fire!" Loberg shrieked. "That's one of our own B-29s."

I looked over the colored glass of the sight and saw a Superfortress bearing down upon us, on the wrong heading, just above our level. My hands shook as I stowed the sight to one side. I was too ashamed to look around.

"Radar to pilot. We are just about at the IP. Take a course of 60 degrees."

Loberg turned the plane to the left.

"Bombardier to radar."

"Go ahead."

"I still can't see the ground. I'm opening the bomb bay doors. You'll have to drop them."

White acknowledged, and we started the run. B-29s were all over the sky, many of them not on their prescribed course, but making runs from every direction.

"I never saw such a fucked up mission in my life," Loberg said with disgust. "You'd think this was their first training mission."

Nothing could be seen below us, and as we headed into the target no enemy planes were in sight.

A series of stepladder bursts filled the air half a mile away. I stared with a kind of tortured fascination at these white puffs of anti-aircraft fire seemingly coming from nowhere. There were still no enemy planes. I almost wished one would appear because it was unreal to be flying over the heart of one of Japan's strongholds and not be attacked.

"Bombs away!" Whizzer yelled. The light flickered on and off on my panel as the counter of the intervalometer ran down to zero.

With a thrust of my left hand I pushed the salvo lever to clear any hung up bombs and called to the gunners. "Are the bomb bays clear?"

There was a brief pause, and then Staff Sergeant Isodore Scheinman, our left gunner said, "All clear, sir."

No sooner were these words out of his mouth than I had the doors up and we pulled away from the target.

I settled back with a sigh of relief. Everything had gone along fine, up to that point, but we had many miles yet to fly before we would be away from possible enemy attacks. We scanned the sky so as not be caught unaware.

"Enemy planes closing in from 7 o'clock!" the left gunner roared over the interphone system.

"How many?" Loberg said quietly.

"Fifteen to 18." Scheinman said with a gasp.

My hair seemed to stand on end. The hard, rough steel of the gun sight felt reassuring as I waited for what was to come.

The silence that followed was unbearable. "Where are they now?" I asked.

"They're still out there," Schein said. "Here they come!" he screeched. "They're closing in!"

Our taut nerves were on edge — the keen, sharp edge of fear. The faint roar of one of the aft turrets echoed in the forward compartment and split the tense silence as we took a renewed grip on our seat cushions.

Before anyone could admit to the firing, McCleod in the tail broke in. "I don't believe they are Jap fighters. They look too large. I think it's a formation of our own B-29s."

"I think you're right," Loberg said over the interphone. "I realize this is your first mission, but we've got to have more discipline over the target. I want all this yelling and screaming stopped. When you raise your voice, it's not easy to understand what you are saying. And tomorrow I want every gunner to go to Intelligence and study models of Japanese fighters. I thought you knew the difference between a bomber and a fighter by now."

"Planes look different in the air," I said.

"That difference may cost you your life," he replied. "On head-on attacks you only have five to six seconds to fire at a fighter. The rate of closure is close to 600 miles an hour. You've got to know your fighters and know them well."

The clouds parted and there below us the lush green countryside lay exposed to view. The shimmering tropical vegetation looked unnaturally bright in the humid atmosphere. The clouds gathered in fluffy patterns, towering like marble pillars to the roof of the world, as if providing support to the heaven of blue above.

Thicker and thicker the clouds formed, hard gray centers, and soft milky-white coverings to deceive the uninitiated. No attempt was made to hold a straight heading and we weaved in and out, turning away from a thunderhead on our left, only to find another in our path. These massive cloud formations, fashioned like an anvil, could not all be bypassed and we picked the smaller ones to fly through. As it was, *King Size* tossed and turned until we had to strap ourselves to our seats.

The clouds thinned finally and ahead we could see the bay of Bengal. The pitching plane as last rode on an even keel.

King Size was overdue when we arrived over the field. The routine of calling the tower and procuring the necessary landing data was soon dispensed with and we turned into the final approach. A severe windstorm had hit the field while we were on our way back so wind clutched at *King Size* as we rolled down the runway.

"We learned a lot this time," I said to Albert. "The next mission won't be so bad."

A crowd gathered around *King Size* as we entered our parking area.

"How was the flak?" said one friend of mine.

"Were there any fighters?" yelled another.

"Did you get hit?" another friend asked anxiously surveying the airplane.

Although we had seen no fighters, other squadrons had reported nine fighter attacks but all planes returned safely. We answered their questions and walked into the briefing room to give a complete account of the mission to interrogating officers. The mission was retold in detail, and at last we were free to get some much needed rest.

That night, among familiar scenes and faces, the anxieties and fears of the flight to Bangkok slowly ebbed away. We faced the coming months more confidently because combat had not been as terrifying as our worst fears had anticipated. We would soon learn that first impressions can be grossly deceiving.

Chapter 5

"Tonight We Bomb Japan"

"It was a fiasco," Loberg said. "No matter how you look at it, the mission was a failure."

I was riding back from group headquarters with Loberg after the reconnaissance photographs had been processed.

"We did drop a few bombs on the target area," I said.

"They were demolition bombs," he replied. "All our fire bombs landed in the city and on the outskirts. We even hit the King's palace."

"I'm not proud of it," I said soberly. "But if you can't see the target on the ground, you must rely on radar. Radar bombing is still in its primitive stages. When I think of the 1,200 bombs the command dropped on Bangkok that only 18 hit the marshalling yards, I agree it's a poor beginning."

Only 77 of the 132 B-29s that were assigned to the raid released their bombs. Major John B. Keller's crew from Chakulia crashed on take-off, killing all but one crewmember. Fourteen other crews aborted the mission and returned to their bases. One plane ran short of fuel and headed for Kunming. Sixty miles short of the Chinese city their tanks went dry and they bailed out. Five B-29s in all were lost, plus the lives of 15 airmen while two other B-29s were reported missing.

Colonel Carmichael set up a practice bombing range on Halliday Island at the mouth of the Ganges and we went out every day following the mission to improve our bombing.

The long hours that followed over Halliday Island were tiresome and uninteresting at first, but as time went on we came to enjoy the flights at 20,000 feet away from the dust and heat of the base. The experience gained by all crews renewed our confidence. Hundreds of millions of dollars had been invested in the 20th Bomber Command. We could not think of failure.

I routinely checked the bulletin board the evening of June 13 and noticed a list of five crews who were to report in front headquarters at 3 o'clock the following afternoon. No indication of the purpose of the meeting was published, but I thought I knew.

The briefing room was too small to hold the throng gathered under the big tree near headquarters. So, with guards to keep the inquisitive away, we waited eagerly for the group commander. We were excited and keyed up beyond measure as we sat beneath the tree in the sweltering heat of the afternoon.

Colonel Carmichael and the group staff at last made their appearance. The hubbub ceased and quiet reigned as the colonel addressed us.

"Tomorrow morning we will fly to our forward base in China for a mission," he said. "Don't ask any questions about it. You'll know soon enough."

What he did not tell us was that the day after the Bangkok raid, General Wolfe had received an urgent message from General Arnold that the Joint Chiefs of Staff wanted an early mission against the Japanese homeland to help relieve the pressure of the Japanese drive in eastern China, which was threatening General Chennault's airfields. Such a mission, Arnold said, was needed also to coordinate with an important operation in the Pacific. Wolfe learned later that the latter was the invasion of the Mariana scheduled for mid-June.

Wolfe resisted Arnold's call for a mission on June 15, saying he could get no more than 50 B-29s over a Kyusha target on that date. He advised Arnold that he had delayed the first strike against Japan until the fuel supply at the China bases was adequate for 100 Superfortresses.

Arnold insisted on June 15, and demanded to know how many planes Wolfe could provide for that date — or June 20 at the latest.

Wolfe tried to explain his problems, telling the Air Force chief of staff that the Bangkok mission had diverted some tanker operations, and that General Stilwell had appropriated B-29 fuel stocks normally carried by the Air Transport Command for Chennault's 14th Air Force. He said his gasoline supplies were now too low for a 100-plane mission but he promised to put 50 planes over a Kyushu target on June 15, or 55 on the 20th.

Arnold had always been an impatient man, wanting things done without a lot of explanations, and Wolfe's attitude irritated him. He told Wolfe that at least 70 B-29s must be on a mission to Japan on June 15, and demanded even greater transport efforts. He implied that Wolfe had been negligent in that respect.

Wolfe initiated an all-out effort to get more fuel to China, increasing the number of B-29 tankers, and reducing most other Hump traffic to the barest minimum so transport planes could carry more gasoline. Drastic measures were needed and strict rationing of fuel in China was imposed on all other operations. Arnold was advised that his schedule would be met. To keep the bombers in commission, Wolfe converted C-46 Commandos into flying machine shops that could fly almost anywhere in the CBI and make necessary repairs.

Carmichael concluded his remarks by saying, "I want you to go to your respective airplanes and prepare for the mission. Check everything. Leave nothing undone because once we are in China, there will not be sufficient time for maintenance work. If your plane isn't ready, you won't go."

Lieutenant Rosenberger, the 770th Squadron's armament officer, stopped by my office. He said he was apprehensive because he had not received any of the five computers needed in each plane for the Central Fire Control System. I shared his concern, but it was another month before they were installed. Armament men worked the night of the 12th and 13th to lead each of the group's planes with bombs. Auxiliary power was in short supply so visibility was poor in the bomb bays and the work had to be accomplished without electric hoists.

At daybreak the next morning the first Superfortress took to the air and the rest followed a tone minute intervals. Gunners in the central fire control section barely had room to sit. Five-gallon cans of gasoline, and crates of food surrounded them. Those thought of these loose gasoline cans tumbling about in rough weather made them wince. The now familiar terrain passed beneath us as *King Size* headed northeast.

For once the Hump was clear of clouds and we could see plainly the world's most rugged terrain for miles on all sides. There were mighty rivers, great chasms, and high plateaus where the feet of white men had never trod. The unbelievable was there to see. Houses and cultivated fields nestled thousands of feet above sea level. The people who lived there had a life that staggered the imagination.

The mountains sloped down to meet the rivers and plains of China and the ever-changing scenery looked more real and habitable. We were making good time and reached A-5 ahead of the flight plan.

The passive faces of the Chinese broke into broad grins as we opened the bomb bays and they saw the bombs. Our Chinese guards were dressed in ragged uniforms and carried outmoded rifles of World War I. They looked cold and half starved.

"Ding Hao! Ding Hao! Ding Hao!" they shouted, with their thumbs in the air.

After chow the bombardiers returned to their planes, took the fuses out of their cartons, and fused the bombs. Other members of the crew drifted out from time to time to check equipment. Excitement mounted and sustained us in a glow of exhilaration. Several photographers were in attendance and pictures were taken as we checked out our airplane. We felt like movie stars on a set, and rather liked it.

The B-29s were refueled as fast as possible with the precious gasoline we had carried over the Hump so many, many times during the past month. What we had ferried over had not been enough. Planes of the Air Transport Command were constantly landing and taking off after depositing barrels of gasoline. These barrels had to be rolled to small tanks and emptied by hand by Chinese under the supervision of our own men.

"Go to bed early," Loberg advised.

Still, sleep did not come as easily as that, and we lay wakeful until long past midnight, until fatigue caught up with us.

In the morning we met Loberg in the mess hall.

"What time is the briefing?" Albert asked.

"Two o'clock. Pass the word around."

Albert went out to *King Size* to check her again and came back with the report that she was in tiptop condition. So far, so good!

We whiled away the rest of the morning restlessly and nervously. Our appetites were slim and at lunchtime we didn't linger long at the mess hall but started walking the mile long road to the briefing room on the line.

The low wooden building with its tile roof was jammed with shouting, milling throng. Words were bandied back and forth until the place was a bedlam. We found the wooden bench with our crew's name on it, and sat down while Loberg checked to see if we were all there. We had a new top turret gunner, Staff Sergeant James O. Bush. Our first man, much to Loberg's disgust, had gone to a native whorehouse in India and was promptly relieved of his wallet while he was in bed with a young Indian girl. He returned to base, procured his automatic, and returned to the place and shot it up. He was remanded for court martial and Bush joined our crew. A slim, quiet fellow, he had worked on the ground in the armament section before volunteering to join us. He had very little to say on his first trip over the Hump, but watched with wondering eyes everything that went on.

A large curtain of cheesecloth screened the front of the briefing room. We gazed at it as if trying to penetrate the covering and learn the vital secrets it withheld from our view.

The outer door opened and the buzz of voices ceased as Colonel Carmichael and the deputy commander, Colonel Kalberer, entered. They talked with Major Fawcett and then looked over the throng packed into the room. The preliminaries were over. We would soon know the worst.

Carmichael ascended the raised platform amid exploding flashlight bulbs (11 members of the news media were present and going on the mission) and began to speak.

"Gentlemen, I know you have waited a long time for this. But the months of training and the sacrifices you have undergone will bear fruit tonight. At last we can say, tonight we bomb Japan!"

A roar welled up and thundered against the rafters. I felt a mixture of emotions: joy, fear, and consternation. As I looked at the others, I could see they felt them too. We had known since we arrived in India that ultimately we would fly to Japan, but the sudden shock that it was tonight was overwhelming.

"Our target is the Imperial Iron and Steel Works at Yawata, on Kyushu," the colonel continued. "We shall hit the target with the first plane about 11 o'clock tonight. Take-off is at 4:45 this afternoon. A certain number of planes will take off first to act as pathfinders to try to light up the target so the planes following can bomb visually. Major Fawcett will give you the details."

"The Imperial Iron and Steel Works is Japan's Pittsburgh," Fawcett began. "It produces 20 percent of the nation's steel, or approximately 900,000 tons a year by 20,000 workers."

We were shown pictures and drawings of the target on a screen. The aiming point was described and I could see it was a perfect target. It would have presented no problem of identification in daylight, but at night, who could say?

King Size was parked about an eighth of a mile from the briefing room so it was just a good walk to our plane. All during the briefing I had thought about the long flight and the possibility of getting back to base. The chance's didn't look too good because the round-trip flight of more than 3,000 miles, with approximately 15 hours of flying was more than we had ever accomplished with the 8,000 gallons of gasoline on board. On paper it had been proven that the flight could be made easily with 500 gallons in reserve. Our paperwork hadn't held up in the past. We were frankly skeptical and fearful of the consequences.

We met Bernard Hoffman at the plane. The *Life* photographer has been assigned to fly with us because we were the second plane of the entire command to take off as a pathfinder.

I checked the bomb bays to make sure that our eight 500-pound bombs were properly secured and the pins and arming wires were in place to prevent a premature detonation. Hoffman took a number of pictures of the crew in the bomb bay but they were later disapproved by the censors and destroyed because they revealed the possible size of the B-29s bomb load.

General Wolfe had sought Arnold's permission to fly on the mission but his request was denied. Instead, General Saunders represented command headquarters.

At 4:45 Colonel Carmichael lifted the first Superfortress off the gravel runway, his tail so low at the far end that he barely made it. I glanced back at Loberg and shook my head. He had once told me that Carmichael had a tendency to dray the B-29's tail on take-off. I said, "He's still doing it."

We were second in line, and I counted the seconds for Loberg so he would be ready when the light from the tower flashed on. This was to be our second heavy take-off, the first from India, and now here.

With the light we started our roll, *King Size* gradually gained momentum as her wheels rolled across the crushed stone runway. As we reached the tower, we were doing 90 miles an hour. Loberg held her down until the indicator read 135 and slowly eased back on the wheel. The plane lifted reluctantly, settled down again, and then slowly pulled herself into the air. The trees at the end of the field whirled past, the wheels retracted, the flaps were eased up and we picked up flying speed.

King Size circled to the left and I looked back at the field and counted the planes at the end of the runway. There were only 14 there now. Two had taken off while we were circling, making 18 planes in all from our group. We settled back for the long journey ahead, and adjusted our gear and ourselves until we were more comfortable. I listened anxiously to the engines, but they were purring smoothly.

"All's well that ends well," I prayed silently.

Rugged mountains surrounded the valley and we had to climb quickly to protect ourselves from the rocky slopes of the 10,000-foot mountains to the east of us. We flew in daylight for three hours or so, watching the changeless scenery below us, worrying about the gasoline, and not thinking too much about the target itself. We had been told about the hundreds of guns and the idea of going over Kawata at 8,000 feet had sent shivers down our spines. However, with the exception of Loberg, we were all ignorant of combat conditions and for once ignorance was bliss. From time to time Albert recommended lower power settings and he and Loberg worked in complete harmony throughout the trip.

The sun set behind us and the deepening shadows obscured our view except for tiny blinking lights from the towns and villages below us. Riding on top of the clouds, with a universe of thousands of stars above us, we felt cozy and warm in our pressurized cabin. It was dark, except for the flashing lights of the automatic pilot and the fluorescent lights of the instrument panel.

At the coast White picked up a checkpoint by radar that indicated we were on course, so we set out across the Yellow Sea with renewed confidence. Now and then lights blinked on and off below us as some unsuspecting Japanese ship passed beneath.

A darker mass appeared ahead in the enveloping blackness of night. A blue of solidity, with a few scattered lights, was visible as we drew closer.

"Dick," I called.

"Go ahead."

"There's a large island just below us."

"That's Saishu. We're not far from Japan."

We made a turn to the left. I noticed a bright glow off to the right and called Loberg's attention to it. "I wonder what that is?" I asked curiously.

The interphone clicked and Loberg's deep voice said, "That's the target. Those are searchlights."

I was fascinated, with a peculiar tense feeling forming in the pit of my stomach.

"Pilot to crew. We're coming up on the target. Put on your flak suits and helmets."

After turning on the IP, the lights separated and formed distinctive beams of light, shooting higher and higher until their brilliance was lost in the atmosphere. Mingling with the searchlight beams were curving arcs of tracer bullets and wicked red flashes of heavy ack-ack.

The clouds had dwindled and there was no protecting screen to hide us, except for the cover of darkness that still surrounded us.

"Radar to bombardier, over."

"Guy ...," my throat was stiff and tight, but at least the words came out. "Go ahead, Whizzer."

"We're coming up to land. The target should be just ahead." I leaned over the bombsight and peered down. But the searchlights had been turned off and I could see only an indistinct blue below, with nothing to indicate where the target lay.

"It's too dark to see the target," I said. "You'd better count on a radar run unless I call you."

"I'll see what I can do. The return isn't very good."

The darkness was rent wide open and batteries of searchlights combed the sky for us, wavering for a few seconds, then swinging straight towards us with unerring accuracy. They enveloped us in blinding light. We felt naked and alone in an unfriendly world, but the intense light was no help in locating the aiming points. In the contrary, the land below seemed to be covered with a milky white film, interrupted here and there by flashes, which went off and on with precise regularity.

"Bombardier to radar."

"Yes."

"I still can't see the target. You'll have to make the run. I'm opening the bomb bay doors and setting up the racks for release."

"Roger."

King Size lurched violently and then rolled to an even keel. I glanced nervously at Loberg but the cause of it was soon evident. Red flashes appeared all around us and long strings of tracers arched up from the smaller-caliber guns on the ground. The searchlights never wavered but followed us with maddening intensity. Giant mushrooming flares floated down on parachutes, lighting up the night in ghastly yellow.

"Left gunner to pilot."

"Go ahead Scheinman."

"I just saw a night fighter fly over us."

"Keep a good look out," Loberg cautioned. "The fighters can see us a lot better than we can see them. Make sure it's not a B-29."

The red flashes and the gray puffs of smoke were closer now and more intense. We were getting into the inner-defense zone and could expect to receive everything they had to throw at us.

King Size rocked and rolled, and the bursts echoed against the sides of the fuselage. It seemed impossible we had not been hard hit, but we were not through it yet.

Making a quick decision, Loberg called White, "Will it be all right if I turn off a bit and then go back on course?"

"Yes sir," Whizzer replied.

Loberg turned *King Size* first to the left, and then to the right, before turning back on the target heading.

Thicker and thicker grew the puffs of anti-aircraft fire as we neared the bomb release line. I glanced back at Loberg and it was then I became really scared. The white light accentuated the tight lines in his face, and his mouth was drawn rigid about his teeth. It wasn't a frightened look, but those lines expressed the emotion of a man cornered and fighting for his life.

The doors were open and the switches were on so I had nothing to do but sit and wait for bombs away, with my feet beating rhythmic tattoos on the floorboards and my heart pounding like a trip hammer.

"Bombs away!"

I quickly salvoed and pulled the door handle up as Loberg put *King Size*'s nose down and we dived away from the target. After what seemed like an eternity the refreshing blackness closed in on us again and we were safe.

We turned south, still inland, intending to pull out to sea as soon as we were clear of the target, but fate intervened in the form of more searchlights. A whole battery erupted into light below and those moving fingers were again probing for us. They swept the sky for a few seconds, and then swung directly towards us, forming a cone with us at the peak. Loberg wheeled *King Size* violently, trying to shake them, but it was no use. They clung obstinately, I felt the nose of the plane go down and I glanced at the air-speed indicator on my instrument panel. My heart seemed to jump into my throat as it registered 300 miles per hour — the B-29s redline indicated air speed that must never be exceeded. But the indicator continued to climb. It reached 310, wavered a bit at 320, and then rushed to 340 where the needle shuddered uncertainly.

I glanced apprehensively at the ground and could plainly see houses and fields. "We're pretty low," I said to Loberg. "I can see the ground."

He pulled up sharply and the indicator fell off until it read 175 mph. *King Size* groaned and creaked at this rough treatment, but we were out of the searchlights at last. Now we were too close to heavily defended Nagasaki for comfort, so we headed for the coast and flew out to sea for the return trip.

Our relief at getting away unscathed was inexpressible. We laughed and kidded one another until we were almost hysterical.

"What did you think of the mission?" I asked Loberg.

"That flak was wicked."

Loberg's reply told the story. He was more or less an authority on Japanese anti-aircraft fire. He had flown 87 missions in B-17s during the early days of the war in the South Pacific under the most trying conditions.

The quiet peacefulness was unbroken as we re-crossed the Yellow Sea and sleep was impossible to postpone and I dozed off, oblivious of everything.

I slept for two hours and woke refreshed. Then I remembered something that had slipped my mind. "How is the gas holding out?" I asked Loberg.

"Albert tells me we should have a thousand gallons in reserve," he said with a smile.

Renz, Albert, and Loberg were hollow-eyed with fatigue as we entered the Chengtu Valley. They had stayed wakeful and alert throughout the whole trial while the rest of us had dozed off.

There were only a few B-29s on the fields as we circled and came in for our landing. After taxiing to the parking area, we climbed wearily from the plane to meet the grinning faces of our mechanics and Chinese guards.

Our crew chief, Master Sergeant James L. Alexander, asked anxiously, "Did you get hit?"

"We must have a few holes," Loberg said.

"I don't see any," Alex said. "Wait a minute. What's this?"

He pulled a jagged piece of metal out of the main frame of the left landing gear where it had spent itself after penetrating the thin outer skin. It had made a ragged hole about the size of a 50-cent piece. We looked at it with avid curiosity.

"Here's another one," he said.

It was remarkable that it was the only damage we suffered.

At the interrogation we learned that we were the first to land on Japan since the Doolittle raiders dropped bombs on Tokyo in April 1942. Late arrivals over the target reported huge fires started by the pathfinders and we all agreed the mission was a success.

Thirty-two crews had to rely on radar, and 15 B-29s tried to sight visually. Twenty-one B-29s bombed other targets.

En route back, one crew was lost in a crash while two others were initially listed as missing, but it was learned later they had crashed, killing all on board, including *Newsweek* correspondent Robert Schenkel.

Only one B-29 was lost due to combat operations. Captain Robert Root had to make an emergency landing at a friendly Chinese airfield close to the battle lines. In the clear, he called for American fighter cover while he and the Chinese tried to repair his B-29 to get it ready for flight. The Japanese heard the call and sent their fighters and bombers to the scene where the B-29 was destroyed on the ground. Root's crew was rescued by a B-25 from Hsinching. Among those saved was Harry Zinder of *Time* magazine.

One of the B-29 photoreconnaissance planes dispatched over the target following the mission was lost, bringing the total loss to seven B-29s and 55 airmen.

Despite the fact we were dead tired, we were not inclined to go to bed. It was announced that an eyewitness account of the raid would be broadcast from the Chungking radio station, short-waved to the United States by a correspondent who had flown on the raid.

Long before 10 P.M. that night the radio shack was crowded with crewmembers anxious to hear what he had to say.

"I'll bet we really clobbered that plant," Albert said to me.

"I don't see how we could have missed," I said confidently.

"Quiet!" someone yelled.

The Chinese program ended as an American voice came through the loudspeaker. "The Empire of Japan is no longer isolated from the battlefronts of the world," the reporter said. "Tonight waves of B-29s attacked Yawata's large steel plant successfully despite heavy flak and night fighters. The strategic bombing of Japan has begun."

We listened until 11 o'clock for more news and finally were rewarded by a 15-minute analysis of the day's happenings. It appeared that the Japanese had been taken by surprise and were caught off guard. They announced to their people that four and six engine bombers, probably B-29s, had been over Japan but that most of the raiders had been driven off before dropping their bombs. Then they said that half of the hundreds of raiders had been shot down, which amused us because only five planes had been reported lost, with two missing, although later we learned that they had crashed, of the 47 that had taken off.

The Japanese broadcast a first hand report by a Yawata journalist following the raid. "Now all the city was black. Suddenly in the north we heard the sound of plane engines. The orders were flashed everywhere and all the sounds on the street stilled. The propeller nose of the enemy planes spread over the whole sky. Minute by minute the noise approached. At this moment there was a shot, like a skyrocket, into the air. Several tons of shots. I could see clearly the figures of the enemy planes. At once anti-aircraft began to shoot. The guns shouted like lightening. But the hateful enemy planes flew on. Suddenly fire dropped from them — one, two, three."

We had heard enough. Feeling quite pleased with ourselves, and in good spirits, we went back to our tents and promptly fell asleep.

The next afternoon a delegation of Chinese from Chengtu visited us and threw a party. There was a mound of peanuts on a platform and Chinese whiskey and plum wine was served. One drink of the orange whiskey was enough. It was about as rough as any liquor I had ever consumed. Carmichael and Chinese base officials began to salute one another, their countries, and then its officials in a time honored tradition that each person so honored must be saluted with a small glass of the orange whiskey. The Chinese soon began to falter, trying to end the ceremony, but Carmichael was remorseless and one drink followed another until I marveled at their capacity.

That night, at the warlord's residence in Kiunglai, the top officers were honored at a huge banquet. Some of our officers had to be carried home long before the banquet ended. They found that their capacity for alcohol was more limited than they thought.

The news was still coming in about our mission to Yawata as we prepared to leave for India on the 17th. General Arnold, in London attending a conference, had followed Wolfe's reports avidly, although Wolfe had noted the insignificance of the damage once the post-strike photographs were available. Arnold stressed the psychological impact on the Japanese people now that their home islands were no longer immune from attack.

The War Department issued a statement in Arnold's name saying, "This strike is the start of truly global aerial warfare." The statement revealed the formation of the 20th Air Force, which had been kept secret until now, and that it would be directed by General Arnold from Washington answerable only to the Joint Chiefs of Staff.

With Allied troops moving slowly inland from the Normandy beachheads they had invaded on June 6, the B-29s had struck Japan for the first time simultaneously with Admiral Nimitz's landing in the Marianas. Knowledgeable Japanese now realized that these events increased the danger to their homeland as nothing had ever done before. For those who honestly appraised Japan's inability to prevent such a B-29 raid against a vital target, they knew it was the beginning of the end.

Chapter 6

Arnold Fires Wolfe

Our jubilation over the success of the mission was short lived. The reconnaissance photos were clear and unmistakable. The damage to Yawata's Iron and Steel Works amounted to only two percent. Bombs had destroyed a powerhouse 3,700 feet from the coke ovens, which had been the aiming point.

"It doesn't seem possible," I argued with Loberg.

"You saw the pictures."

"I can't understand how we could have missed so badly."

"We've been counting too much on radar bombing," he said. "It has not been perfected to the extent where you can knock out such a plant."

"When are we going out again?"

"Not for some time. We've got two missions now and more crews have none. We'll just have to let them catch up."

The relative inactivity that followed was hard to take after the excitement of the last month but the group was not idle. Sasebo, on Kyusha, was bombed on July 7, a mission also doomed to failure. Meanwhile, practice-training missions were flown every day.

Our efforts had been more or less futile. We sorely needed a successful mission to reinforce our belief in ourselves and our equipment.

After the Yawata mission, General Arnold pressed Wolfe to increase the pressure against Japan by setting up a major daylight raid on an important steel plant at Anshan, Manchuria, several smaller raids against targets on Kyusha, and a strike against the oil refinery at Palembang, Sumatra.

Wolfe pointed out that a mission to Anshan was impossible because of the low fuel stocks in China and that such a mission could not be flown until August. In regard to the Sumatra mission, he told Arnold that the Ceylon airfield would not be ready until

July 15 or later. He advised Arnold that if he insisted on the Palembang mission, or the night raids to Japan, a large effort to Anshan would be impossible even in August.

Arnold sincerely believed that Wolfe and his 20th Bomber Command were not using the available C-46s and B-29 tankers to maximum advantage, and he demanded that Wolfe improve his operations. In no uncertain terms he ordered Wolfe to attack the steel plants in Manchuria and Kyushu, and the major oil refinery at Palembang.

Arnold was outraged when he was advised there were only 5,000 gallons of gasoline at the China bases. He bluntly demanded that Wolfe demonstrate immediate improvement of his operations. He not only spelled out a series of missions, but also insisted on the number of B-29s assigned to each mission, and he gave Wolfe a choice of dates in July.

General Chennault now wrote Arnold that he could no longer be responsible for defense of the Chengtu bases because fuel supplies for his fighters had been reduced below the safety level after they were diverted to the 20th Bomber Command to get the B-29s back to India following the Yawata mission. After some vitriolic exchanges Arnold agreed to restore the monthly guarantee of 1,500 tons of fuel and supplies to the 312th Fighter Wing, and the 20th Bomber Command relinquished its logistical responsibility to the fighters.

Arnold now ordered Wolfe to send 15 B-29s to Japan in early July and set up a major mission of 100 airplanes to Anshan between July 20 and 30, with another 50 Superfortresses to bomb the oil refinery at Palembang in August. Wolfe refused to commit himself. He was convinced that Arnold and the 20th Air Force's staff in Washington had no appreciation for his problems in the Far East. As he reminded his staff, the 20th Bomber Command was maintaining a new and untried airplane in the hot, humid climate of India under circumstances different than in any other theater. He readily admitted his in-commission rate was far below any other Air Force, but he believed the circumstances were primarily responsible.

Wolfe forwarded to Arnold his own estimate of the situation. He said he would need more B-29s and a guarantee that the Air Transport Command would commit itself to greater airlift of fuel and supplies. When Arnold reviewed Wolfe's proposal July 1, noting that his field commander would commit himself to only 50 or 60 airplanes for Anshan, instead of 100, even if all other requirements were met, Arnold decided he had had enough. He wanted action, and not excuses. He sent orders removing Wolfe on July 4, saying he had another important command for him. Wolfe left two days later and General Saunders, head of the 58th Wing, was named acting commander until a replacement could be assigned. It was a kick upstairs for Wolfe because he was given another star and named to head a reorganized Material Command where his excellent engineering background and knowledge of the B-29 and its problems could be put to better use.

Wolfe had been given an assignment as head of the 20th Bomber Command for which he was not qualified because of his lack of combat experience. But Arnold had no one else. Top commanders with combat experience were few in number in 1943 and 1944 and those who had proven their worth were already too thinly spread throughout the combat theaters.

Sufficient fuel was airlifted to China for a mission on July 7. Seventeen Superforts bombed a variety of targets, including the naval dockyards and an arsenal at Sasebo, the Akunoura Engine Works at Nagasaki, and an aircraft factory at Omura. Very little damage resulted from these attacks, although the Japanese were shocked by the wide dispersal of these attacks on Kyushu.

Unbeknownst to us, the Joint Chiefs of Staff met on July 11 to consider overall war plans. They decided that sea and air blockade of Japan's home islands, and massive air attacks, would not guarantee an early surrender of Japan. It was concluded that the destruction of Japan's naval and air forces conceivably might cause her to capitulate, but at a much later date than was considered acceptable. It was agreed, therefore, that an amphibious assault on Kyushu would be necessary on October 1, 1945, with another attack on Honshu in the Tokyo area for late December. Planners estimated that Japan could be defeated 18 months after Germany's surrender. Roosevelt, Churchill, and the Combined Chiefs endorsed these plans when they met at Quebec for another conference in September 1944.

When it became clear that the Japanese were unable or not interested in challenging the B-29s over the Hump (there had been only seven contacts by the end of July), a more direct rout that bypassed Kunming was initiated. This shorter route called for flights up through the Assam Valley. Although Japanese fighters were not a problem, the uncertain weather, primitive communications, and uncharted peaks made flying hazardous so crews were given credit for combat time although the hours were cut in half. In other words, an individual had to fly two hours to receive credit for one hour of combat time. This was only fair because crews were flying under the most dangerous conditions of any place in the world. In the first four months of operations, 12 B-29s were lost over the Hump, mainly due to engine failures. Men of the Air/Ground Air Rescue Service, commanded by Captain Frank Mullen, saved a number of crewmembers that were picked up by the Lolos and the Naga warriors in the hills of Assam.

By the middle of July, the monsoon season was on in full force. It rained constantly, and the high humidity and the ever-present stifling heat made living all but unbearable. The base theater consisted of a sheet stretched across uprights in the middle of a field. Regardless of the movie — and most were not very good — they were well attended even when it rained, as it did every afternoon and evening. The men sat on their log benches trying, for the time being, to drive away the constant boredom and thoughts of home and family.

Carmichael and Kalberer, and several other group staff members, used their own money to build more adequate quarters for themselves than were provided by the base. Each had a private room in the wings with bathrooms and showers with a concrete floor throughout. The central section was large enough for a social gathering for 20 people, with cushioned chairs. The place became known as the Taj Mahal and none of us objected to their better living conditions. But when it was learned that Carmichael and Kalberer were living with the two prettiest American nurses assigned to the base hospital, resentment threatened to get out of hand. This was a flagrant violation of military codes, and of questionable decency for all concerned. The others, who shared these living quarters, found the situation embarrassing but they could do nothing about it.

I talked to our group surgeon, Major Burnett S. Rawson, about the matter. I was from upstate New York and he had grown up in Vermont so we had a community of interests. I explained that the situation was becoming intolerable, and that it would soon become a nasty scandal.

"I know," he said. "I've talked to Colonel Carmichael several times, but he laughs at my concern. I've explained that he and Kalberer's flaunting of propriety was destroying the morale of my hospital staff. He replied that this was a personal matter, and none of my business."

"How does he think he can get away with it?" I asked indignantly.

"He won't," Rawson said stubbornly. "I told him yesterday that I would complain to General Arnold unless he and Kalberer stopped living with my nurses."

"You think he will?"

"The nurses are back in their own quarters today. I've threatened disciplinary action, unless they behave themselves. Carmichael is mad, but once he realized that I was serious about a formal complain, he backed down."

Our daylight missions had been limited, and fortunately so, as Captain Rosenberger reminded me the month after he was assigned as group armament officer. "We were all aware of the computer total correction motors in our fire control system," he said, "but until now no one knew where they were located." He chuckled. "We found three of them under the floor boards, and another in front of the navigator's position. They're worth about $10,000 a piece, and each weighs about 110 pounds. General Electric technicians found them for us. They are the first computer trained men we've had. We hope to improve our firing accuracy now that we can test the full system."

I shook my head in disbelief. The absurdity of taking planes into combat without fully operating fire control systems boggled my mind. It was so typical of much of our haphazard operations.

With intense 115-degree heat outside our B-29s it literally became impossible to work on bare metal without gloves. If fuel tanks were filled, the heat made the gasoline expand and overflow, creating the danger of an explosion. Finally a siesta period from 12 noon to 3 P.M. was declared when no work was expected. The fact that 40 percent of our group's ground personnel were routinely reporting to the hospital precipitated this new order.

General Saunders had resisted Arnold's demand that he send 100 B-29s to attack the Showa Steel Works at Anshan, Manchuria, pleading lack of fuel in China for so many airplanes. But this time he found that the problem was not fuel but aircraft, because his command was down to 127 Superfortresses, instead of the 160 authorized (10 planes to a squadron, 40 to a group). He advised Arnold that his command would make the attack on July 29. To save his bombers for the mission, he eliminated all flights over the Hump to China for 10 days prior to D-Day. His greatest concern was the exposure of his bombers at their China bases to Japanese bomber attacks. He had expected the Japanese to retaliate long before, and he was amazed that they had not done so.

Prior to the Anshan mission one B-29 crashed in Midnapore, killing eight of its crews. With those out of commission at the rear bases, Saunders had 107 bombers in China available to take part in the Anshan mission.

Each year, the Showa Steel Works produced one third of the empire's metallurgical coke, so it was a vital target, with a top priority. With two tons of bombs in each airplane, Saunders believed they could destroy the battery of coke ovens that constituted the aiming point and cripple the operation for months.

We were so dispirited about our lack of success that when our group's planes reported good hits, we were pessimistic. Photo reconnaissance, however, confirmed the crew reports and we felt a lot better.

But the mission was beset with difficulties. Out of the 96 B-29s that took off, 80 bombed targets. Only 60 bombed the primary target at Anshan, but they caused considerable damage. The 444th Group at Kwanghan was able to take off on time because a heavy rain the previous night had softened the runway's surface and 16 B-29s were directed to Taku on Formosa where they bombed without opposition.

There was little fighter opposition over Anshan, and although the flak was heavy it proved inaccurate. Two planes were lost, one over the target, from which eight bailed out, and another that cost the lives of eight crewmen from the 444th when it crashed shortly after take-off.

Arnold's confidence in the 20th Bomber Command was reaffirmed. He still believed that daylight, high-altitude missions against strategic targets could be made with acceptable losses. He now insisted upon an early mission to bomb the refinery at Palembang and to mine Sumatra's Moesi River. The Combined Chiefs of Staff had assigned a top priority to Palembang at the Cairo Conference. As a diversionary move, a small group of B-29s would fire bomb Nagasaki. Arnold told Saunders that these targets, 3,000 miles apart, would demonstrate for the first time the versatility of the Superfortress.

Arnold sought a daylight mission but Saunders explained that there was only one Royal Air Force field at China Bay, Ceylon, available for the Sumatra mission, and it could not accommodate his proposed B-29 strike force. Arnold reluctantly agreed to a dawn or dusk attack by at least 50 aircraft.

The refinery at Palembang was of great strategic value, producing 22 percent of Japan's fuel oil and 78 percent of its aviation gasoline. Some Air Force planners argued against the mission because Japan had such a shortage of tankers now that the United States Navy dominated the sea-lanes in the South Pacific that little oil was reaching the homeland. However, the Sumatra oil was vital to Japanese operations throughout the western Pacific.

Our crew arrived at China Bay August 9, among 56 B-29s assigned to the mission. We were parked according to our take-off order because the 7,200-foot runway was too crowed for maneuvering later.

Loberg joined aircraft commanders late that afternoon for a special briefing. When the crews departed India they were not told where they were going other than that they would be based temporarily at China Bay, Ceylon. Lieutenant Colonel Donald A. Roush reviewed the reasons for the mission in relation to the total war effort in the

Pacific, and how it was the start of a large B-29 mine laying campaign. Roush paused and looked at them solemnly. "General Arnold is prepared to sacrifice every B-29 on the mission to achieve success."

The pilots were shocked by his disclosure, listening to Roush in disbelief as he said that the round trip of almost 4,000 miles was expected to be beyond the capabilities of the B-29 so the British had positioned destroyers and a cruiser 600 miles from Ceylon along their return route. "When you reach them," Roush said, "you should know you have fuel enough to make it all the way. If not, ditch near the ships and you'll be picked up."

The gravity of the situation was evident when Roush told them that each crewmember must have his papers in order such as his last will and testament, insurance, etc.

The 462nd Group was assigned the job of mining the Moesi River. We bombardiers were briefed long before we left Piardoba because we were unfamiliar with the 1,000-pound aerial mines we would drop.

Lieutenant Commander Kenneth L. Veth of the United States Navy had briefed us about their inner workings, (various devices were built into the mines to delay detonation) how they were set and that they must be dropped at least 400 feet apart so the detonation of one of them would not set off another. He said drag chutes from altitudes below 1,000 feet would release the mines.

Loberg joined the rest of his crew for the briefing that night and he was unusually solemn. He did not mention the possibility of it being one-way mission, nor did the briefers. But they also did not minimize the risks and there were sober glances and a hush throughout the briefing room. We were told that the 462nd would mine the Moesi River while the other groups would attack the Pladjoe Refinery to draw attention away from the mine laying. Major Fawcett said it was hoped that such a distraction would prevent the Japanese from knowing that the river was being mined, and not learn about it until ships were blown up.

Forty-two aircraft were assigned to attack the refinery while 14 B-29s from our group would come in low, following the contours of the river, and drop two mines from each aircraft. The bombsight wasn't required because the mines would be positioned by the navigator using radar, or dropped by the bombardier visually. Each aircraft was assigned specific points on the river to place the mines.

The flight plan called for the longest mission ever flown by the Superfortresses. Actually, it proved to be even longer for the mine laying B-29s because they had to climb to more than 12,000 feet to get over the mountains, descend to the target at sea level and then climb back to their original altitude on their return flight.

Our crew's part in the mission was brief. Just after take-off a door on one of the wheel cells was ripped off so we had to abort.

When the crews returned, they were red-eyed and completely exhausted. From them we pieced together the results of the mission. One plane, piloted by Colonel Carmichael, had flown an unbelievable 4,327 air miles. (This later proved to be the command's longest mission.) Another plane made it back only after jettisoning all loose equipment, including the radar set, the gun barrels, and many other items to lighten

Chapter 6: Arnold Fires Wolfe 81

the load. They landed at China Bay with almost dry fuel tanks. Only a miracle got them back at all. Major Thomas R. Vaucher's crew mined the Moesi just as they had been briefed but ran into trouble on the return flight when his number three engine caught fire. Fortunately, it was put out. He was so low on fuel that another engine quit 10 miles from China Bay and he quickly feathered the propeller. He landed with almost dry tanks after flying 4,030 miles in almost 19 hours.

After the mission Vaucher realized how primitive their cruise control techniques were, and that if properly flown the B-29 could fly farther than anyone had imagined. He was convinced that the Superfort actually could fly farther on three engines than four once its bomb load was released to reduce the gross weight.

Only eight B-29s dropped mines, but none were lost. Twelve B-29s failed to find any target but 39 others did. Carmichael's plane was one of those that dropped its mines. It was the first to take off and the last to get back, flying 18 hours and 54 minutes.

There were 37 fighter attacks, and some Japanese pilots followed the bombers 350 miles out to sea. Only one B-29 was forced to ditch, and the crew, minus a gunner who was killed in the ditching, was picked up 90 miles from China Bay.

Only one small building of the refinery was destroyed but it was learned after the war that three ships were sunk in the Moesi River, and four damaged by the 16 mines laid by the 462nd Group. Oil shipments were delayed a month before the channel could be cleared of mines.

That night, another mission, 3,000 miles away, was flown from the command's forward bases in China.

Captain George Hadley's voice was low but tense at they neared their IP close to Nagasaki. Their route from their base in China had been uneventful, and he hoped that the rest of the trip would be equally so. "Pilot to crew. Put on your flak helmets and vests."

They droned through the night, seemingly alone, although there were nine other B-29s assigned to the mission, with tension mounting every minute.

At the IP, Hadley called, "Pilot to bombardier. It's all yours."

Lieutenant James C. Whitehurst replied tensely, "Roger."

With the airplane now on autopilot, Whitehurst controlled its every move as it weaved back and forth as he lined up their aiming point. In the rear of the airplane, Radar Operator Lieutenant Francis J. Boyer worked closely with the bombardier to make sure they were aimed at the city, shown only by a bright spot on his radar scope. The B-29's front bomb bay was filled with two fuel tanks while the rear bay had 20 500-pound firebomb clusters. During the briefing they had been told that Nagasaki was an ideal target for firebombs because there were no discernable fire breaks despite the inflammatory nature of the city's wooden structures.

"Bomb bay doors open?" Whitehurst called. Left Gunner Sergeant Thomas F. Walsh quickly confirmed that the rear doors were open.

Flashes of exploding anti-aircraft shells reminded them that they were approaching the city, and some fragments slashed through the thin outer skin of the aircraft.

One penetrated the wall near Boyer, creasing the top of his helmet before it embedded itself in the wall behind him.

"Bombs away!" Whitehurst called. "Check to bomb bay."

Right Gunner Sergeant Kenneth Crowell, monitoring the rear bomb bay through its round window, immediately called, "Sir, the bombs are still in the bomb bay."

Hadley glanced at his co-pilot, Lieutenant William J. Meader, and there was heightened concern in his eyes.

"Pilot to bombardier. What went wrong?"

"I think we have a burnt out fuse," Whitehurst replied.

Hadley started to turn the airplane and Lieutenant William J. Meuwissen called anxiously, "Navigator to pilot. Why are you making the turn?"

Hadley replied, "We are going to make another bomb run as soon as the bombardier checks his equipment."

Meuwissen warned, "Your heading for Yawata!" At briefing they had been advised that this was a heavy flak area and should be avoided. He gave Hadley another heading that would return them to their initial point. After they returned over the ocean, antiaircraft fire ceased. It had been intense although largely erratic.

They made another run, and still the bombs refused to drop. Then as the crew faced a third run over the target apprehension gripped them because the Japanese gunners were now getting their range. Members of the crew repeatedly reported hits but they were grateful the shells hadn't reached a vital spot.

After completion of the third run, with the bombs still hanging from their shackles, Hadley almost exploded with exasperation but he kept his voice down so as not to panic the crew. But his irritation with the bombardier could not be disguised. "Salvo the bombs on the next run!"

For the fourth time they flew the dangerous track over the city while exploding shells highlighted them for the gunners on the ground, and searchlights kept them bracketed. Miraculously none of the shells found a vulnerable spot.

For the fourth time that night Whitehurst announced, "Bombs away!" This time the left gunner, Sergeant Thomas F. Walsh, reported they had left the bomb bay, but at the same instant, radio operator Sergeant Wilbur W. Cipperly heard a loud crash in the front bay. He hurried to the window and noticed with shock that the lower bomb bay fuel tank had released, ripping through the bomb bay doors, and that the second tank was hung up on one end, swinging down and battering the radome. As he continued to watch, the second tank broke free and disappeared. He reported his findings to the pilot.

Hadley had only a moment to give his co-pilot a look of desperation. He called the radio operator, "Are the front bay doors closed?"

"No sir," Cipperly replied. "Evidently they've been damaged so severely that they cannot close completely. The radar dome is smashed."

Boyer called from his radar position, "My return's gone."

Hadley called Meuwissen, "We may not have enough fuel to make it back. Give me the shortest route to our China base. I've noticed that our fuel consumption has increased, probably due to the additional drag caused by the partially opened front bomb bay doors. And we expended extra fuel over the target area on those three extra runs."

Meuwissen quickly figured out a straight route and gave the heading to the pilots.

Hadley called the flight engineer, Sergeant John K. Evans, "Keep me informed about how much time we have before we run out of fuel."

Hadley addressed the crew. "I want all gunners to be extremely alert after daylight over occupied China. Any fighter attacks will probably come from the rear, so Lewison, be on particular alert." Sergeant Stanley K. Lewison acknowledged. He had a 20-mm cannon and two .50-caliber machine guns with a lethal range to protect their rear.

There was a solid undercast over much of the route back so Meuwissen relied on dead reckoning and shot an occasional star fix before daylight chased away the stars.

By then the clouds began to dissipate. Co-pilot Meader called the navigator to announce that he had spotted a large river.

The navigator quickly asked, "Is there a bend in it?"

"Roger," Meader replied, "about a 90 degree turn."

Meuwissen breathed a sigh of relief. Now he knew where they were. He gave Hadley a new heading to bring them directly to their base.

There was just a trace of panic in the flight engineer's voice as he called the pilot, "Fuel gauges are registering almost empty."

Meader called, "There's the base. It lay directly ahead."

Hadley kept an eye on the fuel gauges as he pulled back the throttles at 4,200 feet and made a straight-in approach. No sooner did the wheels touch than the right inboard engine quit. While taxiing off the runway, the left inboard went off. Both engines were out of fuel. Their nerve-wracking flight had brought them close to disaster but the crew's growing experience helped them to get back safely.

Hadley now demanded to know what had happened to the bombing equipment whose failure had nearly proved catastrophic. It was learned that bombardier Whitehurst had not followed proper procedure of immediately using the emergency salvo lever, which would have manually released the bombs on the first run. Under combat conditions bombardiers had to know their equipment thoroughly but a failure at this early stage unfortunately had been all too common. In addition, the forward bomb bay tanks would not have jettisoned if he had left the bomb bay switch off in the front bay.

The mission proved a failure because no fires were started in Nagasaki. It must have been disconcerting, however, to have two missions so far apart hitting Japanese targets simultaneously.

Day in and day out sullen skies hovered over our base in India. Training missions were flown in all kinds of weather through thick overcasts and around towering thunderheads. I was on one such flight to check out a bombardier when we encountered severe turbulence. Our B-29 rose and fell 5,000 feet a minute. I was sitting on the trap door, or bouncing off the ceiling, during these express-elevator maneuvers. But the business of destroying Japan's ability to wage war went on slowly but surely.

August 20 was an anxious day for those of us who remained behind after crews left for China the day before. I talked to Loberg at Operations, "Where is the mission today?"

"Yawata again," he said soberly.

"Not in daylight!" I said incredulously. He nodded.

Carmichael's formation continued on to the target and bombed it. Sixty miles from Japan on their return flight to China, Japanese fighters appeared in large numbers. Carmichael's plane was hit by a phosphorous bomb on the top of its fuselage above the internal bomb bay tanks (B-29s on this mission carried 2,400 gallons of 120-octane fuel in bomb bay auxiliary tanks in addition to the 5,400 gallons in the wing tanks). The phosphorus bomb burned through the thin skin and set the tanks on fire. Major Harold J. Mann, the bombardier, tried to salvo the tanks (they were mounted on bomb racks), but they refused to release because of the damage to the release mechanism.

Now other fighters bore in and Central Fire Control Operator and Group Gunnery Officer Captain Chester E. Tims, was hit in the shoulder. In the nose section, Mann fired short bursts at a "Tony" fighter and it exploded. He called to Carmichael, "Hey, did you see that?"

"It's a little too late," Carmichael said, "Bail out!"

Four gunners in back left the plane. Three landed in the ocean two miles from Iki Island but Tim's parachute failed to open. Japanese fishing boats picked up Joseph B. Datarra, Jr., Gerald B. Livingston, and John A. Fisher.

The B-29's navigator, Major Edward A. Perry had tried to put out fires in the bomb bays without success. Now he got into the co-pilot's seat, vacated by Lieutenant Carl A. Skedsvold who had followed Carmichael's order to bail out. Skedsvold was machine gunned in his parachute and killed. Carmichael looked at Perry, "What the hell do you think you are doing?"

"I'm going to help you fly this thing."

Carmichael swung the yoke back and forth, "The hydraulic lines have been burned out. I have no control. Get out!"

Radio Operator Sergeant Remick Wallace alerted the two American submarines on lifeguard duty. In the clear, he used their code names, "Clever Clarey" and "Larapin Lulu." Carmichael's plane was only 146 miles from USS *Pintado* under Lieutenant Commander Bernard A. Clarey while USS *Crosker,* commanded by Commander John E. Lee was 110 miles from Iki Island.

Meanwhile the attacks continued and the three B-29s fought with a desperate urgency. Carmichael's two wingmen moved closer while gunners fought off repeated attacks, the plane's cabins reeking with the smell of gunpowder.

Roush glanced nervously at Hoisington when Carmichael's plane for some unknown reason made a steep turn to the right (Carmichael had lost all control of his B-29). The B-29 on the right was forced to break sharply to avoid collision, and dropped out of formation. Roush's B-29 on the high side of the turn, managed to stay with Carmichael's plane.

When the latter's B-29 completed its turn it was headed in the general direction of China. Roush and Hoisington were shocked when Carmichael's plane suddenly slowed down and went into a steep glide.

"Pilot to crew," Roush called. "I'm going out in front to protect Carmichael's plane from fighter attacks. If that fails, perhaps I can direct him to the nearest rescue submarine."

At 10,000 feet, Carmichael's plane headed for Iki Island; a cone of land sticking out of the ocean off the coast of Japan.

After Perry bailed out at low altitude, he hit the ground hard. Mann, sitting with his legs hanging out of the nose wheel well, saw Wallace coming around the turret, just before he released his hold and dropped out. After his chute opened a Japanese fighter made a pass at him firing all his guns at the helpless Mann. He slide slipped his parachute canopy to dump the air and let himself free-fall several hundred feet. Evidently Wallace never left the airplane and was killed in the crash. His body was found later in the wreckage. After the war Flight Engineer Paul M. Clark buried Carl Skedsvold's body on Iki Island. Tim's body was never found.

Mann landed in a rice paddy and immediately hid his chute. He decided to head for the coast to steal a fishing boat and try to reach one of the submarines. He hoped to meet Perry because the navigator would have a better idea where the submarines were located. After an hour, a Japanese civilian spotted him. His first reaction was to kill him. He discarded the thought because it would make his plight worse now that he realized that further evasion was useless. He followed the Japanese to a nearby village. There he was beaten with clamming rakes and clubs. A Japanese soldier fractured his skull with a butt stroke and he passed out.

While Carmichael's men were bailing out, Hoisington called the crew. "Count the chutes." They reported eight. He watched in horrified fascination as Carmichael's B-29 went into a horizontal fall and then plunged out of control. It crashed on the western side of the island. Their eyes were scaled by tears as they watched chutes collapse on land and some on the water.

Four crewmembers were placed on trial in Japan and charged with war crimes for bombing civilians. Convicted and condemned to death, they were kept in solitary confinement for eight months at Kempai Headquarters and at Ofuna Naval Prison. Those convicted were Carmichael, Mann, 1st Lieutenant Ernest A. Pickett, and Lieutenant Irving Newman from the 468th Group. They were never executed because the growing number of prisoners would have lessened the impact of their deaths.

Carmichael, and those members of his crew who survived, emerged at the end of the war so emaciated and ill that it was a miracle they had survived. Carmichael, along with tree other officers, was held in solitary confinement for six months. They were kept in small individual cells where they could not sit up straight or stretch out. Some officers were almost beaten to death. With indomitable courage Carmichael refused to let his tormentors destroy him. Several times his body was subjected to the full swing of a piece of wood like a baseball bat. He was beaten so badly that some of his ribs were broken. They even hit him in the head. He said he was fortunate because the Japanese bat wielder was small without the strength to cause him a lasting injury.

In April 1945, they were sent to Omori to a camp on a small island in Tokyo Bay. This island is connected to the mainland by a small bridge. Thirty-eight "special prisoners" were separated by a wall from other prisoners. They were all Americans but not necessarily B-29 fliers. Not included as "special prisoners" were eight men who had survived the sinking of the submarine *Tang*. Two Marines, including Gregory "Pappy" Boyington, and several Navy flies and B-24 crewmembers made up the rest. No distinction was made between officers and men and they were all treated badly.

After the fire raids on Tokyo in 1945, Carmichael was one of those forced to carry the "honey buckets" containing human waste through the streets of Omori. Before he was shot down, he was a 220-pound, raw-boned Texan without an ounce of fat. After, his weight was down to 140 pounds. He hadn't lost his sense of humor. He said he was proud that during his "honey bucket" period he never spilled a drop.

Carmichael's crew was liberated August 29, 1945 by sailors under Commander Harold E. Stassen. Major Mann was down to 118 pounds from 212. He had flown 30 missions with the 93rd B-24 Group in Europe and North Africa prior to his service in the Far East.

After his return from China, Loberg told us in India that the B-29s on the daylight Yawata mission were attacked by swarms of fighters. "A good many of the command's aircraft were shot down. Crews said the anti-aircraft fire was deadly and planes blew up right over the target."

"I can't believe it," I said, as the horror of the mission slowly crept into my consciousness. "How many planes did we lose?" My voice was just a whisper.

"Eighteen out of 70," Loberg said. "Some crews were saved when they bailed out over China."

"This blow will finish us," I said.

"No, it won't," Loberg said. "But my worst fears were confirmed about daylight missions over Japan."

"Did they get the target?"

"It's been hit, but far from knocked out."

"Then we'll have to go back and get it," I said with no enthusiasm.

"That's right," Loberg said.

"Who's going to take over the group?"

"Colonel Kalberer. He's a good man. Despite this mission, we'll pull out of this. I've seen outfits hurt worse than this one."

Our new group commander, Colonel Alfred F. Kalberer, was a veteran of 40 missions in the Near East who had volunteered to return to a combat theater. He was truly an outstanding pilot with more than 18,000 flying hours.

"If we'd only knocked out a few targets," I said miserably, "it wouldn't be so bad. It seems so useless."

"Rice Paddie Hatties" plying the world's oldest profession, found more eager patrons after the two Yawata missions, as tense airmen sought their services. While their daughters were providing comfort and solace for young Americans the mothers were fleecing their discarded pants for whatever valuables they contained. The rising venereal disease rate in India and China prompted base commanders in China to propose the establishment of off-base whorehouses. Lovely young girls would be imported, placed in secluded quarters where they would have contact only with Americans, and be checked regularly by American doctors.

Chinese officials reported to the base commanders the day before the houses were to be opened that the girls were fine — they had professionally checked them out. This was not what the American officials had in mind, and they told their Chinese hosts that the girls must have relations only with Americans; otherwise they would disapprove of the house. It was a delicate situation, involving relations with some of the area's highest-level civic leaders, but before the girls could be re-examined by American doctors the chaplain of the 20th Bomber Command heard about the plan. A strict Catholic, he expressed his opposition, warning base commanders that he would carry the matter to the higher authorities. The chaplain's popularity — never very high in the first place — plummeted once the word got out that the houses would not be opened.

A brother-in-law of the local Chinese commander set up wine shops near each base, between the barracks area and the airfield, but outside the base itself. This enterprising businessman did a huge business despite the efforts of base commanders to stop the practice by fliers of taking a few snorts or more of orange whisky or rice wine en route to the flight line.

Much to my surprise, I received a letter from the head of Armed Forces Radio in Washington, D.C. that they were in desperate need of men who had served as radio announcers and newsmen on pre-war commercial radio stations. It stated that General Arnold had personally authorized the immediate transfer of any man with such a background who agreed to be reassigned, and that all I had to do was to sign the accompanying request. My six-year background in radio would have been valuable to them, and quite possibly have opened up better opportunities in the industry following the war, but I did not hesitate. I had tried very hard to become a skilled bombardier-navigator, and I was a proud member of a great outfit. I refused the offer, much to the surprise of some of my squadron mates, but I have never regretted it. What I could not conceive at the time was that my wartime experiences in combat would open up for me a whole new career as a historian that far exceeded my postwar radio expectations. Besides it didn't seem right to leave comrades for whom I had developed a growing respect and admiration, and who might need my growing experience and capabilities, and that in the coming months, I was sure would have their manhood tested to the utmost.

Since the middle of July each of the original crews had been given a three-day pass to Calcutta. Airplane commanders drew lots because only one or two could be spared at any one time.

Our crew's turn came in late August. We had to get up early to meet the train at the Piardoba railway station. Fortunately we were lucky in getting a compartment in a first-class car. All other cars were jammed with people, with several standing on or off the boarding steps and on top of the cars. There was little risk for them because the train just crawled along and it took us 10 hours to get to Calcutta, a distance of approximately 80 miles. This was considered a fast train because it averaged 11 miles an hour when it was underway.

In Calcutta swarms of natives in reddish shirts started to climb in the windows and doors.

Some were villainous looking. Although they were unarmed, at first we feared they meant us harm, but they only fought amongst themselves for the privilege of carrying our bags — for a fee, of course. The ten of us strode single file though the station, each with a bearer carrying a bag on their heads, while a string of urchins and filthy beggars tagged along hoping for a handout.

We finally paid them off and whistled for a taxi. In these days, Calcutta was one of the largest cities in the British Empire and quite cosmopolitan. It had paved streets, some tall buildings, huge bridges, streetcars, buses, horse carts, rickshaws, ox-drawn carts, and millions of people on foot. Taxis were driven by bearded Sikhs with huge turbans on their heads. While we rode to our destination at the Grand Hotel, where the officers were staying (the enlisted men were booked into the Continental), the drivers drove their cars through mobs of people with their horns blaring constantly.

The Grand Hotel was packed, but we were lucky to obtain part of a room (10 to 20 men to a room depending upon its size) and we moved right in. We badly needed a shave, and to put on clean clothes before we went to dinner. We were starved. It had been almost 12 hours since we had breakfast at the base.

Calcutta's hotel operated on the American plan with meals included in the price of the room, so we decided to eat most of our meals there. The ornate dining room of the Grand Hotel was filled with officers from all nations fighting in the Far East. Our table that night was fringed with red sashed, turbaned men anticipating our every need. When one course was finished, a hand quickly reached for the plate and it disappeared as if by magic. I told Bob Albert and a navigator friend, Joseph Buchta, "I don't think I could have stayed another day in that malaria hole of Piardoba. After three days in Calcutta I was almost ready to go back and fight some more."

"The sign in our room said we can be served toast and tea in bed tomorrow morning," Buchta said. "Just call one of the porters. How about that? Then, after we're dressed, we can go down to breakfast."

"And there's tiffin in the afternoon," Albert said. "A porter will bring tea and cakes and toast."

I smiled. "A room and five meals a day for $3 in a very nice hotel is the best bargain I have ever seen."

After dinner we went into the ballroom where a string orchestra played familiar waltzes.

I looked at my friends across the table and I could see the music was recalling fond memories of home. Albert had a solemn look on his face and, with his thick glasses, he looked like a preacher. Joe's high Slavic cheekbones protruded even more than usual because he had lost pounds he could hardly spare. His blond hair was slicked back in its customary neatness.

"I need some fresh air," Albert said. "Why not take a walk before going to bed?"

We agreed and walked out into the darkened street. There were people from all walks of life. Lovely Indian women of the higher castes in beautiful, flowing saris and wretches dressed in rags. Taxis roamed the streets weaving in and out of rickshaws, scurrying pedestrians and horse drawn carriages similar to the type that still cater to a small clientele in New York's Central Park.

Car headlights were blackened except for a slit in the middle and I wondered how the drivers could see.

I marveled at the rickshaw pullers who never seemed to tire even with two heavy-set people riding in their conveyances. Small of stature, most were young, but there were older men who obviously had done this work for years despite their corded legs and thighs and obvious undernourishment.

There were people everywhere, many sleeping on the streets, the sidewalks, the gutters, and any place where they could curl up. The sheer mass of humanity was over-whelming and their poverty was depressing. In the park, thousands of people flocked around benches or lolled on the grass while ancient trolleys roared along the side of the road with passengers clinging to windows and railings. Like the railroad cars, Indi-ans hung all over the sides of the trolleys. They seldom bought tickets, and large crowds waited at the stations to catch already overcrowded trains and trolleys. After we had been out for two hours we headed back to our hotel.

"I'm beat," Buchta said. "I'm going to crawl into the sack."

Albert agreed, but I had other ideas, "I think I'll have a night cap before I turn in."

Buchta looked at me quizzically and shrugged, "You take care."

After they entered the hotel, I hailed a horse drawn vehicle. I had other things on my mind than a drink. I had been intrigued by stories in some American publications, and from crewmembers that had preceded us to Calcutta, about a notorious woman by the name of Margo. One publication had described her as a beautiful Anglo-Indian with jet-black hair, a coffee-cream complexion, and green eyes whose house of prostitution catered to officers only. The magazine said her house was filled "at all times with rank and determination." She supposedly had been married to a British major who abandoned her, and to support herself, she offered her most saleable asset — her incredible beauty. In India, her mixed parentage shut her out of respectable employment and, even worse, both the British community and the higher castes of her Indian forebearers despised her.

I gave the driver her address and rode expectantly through the darkened streets, concerned by my impulsiveness in embarking on such an adventure all on my own, but other thoughts overrode my more cautious instincts.

I ended up in a nice section of the city, with neat homes jammed together, and the driver stopped. He pointed to the number and I gave him some money and promised more if he would wait. He eagerly agreed to do so.

I hastened out of the carriage and rang the doorbell. When the door opened an Indian maid said, "We're closed." And she shut the door in my face.

Chagrined by my reception, with my emotions so high, I returned to the carriage. The driver explained that there was another very nice place on Krier Road if I was interested. I agreed.

As the old horse clip-clopped his way through the almost empty streets I recalled a long story about Margo that some American reporter had written. A young American private, who had been fighting in the Imphal-Kohima area, had come to Calcutta on a pass. The sheer horror of his experiences on this savage frontier had taken its toll on his nervous system and emotions. Like most of us, he had heard about Margo and, after a few drinks, had decided to visit her.

She answered his ring, and noticing that he was not an officer, gently explained that she could entertain only officers. He looked at this gorgeous creature and tears welled up in his eyes. "I'm not interested in sex." He blurted out. "Can't I just talk to you?"

"I'm sorry," she said, noting the distraught youth's face, "but the authorities won't permit it."

He began to cry and turned away. On impulse, she locked her door and sat down on the steps. "Come here," she said softly.

He walked back slowly to her and she cradled him in her arms like a baby, as his tears flowed, and some of the horror of his life in the jungle and the fears that possessed him poured forth as she gently rocked him.

She remained with him throughout the long night, brusquely telling high-ranking officials that her place was closed. They looked at her with amusement, wondering at the scene, and their own thoughts about Margo underwent a change. A few of them saluted her in respect of her compassionate womanhood. I've often wondered what happened to that nameless G.I., and if he long remembered the lady who had shown so much more kindness for a fellow human being than those who considered themselves her superiors in upright character. I like to think he did.

My driver stopped at a similar establishment and this time I was ushered into a sumptuous drawing room with deep upholstered chairs of brightly colored fabrics.

A nice looking English woman dressed beautifully in an evening gown bade me welcome. "I'm Alice. Would you like a drink? We have British Scotch but I'm afraid it's terribly expensive. We must charge three American dollars for a drink."

I agreed, and a bearer brought me a tall drink that I slowly sipped. I was on guard because we had been warned that Japanese spies were active in Calcutta, and reminded myself to answer no questions about my war activities.

My concern proved unnecessary. She made it clear right from the start that there would be no questions of a military nature. Now I had a more personal concern. Most of the men from our group had ruefully admitted that under similar circumstances they had found themselves unable to perform in bed. Several had sought the advise of our flight surgeons who explained that the high temperatures under which we lived, and the constant stress, were devastating to a man's sexual prowess.

But after she led me to a gorgeously appointed bedroom and I lay down beside her, I was pleased to find out that I would have no such problem. Kind and considerate, Alice made me momentarily forget the harsh, often brutal masculine world of death and destruction of which I was a part, and the uncertain months that lay ahead of me. I was grateful despite the $14 that she discreetly accepted from me.

Buchta eyed me speculatively the following morning, but I kept my evening's adventures to myself.

"I'd like to see the Jain Temple today," he said.

We had been told not to miss this fabulous temple in the midst of Calcutta's slum district and I wanted to see it very much and readily agreed.

We toured a maharajah's palace first before going to the temple. It was now a public museum but the original paintings were still hanging on the walls. We luxuriated on thick carpets and admired the ornate statuary and fixtures.

"I wonder what the average Indian thinks of this place?" Joe said. "It's such a contrast to the miserable slums around here."

"Whoever owned it spent a large fortune for his personal pleasure," I replied.

The Jain Temple was a marvel of beauty and symmetry. Bits of colored glass were formed into mosaic patterns so that the coloring and artistry were overwhelming. The beautiful grounds contained pools reflecting the color of the statues and the temple. Elephant statues, and many other different types, surrounded the area.

We started to walk inside but were reminded to leave our shoes outside and walk in barefoot. The perennial ragged boy watched our shoes for a few annas while we inspected the interior. We were overwhelmed by the massive statue in the middle of the room that was ornately and brightly beautiful.

On our way out Joe pointed to an Indian brushing a bench with a tiny wisp of straw.

"I understand that the Jains take vows not to injure any living things," Joe said. "They even dust a chair or bench before sitting down so as not to crush an insect."

"Their religion is certainly unusual," I said. "I've heard they won't lie, kill, or take what isn't given to them. Furthermore, they have renounced pleasure of all material things."

"But why?" Albert said.

"Jains seek to become independent of all earthly objects," Joe said. "I read about them in a book at the hotel."

"The peculiar part of their belief is that a Jain may take his own life by slow starvation," I said.

"I wonder how many Jains there are in India?" Albert said.

"About a million," I said. "I don't think I would like to be a Jain."

"Me either," Albert said.

We rode back to the hotel in a taxi. "Despite the contradictions in India," I said, "its an enormously interesting country. They have perhaps the oldest civilization in the world and they, like the whole Far East, are emerging as if from a deep sleep. I've been pleased with their friendliness, and I hope after the war it ripens into a lasting respect based on mutual exchange of ideas and commerce."

Chapter 7

LeMay Assumes Command

Several days after we returned from Calcutta we learned that Major General Curtis E. LeMay was taking over command of the 20th Bomber Command.

Tragedy struck in Piardoba when General Saunders and a nurse took off in a B-25 medium bomber and crashed shortly afterwards in the jungle. He never had time to radio the tower and hours went by before it was realized that his plane was missing. Saunders and the nurse lay on the ground seriously injured while they waited for help to arrive. It was before dawn before they were found. Saunders was returned to the States for a long convalescence.

When Loberg returned from Kharagpur after his first staff meeting with LeMay I asked him, "What kind of man is LeMay?"

"He's brusque and to the point. He told us he didn't like the way we were running missions and he's going to make a lot of changes."

"Who is this hotshot anyway?" I asked indignantly.

"He has a fine record with the 8th Air Force."

"So what?" I said. "It's different over here."

"He says not. For one thing, we're going to fly 12 plane formations over Japan, not only to increase the chances of knocking out a target, but for mutual protection."

"That's ridiculous," I said. "Everyone knows you can't fly a large formation with B-29s. You'd use too much gas."

"He says he thinks we can. And we're going to do it."

"He'll learn," I said.

"He impressed me a great deal," Loberg said. "I think he may be the answer to our problems."

"Just what did he do in Europe that was so outstanding?" I said bitterly.

"He initiated the straight-in bombing run, without evasive action for one thing."

"That's suicide," I cried. "They'll blow us out of the sky."

"It didn't work that way over Germany. The general believes that a straight-in approach to the target increases the number of hits and is more economical from the viewpoint of aircraft and crew loss. He told us they learned that in most cases a target is knocked out the first time."

"He's a fine one to talk," I said. "He won't have to fly the missions."

"He did in Europe," Loberg said. "As a matter of fact, he led the initial missions employing the straight-in approach. He proved it could be done and now the 8th Air Force has adopted this system."

"Maybe he's right," I said doubtfully. "We're certainly wasting our time as it is."

"The general plans to bring some specialists from Europe to teach our crews the radar-bombsight procedure. And lead crews will be chosen to take a special course to prepare them fully to lead squadron and group formations."

"You mean that one crew will do all the sighting for a whole formation?"

"That's right. All planes will drop on the leader. LeMay says this method is more effective because it places the responsibility on the best crew in the formation."

"I still don't like flying into a target without evasive action."

"The general brought up a good point. He said when evasive action is used, the time of the formation in the flak area is increased and so the planes have a greater change of being hit. He also said that evasive action on the bomb run prevents formations from scoring hits."

"I hope we don't have to try out his system first."

Loberg replied, "At the rate we're going, we'll never finish the job."

"I agree. And, with 12 planes in a formation we should be able to fight off Jap fighters."

"I believe his ideas are sound," Loberg said. "At least they are worth a try. He believes in the B-29. He realizes the plan has a lot of bugs but thinks that we can work them out."

"They'd better do something about these engines overheating."

"They are working on it. The engines were never designed for the temperatures of an Indian summer."

Our training program was stepped up and we flew of Halliday Island more frequently on practice missions.

A matter of personal importance demanded my attention as I passed my second year as a lieutenant without a promotion, although my position as squadron bombardier called for a captaincy. I had been in this staff position for almost a year and when a new promotion list came out without my name on it, I could contain myself no longer. Other bombardiers and navigators, plus a number of pilots without squadron positions had been promoted over me because they had the time in grade for a promotion. I felt that I had earned a promotion because of my staff position and the fact that I was also a lead bombardier. Furthermore, I had more than the required months in grade for a promotion.

Loberg was taken aback when I challenged him, and he was literally speechless by my indignation. "I'm fed up with being passed over for promotion while I'm in a position that calls for a captaincy. Put someone else in the job, and I'll just be another bombardier. This is no way to run an organization. I'm putting in for a transfer."

"Now, now," he said placatingly. "Don't go off half-cocked. I'll get your promotion. Give me more time!"

"Time! Hell!" I was much too mad to worry about the consequences. "I just want out of a squadron that treats its staff officers in this manner."

"Don't do anything hastily," he said. "I'll handle it." I stood my ground glowering as he hastened away.

I had no plans to remain in the post-war Air Force, so a captaincy was not important in that respect. But there was a considerable increase in pay that did matter to me. Basically, my outrage was triggered by the injustice of the situation.

Shortly thereafter I received my promotion, but the matter rankled in my mind. I believed then, and I still do, that promotions should be for merit only. Through favoritism or friendships, many poorly qualified officers were promoted to ranks they did not deserve. This situation not only did a disservice to fellow officers who were deprived of promotions, but reduced the quality of the nation's armed forces. Many of those promoted under such circumstances later had to be sent home for incompetence.

The next scheduled mission to the steel plant at Anshan was postponed twice. Once because of General Chennault's fear that the Japanese would attack Chengtu's airfields, and the second time because of bad weather. Finally the date was set for September 8, the day that LeMay was scheduled to take over the command. LeMay had been restricted by Arnold to fly just one mission, and he chose to go along on this one because Intelligence had told him the best fighter outfit in the whole area was at Anshan and he was particularly anxious to see firsthand how efficient Japanese fighters were against Superfortresses.

On this same date General Hayward S. Hansell, Jr. was appointed to head the new 21st Bomber Command at Salina, Kansas. But it was not until October 12 that "Joltin Josie, the Pacific Pioneer" led the vanguard of 73rd Wing B-29s to Saipan in the Marianas, while we carried on the only other B-29 operations in the China, Burma, and India theater.

Arnold had been pressing for weeks to get more B-29s over targets, so for Anshan every B-29 in commission was assigned to the mission.

Loberg's crew was set up for the mission and we were among the 108 B-29s that took off for China, leaving seven on the ground. The route to the coast was routine and it was not until we saw the sea ahead of us that we showed much interest. We had flown over Mao Tse-tung's Communist Eighth Route Army that controlled a vast area of north China. The Japanese controlled China's large cities and its railroads and rivers. Thus only a decreasing area in the south was still held by Chiang Kai-shek's armies while an increasing section of the north was coming under Communist control in their battles with the Japanese field armies. I saw we were headed for a jut of land that swung out to sea. I didn't pay much attention at first but then it suddenly dawned on me that this landmark was not on our prescribed course.

"Dick," I called.

"Yes."

"I believe we're off course. There's a large peninsula up ahead."

"I'll be right up."

We talked it over with Loberg and after another perusal of the maps we decided that it must be the Shantung Peninsula. We were considerably south of course but inasmuch as we knew where we were, we continued on a straight line with the idea of turning north to the assembly point after we had gone some distance out on the peninsula. It was obvious that our compass was off and we wanted to be able to see the bay up which we had to fly to reach our turning point.

We left the peninsula and turned north over the open sea where we assembled our formation. Three 462nd Group planes joined us as we headed north in a loose formation.

We were still several hundred miles from the target and distant from any interference by Japanese fighters, so I decided to have a last smoke before we entered the target area. I lit up my pipe and sat contentedly puffing on it, until the strangest thing happened. The tobacco in my pipe rose to the roof of the cabin in a neat column. My eyes popped at this strange occurrence, and so did my ears.

"Get your oxygen masks on!" Loberg shouted. "We've lost pressure."

At 20,000 feet a life can be snuffed out in a matter of minutes without oxygen.

"What happened to the pressurization?" Loberg called to Albert.

"Scheinman's blister blew out," Right Gunner Guido Bianchi called from the rear. "He almost went with it."

"Are you alright, Scheinman?" Loberg called.

A shaky voice replied in a high-pitched tone. "Yes sir. It just scared me for a moment."

"Navigator to pilot. You almost lost your navigator. When the blister blew I grabbed for my oxygen mask but couldn't find it. I was beginning to pass out until Knight found it and fastened it to my face."

It was a momentary relief from the strain of entering the target area, and we laughed. It wasn't funny of course, and it would have been a deeply felt tragedy if Isidore Scheinman had been lost. In as much as he was not, we chuckled to ourselves when we thought of Schein sitting there quietly until an unseen force tried to drag him out of the airplane. Humor takes strange forms under duress.

The mountainous terrain of north China was on our left and the Great Wall of China crept serpentinely across the countryside. The Liaotung Peninsula on our right was in clear view as we proceeded up the middle of the bay where a river emptied into the ocean. Visibility was good as we turned on the target heading. As we progressed inland to Anshan, the cloud cover obscured our view of the ground most of the time. Radar was useless because of the terrain below.

"I can't see the target," I said anxiously to Loberg. "We should be just two minutes away."

We all looked but failed to find it. Anshan was nestled in a valley completely surrounded by hills so when we started to see the hills below us we knew we had missed the target. Our compass was off but we didn't think it would make that much difference in 50 miles.

"There it is!" Loberg called.

I looked back and he was pointing off to our left. We had passed 20 miles to the right of it. Using the automatic pilot, I swung the plane around until we were on a reciprocal course to the one we were supposed to fly. The run was short, and I buried my head in the sight to pick out the aiming point, but it was completely obscured by a smoke screen. A huge smoke cloud hung suspended for thousands of feet above the target area. I synchronized on checkpoints and offset the bombs into the smoke.

"Bombs away!"

The flak was feeling for us a few feet away and we quickly swung back to the coast.

"That wasn't so bad," I called to Loberg. "Very little flak and no fighters."

"Fighters at 10 o'clock!" the left gunner yelled.

I was jolted to instant readiness and reached for my gun sight. There, unbelievably close was a Japanese fighter circling 400 yards away in front of our formation. I watched him with intent eyes as this sleek fighter with the red balls on its wings and fuselage passed by. By the time I had gathered my wits he was gone.

"Why didn't you shoot him down?" Loberg said with disgust. "I could have knocked him out with an air rifle."

Despite his exaggerated comment I was surprised myself and had no answer to make, except that he wasn't attacking, and I didn't see any sense in shooting. The logic of this argument was open to sharp dispute. The truth of the matter is that the fighter's appearance was so startling that it momentarily threw me off balance.

We checked the compass on the route back and found it was off by 10 degrees, so we applied the correction and the return trip was uneventful.

Four planes were lost on the mission but 90 B-29s hit Anshan with 200 tons of bombs. Target specialists reported that three of the 16 coke ovens would be out of service for a year, while another three were damaged and would be out for six months. The two successful attacks cost the Showa plant 35 percent of its coke output, reducing Japan's steel output by 9 percent.

LeMay was not impressed by the way the mission to Anshan was run. He called it amateurish and ineffectual. He told group commanders the flak was accurate over the target, and his own B-29 was hit, but he spoke contemptuously of Japanese fighter pilots. "They were up there, in position to make a beautiful attack on us, and then turned the wrong way! Only one guy got a fleeting shot off, but the rest of them never could catch up." He told the group commanders that he was grounding the command until crews were completely retrained.

That night in China we all turned in early. I quickly fell asleep and slept like I was drugged. Then I heard, "Get up!" It was Loberg. He shook me hard. "The Japs are going to bomb us!"

When I turned over, he demanded. "Will you get up!"

"Alright! Alright!" I said sleepily, not realizing the seriousness of staying in a tent close to the field during a bombing attack.

I was completely exhausted from the mission and had no command over my senses. Loberg started to go but noticed that I was sound asleep again.

"Come on!" Loberg said roughly, as he pulled me bodily out of bed. "There's a red alert and the Japs will be bombing any minute."

"I'm so tired I think I'd almost rather stay here," I mumbled.

We trooped toward the river and plunked ourselves down in a rice paddy to await the Japanese. The mile long march had awakened me but the soft, fragrant straw in the paddy felt good, and I was soon sound asleep.

"Here he comes! He's flying right over us!" someone yelled.

At these words I was wide awake and watching the heavens with a straining eye. The Japanese twin-engine bomber nicknamed "Betty" was silhouetted against the moonlit sky. When he made his second turn over the field a stream of fragmentation bombs poured forth from the bomb bay and popped like firecrackers as they hit the ground.

Major Roscoe L. Norman had just been assigned as commander of the ground echelon in China. He was appalled to find that no base defenses had been established by his predecessor. Personnel were told to head for the rice paddies in case of attack. He soon made changes but the field was defenseless in this raid.

The bomber made several attacks at infrequent intervals. It was not until 3 o'clock in the morning that we finally were permitted to go to bed. The bombs caused little damage at our field, so it was a wasted effort on their part. This was due in part to the fact that the anti-personnel bombs were released too close to the ground and failed to arm themselves. The runway was full of them the next day.

Many of our people grabbed them for souvenirs despite the fact that they were extremely unstable and dangerous. The bomblets were so crudely made that no one in the right mind would touch them. I warned our people but some did not listen to me. The Chinese soldiers were ordered to get rid of the bomblets and they picked them up and casually threw them into gunnysacks. I shuddered at the risks they were taking.

"Attention!"

We rose to our feet as a short, thickset, dark complexioned officer with rows of decorations, strode into the room flanked by his chief of staff and other high-ranking officers. A stubby cigar protruded from his mouth, his face expressing no emotion whatsoever.

Major Thomas R. Vaucher stood beside me. I had a new pilot. General LeMay had ordered all squadron commanders off of combat crews. He felt they had enough to do without flying missions. Lieutenant Robert G. Fessler and Sergeant Clayton K. Knight, had been transferred to another crew. Lieutenant Ralph Todd and Technical Sergeant Albert I. Carmona replaced them. They had been with Vaucher and he was reluctant to part with them. We had come to Dudhkundi, home of Colonel Alva L. Harvey's 444th Group, to attend lead crew school.

"Rest gentlemen," the general rasped.

"I flew to Anshan as an observer on your last mission," he said. "The mission was completely disorganized and the results were negligible."

"The B-29, with its long range characteristics gives us a chance to open a new field in the strategic employment of air power. Our major problem is supporting our operations from India and China, thousands of miles from the United States. The tactical problem of employing the B-29 is not difficult. I intend to use it much as the B-17s and B-24s are used in England."

We hung on every word, knowing that his plans for us would determine our fate.

"I have asked the group commanders to take the best crewmembers of their respective organizations and send them here for lead crew training. You men have been chosen to take this course. Some of you will not make the grade. I feel sorry for those who do not have the necessary qualifications, but there is no place for a crewmember in front of a formation who cannot get the desired results. You will be trained under the guidance of an instructor who has been with the 8th Air Force for two years working on the procedure, which you are about to learn. Those of you who finish this 10 day period of training will be assigned as lead crews in your organizations, and will have the responsibility of destroying the targets to which you are assigned. If you fail us, someone else will take your place. We have a definite job to do. If you can't do it, we'll find someone who can."

"The old boy doesn't mince any words," Vaucher said.

"He'll be a hard man to meet after a bad mission," I said as we walked out.

The procedure was easily learned. The actual operation took time and patience. It was a matter of coordinating the work of the bombsight and the radar set in dropping bombs.

Vaucher's crew did very well. The procedure that White and I developed worked perfectly, and we had a high score when we finished training.

LeMay ordered the elimination of two crews per aircraft, and we soon learned this step was the first of many that completely reorganized the command as new men were selected by LeMay for top positions. Double crews were considered mandatory at first because so many missions were anticipated. Actually the B-29 proved to be the limiting factor because it could not be kept in commission due to constant engine problems.

Group commanders were told by LeMay to fly hell out of the airplanes. "They get out of commission quicker sitting on the ground than they do in the air."

The first of many changes occurred as Colonel Engler, commander of the 468th Group was transferred to bomber command, as deputy chief of operations. Colonel T. S. Faulkner was placed in command of the group with Lieutenant Colonel James V. Edmundson as his deputy. The two complemented one another because Faulkner was a rugged personality — a no nonsense officer — and Edmundson was a quietly efficient, always smiling, popular officer. Faulkner was later lost on a mission to Singapore and Edmundson became group commander. Colonel William H. Blanchard took command of the 40th Group, replacing Colonel Leonard F. Harman, who was promoted to another job.

We felt confident in ourselves as a lead crew when we returned to Piardoba and firmly believed that we would give a good account of ourselves.

I told Vaucher as we separated in the barracks area, "I can see why they call LeMay 'Old Iron Pants.'"

"Have you heard the new names they're calling him?" Vaucher said with a grin.

"I can imagine it's good. Some of the one's I've heard aren't spoken in polite society."

Vaucher laughed. "Some of the men have nicknamed him 'Old Smiley.'"

"That's the best one yet," I said with a chuckle. "It's a perfect nickname with that deadpan expression of his."

Vaucher's crew started out on another mission to the steel plant at Anshan on September 26. Our part was brief. A two-bit toggled switch, controlling one of the propellers, failed to function, and we had to return to base. The lead crew of our flight also came back and an inexperienced crew took over at the target and the whole formation dropped its bombs, accidentally, miles from the target. The other three groups did little better, and Anshan needed still another pummeling before it could be taken off our list. LeMay had promised Arnold 100 B-29s over the target but only 73 made it all the way. Fortunately there were no losses.

Day after day we flew training missions, checking out promising new crews in the radar-bombsight procedure, while increasing our proficiency. Our gasoline hauling days were now a thing of the past. The Air Transport Command took over the job, but we still had to haul bombs in case several missions were planned during our stay in China.

LeMay had transferred excess B-29 crews to fly converted B-24s as C-109 tankers. Supplies increased to a remarkable extent in a short time.

Captain Allen B. Rowlett, operations officer for the 769th Squadron was ordered to run a filmstrip of the entire west coast of Formosa on September 30 to prepare target folders for future strikes against military targets.

After a routine take-off and flight to the northern tip of Formosa, Rowlett noted with satisfaction that he could see for miles so their mission was assured of success unless they encountered aggressive Japanese fighters in large numbers. But they were flying at 30,000 feet, which he knew gave them a measure of protection. He no longer had a regular crew because he was assigned to a staff position so he barely knew any of them.

The filming progressed routinely until they were half way down the island when two single-engine Japanese fighters appeared. They didn't attack, just looked them over out of range of the B-29's guns and then turned away.

"Tail gunner to pilot, over."

"Yes, Setter."

Staff Sergeant William Setter, a rawboned westerner who prior to the war had been a bronco buster, said, "There are six twin-engined fighters climbing on our left while another formation is 5,000 feet below us at 12 o'clock and climbing. My turret is out and I have smoke in my compartment from an apparent electrical short. That's all right. I'll get the son-of-a-bitch fixed."

With deepening concern Rowlett looked out his window and spotted them. The fighters were getting into position for a frontal attack. Deciding that offense was the best defense he told his gunners to prepare for action. He thrust all four throttles forward to increase engine power and turned right into the formation while all six top turret guns blazed away at the diving fighters. They made a starburst maneuver and scattered like a covey of quail that had been flushed despite the fact that they outnumbered Rowlett's lone aircraft 14 to one. Rowlett deciding that discretion was the better part of valor turned his Superfortress to a westerly heading. He dropped the nose wheel to increase their rated of descent and they began to lose 500 feet per minute under full power. The Japanese fighters soon lost heart in the losing chase and ended their pursuit. It wasn't long before Setter reported they were just small dots in the eastern sky.

Back in Piardoba, India, Albert and I were taking some sack time but both of us were wide-awake, wondering when we would hear about our next mission.

"I wonder why they are hauling so many 500-pound bombs to China," Albert said. "There must be enough for a dozen missions up there."

Loberg called from his adjoining room. "We're leaving for China tomorrow morning. Plan on staying awhile."

Later in the bombardier's briefing, Group Bombardier Mitchell told us, "We've got a juicy target for you this time. It's the modification center for airplanes destined for the Philippine area and the southwest Pacific."

"Where is it located?" I asked anxiously.

"Okayama, Formosa. It's inland just a few miles and should be easy to locate."

"Sounds good."

The original list of target systems for the 20th Air Force, drawn up in late 1943, a year later were now considered outmoded. Arnold called upon the Committee of Operations Analysts in Washington, September 8 to recommend new targets.

MacArthur's forces were bypassing islands once thought crucial in a step-by-step approach to the main islands of Japan. By leap-frogging over great distances, huge enemy held areas were left to stagnate in the backwash of a rapidly changing war.

Admiral Nimitz's Central Pacific forces were making plans towards Japan along its seaways now that the Mariana Islands were in Allied hands, and being readied to serve as bases for the B-29s of the 20th Bomber Command.

Arnold grew impatient when analysts failed to come up with a new list by late September, and LeMay voiced his own concern at the lack of recommendations. Arnold told him that he was considering transfer of the 20th Bomber Command from India because the ground war in China was deteriorating rapidly as the Japanese drove into south China. When LeMay insisted on some direction, Arnold's staff told him that priority should be given to aircraft plants at Omura, Mukden, Watanabe, and Okayama. There were more important plants in Japan, but they could not be reached from China. Therefore, LeMay decided to attack air depots in Okayama. The target was a strategic one because its facilities provided direct aid to Japanese forces preparing to resist MacArthur's projected invasion of Leyte as the first step towards the recapture of the Philippines.

Mitchell closed his bombardier briefing by saying that two strikes were planned to make sure the modification center was destroyed.

It was cold in China on the morning of October 13, and the unheated briefing room was damp and oppressive. I was eager for some action and studied every detail of the target until I could draw if from memory. The mission would be relatively short, and would be a welcome relief to the three missions I had flown. I walked to the final briefing with Captain Michael P. Egan, our navigator. Renz had to leave the crew because his duties as a squadron navigator prevented him from participating in missions.

Mike Egan was a slim, blue-eyed Irishman with a poker face who had chosen prior to the war to enter the Catholic priesthood but who had changed his mind before he was ordained.

"We're really carrying a load of bombs for a change," I said. "There's only one bomb bay tank and they've loaded 28 500-pounders. Half of them are incendiaries."

"That's what the B-29 was built for," Mike said.

"I know. In the past we've had to carry so many bomb bay tanks that there was hardly room for bombs. No wonder it takes so many missions to knock out a target."

Colonel Kalberer walked to the front of the briefing room after we were all assembled. "You have a wonderful target," he said. "It's an easy mission without much flak and very few fighters."

He explained that Admiral William P. Halsey's Task Force 38 had roamed from the Ryukyus to Formosa on a sweep that included attacks on Luzon on October 11 prior to the attacks against Formosa's airfields.

I looked with respect at the colonel as he stood before us, speaking authoritatively with nervous gestures. There were patches of gray in his hair, and many of them had come since Pearl Harbor.

"Weather permitting," Kalberer continued, "I have the utmost confidence that you will do your part to destroy Okayama."

The first mission on October 14 was uneventful as we flew in deputy leader position. The target was well spotted with hits as the last B-29 headed home. We returned to base jubilant over our success and looked forward eagerly to the next strike.

Captain Allen B. Rowlett had just landed after the October 14 mission to Okayama when he was ordered to report to Colonel Kalberer. He and his crew were dirty and exhausted from the mission. They cleaned up, ate dinner, and reported to Kalberer at group headquarters. Rowlett was down to 120 pounds after bouts of dysentery and malaria but he made no attempt to get out of the mission.

They were briefed by Kalberer who impressed upon them the need for secrecy. "You will take off late today and fly to Luzon in the Philippines. There you will make photographic strips from the northern end of Luzon to the Lingayen Gulf. General MacArthur's staff will use these photographs in planning his army's return to the Philippines in the near future. (The invasion of Leyte Gulf was scheduled for October 20.) You will be one of two aircraft. A different group will fly the other."

He pointed to a map of the Philippines. "You will start your run from the northern tip of Luzon while the other aircraft will begin at Lingayen Gulf. Your take-off time is set for early tomorrow morning to obtain the best visibility. The weather should be clear. I can't emphasize too strongly the importance of secrecy prior to your departure and after your return. You must not discuss the mission with anyone but me! You'll take off about midnight."

After a routine take-off, Rowlett's crew encountered good weather to the coast of China with no enemy action. Their B-29 developed no problems, which was unusual at this stage of operations.

At dawn they noted that the sky was clear as far as their eyes could see with unlimited visibility. This condition prevailed all the way to the northern tip of Luzon. From their 30,000-foot altitude they could see a native with a water buffalo on an otherwise deserted beach. They met the other B-29 at the halfway point, waggling their tails in recognition.

At Lingayen Gulf there was still unlimited visibility in all directions as they completed their filming without once encountering a Japanese fighter over one of Japan's most heavily defended occupied territories.

Their return trip proved equally uneventful. After they landed a courier picked up the film and flew it to Australia via India and Ceylon.

The filmstrips from both B-29s gave MacArthur a clear picture of what awaited his troops in his upcoming invasion of the Philippines at Leyte Gulf. The groups that furnished the B-29 crews for this 3,800-mile mission received a personal recommendation from MacArthur for their invaluable assistance in gathering up-to-date intelligence.

Lieutenant General Stilwell came to LeMay's headquarters in China, October 13 while LeMay was preparing his command for the first strike against Formosa. He told LeMay that he would like a briefing about the 20th Bomber Command while he was there.

"Follow me around, and let me get the work done," LeMay told him, "and once the mission is off I'll have time to give you a good briefing about what is happening here. And this way you will pick up a little something of what we're doing."

Stilwell agreed. After the bombers were off on their October 14 strike LeMay invited Lord Mountbatten's deputy in the Southeast Asia Command to join him for dinner. Afterwards, and for most of the night, LeMay briefed him about his operations and their importance in the context of global air strategic warfare.

"It is General Arnold's belief," he told Stilwell, "that strategic airpower, when properly applied, can reduce a nation like Japan to military impotence. And force her to surrender without an invasion of her main islands."

Stilwell looked at him with skepticism. He told LeMay he had heard such theories for years, and he reminded him about the failure of the strategic bombing to be decisive in Europe. "The army still had to invade the continent."

LeMay agreed. "You must remember that at first we did not have the airplanes and the trained men. Only now is airpower effective because we have sufficient resources to do the job. The same is true in the Pacific. We're just beginning to create serious problems for the Japanese in their control of the air. I agree with General Arnold that selective destruction of vital industrial, logistical, and military targets will force Japan to sue for peace without a costly invasion of her home islands."

He noticed with chagrin that Stilwell was only half listening, so he spoke more forcefully. "Our Navy is rapidly winning the war at sea, and once it starts to blockade Japan, and we use our B-29s to help mine her inner sea lanes and harbors, Japanese leaders will be forced to sue for peace. We in the Air Force believe that such a victory is possible, and a lot sooner than most people think."

With dawn breaking, LeMay was exhausted after a day and night on his feet without sleep. He felt frustrated because he could tell that Stilwell was not convinced of the logic of his arguments about strategic bombing. He admired Stilwell, knowing he was a fine field commander, perhaps somewhat old fashioned in his views of warfare, but who was doing a difficult job under trying conditions. When he said goodbye to him, LeMay was convinced that he had failed completely to give Stilwell an appreciation of the value of strategic bombing in shortening the war, and making an invasion of the Japanese homeland unnecessary.

Early in the morning of October 16, we were headed east again, this time to lead a formation of 12 planes over the target. Loberg, recently promoted to Lieutenant Colonel, was along as formation commander.

"We saw only one fighter the last time," Vaucher said to Loberg. "Hope we have the same luck today."

"Don't count on it," Loberg said grimly. "We caught them by surprise on the first mission. We can't expect them to be caught unprepared this time."

We accomplished our assembly with the other planes in our formation and headed seaward. Later on two more planes joined us giving us a total of 14.

"That's a beautiful sight," I said to Loberg as I looked out both sides at the B-29s around us.

"You've got a good chance of finishing off the target," he said, adding with a grin. "If you can hit it!"

Ahead the outline of Formosa came into view, with clouds piled on top of the mountains on the east coast. It was difficult to tell whether or not the target was clear because there were scattered clouds below us.

We weren't sure when we turned on the IP, and island near Formosa, that it was the correct island, but we went on nevertheless.

"Do you see it?" Egan asked me anxiously.

"Not yet. If these clouds would only blow away," I said desperately. "Hey! What's that?" I pointed to the harbor to the right. "That's Takao," I said after a moment's study. "Takao is far to the south." I looked off to the left. "There's the target. It's clear!" I cried jubilantly.

"You make the turn," Vaucher said to me. "And take it easy. This is a big formation."

I took over flying the airplane on automatic pilot. I grabbed the turn knob on the stabilizer and anxiously turned the airplane.

"Not so much!" Vaucher yelled. "The formation is having trouble staying with us!"

"I've got to get lined up," I said. There was a note of desperation in my voice because the target was still to my left and rapidly getting closer.

I kept turning the airplane, despite screams of outrage from pilots in the formation who were having difficulty making even tighter turns to remain in formation with us. At last I looked over the sight and we seemed to be in the line with the target. Looking down through the telescope, I used the turn handle to bank the plane until the vertical hair in the telescope split the target.

"Pilot to bombardier," I said tensely, feeling the drama of the moment, and knowing that 14 planes depended on my few seconds of work.

"Go ahead."

"On course and level! Target in sight."

I watched for drift to see if the vertical hair moved off the aiming point. Yes, we were drifting off, so I made a slight course correction and watched intently. It looked good, I noted with satisfaction. Carefully, with hands that trembled, I adjusted the rate knob until the cross hairs stared on the aiming point. A glance at the bubbles on my bombsight gyro showed they needed leveling.

"Bombardier to pilot."

"Yes," he said. His voice muffled on the interphone as he spoke through his oxygen mask.

"Level please."

"Just a second. All right. Straight and level."

I leveled the bubbles, then went back to the sight, and moved the cross hairs back on the target. The telescope was moving faster and faster as the rate of closure increased the closer we got to the target. I could plainly see holes in roofs and workshops and the bomb-studded runway from the previous raid.

Ten more seconds to go, and nothing more could be done. It seemed an eternity. I glanced anxiously back into the sight, noticing the rate was off slightly, and carefully readjusted it.

My voice was tense but controlled when I called, "Bombs away."

I salvoed quickly and called the gunners. "Check the bomb bays."

"Rear bomb bay clear," Scheinman called.

I waited impatiently for Carmona to announce the front bomb bay was clear and I could close the doors. After a few moments I called impatiently, "How about the front bay?"

Mike Egan replied. "Eight bombs are hung up and the arming wires are pulled out," he said excitedly.

I knew it! I said bitterly to myself. Eight bombs had been tied together with heavy wire, two to a shackle, to increase the bomb load. I had feared that this would happen and had argued against it.

"Are the bombs release by the shackle?" I asked.

"Yes," Mike said. "They are just hanging there, nose known, with the arming vanes turning back and forth."

This was worse than I had feared. I pressed the salvo lever several times in desperation, but nothing happened.

I called Vaucher. "We'll have to wait until we get out to sea again before I can go back to the bomb bay and try to kick them out."

Vaucher's face reflected his deep anxiety. "Isn't it dangerous to leave them that way?"

I nodded soberly.

"Leave the bomb bay doors open," Vaucher said. "They may tumble out."

I had been oblivious to the slight flak that we had encountered but now, as I looked over the sight to spot the bombs, I could see it exploding around us. The buildings stood out in stark relief until tiny puffs of smoke began to obscure them, spreading throughout the whole area. The steel plant seemed to rise up in an eruption of smoke and debris.

Words can never express my feelings at this moment. Relief and a growing excitement pervaded my very being. The worry and misgivings that had prevailed previously were suddenly thrust aside and I felt confident and sure of myself. I had often wondered how I would react at the head of a large formation, and worried whether I was capable of doing the job, wondering whether I would fail when so many counted on me.

"Captain Morrison, that was a wonderful job," Scheinman called. "Not a single bomb missed its target."

The past months of futility passed away as if they were but a bad dream, and we all felt proud of the job we had just done. Our tedious work in training had not been in vain; the fires and smoke of the buildings below confirmed it.

We swung in a wide circle away from the target and proceeded unmolested toward the coast of China.

I called anxiously to Egan. "How are those bombs?"

"They're still in the same position."

I was almost afraid to ask my next question. "Have the arming vanes turned off?"

"Not yet."

This was our biggest worry because if they spun off, and the bombs dropped, they would explode if they collided with one another as they almost surely would.

"Fighter at 9 o'clock!"

There were more pressing problems to worry about and I forgot the bombs and searched the sky. Up ahead I noticed two fighters, one on each side of the formation, circling and waiting for an opportunity. I watched them closely because it was a familiar tactic of the Japanese to attract our attention in one quarter, only to have another Japanese fighter appear unexpectedly from a different direction.

The fighter high above us on our right leaped and rolled and put on a good show, but I watched the other closely. Suddenly the tiny speck grew larger as he dived at us from the left. I tracked him closely and when he was in range let go with a long burst, but still he came on. The whole formation moved up in line abreast and the forward top turrets of 14 airplanes sent streams of tracers toward the fighter. Still unscathed, he closed in on us, firing all the way, and flew over the right side of the formation.

"What's that?" Ralph Todd, our co-pilot yelled.

A little above us and to the right a huge blossoming yellowish mass descended in a cloud of streamers.

"That phosphorous bomb almost got us," Bianchi said tensely.

The fighters followed us out to sea and then broke off and returned to Formosa.

I called Vaucher. "I'm going back to the bomb bay and see if I can't pry those bombs loose."

He looked at me with deep concern. He said softly, "Take it easy."

"You'll have to depressurize the cabin."

He nodded and warned the crew. We had been flying at 23,000 feet and the cabin pressure was 8,000 feet. Our ears popped and our lungs exhaled violently as the pressure was released.

I edged my way out of the cabin and into the navigator's compartment. My Mae West and parachute made every movement slow and methodical. I was also burdened with a portable cylinder of oxygen for my mask.

The round door into the bomb bay resisted my mightiest efforts and when it did pull loose I fell back sharply against the top turret.

I crawled out on the narrow 10-inch catwalk on the left side, looked down 23,000 feet to the white caps of the ocean, and shuddered. I looked quickly away and reminded myself not to look down again, then went to work on the bombs.

I pulled cotter pins out of my pocket — some of those I had removed after take-off to arm the fuses — and leaned far into the bomb bay, with my left hand clutching the rack, and felt for the nose fuse of the first bomb. With fingers stiffened by the cold, I placed the cotter pin in the fuse and sighed with relief. Fifteen more to go.

I was vaguely aware of tense faces peering through the portholes in the cabins watching me at work. I carefully unscrewed the fuse from the bomb and dropped it through the yawning hole of the open doors. I went back and repeated the procedure, removing the tail fuse from the bomb.

When the bombs were all defused on one side, I motioned for the doors to be closed. Then I crossed over on the narrow catwalk to the other side. Before I motioned for the doors to be reopened, I rested by clinging to a bomb rack support. My heart was pounding and I knew I had to get my emotions under control if I was to finish the job. I took deep breaths of the pure oxygen and it restored my equilibrium. I motioned to reopen the doors.

It was slow, methodical work requiring every ounce of energy I possessed and my arms shook with fear and the extreme exertion of reaching down into the bomb bay from that narrow catwalk while clinging to the rack. One misstep and I would go plunging toward the ocean so far beneath me.

At last it was done, and I was so exhausted that I stood for a moment on my precarious perch to calm down before I tried to kick the bombs out. They weren't dangerous now, with their fuses removed, but they might spring loose when the plane hit rougher air and go tearing through the bomb bay doors. I tried to pry loose the wires that held the bombs in place with a screwdriver. Desperately I worked, but it was no use. The weight of one bomb pulling on the cable held the release in place so that none would drop. I finally gave up and edged my way back toward the forward cockpit.

"Couldn't you get them out?" Vaucher asked with a worried look on his face.

I shook my head. "I did my best. The fuses are all out and they are not quite as dangerous as they were."

"Won't they go off without the fuses if they are dropped on the runway when we land?"

"They are not supposed to detonate unless they are dropped from 8,000 feet. I don't think they will."

Worry lines crinkled Vaucher's face. "A crew dropped a load from very low altitude not so long ago and they went off."

I nodded. I said grimly, "That's the chance we'll have to take."

We headed home and watched the front bay constantly but the bombs remained in position. We felt we were riding a keg of dynamite as our plane approached the field.

"Grease her in," Loberg said to Vaucher. "Land her like you would a case of eggs."

Vaucher glanced at him soberly. "You're right. This is no time to bounce 10 feet in the air."

Vaucher eased her in and Egan, his eyes on the bombs through the bomb bay window, called. "They're still in place."

We breathed a sigh of unutterable relief.

Vaucher taxied to our parking area, ran up the engines, and then cut them. "Stand clear outside!" Vaucher yelled. "We've got some hung up bombs in the front bay."

The ground crew scurried for cover.

"I'm going to open the bomb bays," I said.

The doors snapped open and with a crash eight 500-pound bombs thudded to the crushed stone parkway.

Time seemed to stand still for a second and my pulse stopped beating.

"Phew!" Vaucher breathed. "I'm sure glad this day is over!"

"Oh, so we're safe again!" I said flippantly to disguise my true feelings. I climbed down out of the plane and headed for the briefing room.

We flew back to India the next day, buoyed up by the fact that reconnaissance photos for once confirmed the most optimistic reports. The target was completely wiped out with the installations practically obliterated. We learned later that they were never rebuilt. Although 12 B-29s had to make emergency landings in China, only one crashed and all but one crew was saved.

Shortly after General LeMay arrived he sent staff officers to Yenan in a C-47 transport plane to make contact with Mao Tse-tung and enlist his help in rescuing B-29 crews who had to bail out in his area. They were greeted cordially and Mao requested the establishment of a radio station up there with Americans to operate it. He promised to aid crews who bailed out in areas under his control. He even volunteered to build some airfields for B-29s but LeMay rejected this offer because he couldn't supply them.

LeMay sent a C-47 load of medical supplies to Mao in appreciation for his offer of assistance. The Chinese doctors had never seen such medical supplies, and had never heard of sulfa drugs that were included. In return Mao sent LeMay a Japanese sword and some woodcuts. The Communists fulfilled their part of the bargain by rescuing a number of crews. The Russians had been uncooperative in supplying weather forecasts so Mao's men in Yenan set up a weather station.

B-29s had crashed north of the Himalayas in a wide area of western China inhabited by tribes that were not Chinese, and were antagonistic to them. Actually the Chinese feared these fierce tribes.

After a few crews had been rescued by the Lolos on the Hump route LeMay realized that he had to convince all tribes in China's remote areas to help to rescue downed airmen. He sent Americans to establish contact with some of these tribes and convince their leaders it would be worth their while to help airmen. As an added inducement, these leaders were advised that the Americans would pay well any time they offered assistance to downed fliers.

Some leaders promised to help but they refused to be paid in cash. They insisted on opium. The officer that LeMay had assigned to the operation told him, "What am I going to do? They won't accept money, and I haven't got any opium."

"We have to get the crews. Get the opium. Go buy it."

"I can't put opium on my expense account," the officer said in protest.

"I don't give a damn what you put down," LeMay said. "Get those men out. Pay these people, and let them know they are going to be paid in anything they want if they help our men."

The officer told LeMay later that he had entered "fertilizer" on the manifest for the opium he had purchased. The tribes helped, but most of the men who crashed in the Himalayas were never heard from again. This was one of the most primitive areas in the world, and navigation aids then were inadequate to fly over mountains that are the highest in the world.

On the fourth day after MacArthur's invasion of the Philippines Captain David A. DeLong, Jr., and his 462nd Group crew, was assigned to patrol the Yellow Sea north of Luzon to report the presence of any Japanese warships that might interfere with the invasion.

Up front, his co-pilot, Lieutenant Donald R. Anderson, his navigator Lieutenant Theodore P. Banks, and bombardier Lawrence G. Devine kept their eyes alert for any sign of Japanese warship activity, while the rear gunners searched their areas of vision. They saw nothing in this vast expanse of sea until a large number of Japanese ships appeared on the horizon, including a carrier. The crew was unaware that this fleet was under Vice Admiral Jisaburo Ozawa and included one large carrier and three smaller ones that were almost without planes. By now, Japan's carrier aviation had lost most of its planes and Ozawa's planeless carriers were being used as decoys to lure Admiral Halsey's Third Fleet away from Leyte Gulf. Meanwhile, another Japanese fleet under Rear Admiral Takeo Kurita, plus two smaller task forces under separate commands, was ordered to penetrate the defensive perimeter around Leyte Gulf and destroy the American invasion fleet. The clever plan almost worked because Halsey was drawn away in pursuit of the Japanese carriers. The plan failed only because older American battleships heroically forced Kurita to retreat before his fleet could destroy the invasion ships.

After reporting the Japanese fleet, DeLong headed for his base at Kiunglai in the Chengtu Valley.

His radio operator, Staff Sergeant Arthur Lazeroff, after receiving a radio message from their base in western China, passed it to DeLong. It revealed that their field was closed due to unfavorable weather, and he was advised to proceed to a field at Hanchung. En route to the designated field, their B-29's direction-finding instruments failed. Even worse, after arriving in the vicinity of the field, DeLong found that it was covered by a solid undercast of clouds. It was 6:20 P.M. China time, and dark, with his gasoline supply dangerously low.

DeLong told his crew they had two choices; to bail out or to try to land on the 3,400-foot dirt runway. (Normally B-29s need an 8,000-foot runway.) He elected to land because he knew he had to get on the ground quickly or his fuel supply would be exhausted. He flew his B-29 through the clouds, breaking out into the clear at 400 feet, but in a snowstorm. The field was not in sight, and no other landing spot appeared as he flew back and forth, often at 1,000 feet.

Flight Engineer Lieutenant Charles Ruszin, Jr., warned DeLong that their gasoline level was dangerously low so the pilot started to climb to a safer altitude and to fly farther inland before ordering his crew to bail out.

Meanwhile, radio operator Lazeroff heard a call from the field they had been seeking that the weather had cleared slightly and directions were given to find it.

DeLong advised the crew that he intended to get as close to the field as possible before giving the order to "Take to the silk."

The ground radio operator warned DeLong that this was very rugged country. He asked DeLong to shoot some flares, and they would shoot from the ground.

DeLong reported that they could not see the ground flares, and that they did not have any flares on board but he said he would fire their machine guns in the hope that ground personnel would see the tracers. But the tracers were not seen by those on the ground.

The ground operator advised DeLong to hold his course and watch for a searchlight that they had just turned on.

With his gasoline almost gone, DeLong spotted the field momentarily. Automobiles with their headlights on, lined each side of the runway.

He was told to land on a northwest heading, but he lost sight of the field. One gunner called DeLong to tell him he had seen the field at the seven o'clock position. Now the ground searchlight was turned on directly over the field and DeLong was instructed to let down from 12,500 feet. He was reminded again about the nearby mountains.

The ground operator at Hanchung's Army Airways Communications Systems talked DeLong down, telling him how to make the let-down, and gave him the altimeter setting as the B-29 passed over the field. Still talking the airplane down the operator requested the plane's altitude and then told DeLong to circle the field once and to let down faster.

DeLong protested, saying he could not do it in one circle.

"Don't widen the circle," the operator replied.

DeLong increased his let-down angle, noting that his speed was too high for the short runway. He quickly pulled back the throttles. Then two engines quit as their fuel was exhausted. He dove for the ground and landed on the last third of the dirt runway. He jammed on the brakes and the heavy bomber screeched to a halt just a few feet from a 16-foot ditch at the end of the field. When he tried to taxi off the runway, his other two engines quit from lack of fuel. He had to be towed off the runway.

After refueling the next day, DeLong flew his B-29 back to the Chengtu base, marveling that they were still alive.

Chapter 8

Pin-Point Bombing

After General Arnold officially confirmed that the Japanese aircraft industry had first priority, the Omura Aircraft Factory on Kyushu was assigned to the 20th Bomber Command.

Operations against Formosa had exceeded the command's quota of fuel so LeMay was unable to get a maximum number of Superforts assigned to the October 25 mission.

Vaucher's crew was named deputy leader and we flew across the Hump two days prior to the mission. Several of us decided to explore the neighboring community of Kiunglai. Joe Buchta, Bob Fessler, and I hired rickshaws to take us there.

"These rickshaws weren't built for comfort," Buchta said with a grimace as his two-wheeled carriage lunged into a hole.

"It's fun thought," I said. "How are you doing, Fess?"

Fessler's large frame dwarfed the rickshaw. The Chinese coolie strained hard on his two poles as we rode along.

"It's better than walking," Fessler said with a grin. "That's the best I can say for this mode of transportation."

There was a constant stream of humanity along the rutted dirt road that led from our base to the city. All were dressed in blue and some were very well dressed indeed.

"This is an amazing nation," Joe said reflectively. "For thousands of years there has been little change in customs, their way of dressing, their language, or laws."

"China reminds me of the old feudal countries of Europe," I said. "Most of the wealth in this nation of 450 million seems to be in the possession of relatively few people."

"I doubt if there is a nation in the world whose people have been exploited as much as the Chinese by their rulers," Joe said. "They seem constantly on the verge of starvation."

"It's difficult to understand why," I said. "The nation is rich in minerals, land, and personal ingenuity. Look at this Chengtu Valley. I doubt if there is a more fertile valley in the world."

"There are just too many people," Joe said. "The country is so immense and transportation facilities are so poor that even if they have a surplus in one area, there is no way to get it to another area where the people are starving. These peasants live on just a few pennies a day, but many of them don't even have those pennies to buy rice."

As we swayed back and forth in our rickshaws I thought about China. It was ripe for revolution. Conditions had been bad for so long, even before the Japanese invaded the country.

"I sometimes wonder why China continues to fight with such dogged determination," I said. "It seems the common people have so little to gain or lose regardless of who wins."

"The Chinese dislike foreigners," Joe said. "It's more than dislike. Hatred is a better word. In China the family has been the key to stability."

"I've heard a lot about ancestor worship," I said. "These mounds of graves, kept with such care, indicate how much they revere their ancestors."

"Confucius made a strong impact upon the Chinese," Joe said. "He taught them that if the house is built on a sound foundation, the world is more secure."

"There's a lot of truth in that," I said thoughtfully.

I watched with amusement as a woman with a baby stopped by the side of the road, upended the boy, lowered the flap of his behind and let him evacuate into the ditch. It was such a natural action, with no sense of embarrassment on the part of the mother, that I quickly overcame my own initial reaction of disgust.

Joe, who had also watched the scene, spoke up. "The whole existence of the family revolves around children. In China the individual means little, it's the family that is all important."

"They do seem to worship their children," I said. "And they are the most obedient children I have ever seen."

"There are signs of revolt in the younger members growing to adulthood. Passive obedience to traditions is not as strong as it used to be. The institutions that once were so important are being attacked by the younger generation of men and women our age," Joe said.

"It will be a tragedy for the world if their thoughts turn to violent social revolution."

"They are ready for it," Joe said. "China used to be very servile as a nation, but the influence of the West has been profound. The unfortunate part is that our own nation has failed to understand this changing trend. The Communists are now strong in northern China. I'm disturbed because of all the armies fighting Japan; the most fanatical is the Communist Eighth Route Army. World War II won't end the upheaval going on in Asia."

"I hate the smoldering anarchy that is just beneath the surface in China," he continued. "One never knows what explosive form it will take and in what direction."

"There's Kiunglai," Fess pointed ahead. "What a smell!" He pointed to sewage in the ditches alongside the road.

It was sharp and repugnant as we entered the ancient walled city. We gazed with profound fascinations as we eyed the swarm of humanity inside the ancient gate.

Chinese swarmed around us as we left our rickshaws and walked through the narrow, crowded lanes. Shops of all kinds abounded, with fur coats hanging from lines above the shops and strips of meat suspended below them. Over all hung an odor of decay as sweating bodies dressed in rags followed our every step.

Some of our men had been intrigued when told that Kiunglai was called the city of free love. They assumed that the city's young ladies would freely distribute their services to anyone seeking them. Alas, for their hopes, it carried the name because it was the first city in China to break with tradition and allow young lovers to marry without the usual parentally arranged marriage of convenience.

"What's that?" Fess asked.

I looked down and averted my eyes in horror. A creature lay upon the ground, flopping up and down, uttering strange, distorted cries. It was just the trunk and head of a man whose tiny, ill formed legs and hands had never grown from babyhood. He cried out, as if in pain, and beggars beseeched us for alms. We tossed money at them and fled. Later we learned it was common practice to use deformed people to beg for money.

Even the heart of the city was old and dilapidated. We had been told that Kiunglai was 5,000 years old. We could easily believe it. There was an air of antiquity that passed beyond time into the distant past. The people we saw were friendly and cheerful, and we returned their warm greetings in kind. But the city was depressing and dismal, so we headed back toward the gate.

"It's appalling when you think that there are so many millions of people in China, living not only in poverty, but in outright want," Joe said. "I feel ashamed to walk among them in my fine clothes and well filled belly."

I nodded. "But what can America do? These millions must solve their own problems. We couldn't begin to help them with what they need."

"It's an almost insolvable problem," Joe said.

"Back to the war," Fess said as we neared the field.

"Do you know where we are going in Japan this time?" Joe asked me as we headed for our tent area.

"Yes, it's Omura, an aircraft factory."

"Oh no!" Joe exclaimed. "That'll be a hot one. After that last daylight raid in August those Japanese fighters will be spoiling for a fight."

"You're right," I said soberly. "There are 500 fighters in the area and they're not afraid to tangle with our much-vaunted Superfortresses."

Several hours out on October 25 the sun rose over the horizon and chased away the night. It was always a relief to feel the first warming rays of the sun on our faces. I believe it is the age — old fear of darkness and what you can't see that still haunts us.

Arriving at the coast of China, we circled the assembly point hoping to pick up the rest of our formation. We were deputy leader this time. There was no sign of a B-29. (After the mission we learned that we were the only B-29 to navigate to the departure point.)

"What are we going to do?" I asked Vaucher.

"I heard a faint signal on the radio telling us to proceed to the final assembly point and meet them there."

"But that's close to the mainland," I said with consternation. "We'll be sitting ducks if we don't meet up with our formation."

"I know," Vaucher said quietly.

We were disturbed by the turn of events but we headed across the Yellow Sea.

Small, scattered boats broke the monotony of the limitless expanse of sea, but that was all. We passed to the southeast of Saishu Island and headed for the assembly point.

"There's not a cloud over the coast line," I said to Vaucher anxiously. "Do you think we should go in alone? I don't see the formation anywhere."

"I hate to go back," he said. "I'll circle for awhile."

Despite my mounting fear for our safety, I couldn't help but feel admiration for the island of Kyushu. For hundreds of miles the beautiful green hills and mountains lay below us in panoramic display. This was the southernmost island of the main Japanese group.

I nervously scanned the sky for the sight of friendly Superforts or Japanese fighters.

"There's a B-29 returning to China," Scheinman called.

I looked to the left and saw a lone plane heading back with all speed. Farther to the right I could dimly see the outlines of a loose formation.

"There's our formation!" I cried excitedly.

"Where?" Vaucher said quickly. "They didn't even come to the assembly point," he said angrily after I pointed them out. "Wait until I get back!"

"What are you going to do?" I said with alarm, as he turned the plane in a quick maneuver to the left.

"I'm going to try to catch up with them and tack onto the tail of the formation before they reach the target."

I didn't say anything although he must have read the doubt in my eyes.

As we headed for the formation under full power, we could see a tall column of smoke rising from the direction of the target.

"Do you think we can make it?" I asked.

"We'll make it."

The formation was tightening up as we neared, and we finally managed to join the rear end just as they were approaching the target.

"No fighters yet," I said tensely. "Maybe this is our lucky day."

Near the bomb release line a few bursts of flak appeared in the sky but it was nothing to worry about. I could feel the crisp tenseness of everyone in the forward cockpit as our straining eyes searched the skies.

The leader dropped his bombs and I salvoed immediately, checked with the gunners, and closed the doors. I peered over the bombsight and noted with satisfaction that our bombs fell right in the heart of the plant.

"We smacked it good!" I shouted.

We carefully turned in a tight circle to keep away from the heavy anti-aircraft batteries at Nagasaki and started on the long route away from the target.

"Who said this was going to be a rough mission?" I said with glee to Vaucher.

Before he could reply, I noted with consternation that a large flight of fighters was headed toward us from Nagasaki.

"Bombardier to crew. Twenty fighters closing in at 10 o'clock."

They came in a few breathless seconds. With our closing rate of 600 miles an hour I only managed to get in a few bursts before they were gone.

When the pounding of the turrets ceased, the silence that followed was nerve wracking. I clutched the gun sight for reassurance.

"We'll give them the fight of their lives," I said to no one in particular, but primarily to reassure myself.

"Anyone see where they went?" Vaucher said.

No one replied until I spoke up. "They're still out there. They're probably waiting to catch us unawares by diving out of the sun."

I stowed the sight to my right and my eyes roved the sky. Sure enough, a twin-engine fighter was diving from in front for a sneak attack. I traced him carefully, and the top turret of the whole formation — 24 in all — followed the fighter down until it came within range. We held the triggers down, watching tracers curving around him, until he pulled off, untouched as far as I could tell.

The formation was now quite a way out to sea, and although we did not expect further attacks, we watched closely. A tiny speck appeared high in the sky ahead.

"Fighter at one o'clock!" I called.

He was diving at a terrific burst of speed. I tracked him, now and then letting loose a short burst to let him know we had seen him. The tiny speck grew larger and larger. It was a matter of seconds until the plane filled the lighted circle of my sight. I fired round after round in a rapid succession, until the cabin was filled with the acrid smell of powder.

"He's going to ram us!" I yelled.

He winged over and passed beneath us.

"That guy really has guts!" I said breathlessly to Vaucher. "Who said these Jap pilots aren't any good?" We had been highly critical of our previous encounters with most Japanese pilots, many of whom seemed to be lacking in aggressiveness.

"Tail gunner to crew. There's a twin-engine fighter making passes at the rear of the formation. He sneaks in and gives us a few bursts then backs out of range."

"I see him Mac," Bianchi called. "I wish I could get a crack at him."

This hide and seek maneuver went on for about 30 minutes until McCleod called and his voice shook with fear. "I'm out of ammunition. I fired everything I had and he's still there."

I closed my eyes for a moment and silently prayed. "Pilot to right gunner."

"Go ahead sir."

"I'll try fish-tailing. Maybe you can keep that Jap away from us with a few shots now and then."

"Fighter at one o'clock!" I said with a catch in my voice.

I fired continuously as he dived in close. This time I had difficulty holding the fighter in the sights for tracking.

"My sights gone bad," I said with dismay.

"What do you mean?" Vaucher asked anxiously.

I explained about the difficulty in tracking.

"I was pulling up to spoil the fighter's pursuit curve," Vaucher said.

"Don't do that!" Then I spotted another fighter. "Fighter at two o'clock low!" I yelled.

This was a bad deflection shot so I held my fire until I had tracked him for five seconds and then gave him a long burst. A stream of smoke poured from his cowling and streamed behind.

"You hit him! You hit him!" Mike Egan shouted, pounding me on the back.

"I hit him too!" Bianchi shouted excitedly. "He came right in firing all the way, and when he passed beneath me he was pouring smoke and flames."

"Did you see him crash?" I asked.

"I was too busy to watch him go down," he said. "He looked in a bad way when he went beneath us."

Fighters based on Saishu Island made a few more attacks on our formation, but at last we were free to relax.

"Whew! What an ordeal!" I said. "That's the most exciting experience I have ever had. There really wasn't much time to get scared after they attacked. It was almost fun!" I said to Vaucher.

"Fun?" he said with a relieved grin. "I can think of better ways to amuse myself."

Vaucher talked by radio with other planes in the formation. When he was through I asked, "How many were hit?"

"Not one," he said with surprise.

"That's amazing," I said. "I've been tallying up the score and as far as I can figure we were under attack for an hour and 50 minutes. During that time there were 47 attacks on the formation."

"Our turrets must be low on ammunition," Todd said.

"I'd forgotten about that," I said. "We've got occupied China to cross. Hope the Japs leave us alone."

Vaucher warned the crew. "Everyone keep a good lookout when we get over occupied China. Don't waste ammunition. There can't be much left."

"They did their best today," I told Vaucher, "and we beat them at their own game on their own home grounds. I've got to hand it to LeMay, he knows what he's doing."

"That's what I tried to tell you," Vaucher said.

"Here you are, bomb-aimer," Carmona said. "Have a steak sandwich."

I looked into the plump, smiling face of our radio operator. "I don't know how you manage to prepare these delicious steaks out over the Yellow Sea," I said with mock gravity.

"Nothing to it, if you know how," he said with a grin.

Carmona had taken on the job of dispensing the food from our flight rations. His genial face always appeared from behind the turret, after we had left the target, as he doled out our small supply of food. He took pleasure in the job. Of course the steaks that we kidded about were, in reality, dabs of potted meat between crackers. In all the missions we flew together, I never knew Carmona to be grumpy, or irritable regardless of the circumstances. He was a ray of uninhibited sunshine on the darkest day. Short, fat, and with and infectious grin, he was worth his weight in gold.

The flight home was monotonously uneventful, and no fighters rose to challenge us.

"Check my turrets," I said to the armament men when we left the airplane. "There can't be many rounds left. I had a full load."

They opened the turrets and inspected the .50-caliber rounds that were left.

"You fired about 3,200 rounds," the chief said. "You must have had a battle today."

"We sure did. Those Japs were out for blood, but they didn't draw any."

Only 59 B-29s bombed the Omura factory but they caused considerable damage to the plant's fabrication facilities. Nineteen other bombers hit targets of opportunity. General LeMay was pleased with the results and presented Air Medals to several members of the lead crews.

Back in India, preparations were under way for a mission out of our rear bases. During November a shortage of fuel limited the number of missions out of China, but that was not a problem in India. An attack on November 3 on the marshalling yards at Rangoon demonstrated the effectiveness of the B-29 when it could drop a full load of bombs visually on a target. The British had been trying for three years to knock out these yards but a small force of B-29s completely destroyed them in one of the finest examples of precision bombing to date. The Japanese railroad system had always been critically short of locomotives so their losses during this raid were felt acutely.

Our crew was not assigned to the Rangoon mission so Albert, Fessler, and I relaxed on our cots in a good mood.

"We're still carrying the ball," I said. "We haven't fumbled in some time."

They both grinned, and there was an air of satisfaction on their faces that was good to see.

Our optimism reached new heights when the reports were in about the Rangoon mission. Photographs demonstrated that the marshalling yards were completely demolished.

"That shows you what the B-29 can do when it carries a full load of 500-pounders," I said to Albert when we learned the results.

Lieutenant Thurman W. Sallade, the newest lead bombardier of our group, placed his formation's bombs all within 1,000 feet of the aiming point after a short and difficult bombing run. On this exceptional mission, Sallade's score was not unusual but typical of what occurred throughout Bomber Command.

I looked at Bob Albert and grinned. "I understand 'Old Smiley' LeMay made a wager with the British commanders that we could do the job with just a small effort on one strike. Loberg said he returned from headquarters and that LeMay's cigar was at a jaunty angle."

Two days later, B-29s were loaded with 1,000-pound bombs for an unusually long mission to Singapore. The target was only 10 feet wide and 200 feet long, and the bombardiers were told that only precision bombing at its best could knock it out. The aiming point was the sliding gate of the main dry dock; a dock the Japanese inherited from the British and which was now being used to repair Japanese warships.

Our group bombardier gave us the details. Mitchell said, "On November 5 you'll take off to bomb the sliding gate of the main dry dock at Singapore."

We drew in our breaths and stared popeyed at Mitchell as he leaned against the drafting table in the briefing room.

"This is a difficult mission in more ways than one," he said. "The gate is only 10 feet wide. Only superior bombing can knock it out."

"What's so important about a dry dock?" I said.

"The Japanese use it to repair their warships. It's in constant use. Here are the charts and photographs of the target. I want you to spend the rest of the day familiarizing yourselves with the area."

"How far is it to Singapore?" one of the lead bombardiers asked.

"Approximately 3,800 miles down and back," Mitchell said with a smile.

"That will keep us in the air over 18 hours," I said unbelievingly.

"That's right," Mitchell said.

I turned to Lieutenant Wilbur H. Boseling next to me. "I'm not looking forward to it."

"I saw the flak charts," he said. "It looks pretty bad. On top of that they always have a number of warships in the Strait and their fire is deadly."

I looked through my target folder and arranged the material. I felt no enthusiasm, just a dread fear of what lay in store for us.

Mitchell pointed to an enlarged mosaic of the Singapore area on the wall.

"Singapore is an island, roughly shaped like the head of an elephant, connected to the mainland by a narrow causeway across the Johore Strait. Our target is on the topside of the island, surrounded by warehouses and workshops."

The day was spent in studying the area with mounting tension, drawing it from memory and planning our attack to the minutest detail.

Little new was added to the final briefing but we were advised that the Office of Secret Services (OSS) had buried survival equipment in two graves on the Andaman Islands, and they gave us the fictitious names. We were told that if we had to bail out, this material might save our lives.

The moon silvered the waters of the Bay of Bengal as we headed on our way November 5 at about one o'clock in the morning.

"I hate to think what a flak hit would do to our bomb bays," Vaucher said.

"Those three bomb bay tanks are filled to the brim," I said. "We hardly have room for the three 1,000-pound bombs. A hit would make us a flaming torch."

The Andaman Islands showed dimly despite the darkness, and we knew we were on course. I reminded myself of the graves with their survival equipment and marveled at the OSS's forethought. After the sun rose out of the east, planes appeared around us.

"We've got company," Vaucher said with a grin.

"They're a welcome sight," Todd said. "I've been worrying about heading for Singapore with just a few planes. That's no place to be without a large formation."

Out of the haze ahead we could see the outlines of land extending on either side of us. With the Malay Peninsula on our left and Sumatra on our right, we flew down the middle of the Malacca Strait to the assembly point. We were flying deputy leader so we joined a large formation on the second turn.

The Straits were narrow at this point and the beautiful greenness of the surrounding countryside was refreshing. We knew that this wooded country was deceptively inviting because of the many stories we had been told of the steaming jungle, unfriendly natives, and rugged terrain.

"I'd hate to have to bail out and walk out of that country," Todd said with awe. "My chances would be practically non-existent."

As we turned on the IP, we could plainly see the Straits of Johore, and we knew the target was clear. We could see for miles and every identifying mark was visible.

"That formation ahead of us is really catching it," I said to Vaucher. "There's a wall of flak shielding the target."

He nodded to me with troubled eyes. I pulled my flak helmet tighter as we passed the 25-mile radius from the target. The sky over the target and on the approach was filled with black and white puffs of anti-aircraft fire.

The formation hugged together protectively and during the last two minutes of the bombing run the seconds ticked by with spectacular slowness.

I opened the bomb bay doors, searched the sky for fighters, and then riveted my eyes on the lead plane. Boseling guided the large formation as we weaved back and forth while he put in his corrections. Seemingly, from out of nowhere, the sky around us filled with bursts. They were so close that we could see the red flashes as the shells exploded.

"They've got our range down pat," I announced grimly over the interphone.

The sides of the plane echoed the bursts and it sounded as if someone was beating on the fuselage with a baseball bat. I flinched at each close burst and tried to make myself as small as possible in the cramped nose. I took a quick look down and could see the shore batteries firing. A glance at the Strait was revealing. "Wow!" I exclaimed.

"What's the matter?" Vaucher asked nervously.

"There are several warships in the Strait. They're lit up from stem to stern. They must have every gun trained on us."

The seconds seemed like hours while the bursts multiplied in intensity. Two or three resounding wallops told us all too clearly that we had been hit. I licked my dry lips with a tongue like sandpaper. Vaucher edged us closer to the lead plane.

Three large objects parted from the lead plane and I quickly salvoed my thousand pounders with a feeling of tremendous relief. After closing the doors, I leaned over the bombsight to spot the bombs, but those wicked flashes were too much for me and I quickly regained my seat.

"Where'd they hit?" Todd called.

I turned to him with a blanched face and said, "I didn't see. That flak looks awful."

The guns followed us as we turned away from the target and quickly passed the Johore Straits. At last we were out of range of those murderous guns, and we all breathed a sigh of relief.

"Fighter at 11 o'clock high!" I called.

The need for immediate action calmed my jangled nerves and I spun the top turret and tracked the tiny speck diving straight in for a head-on approach. Arc machine gun bullets swirled toward the plane like roman candles on an old fashioned Fourth of July. Defying the massed fire of our guns, he held his curve, never wavering for a second, until an object fell from beneath the fighter's fuselage and a bright yellow blossom appeared just above the formation. My heart constricted as I watched the phosphorous streamers fall toward us.

"That was a close call," I said with a voice that shook. "If he had not released the bomb just a second too soon, he'd have hit us."

"I hate those phosphorus bombs," Vaucher said. "The flak and the fighters are bad enough, but if one of those phosphorus bombs hit near an engine nacelle, this plane would be a flaming inferno in no time."

"We didn't hit him with our fire," I said. "But I believe we forced him to drop sooner than he intended."

"Thank God for that moment of indecision," Todd said mirthlessly.

Formation after formation hit the target behind us. We received only desultory attention as our formation left the target area and headed out over the green hills and luxuriant valleys with huge estates dotting the countryside.

We now had time to survey the flak damage.

"Check the wings and fuselage," Vaucher told the crew. "All engines are operating efficiently, but I think we must have been hit several times over the target."

When the reports were in from all stations, Todd said, "Doesn't appear to be too bad, Skipper. The wings have some ragged holes in them, but otherwise no serious damage seems to have been done."

We flew directly over several Japanese fighter strips before we reached the west coast of Malay Peninsula, but we were not intercepted again.

"How many hours back?" Vaucher called to Egan.

"Approximately eight hours," Mike said. "By the time we return to base we will have been in the air over 18 hours."

When we landed at Piardoba our faces were gray and puffy with fatigue, and dark circles accentuated the bags under our eyes. We climbed stiffly from the nose of the plane to meet Loberg and Durbin. They were grinning with relief at our safe return.

"How was it?" Durbin asked. "Did they give you a bad time?"

"I never want to go down there again," Vaucher said. "That flak is worse than at Yawata. Everyone accounted for?"

"So far, so good," Loberg said. "You're the first plane back, but all the others have reported."

"I'll bet some of them are short on fuel," Vaucher said.

"They are," Durbin said. "But they'll make it all right."

The mission was a spectacular success because the gate was knocked out, and the stern of a ship in the dry dock was seriously damaged. It was an example of the kind of precision that was expected but seldom achieved.

Boseling, our formation's lead bombardier and I reviewed the strike photos. "That's the greatest job of bombing I've ever seen," I said. "You knocked that 10-foot wide gate completely."

"I was lucky," he said modestly.

"That wasn't luck," I said. "On top of that, one thousand pounder knocked the stern off the ship in the dry dock. That's what I call precision bombing at its best."

The top priority given to the Omura Aircraft Manufacturing Company factory made it mandatory to schedule the next two missions in November out of China in further attempts to knock it out.

Our crew headed out over the Yellow Sea on November 11 to lead a formation against it. The mainland was completely cloud covered and we realized with deflated hopes that the target would be obscured by clouds. As we penetrated a huge frontal area of dark, billowy clouds, our formation disappeared. Ice formed on the wing and the plane lost speed and became unsteady. Then it began to pitch violently as we neared the center of the disturbance. We learned later that a recall message had been sent with orders to bomb Nanking instead, but only half the crews received it.

Our bombs were dropped by radar, and we had little hopes of success. Some crews had turned back after receiving the recall message and bombed Nanking in China. Others had simply jettisoned their bombs and gone home. Five crews were lost, but none to Japanese defenses.

The storm was much worse than we had imagined at the time. Winds of 150 to 175 miles per hour were recorded. They buffeted our B-29s like matchsticks whirled in an autumn breeze.

Photo reconnaissance later proved that the November missions had caused no new damage.

Captain Weston H. Price in the "Gen. H.H. Arnold Special," the airplane Arnold had personally selected off the factory lines in Kansas for earlier delivery than scheduled, was so low on fuel that he headed for Vladivostok in preference to crash landing in Japanese-held China.

Once they were over Russian territory, they were escorted by 10 fighters and led to a naval air station. On the ground they were ordered peremptorily out of their plane and taken to naval headquarters, and they never saw their B-29 again. They were treated almost like enemy airmen, and they resented it.

After the Department of State protested their treatment, they were allowed to leave through Iran on February 2, 1945.

Arnold was bitter because he considered the Russian actions inexcusable, and hardly what one would expect from an ally. He told his staff that the Russian action was the easiest way he knew for them to acquire one of the world's most advanced bombers without cost. Privately he expressed his conviction that the State Department had not tried hard enough to get the airplane back.

Arnold wired LeMay that he wanted another attack on Omura on November 14 to coordinate with a Navy carrier sweep against Honshu, and the 21st Bomber Commands' first strike at Tokyo. When the Tokyo strike was delayed for 10 days because of a typhoon, LeMay told Arnold he would send 11 B-29s to Omura on the 21st, or three days before General Hansell's new command on Saipan was scheduled to hit Tokyo. Although 109 airplanes took off, one crashed after take-off, killing all but one crewman, and then bad weather closed in on the target. Sixty-one B-29s bombed by radar but it was a chaotic release as two formations broke up when lead planes switched on the bombing run. Anti-aircraft fire was inconsequential but the new "Frank" and "Jack II" fighters made their first attacks against B-29s. They proved aggressive and deadly as they closed within 100 yards. One B-29 was shot down while four others were lost. Twenty-three other B-29s bombed targets at Shanghai and other cities with some success. But it was a costly mission for the limited damages done to the targets.

The first mission of the 73rd Wing at Saipan was assigned to attack the Nakajima Musashino-Tama plant in northwest Tokyo. It was the number one target in Japan because it produced almost half of all Japanese combat engines. Intelligence estimates predicted 500 fighters in the target area. (Later, more accurate data indicated there were only 375 in all the home islands.) But the projection of heavy guns proved accurate. Five submarines were positioned at sea between Iwo Jima and Japan prior to the raid while destroyers were stationed between Iwo Jima and Saipan. All search planes were placed on alert November 17.

The Navy's fast carriers planned to strike Honshu between November 12 and 17, and Hansell scheduled B-29s to arrive on the last day, supposedly at a time when Japanese fighters would be exhausted. Hansell welcomed the diversion by the Navy's Pacific fleet but Japanese Navy attacks against American forces at Leyte Gulf threw the Navy's time schedule off. Admiral Halsey was forced to cancel the Navy strikes against Honshu, and he and Admiral Nimitz recommended that the 21st Bomber Command attacks be cancelled also, or postponed until the Navy was ready. Despite the delay and lack of coordination with the Navy, Hansell was anxious to launch the mission alone without its help. He was concerned that a delay would be perceived as indicating that his operations were only possible with Navy assistance.

There was still only one operational runway on Saipan, and it had no lights for returning aircraft, only smudge pots, instead of the four runways Hansell had expected when he arrived in the Marianas. He knew that if there was a mishap on that single runway that all returning aircraft returning from the mission would be lost. The only other runway was at Kwajalein 1,200 miles away.

Just before Hansell had departed Washington for Saipan, Arnold had sent for him saying that General Marshall wanted to see him.

At their meeting, Marshall reminded Hansell that the first operation of the 20th Air Force in the Pacific was a joint operation, coordinated with surface operations of the Army and Navy. He stressed the importance of carrying out the 21st Bomber Command's mission on time.

Marshall said, "Can you carry out your share?"

Hansell assured him that his command would do so.

Prior to the mission, Major General George C. Kenney wrote Arnold and denounced Hansell's operational plan and predicted failure. He said B-29s could not survive a daylight attack because the Japanese would simply shoot them out of the sky.

Hansell received a copy of the letter, with Arnold's postscript on the bottom. He said that his most experienced advisors agreed with Kenney and that he was inclined to agree with their views. He added that if he still believed his command could make it, "Good luck, and may God be with you."

Then Hansell received a personal letter from his wing commander, Brigadier General Emmett "Rosey" O'Donnell expressing his doubts that the mission could be carried out without excessive losses. He recommended that the first assault be made at night.

Deeply concerned, but knowing that he was committed to daylight operations, he told O'Donnell that he shared his concern about the mission but that the strategic considerations outweighed the tactical obstacles. "I am determined to go ahead with daylight attacks against our prescribed targets."

He studied O'Donnell's face. "Are you reluctant to lead your wings on the forthcoming mission?" Hansell had requested permission from Arnold to lead the mission, but had been denied.

O'Donnell hastened to assure Hansell that he was willing to go ahead although he had been impelled to voice his concern.

Hansell set the morning of November 17 to send his B-29s on their first strike against Japan but a typhoon at Saipan prevented the take-off. For a week of on-again, off-again schedules the crews waited impatiently for the weather to clear. It finally did so on November 24.

The black-haired, blue-eyed Irishman from Brooklyn, General "Rosey" O'Donnell, led the 73rd Wing over Tokyo. Weather was bad over the target as formations tried to get through at altitudes of 27,000 to 35,000 feet. Wind velocities of 150 miles per hour raised downwind ground speeds to 445 miles per hour, making it almost impossible for the 24 bombardiers who could see the target to synchronize.

Lieutenant Sam F. Wagner's crew fought off Japanese fighters after their plane left the target, but a "Tony" fighter was disabled by other bombers in the formation and crashed into their tail. Fighter and bomber plunged to earth, and there were no parachutes. It was the new command's first loss. Another bomber ditched at sea but its crew was picked up.

Japanese fighters surprisingly had not put up a strong defense of their capital and the heavy anti-aircraft guns proved ineffective.

The mission achieved little, with only one percent of the factory receiving damage. But Arnold briefed President Roosevelt, and a statement was released saying, "No part of the Japanese Empire is now out of range."

Although the bombing was understandably poor, the mission proved that decisive air warfare could be carried out from the Marianas.

The same target was attacked November 25 and the B-29s encountered winds of 220 miles per hour. The lead navigator clocked their plane's ground speed at 580 miles per hour, too high to synchronize the bombsight and the Musashino plant again emerged unscathed.

But Hansell's faith in strategic air warfare had been vindicated. Despite Arnold's glowing reports to the president and the press, the B-29s could not have done a worse operational job, and unfortunately, results would continue to be poor for 73rd Wing operations for some time to come.

Although the first two missions against Tokyo targets achieved no military goals, their impact on the Japanese people were great. Disillusionment with their leader's ability to protect the homeland was widespread, and soon would get worse.

Those of us in India were excited by the 73rd's first attack against Tokyo but we were in low spirits. Some of the crews had been sent home, just one or two, but enough to make the rest of us feel sorry for ourselves.

"I wish we could get out of here," I said listlessly to Joe Buchta. "I'm fed up with missions that accomplish so little."

"The weather is our greatest enemy," Joe said.

"It seems so useless to stay here any longer."

At the end of a briefing for a mission to Bangkok, Major Fawcett said, "If you have to bail out be sure to keep away from the city and only approach a native if he is by himself so there will be no way to report the contact."

The mission was flown the latter part of November and tons of bombs were dropped by the marshalling yards to destroy the freight cars and locomotives that were transporting war material to the Burma front. The locomotives were especially valuable to the Japanese because they had only a limited number. Their destruction was a serious blow to their forces fighting Allied troops in Burma.

Tremendous destruction was caused, proving again the power of the B-29 when a full bomb load was carried. There was nothing that could survive under such a deluge of TNT. The mission analysis later proved this theory because the yards were completely wiped out. Never again were the Japanese capable of using the yards as they had in the past. The best they could do was to fill in a bed and lay a single track through the area for trains from the city.

Chapter 9

"Pisspoor Bananas! Chickenshit Coconuts!"

Our barracks had a 10-foot straw covered veranda that was ideal for lounging at the end of a day, particularly now that the temperatures had moderated in India. At night it began to get downright cold.

Often before dark a familiar Indian strode down the road in front of us stepping high while we chanted, "Hut, two, three, four; hut, two, three, four" as the tears rolled down our cheeks. We had seen him many times before with his white wraparound flowing in the breeze, and a tremendous basket on his head filled with fruit and nuts for sale. As we counted cadence, he walked briskly with a sweeping swing to his arms, his legs working like pistons in exaggerated military stride.

"Hut, two, three, four," we roared, and it became a chant that echoed throughout the area. His arms made even greater arcs and his knees came up level with his stomach as he marched along. There was a wide expansive grin on his brown face as his flashing white teeth smiled in appreciation.

"I've needed a good laugh for a long time," I said as I clutched my sides.

"Isn't he a character?" Albert said.

I motioned to the peddler to come over. I motioned to his bananas. "Good bananas?"

"Pisspoor," he said.

I pointed to the coconuts.

"Chickenshit coconuts," he said as if he were extolling their virtues.

I bought some fruit and walked away, disturbed that some of our misguided Americans would make a fool of the man because he spoke no English and only parroted such sayings because they helped to drum up trade. I expressed my concern to a friend, who shrugged it off.

"He's only a gook," my friend said.

"He's a human being," I said indignantly. "And we're taking advantage of his ignorance of our language."

Several days passed while we idled through the dreary hours of training missions. When we were told on December 5 that we should make preparations to cross the Hump, we obeyed with alacrity.

Colonel Kalberer, the group commander, was with us when we took off the next morning.

Toward the end of the flight Kalberer told Vaucher he had a new job for him on the group staff.

Vaucher protested that he wanted to remain with the crew, despite the lure of a lieutenant colonel rank, but Kalberer was adamant.

We were all depressed because our crew would be broken up again. We had come to respect the Skipper not only as a pilot but also as a man. We had been through a lot together, so the mere thought of him leaving was unthinkable. We were in a black mood the rest of the flight.

I tried to buck up his morale with a labored attempt at humor. "You're an armchair pilot now," I kidded.

This aroused only a feeble grin.

A few weeks later we pinned armchair wings on his breast. The enlisted members of the crew had had them made in Calcutta. They were similar to a pilot's wings except for a rocking chair that replaced the shield.

Our thermometers dropped steadily as we climbed for altitude and headed for Manchuria. Even the heavy clothing we wore failed to keep out the sharp cold.

"If you think this is cold," Vaucher said, "wait until we get over Manchuria, the weatherman predicted 40 below, centigrade, at bombing altitude."

We formed up just beyond the Shantung Peninsula with the greatest of ease. Leveling off, my eyes opened wide as I gazed at the free-air thermometer.

"Do you realize how cold it is?" I said to Vaucher.

"It's cold enough," he said with a shiver.

"The outside thermometer reads 52 degrees below zero."

"I hope we don't frost over the pilot's compartment."

We could see the bay around Dairen frozen solid, just a sheet of shimmering ice that glittered in the bright sunlight.

As we approached land on our way to the target, a mantle of white snow covered the earth, with black and gray houses standing out in sharp relief against the white background.

"Fighter at one o'clock, high," Vaucher called as we turned on the IP. We were still 60 miles from Mukden, so I grabbed my gun sight and gave the fighter a quick going over without any tell tale effect.

Then I settled down to the business of locating the aircraft factory to the east of the arsenal. We were still 40 miles away.

"Remember what date it is?" I asked Todd.

"Can't remember anything significant about it."

"It's December 7. Three years ago the Japs bombed Pearl Harbor. I've got an anniversary present for them," I said with a happy grin. "All done up in a special package just for them."

I ignored the fighters that made passes and attended to my job of locating the target. I was in a different world, oblivious to the roar of the turrets, and concentrating on the bombing problem.

The frozen countryside was visible for a hundred miles in the clear, cold atmosphere. Up ahead I could see a column of smoke rising in the air.

"That must be the target," I said pointing ahead.

As we drew closer, there was no doubt about it. Mukden, with its walled inner city was on the left, and the huge arsenal sprawled to the right of the city. I knew the aircraft plant was to the right of the arsenal so I turned the airplane in that direction.

The whole area was covered by a rapidly developing smoke screen, hiding the plant completely from view. A few fires were visible in the arsenal as several buildings burned.

I swung the bombsight to the left and right, trying to find the aiming point through the thick clouds of smoke that swirled high in the air.

"I can't find the aiming point," I said desperately to Vaucher.

"Why not?"

"They've got a smoke screen covering the plant."

A minute and 30 seconds before bombs away I noticed a building in the smoke that I felt sure was the aiming point. I cranked out 12 degrees of drift.

With cold, cramped hands I synchronized the sight and placed the cross hairs on the target. "Bombs away!"

During the 40 or so seconds before the bombs hit I closed the doors and turned off the sight. I looked out over the bombsight to spot the bombs and saw the bursts blossoming in the gray patches at the edge of the buildings and spreading through the whole area.

"Looks like we've done it again!" I cried exultantly.

As we swung to the left over Mukden, the fighters and the flak that I had been too busy to notice now caught my attention. In the frigid sky the fighters were easily recognizable by their long vapor trails. A formation of B-29s on its way out ahead of us had 12 magnificent white streamers streaking the sky.

"Here they come again," Todd called.

The fighters closed on us and we fired back but failed to knock down a single one of them. I looked back over the target. Another formation of B-29s was on its way in, with vapor trails making a beautiful pattern against the blue backdrop of the sky.

Over Mukden the fighters came in close, daring the massed fire of 12 B-29s only to turn away after their pass, seemingly untouched.

"It seems impossible that any human or mechanical contrivances can stand this withering fire," I said.

"These guys are good," Vaucher said. "They must have the first team up today."

"You're not kidding," I said breathlessly, as another fighter roared past us. "This is the best show I've seen them put on since Omura."

Many more formations were on their way to the target and the fighters ignored us as we reached the coast. We were happy to see them go.

"I don't see how some of the pilots can see to fly," Vaucher said. "Most planes are completely frosted over in front."

"I noticed some of the bombardiers scratching holes in the frost," I said. "I don't understand either how pilots can hold such a tight formation."

"It's a miracle," Todd said, "but they are doing it and doing it well."

That night the air raid sirens sounded shortly after we returned and we headed for the rice paddies.

"Do you hear anything?" Mike Egan whispered nervously. "Listen!"

My ears were alert as Mike and I rested against a pile of straw in a field half a mile from our quarters.

"I don't hear anything," I said. "A-I is getting bombed badly but they are leaving us alone."

The alarm had sounded earlier that Japanese bombers were on their way and we had spent hours in a ditch. The thud of bombs and the arcs of tracer shells could be heard and seen in the distance as another one of our fields was repeatedly bombed.

"Don't you hear that plane?" Mike whispered.

I listened carefully and at first could detect nothing abnormal. Then the faint throbbing of a plane could be heard.

"Sounds like one of our C-47s," I said.

"I don't think so," Mike said.

A vague outline appeared in the east, flying low and heading right for us.

"He's flying right toward us!" Mike shouted.

His last words were muffled as he tried to burrow into the rice stack, which put the bomber out of sight but offered no protection. The plane, flying at 500 feet swept over us and circled the field. We relaxed a bit.

"Here he comes again!" I shouted.

The twin-engine Japanese bomber flew directly over us and then down across the length of the field. When Major Norman had taken over as base commander in September he had found no provisions for its defense. He used ground troops to man 20 gun positions around the runway and trained them in the use of .50-caliber machine guns. He scavenged a 20-millimeter cannon and some of the machine guns from the tail of a crashed B-29. Now these guns were put to use. Norman directed the defense at his command post about 200 yards from the runways central tower. He had been ordered by Command headquarters to remove all tracer bullets from his machine guns because they would give away the field's location. So they were shooting at Japanese planes almost directly overhead and not knowing whether their bullets were making contact or not. When one bomber came directly overhead below the clouds at 1,000 feet, perfectly outlined against them, the machine guns blasted away but the gunners couldn't tell where the bullets were going without tracers. Norman noticed splashes of fire on the side of the Japanese bomber; but it kept on coming. It dropped a few demolition bombs, which straddled some of our own bombs alongside a hard stand and a gun position. Through no fault of his gunners, they had lost a good chance to shoot down the Japanese bomber. The next day Norman ordered tracer bullets back in their machine guns.

That night the problem was complicated by planes returning late from the mission. With the field under attack, they were told to orbit the area. Command headquarters had ordered the runway lights turned off but when pilots called in desperately short on fuel Norman ordered them turned back on. Captain John C. Campbell tried three times to land before he finally made it safely back home.

Egan and I watched as one Japanese bomber flew directly over us and then down across the length of the field. The crackling popping of fragmentation bombs could be heard along with the dull thumping, thudding sounds of three demolition bombs. Several more Japanese bombers followed. Some did not drop bombs, but our stationary .50-caliber machine guns on the ground roared defiantly. At last it was over and the all clear was sounded.

The next morning we went out to the field to inspect the damage the bombers had caused. Two of our B-29s were badly damaged. *King Size* was one of them. She was riddled with fragments from the bombs and her radar compartment was a sieve. I looked her over sadly and there were tears in my eyes as I turned away because her combat days were over, and she had served us long and faithfully.

King Size was patched up and later flown to India, and then back to the States. During overhaul it was discovered that the tail section of the plane had been so stressed by Loberg's pull out at 340 miles per hour on that first night raid at Yawata that many of the rivets associated with the interior structure were close to pulling out. It was a tribute to the airplane's structural integrity that she had continued to fly despite her severe damage.

During the mission critique that day, Major Mitchell turned to me. "How did you pick the wrong aiming point, Wilbur?"

"I had a terrible time seeing the target," I said. "I'm not apologizing for missing the aircraft plant but there was a thick smoke screen over the plant."

"The bombs from the right element went into the aircraft plant, but all of the others struck buildings in the arsenal," he said.

"We did some good," I said with resignation, and I gazed at the strike pictures with disgust. Of deeper concern was the fact that against all international conventions the Japanese were using prisoners of war in the arsenal, and my bombs may have killed some of them.

Kalberer decided to fly back with us to pioneer a new route over the highest part of the Himalayas. We climbed quickly to 20,000 feet before setting out across Tibet. The mountains around and below us were tremendous. It took our breaths away just to see them beyond the wing tips, completely snow covered and pointed like daggers toward the plane.

I gazed at this harsh, cruel land of snow and ice and marveled at its incredible beauty. Far to the west I could see Mount Everest, jutting up to 29,028 feet — the world's tallest peak — thrusting its snow-capped spire majestically into the blue sky with its slopes swathed in a mantle of white. We were flying above the border of Nepal and Tiber and the mountain seemed near. In reality it was as least 80 miles away. Clustered around Everest were a number of the world's greatest peaks, all above 20,000 feet.

The Himalayas (Abode of Snow) stretch from Afghanistan in the west to Assam in the east for 1,700 miles but they are less than 150 miles wide as they range through eight countries. There are two principal rivers, the Indus and the Brahmaputra, that rise a few miles from each other in Tibet. They flow 1,000 miles west and east before they abruptly turn southwards to cut through the Himalayas and flow into the Indian Ocean.

The gorges carved by these rivers are the deepest in the world and their foam-flecked waters are marvelous to behold.

Despite savage winters, life endures even in this land of snow and ice where animals and people have learned to survive. After the snow melts in the spring, huge glaciers cascade down the slopes but there are also alpine meadows at lower altitudes that grow lush with green pastures. Even further down the slopes conifers thrive below the tree line and men and beast herald the end of the frigid winter.

The colonel flew so low we were practically flying the valleys in between, with jagged peaks jutting into the sky around us. Large towns, villages, and monasteries could be seen in the high plateaus below us, 18,000 to 20,000 feet above sea level.

"Those aren't mud huts," I said with amazement. "They are constructed of stone and wood."

"I wonder what strange people live there?" Vaucher said.

"I wonder how they live," I said.

"We can't possibly imagine their life," Kalberer said. "This is a part of the Hump never visited by the white man."

As we came out on the other side of the mountains into a huge valley, the winding, sprawling Brahmaputra River appeared on our right. After this breathtaking crossing of the real Hump, the rest of the trip was uninspiring and anti-climactic. We had seen it too many times before.

I stepped off the porch the next morning and started for group operations. Just then I noticed a jeep coming up the road and signaled for a ride. And then all through the area a loud quacking broke out, up and down in rising and descending scale, "Quack, quack, quack." Came the chorus in imitation of Donald Duck.

I chuckled to myself as Captain Everett J. Witt, the 769th Squadron's flight surgeon slowed to pick me up. He was doing his best to look mad but I caught the twinkle in his eye.

"Just wait until those characters come to me with a belly ache," he said. "I'll fix them good."

"Quack, quack, quack, quack, quack, quack, quack, quack."

I could not help but laugh as I looked at the picture of Donald Duck some wag had painted and bolted onto Doc's jeep.

"When are you going to take that sign off?" I asked.

"I've been trying to," he said. "They bolted it on and I can't get it off."

I grinned but said nothing. I knew Doc would never take it off. His face was red but despite the fierce expression he assumed his good nature shown through. We kidded him because he loved it and because there was a bond of affection between Doc and the rest of us that could not be expressed in words.

He sweated out every mission, hoping against hope that he would not have to take the "Meat wagon" out and pick up more charred, mangled bodies when a plane failed to make it on take-off, as happened every now and then. And while we were out on a mission he waited impatiently and nervously to see whether we would make it back safe and sound. He was a flight surgeon and flew across the Hump like the rest of us but he received no particular credit although he accumulated combat time. It was part of his job. He doled out pills, worked in the hospital on all kinds of tropical diseases, sympathized with us, and was ready with a pun when we needed it most. We kidded Doc, but he knew it was all in fun.

A parade of natives walked by and one in particular caught my eye because his skin was blotchy and hanging from his body.

I turned to Witt. "A leper?"

"No," he said. "He's an albino and suffers terribly from the sun. I've seen quite a few." He looked at my face, noting the revulsion, and said, "I've seen some horrible medical cases here. The other day a man came down this road with testicles so enlarged that he carried them in a tiny wheelbarrow."

I looked at Doc with horror. Before I could ask the obvious question, he said, "He had elephantiasis. It's an advanced stage of filariasis caused by the bite of an anopheles mosquito."

Witt dropped me off at group operations and I was in a thoughtful mood when I thanked him for the ride. I hurried to Major Mitchell's office to see why he had called me. There was a serious frown on his face as he watched me walk in. "I've got to go to Bomber Command today."

Mitchell had been made Bomber Command bombardier a short while back. I had been offered his group job but had declined. Captain Walter Dinnison had been named to replace him.

"Word has just come in," Mitchell said, "that the crew Walt was flying back with over the Hump had some trouble. They all bailed out. Will you keep an eye on things until he gets back?"

"Sure Mitch, tell the colonel I'm only temporary," I kidded. "I don't want to get stuck in this job."

"I'll appreciate it. Walter should be back in a few days."

Later that afternoon Lieutenant Colonel Roush called me.

I walked into his office and eyed the depressed group before me.

"Did you hear the news?" Roush asked.

"What news?" I said, with growing uneasiness.

"Dinnison was killed when he bailed out."

"Oh no!" I exclaimed. I was shocked beyond measure by this sudden development. "I understood they all got out safely."

"The early report indicated that they did, but we've just heard that all were killed."

"You'll have to take over the group bombardier's job," Kalberer said.

"I don't want it!" I said vehemently. "I'll take over until you can get someone else."

"Nothing of the kind," Kalberer said. "You've got the job and you're going to keep it."

"I only have a few months in grade as a captain," I said persuasively. "It will be mid-July before I can get the majority the job calls for."

"I'll rush it through as soon as you have served time in grade," Kalberer said. "Now, no more arguments. You're Group Bombardier."

I walked out on the front porch of the operations office and stood watching a plane at the end of the runway. I felt depressed and beaten. I had no plans to make the Air Force a career, and I knew I would need nine months in grade as captain to get a promotion. I had been a captain less than three months. Now there was no chance of going home until the end of the war.

Vaucher followed me out. "It's not as bad as all that," he said. "I felt bad at first, but we're with a fine outfit, and back in the States we could get assigned to some chicken-shit outfit."

The plane roared by in front of us and I casually watched it as it lifted off the runway and the wheels started to retract.

"Oh no!" I said.

"What's the matter?" Vaucher said, who had not been watching the plane.

"He's on fire," I said in a whisper.

"Hit the extinguisher!" Vaucher yelled.

The flames died down for a moment as if Vaucher's warning had been heeded.

"He's flaming again!" I cried.

But the flames died down a second time as the other extinguisher went into action.

"Do you think he'll make it?" I said desperately. "He's turning to the left trying to get back."

"I'm afraid not," Vaucher said. His face was ashen and his hands shook.

"He can't now. He's flaming again."

We watched the burning plane as it struggled to maintain altitude. In a matter of seconds the flames burned the engine mount and the engine tumbled to the ground.

"If they were only a thousand feet," Vaucher said. "They could jump."

"They can't be over 200," I said.

Our horror-stricken eyes watched as the right wing crumpled and fell off.

"Jump!" Vaucher yelled.

It was too late. The plane cart-wheeled and plummeted to earth and a huge column of smoke and flame shot high into the air five miles from the field.

"Doc's got his work cut out for him this time," I said.

Now political controversy erupted in the CBI and added to LeMay's problems. He avoided the clash of personalities by reminding theater commanders that he took orders only from General Arnold and the Joint Chiefs.

Stilwell's dislike of Generalissimo Chiang Kai-shek was mutual. He repeatedly denounced the Chinese leader's corruption and what he termed was false pride, apathy and the military ineptitude of his military staff. Stilwell's tight control of Lend-Lease materials caused some of the antagonism and Chiang Kai-shek wrote President Roosevelt that he was personally affronted by the situation. The cagey president was not about to turn over control of Lend-Lease to the Generalissimo and privately supported Stilwell.

The president sent Vice President Henry A. Wallace to Chungking in June to mediate the dispute. Wallace reported back that the situation in China was explosive, and that Chiang insisted on a personal representative to act as liaison between him and the president because Stilwell no longer had his confidence. The vice president recommended two courses of action: That Stilwell retain his responsibilities in Burma, but that another commander should be selected for China, possibly Stilwell's deputy, with broad responsibilities for acting independently in China. He suggested the Lieutenant General Albert C. Wedemeyer for such a command.

Wallace never talked to Stilwell during his visit, which was shortsighted, and he admitted as much when he met with the president in Washington. But he told Roosevelt that loss of eastern China would cause a violent economic and political upheaval that might collapse the Chiang government.

The Joint Chiefs met in Washington on July 4 and strongly supported Stilwell. They argued that he be promoted to four-star rank, and that the president use his influence with Chiang to get all Chinese forces under Stilwell.

Roosevelt agreed and he advised Chiang Kai-shek that he was promoting Stilwell to full general and that he hoped he would place him in charge of all Chinese and American forces.

General Marshall notified Stilwell of these actions, but chastised him for failing to work harmoniously with Chiang. He told Stilwell that many of his words and actions had offended the president as well as Chiang. "I hope you will make a continuous effort to avoid wrecking your, and our plans because of inconsequential matter or disregard of conventional courtesies."

Stilwell replied July 9. He promised to justify Marshall's confidence, admitting "the load promised to be heavy for a country boy."

Chiang agreed to the president's suggestions the same day although he hedged by saying that the political considerations might delay action.

Wallace's recommendation that Roosevelt send a personal representative to China was acted upon when Brigadier General Patrick Hurley was assigned. After two months of negotiations with Chiang Kai-shek, on September 6, Hurley got his agreement to permit Stilwell to command all forces. By now, the military situation in China had become desperate. Without Hurley's knowledge, Chiang had summoned Stilwell and told him to withdraw the Yunnan divisions to the east bank of the Salween River unless Stilwell advanced his forces from below Myitkyina toward Bahama within a week.

Stilwell was an outstanding leader of ground troops, but he had a stubborn, explosive streak that made him difficult to work with at the highest level. His relations with Chiang from the beginning had been confrontational. Now Chiang's order aroused all of Stilwell's old suspicions about the Chinese leader's basic motives.

He sent a letter to Marshall reporting that his troops were not ready for an offensive. He said Chiang's threat to withdraw the Chinese divisions was another attempt by the Generalissimo to sabotage the Burma campaign. He told Marshall that Chiang would not listen to reason. Whether deliberately or not, Stilwell did not send copies of his wire to either Chiang or Hurley.

Marshall composed a letter for Roosevelt's signature on September 18. The president told Chiang Kai-shek that his cooperation was needed so that a land route to China could be opened early in 1945, and that the Generalissimo must help to press the Salween offensive by placing Stilwell in complete command of all forces. The president said such action would strengthen the British and American decision to open such a land route, and that withdrawal of the Salween forces would also jeopardize the air route to China, and that, if this occurred, he must be prepared to accept the consequences of his actions, and accept personal responsibility.

It was an ultimatum from one head of state to another. To make matters worse, it was delivered personally by Stilwell. Chiang refused to comment for three days, while Stilwell belatedly sent Hurley a copy of the memorandum. The basic problem between Chiang Kai-shek and Stilwell was control of Lend-Lease. Other recipients of such aid controlled distribution, and the Generalissimo insisted that he also had that right — and not Stilwell. But Stilwell's objections to Chiang's control were based on past experiences where such military supplies were diverted to Chinese leaders and favorite members of the Nationalists and failed to reach the forces for which it was destined.

There was no possibility of reaching an agreement between the two men, and as soon as Hurley was convinced he recommended Stilwell's removal.

The conflict of personalities brought China to the brink of chaos, and the Japanese took full advantage of the situation by expediting their drives south and east.

Roosevelt blamed himself for the situation, and now that it was evident Chinese coastal bases would not be needed, he agreed that construction of the Ledo Road was a costly and unnecessary project. Stilwell was recalled to Washington on October 18 and the president told Chiang Kai-shek that he would not appoint another American officer to command Chinese armies. He did not say he was appointing General Albert C. Wedemeyer as Chief of Staff for the Chinese theater. Further complicating the confused and tragic situation was division of the China-Burma-India theater into two parts. Wedemeyer was given command of American forces in China, and the India-Burma theater was given to Lieutenant General Daniel T. Sultan whom Chiang asked to be placed over Chinese forces committed to the Burma offensive.

LeMay refused to be drawn into these political moves, and he continued to resist requests to use B-29s for support of purely China operations. He was upset, therefore, when Wedemeyer strongly endorsed a B-29 strike against Hankow's dock areas. Wedemeyer justified his stand by citing the imminent threat to Kunming by Japanese ground forces, and that the Joint Chiefs' guidelines provided for such emergency action. He asked LeMay for an attack by 100 Superfortresses.

LeMay challenged Wedemeyer's authority and Wedemeyer appealed directly to the Joint Chiefs of Staff. LeMay lost the round and he was ordered to make the attack.

The mission was set for December 14 as part of a coordinated strike with Chennault's 14th Air Force, which agreed to bomb airfields in the Hankow area while B-29s dropped incendiary bombs on the city's dock areas.

The mission was rescheduled to December 18 for operational reasons and LeMay told Wedemeyer that his command probably could supply only 60 B-29s because older airplanes with unmodified engines were being withdrawn from combat.

Lieutenant Raymond C. French, ordnance officer of the 769th Squadron, and Group Armament Officer Captain Rosenberger had gone to China with the combat crews and a few key men to help stage several missions from China.

Rosenberger and French had supervised the loading of the group's planes and were "sacking" out when they got a call about 10 P.M. from Colonel Kalberer's office to report at once.

They walked into his command tent — an old RAF double-walled tent brought from India. Kalberer was seated behind a small table with a lighted candle on each side of him in whiskey bottles.

"I've just received a target change from Bomber Command for our group only. Instead of running a high-level daylight mission with 500-pound general purpose bombs tomorrow, we are assigned on an urgent basis to make an incendiary raid on Hankow dock area where the Japanese have just begun a large scale troop and material unloading operations."

Rosenberger spoke up. "I can see no way to off-load the general purpose bombs and reload incendiaries in time to meet the scheduled take-off."

Rosenberger gaped at the group commander when he merely repeated the new bomb load for each airplane and the next day's take-off time. Kalberer indicated that the discussion was over, so they saluted and walked out.

Rosenberger and French walked back to their tent, discussing the turn of events. Both agreed that there was only one way to get the job done on time and that was to remove the fuses and manually trip each bomb onto the ramp; rolling each bomb aside before the next one was dropped. There were 18 airplanes assigned to the mission, with an average of 10 bombs per airplane. They agreed that if all went well they could off-load those bombs in an hour and a half. By then the ordnance crews would have the incendiaries to place ready to load and hopefully make the take-off time. They decided that the operation should start at dawn, and their men were alerted.

General-purpose bombs had never been dropped in the six to eight feet distance required to unload them. They had been taught in armament and ordnance school that general-purpose bombs were supposed to be safe to drop on concrete without exploding. Theory was one thing but actually performing the act was filled with apprehension. The officers started the procedure while the enlisted men hid behind revetments.

To their relief all went well and the incendiaries were in place with only minutes to spare to meet the take-off schedule.

Three or four months later there was a similar bomb-unloading incident at another B-29 base in India that resulted in an explosion that destroyed two B-29s and killed seven men.

Chennault upset the carefully laid plans a few hours before the B-29s were ready to take off by asking the command to send its bombers 45 minutes earlier. When 40 crews failed to get the message due to the primitive communications network, the prescribed order for B-29s to approach the targets could not be adhered to. Three formations dropped bombs out of sequence so later formations found their aiming points obscured by smoke. Thirty-three planes in the first three formations hit targets and a few B-29s made single attacks. With smoke obscuring the targets, some bombs were dropped on civilian areas. Fifty percent of the target area was burned out, and Chennault claimed that Hankow was destroyed as an effective supply base and the Japanese army's drive inland was seriously handicapped.

Chennault claimed after the war that the Hankow raid was the first mass fire raid the B-29s flew, and gave LeMay the idea months later to change from high altitude, daylight strikes against Japan to night fire raids. Chennault's viewpoint is in error because fire raids against major urban cities had been under consideration for a long time, awaiting only sufficient B-29s to make such raids worthwhile on a massive scale. LeMay's B-29s had made a fire raid on Nagasaki earlier, but it was on a smaller scale.

One of the 462nd Group's planes was damaged over Hankow and crash-landed nearby. Three crewmembers were picked up by Japanese troops and paraded through Hankow's streets. Then, at the instigation of the Japanese commanding general in the Hankow area, they were set on fire while still alive and burned to death.

After the war, during the Japanese war trials in Shanghai, Major General Masataka Kaguragi declared in a signed statement that the humiliating parade of three American fliers in Hankow on December 16, 1944, was designed to force Chiang Kai-shek to demand that the United States halt bombing of the city.

Kaguragi was one of 18 Japanese placed on trial charged with the cremation alive of Lieutenant Lester R. White, Sergeants Henry Wheaton and James F. Forbes. He admitted that he, as chief of staff and Lieutenant General Tadayoshi Sano, commander of the 34th Army had approved the parade of the three fliers to arouse public opinion.

It was revealed at the trial that some of the crowd of tens of thousands attracted to the parade beat the fliers with sticks. Eyewitnesses charged that the three fliers were cremated that night — alive and twitching — after a beating with small fire logs.

Kaguragi said he gave verbal approval for the parade but denied that he had anything to do with the cremations. He and four other Japanese were hanged April 22, 1946, after they were convicted of the deaths of three Americans.

During the war none of us heard of their tragic death, but it was to become an all too familiar pattern once the home islands came under massive bombing attacks.

On December 19, B-29s took off for Omura again but turned back before reaching the target because of complete cloud cover. The shipyards at Shanghai were blasted thoroughly instead. Vaucher and I, along with the group staff, had come to China to brief the crews for two missions.

A group of Japanese collaborators had been active in our China base for some time, sending radio signals with a bicycle driven generator from Kiunglai. Major Norman initiated a trap to capture them because they were alerting the Japanese every time we took off, or returned to base.

Radio operators, combined with men from the communications unit, set up two tracking devices. One was installed in the base communication's shop and the other in a jeep. With radio telephones, and a local map, Norman's sleuths were able to pinpoint the location of the device.

Captain Hann, the base's Chinese commander, and several truckloads of Chinese soldiers, captured the spies. The sending device was located in a Chinese home in the heart of Kiunglai. There were three men and a woman in the compound and they were picked up for questioning.

When Norman asked Hann what had happened to the collaborators, the Chinese commander refused to be specific but Norman suspected they were interrogated to death.

Some Chinese, or possibly Japanese, also had the habit of starting two or three fires around the edge of the base about a mile or so out. When it was realized that lines from these fires intersected in the middle of the base to direct Japanese bombers, a more careful surveillance was made of the entire area. When fires erupted, .50-caliber machine guns opened up on them and they were quickly extinguished.

One Chinese civilian was caught one night on the base by a Chinese guard. After interrogation, he supposedly admitted that he had been hired by the Japanese to either blow up a B-29 or kill a crewman. He was turned over to Captain Hann for further interrogation, but he died during the night.

When Norman questioned Hann, the Chinese captain said, with a half smile, "He must have had a weak heart."

On December 21, Colonel Kalberer addressed the crews who were assembled for a mission. "We're going back to Manchuria. Our target is the same airplane factory that we tried to knock out before."

There was a flutter of apprehension as crewmembers listened to him. They remembered the fighter attacks.

"We have just learned," Kalberer said. "That we are not receiving the cooperation from Russia that we had expected. General LeMay has ordered that no B-29 will make a forced landing at Vladivostok."

"What if we get into serious trouble?" one pilot asked. "That's the nearest place to land in friendly territory."

"What do we do if we have to make a forced landing?" the pilot persisted.

"Fly back into China as far as you can. The underground will bring you back."

This brought a hoot of derision from another pilot. "No Chinese will trust us after what Tom Harmon did."

There was a chorus of agreement. Harmon, Michigan's 1940 Heisman Trophy winner had been shot down in a fighter plane in Japanese-held territory and made his escape through the help of friendly Chinese. He was awarded a Silver Star for "outstanding bravery." Back in the United States, during a newspaper interview, he revealed some of the places where he had been assisted in his escape. The Japanese after learning of his incredible revelations of top-secret information, burnt six villages to the ground and killed more than 100 prominent Chinese civilians. His action, once it became known to us, caused great anger and bitterness throughout the China theater. Those of us who counted on the Chinese to assist us if we had to bail out over Japanese occupied territory were particularly incensed by his thoughtless disclosures.

Kalberer agreed that Harmon's action made our problem worse but he reminded us that the Chinese underground was still saving crewmembers in Japanese occupied territory. This was true, and many were brought back to our base, sometimes more than a thousand miles. We all had the greatest respect for their efforts, entailing as they did the most severe retaliation if the Japanese caught them rescuing Americans.

"I thought we were allies," I said in an undertone to Vaucher. "They treat us as badly as the Japanese."

"How'd the mission go?" I asked Vaucher when I returned to the briefing room just before the planes were due back.

"They had a rough time," he said wearily. "Captain Campbell's plane was hit over Manchuria and they all bailed out."

I had to take a good grip on myself or I would have broken down and wept. Johnny and his crew were some of my best friends.

"Did they get the target?" I asked hoarsely.

"That's the worst part of it," Vaucher said. "The arsenal was hit again but the target was missed."

"Did Johnny and the boys get down safely?" I asked, fearing to hear the worst.

"We don't know. Jap fighters were seen shooting at the men as they floated to earth."

I walked away with leaden feet and a troubled heart.

After the crews returned I talked to Guido Bianchi, our former right gunner, who was now assigned to another crew. His plane, I knew, had flown as deputy leader. He described the circumstances leading to the loss of Campbell's crew. "A Japanese fighter dove on the formation aiming at the lead aircraft. In pulling away to its right the fighter fired at Campbell's B-29, which immediately dropped below the formation. I watched it continue to dive and noticed that it was trailing smoke. Then guys began tumbling out and I counted nine parachutes. They had no extra flight engineer on board so there were 12 crewmembers on board the plane."

While the command flew the maximum number of missions out of China in late 1944 with the fuel available in the forward areas, it continued to support Allied Forces in Burma with attacks against railroad systems.

The 1,500-foot steel Rama VI railroad bridge over the Chao Phrayam River had long been considered a prime target despite its small size because it was a vital link in Burma's rail system. Bombers went out December 14 to try and knock it out but the weather was bad so the Central Railroad Station in Rangoon was hit instead.

Crews of the 40th Group had protested the loading of their airplanes because 500-pound bombs, with a new explosive called Composition B that was far more powerful than TNT and much less stable, hung on racks below 1,000-pound bombs. Some crews threatened to refuse to fly the mission. They claimed this loading sequence was in violation of the field order from Bomber Command, and that the lighter bombs had a different ballistic coefficient than the half-ton bombs hanging over them. The fear was that they might collide after release and with their instantaneous fuses, cause an explosion beneath the aircraft.

Group Commander Colonel William Blanchard threatened to court martial any crewmember that refused to fly the mission so they reluctantly agreed to go.

After the mission eyewitnesses reported that four of the group's 11 aircraft had gone down after one of them exploded over the target. Two crashed into the city of Rangoon on a troop train, killing 753 Japanese. They learned the figure later from British prisoners of war who had been forced to bury the Japanese. Several Americans were taken prisoner and brutally treated.

Whether the bomb loading caused the tragic accident that killed so many men, and made prisoners of others, or whether a stray Japanese shell exploded in the bomb bay of one of the B-29s, blowing three more out of the sky, will never be known. Not one member of the crew of the exploding bomber survived. The episode lingered for years in the minds of some survivors with and unquenchable bitterness.

The strike by all groups was one of the best ever flown for bombing results but it cost the 40th Group five B-29s and their crews.

Kalberer offered a bottle of rare Scotch to an individual who came up with a name for our 462nd Group. There was a vigorous competition and one of the enlisted men won the prize for recommending "Hellbirds" with a subtitle "With Malice Toward Some." A special insignia was designed similar to the 20th Air Force insignia with the silhouette of a B-29 superimposed on the world with the new name of the group.

The huge rudders of our B-29s were painted a brilliant red so that everyone could identify us as the "Hellbirds."

Vaucher lodged a protest. "The Japs will spot us with those red rudders. They'll identify us every time we fly."

"They have reason to know us now," Kalberer said.

The Japanese had seen enough proof of the destructive capabilities of the B-29 Superfortresses and they cursed our existence. Now, in their propaganda broadcasts they began to call the B-29 Superfortresses "the birds from hell."

Chapter 10

The Hellbirds Lament

Japanese bombers penetrated British defense around Calcutta Christmas Day and four planes strafed and bombed command headquarters at Kharagpur. Their bombs caused only a few injuries but several B-29s were damaged.

We were eating Christmas dinner at our group when Captain Matthew H. Farrelly, base defense officer for our group, was called to the tower by Captain B. K. Thurston after an alert was sounded by an unidentified plane flying overhead.

Farrelly hated to give the word to the trained British anti-aircraft crews, some of whom had been in London during the Battle of Britain in a similar capacity, because he was fearful that it was an American plane that had failed to identify itself. He knew that the RAF crews were following his orders and had their radars locked on that plane overhead. One word to him, and it would be shot down. He continued to hesitate, reluctant to order guns into action unless the plane committed some overt action. He quickly checked the base's defenses, noting everyone was on alert. The plane solved his problem by leaving the area.

The next day Farrelly learned that the plane was an American C-46 cargo carrier that was unable to establish radio contact with the ground due to a malfunction of the plane's radio.

Those of us not on duty during the alert caused by the Japanese bombers — the Japanese planes never got beyond Kharagpur — headed for the officers club that night. No missions were scheduled until after the New Year so it promised to be a lively party.

I walked into the club about 9 P.M. and stopped by a group of friends in a corner trying to harmonize like a barbershop quartet. We had some fine singers in our group, and I had taken voice lessons myself, although I had never sung professionally. They were in a mellow mood, their faces flushed with too much alcohol, when they began

"The Hellbirds Lament." It was sung to the melody of the *Washington and Lee Swing*. I listened with a smile on my face.

> *"The 462nd is a Hellbird team*
> *It dates way back to Hap Arnold's dream.*
> *The song we sing is of a gallant plan*
> *To annihilate the little isle of Japan."*

I put my drink down and joined in the rollicking chorus.

> *"I am a Hellbird superman;*
> *I fight the war against Japan.*
> *I know no word such as abort*
> *And when I drink — I drink at least a quart.*
> *We are old soldiers, each and every one.*
> *We won't go home until the battle's won.*
> *We can't fly low enough for Curt LeMay*
> *Bombs Away!*
> *We Hellbirds."*

I looked at them with pride and affection. They were out of the heart of America — not members of its rich and privileged class — but it's middle class, who formed the backbone of America. Each was a volunteer and no one had forced them to join the Air Force. They had grown up during the period of the nation's worst and most debilitating depression, never losing faith that their nation would survive. Now they were doing a job that needed to be done. Like each generation before them they were fighting not for some vague idea of democracy but for the freedom of all people to make their own decisions and live their lives without dictation. These were not young men in their late teens, but mature adults whose average age was 26 with many like myself a few months short of our 30th birthday. At heart we were civilians in uniform. Through necessity we had become a tightly knit organization of fighting men and a fraternity of individuals bonded together by a common purpose. Through the efforts of men like Colonel Kalberer we had become something special — an organization with a unique character.

They continued The Hellbird Lament as I sat down.

> *"The Mukden Japs, they hate our guts*
> *But we'll go back to get their butts.*
> *When Jack II intercepts*
> *We'll give him hell, boys — hit those trigger trips.*
> *And when those frozen fifties fail to roar*
> *You'd better open up that nose wheel door.*
> *For just remember boys that life's serene*
> *In a submarine*
> *We Hellbirds."*

Colonel Kalberer walked in and there were shouts of greeting. Never stiff and military, the colonel was slapped familiarly on his back as he walked to the bar and ordered a drink. No one was sacred to this group and any commander who tried to rule them with a strict military hand would have been laughed out of the outfit. The irreverence was always there, but in a respectful way.

When someone stood up to lead the gang in a few special words for Kalberer to the tune of McNamara's Band, most everyone joined in.

"I am the group commander,
I'm the leader of the group.
I tickle all the nurses
And I pass out all the poop.
Tra-la-la."

Kalberer roared with laughter as the verses became more ribald until they tired of the game. We were just getting warmed up on some of our favorite songs, particularly, "On the Road to Singapore" that was sung to the tune of "On the Road to Mandalay."

"Send me back to Uncle Sugar,
Put me on rotation list,
For I've packed my bag and baggage,
And I'm sure I'll not be missed.
When they're setting up a mission,
And you're bombing up your ship,
I'll be back in Uncle Sugar,
When you go against the Nip."

Everyone loved the choruses.

"On the road to Singapore,
Where the angry Hellbirds roar,
And the flak comes up like thunder,
From the batteries off Johore"

We waxed nostalgic when we sang:

"I'll be back in uncle Sugar,
By a silver-plated bar,
With a little cutie by me,
For I'm tired of making war.
And when number four is feathered,
And your gas is running low,
I'll be warming up that cutie,
While you hot-shot pilots go."

Then, in the rousing chorus, we sang our hearts out until the club was a bedlam.

Toward midnight the straw covered club was thick with cigarette smoke and the party began to lose its original buoyant gaiety. Most of the men had drunk too much, and the effects of the alcohol depressed their spirits. The homesickness that they had tried to drown now began to overwhelm some of them. Even the singing was more subdued.

To the tune of "My Merry Oldsmobile" most of the officers joined us in singing:

"We will get Yawata yet,
In our B-29s, you bet.
High above the Yellow Sea
Just as pretty as can be.
We've got plenty of time,
We'll be here 'til forty-nine.
O Mr. Jap, you sap,
You know we'll be back
In our Suuuper 29s."

I started out of the club, intending to get some sleep, after midnight. The celebrants had become maudlin, and the fun was gone out of it. Someone grabbed me and pulled me back. "One more song," he said. I tried to pull away, but he was insistent and I reluctantly joined a group just as someone handed out sheets of a new song. "This is sung to the tune of 'That Old Gang of Mine,'" he said thrusting a copy into my hands. I joined in good-naturedly.

"Gee, I get that lonesome feeling
When I take off for Japan.
Those ack-ack guns are breaking up
That old gang of mine.

There goes Bill and there goes Al
Off into the blue.
Your old friend and my old pal
Lots of luck to you.

Gee I get that lonesome feeling
When I take off for Japan
For Curt LeMay is breaking up
That old gang of mine."

I waved and hurriedly departed before I got sick, as were some, who were retching their insides out after imbibing more than their usual quota of cheap Indian liquor. Only a few of the men were heavy drinkers, and the rest of us were not used to large quantities of alcohol.

Our operations officer, Lieutenant Colonel Roush, thought I needed a leave in Calcutta shortly after Christmas and I readily agreed because I was having difficulty holding a cup of coffee steady.

Inasmuch as a 769th pilot could fly a B-25 down to Dum Dum near the big city, I checked with the assistant operations officer in the squadron. When he learned of my plans, Lieutenant Arthur B. Tuttle decided to join me.

The enormous fan overhead in our room at the Great Eastern Hotel turned slowly and whispered softly.

"This is the first time I've been able to get a room here," I said. "This is a magnificent hotel."

"I just wish we had more privacy," he said.

I agreed. There were no beds, just cots spaced tightly throughout the room for a dozen or so other officers. Demand for rooms was so great that private rooms in Calcutta were a thing of the past.

The lobby downstairs was large, and swarms of native boys hurried barefooted to tables where elegantly groomed Indians sipped soft drinks, and officers of the Allied nations gathered in complete relaxation.

"What shall we see first?" Tuttle said as we prepared to leave the hotel.

"I've been fascinated by all the stories about the burning ghats," I said. "I'm sure they're not pleasant, but curiosity has gotten the better of my commonsense."

"Why not? I'll try anything once."

The street was jammed with vehicles of all kinds and swarms of children clustered on every doorstep. It was an unbelievable sight to my western eyes.

"I've known slums in America," I said, "but nothing compared to the worst parts of Calcutta."

"I'm surprised how modern it is downtown," Tut said.

"It compares with many European cities. It has the usual tall buildings of brick and stone and some of the department stores are modern."

"These people have a long way to go before they even begin to attain the lowest standard of living in America," Tut said.

"Give them time," I said. "They face problems that no other nation has had to face. They've pulled themselves up a great deal in the past 50 years. I like their spirit. A proud people will never be humbled for long."

Our rickshaw stopped and the driver asked for 10 rupees. We gave him one, which was twice the usual fare. Now we could see the Ganges beyond the row of gates leading to the burning ghats.

"Look at these people," Tut said in a hushed voice.

I was staring at the blank, expressionless eyes of emaciated men and women leaning against the outer wall. Their ribs showed and their eyes were deep caverns in sunken faces.

Upon inquiry of a well-dressed Indian, we learned they were waiting to die.

"But why?" Tut asked.

"They are from the poorer sections, probably have no relatives, and can't afford to pay for the wood necessary to burn their bodies when they die."

"But what are they doing here?" I asked.

"They come here to die because the city burns unclaimed bodies."

We watched as dead bodies were brought to the sacred Ganges on litters. They were lowered into the muddy, filth polluted water as part of their purification process. Each body was washed with care and then carried to a prepared bed of wood. More wood was piled on top and the pyre was set on fire. A pair of feet stuck out from one side of a funeral pyre and the head out the other. They were in various stages. Some had been lighted and others were merely smoldering embers that were raked together by attendants so that the bones would be completely burned. The entire proceeding took about four hours. Then the survivors of the deceased waded into the river and washed themselves to purify their own bodies. Throughout the long process a deep respect for the departed was maintained and somehow the grotesqueness of the funeral (at least to western eyes) was dissipated.

"Doesn't smell bad," Tut said.

Our informant broke in. "The wealthier Indians can afford to buy scented wood for cremation. Notice that body over there. He has just a pile of faggots over him. He must have been very poor."

"What do they do with the ashes?" Tut asked.

"They are scooped up and thrown into the Ganges," he said.

"It's a gruesome place," Tut said in a whisper to me.

"In a way it is, but it seems an ideal way to be buried. I've always had a horror of bodies placed in boxes and put in the ground. I like this way better."

"I've noticed there isn't any mourning of the dead," Tut said.

"The body is nothing to these people," I said. "Once a person dies, the soul departs, and the body is disposed of as if of no consequence."

"Let's go back to the hotel," Tut said.

As we got off in front of the hotel, beggars descended upon up and cried. "Baksheesh, sahib. Baksheesh!"

"What do they want?" Tut said.

"Money. I don't know the literal meaning of baksheesh but believe it means presents."

"Look at that poor blind girl," Tut said with sympathy.

I noticed that she was watching us with horribly distorted eyes and supplicating hands.

"I'm going to give her something," Tut said.

He walked over and several of the native boys sniggered and turned their lower eyelids inside out, and I noted with surprise that they looked as awful as the girl.

"Hold it!" I said. "She's putting on an act."

I explained what she had done with her eyelids and he walked away without giving her any money.

"Despite the poverty and disease in Calcutta, I enjoy these visits," I said.

"I do too. It's like finding an oasis in the heart of a desert after Piardoba."

We entered the luxurious ballroom New Year's Eve and sat at a table. We reminisced about the year just passed and all that we had gone through. The room was filled with British officers and we felt like outcasts.

"What would you be doing tonight if you were at home?" I asked. Home, I knew, was Brooklyn.

"I'd take the little woman out for a good New Year's Eve party."

Tut and I listened sadly to the music with our thoughts thousands of miles away. At midnight they played "God Save the King" and we remained seated as nearby officers glared at us. There was no thought of disrespect, just our way of expressing our defiance at a world that had turned our lives upside down, with little hope of an early improvement. It was a silly gesture; a momentary revulsion against world leaders who should have prevented the murderous holocaust that had engulfed the world. At the time, it gave Tut and I an enormous satisfaction.

"Babulal!" I called.

"Yes, sahib."

Our bearer came running with his bare feet slapping the concrete floor in his excitement at my return from Calcutta.

"Take this bag of clothes to the laundry."

He nodded and bent over and counted out the pieces of clothing, making a list. I watched his fine, intelligent eyes as they efficiently sorted out my things. He was rather old for an Indian, about 30. But his face was smooth and firm, and a dark mustache draped his upper lip. I thought if only he had had some education his lot might have been quite different.

"Today's payday, isn't it?"

"Yes, sahib."

"Here you are."

I handed him three rupees. It was 90 cents for his weekly wages, but we were not allowed to pay more. But he worked for four of us, getting the same amount from each officer, so his total amounted to $3.60 per week. For that, he worked a 10-hour day, seven days a week. He was worth many times that amount and we often slipped him tips.

"Wilbur!" one of my roommates said with surprise as he walked in. "Glad you're back!"

Since I had become a member of the group staff, I had moved my quarters and shared a room with Captain Raymond O. Oprzendek, the group's ordnance officer. His name was difficult to pronounce so "Murphy" became his tag to everybody.

General Arnold now advised LeMay that the Japanese Navy had suffered grievous losses in the last few months, saying the Japanese fleet had ceased to exist as an effective fighting force. The loss of 1,500 Japanese carrier pilots during the Allied invasion of the Marianas and the Battle of the Philippine Sea was particularly acute.

Arnold stressed to LeMay that with extensive damage inflicted on the Japanese fleet, the dock and repair facilities at Singapore should continue to have top priority. LeMay's planners objected because Singapore was at the maximum range of our B-29s. They had to carry three bomb bay tanks and only a ton and a half of bombs in each airplane. Despite their protests, Arnold insisted and more attacks were scheduled. The November 5th raid against the King George Graving Dock, the area's largest dry dock, had knocked it out for three months.

Arnold advised LeMay in December that the Joint Chiefs insisted upon another attack "Because the Japanese fleet was in such a crippled condition, and repair facilities such as those at Singapore continue to have top priority." But other priorities in December postponed another attack on Singapore.

On January 11, 1945, LeMay divided his command to strike the Admiralty IX Floating Dock and the King's Dock at Singapore. But no hits were scored this time, and two B-29s were lost.

In the Marianas, General Hansell's 21st Bomber Command on Saipan had accomplished very little since their first Tokyo mission. Airplanes frequently could not stand the drastic change in temperature from tropical conditions on Saipan to freezing temperatures at high altitudes over Japan. All kinds of problems developed. The long haul to Japan, without the security of friendly fields to fall back upon, going or coming back if trouble developed, created a constant pressure on crews that was worse than the Japanese opposition. The number of B-29s bombing primary targets kept declining and crews either bombed secondary or last-resort targets or salvoed their bombs and returned to base.

Arnold dispatched 20th Air Force Chief of Staff Lauris Norstad from Washington on January 6 to tell Hansell he was being relieved, and LeMay was ordered to Guam for a conference. The latter was ordered to take over the 21st Bomber Command on January 20. The meeting was embarrassing for all concerned because they were old friends, so formalities were quickly dispensed with. Hansell requested a minor job in the training command back in the States, which was approved, and one of the Air Force's most imaginative planners lost a coveted job to a man who had once served under him as a group commander.

It was small comfort for Hansell that the last mission under his command was one of the most successful of the war. The 21st Bomber Command attacked the Kawasaki Aircraft Industries Company on January 19 and production of engines and aircraft was cut 90 percent. So severe was the damage that only limited assembly of aircraft was accomplished there for the remainder of the war.

Hansell wrote Arnold a letter on his last day in office and he did not minimize his command's shortcomings. He listed four major problems. He said originally the 73rd Wing had been trained for nighttime radar bombing and then switched to precision bombing for which it was not qualified. He admitted that bombing accuracy had been deplorable, but that he had been making progress in improving it.

When LeMay took over the 21st Bomber Command, January 20, he selected top managers for his staff. He chose as his Chief of Staff, Brigadier General August W.

Kissner, who had learned to fly with him at Kelly Field in 1929. Colonel James D. Garcia, a dark, fastidious officer was placed in charge of intelligence operations. For Deputy Chief of Staff of Operations, LeMay selected the energetic, 33-year-old Colonel John B. Montgomery. The slim Montgomery had flown as LeMay's copilot during the classic interception of the Italian liner *Rex* in 1938 when a B-17 piloted by LeMay demonstrated airpower's ability to intercept ships 600 miles at sea.

Colonel C. S. Irvine, the bluff, tireless man who did more to win the "Battle of Kansas" than any other man, was the eldest of LeMay's staff, at 46. He was an ideal choice to be in charge of supply and maintenance. An intimate of General Arnold, Irvine had served in World War I as a Signal Corps private.

LeMay found the 21st Bomber Command in about the same condition that the 20th Bomber Command of India had presented. He quickly realized why he had been selected by Arnold to handle operations in the Marianas. He was senior in rank and his combat background was more extensive, in comparison to Hansell's, with almost two years in England, first as a group commander then later in command of an air division. Hansell had been a wing commander for only a short time in England, and had flown a number of missions, but his combat experience level was not as extensive because he had been called back to Washington where his talents as a superb planner were needed even more.

LeMay had improved operations out of India and China so he was now given a chance to show what he could do on a much larger scale. Changes were needed quickly to get some payoff for all the things Arnold had fought for in getting a semi-independent strategic air force into combat.

Brigadier General Roger M. Ramey, an experienced bomber man from Hansell's staff, replaced LeMay as head of the 20th Bomber Command at Kharagpur. Some of LeMay's top personnel went along with him to the Marianas, including Colonel Blanchard, commander of the 40th Group, so personnel were promoted. Colonel Henry R. Sullivan served temporarily as the new 40th's commander but he was replaced by Colonel Kenneth Skaer.

Ramey informed his new command that the 20th Bomber Command would no longer report to General Arnold but would be assigned to the Southeast Asia Command under Admiral Lord Louis Mountbatten.

Prior to the first mission, Kalberer advised crews forced to bail out over Saigon to go to a specific address, which he identified, and tell the woman living there, "Kal sent me. She'll take care of you," he said. He warned, "But for God's sake don't do anything to compromise her!" Kalberer frequently gave the crews similar information about other cities and each time he did the news was greeted with raucous laughter. It was obvious that he was like the proverbial sailor, who had a girl in every port. Kalberer had one in every Asian city.

Vaucher, who had taken Roush's place as operations officer for the 462nd Group, had been trying for months to figure out a way to devise a formula to predict B-29 fuel consumption. It had long been obvious that Boeing's fuel consumption graphs were incorrect. Some planes used more fuel, some less, at high altitudes. Ever since the Palembang mission, when Vaucher flew most of the way back to Ceylon on three engines — impossible to accomplish according to Boeing's fuel consumption charts — it was clear to him that the amount of gasoline in his plane's tanks was greater than the charts indicated. His flight engineer had transferred fuel from one tank to another and Vaucher had landed normally, although he almost didn't make it.

After that mission, he decided that a B-29 could fly farther on three engines than Boeing believed was possible. Within the 462nd Group he promoted the idea that B-29s could unload bombs on a target, cut off one engine to conserve fuel, and thereby increase the aircraft's range. This theory was met with disbelief by those in authority.

But the more Vaucher explored his theory, the more he became convinced that he was correct in his assumption that their B-29s were expending a lot of gasoline unnecessarily to carry more fuel, thereby adding to the plane's gross weight and reducing its bomb tonnage. He developed the idea of loading more bombs by reducing the amount of gasoline, and thus keeping within the maximum allowable weight of the aircraft. He reasoned that once the bombs were dropped that the aircraft's weight would be less than normal and would require less gasoline to fly it back to base. He worked on the assumption that a minimum reserve of 300 gallons must be retained — but he focused on a 500-gallon reserve for safety reasons. He realized that even 500 gallons, spread in all of a plane's tanks, was not a lot of gasoline, particularly because gauges were inaccurate. He knew it was imperative for pilots and flight engineers to carefully monitor their gas consumption and transfer fuel from one tank to another to equalize the amount for each engine.

All fall, while he continued to fly missions, he quietly explored his theory that B-29s could fly farther, carry more bombs, and use less gasoline, but he had to find a way to prove it. He needed a mathematical formula, but he didn't know how to develop one. One night in December while he was having a drink at the officers club with Captain Zimmerman, who was mathematically inclined, they discussed Vaucher's theory. He explained to "Zim" that he needed a formula that would include altitude, weight, and temperature factors. Zimmerman was intrigued and it did not take him long to develop such a formula.

When the Bomber Command's operations order came in prior to the first mission to Saigon, Vaucher asked Zimmerman to use his formula to delineate the fuel load for the mission. He gave him the approximate gasoline and bomb load — it varied by airplane because some of the B-29s weighed as much as 1,000 pounds more than others.

The equivalent of two crews from each squadron now were authorized to return to the United States on February 25 and Loberg was one of those who went home. Individuals in each category with the greatest number of combat hours were picked to make up the two crews who would fly back in older B-29s. I watched sadly as most members of Loberg's and Vaucher's crews departed for home. Only Vaucher, Ralph Todd, and myself remained.

After our last mission was flown out of our forward bases in China, Arnold ordered their abandonment. Several missions had been flown to Formosa in support of the invasion of the Philippines after MacArthur's forces bogged down. We struck hard at the airplane modification centers and did a particularly good job at Kagi.

Bad weather disrupted many of these missions, but the best strike was against the airfield installations at Shinchiku, which were completely leveled.

Men and planes were lost on their vital missions and we were slowly losing the best men in the group. Men such as Lieutenant Colonel Roush and Major Slack lost their lives on a mission to Omura Aircraft Factory on Kyushu on January 6 and their sacrifices were typical of what was happening to group personnel.

Slack's plane was hit by enemy fighters after leading a formation against the factory. The bombing was made by instruments through thick clouds. The formation then turned away from Japan towards the sea, but both engines on one side had been knocked out. The fighters used small phosphorus bombs along with their guns.

Roush called Major Laidler B. Mackall, in a B-29 on their plane's left and described their situation. In a calm voice he said, "None of our crew has been seriously wounded except for a slight arm injury to Boseling."

The plane continued to lose altitude and the other planes stayed with it to cover it from further attack.

Ten minutes later Roush called again. "I'm afraid we'll have to bail out." A few minutes later he called, "John seems to have the plane under control, so we are continuing to China."

After the formation shot down two fighters, Japanese pilots lost their aggressiveness and no longer pressed their attack.

Thirty minutes later, Slack's plane entered into an undercast at 15,000 feet still under control. He was attempting to get as far from Japan as possible and perhaps make a successful landing in the sea. He was aware that Japanese patrol boats would almost certainly pick up the crew and make them prisoners. It is surmised that he tried to make a landing near a small rocky island where American submarines could pick them up. This had happened before. The submarine *Sea Wolf* had been pre-positioned in the area for just such a rescue. It found only wreckage on the surface and found no bodies. Forever afterwards, Mackall was haunted by Roush's last words, "Say goodbye to my wife."

Lieutenant Wilbur Boseling, one of my best bombardiers, was lost on this mission. For months he had been convinced that he would not survive the war but it never impaired his performance.

The days and weeks dragged with the kind of tiresome missions that were necessary but uninteresting. Crews were briefed for three successive missions the latter part of January to mine the river leading up to Saigon in French Indochina, and Camranh Bay farther north, and to bomb Saigon's port facilities in daylight. Saigon was a major shipping port between Singapore and Japan. The night missions were assigned during a full-moon period at altitudes of 2,000 and 6,000 feet.

Not all missions were praiseworthy. During a mission February 7 to Bangkok to bomb a navy yard and arsenal, the bombs had to be dropped by radar and many bombs fell into residential areas.

The 40th Group distinguished itself when it joined small formations from the 468th to attack the Rama VI Bridge. Four direct hits destroyed the northeastern approach and 65 percent of the central span collapsed. Finally, during the commands final missions out of India, the bridge was knocked out for good.

Many of these missions had been flown at the request of the Eastern Air Command's Strategic Air Force, particularly the coordinated attacks against the huge military dumps in the Rangoon area where 75 percent of all Japanese supplies were stored. Vast destruction was caused to the dumps, worsening a supply situation for the Japanese that had already become acute.

In February our ground personnel, minus a few specialists and a crew chief for each airplane, departed for Tinian in the Marianas. We were told we would follow in April. Meanwhile, the combat crews maintained their own airplanes.

Joe Buchta was named group navigator this month so we were called to Vaucher's office for an important meeting. He had replaced Roush as operations officer.

"What's up?" I asked.

"We've got to fly a series of photographic missions along the Malay Peninsula."

"What for?" Joe said with surprise.

"This is top secret but Mountbatten is planning an invasion."

"What do they need from us?"

"A series of photographic strips around Georgetown and another area south of there."

I helped to plan the mission, working with the Intelligence staff, and day after day strips of films were taken of the invasion areas despite persistent Japanese fighter attacks. The war ended just as Mountbatten's fleet was ready to land troops, but we never dreamed at the time that our painstaking work would be in vain.

This was our first experience of flying photo reconnaissance and it gave us a new appreciation for the men who flew modified B-29s, (F-13s) as members of the 311th Wing's first Photo Reconnaissance Squadron. They were truly unsung heroes, because they mapped most of Asia, including all of Japan, flew surveillance and search missions at sea, and provided up-to-date information and photographs for MacArthur's command. Many planes were lost. Some went out and were never heard from again. Their missions were extremely dangerous as they flew alone at high altitudes straight and level for minutes at a time to take an overlapping sequence of photographs. Without their photos our operations would have been impossible.

Admiral Halsey's carrier strikes against Okinawa were possible only after these specially designed B-29s provided detailed photo coverage.

MacArthur had sought their assistance prior to his landings on Leyte, and despite the loss of two airplanes, vital photographs of northern Luzon were taken and wet prints rushed to MacArthur.

Their flights averaged 15 hours, and along with boredom their greatest hazard was Japanese fighters who were well aware of what they were doing, and considered them prime targets.

Combat B-29s of the 3rd Photo Reconnaissance Squadron also flew photographic missions out of China on behalf of Mountbatten, and later moved to Guam.

Admiral Mountbatten announced that he would visit our group, saying in advance that he did not want any formality upon his arrival.

There was some anti-British feeling among the men, all of it wholly unwarranted. It was probably brought about by the tall tales spread by malicious gossip of how the British had charged fabulous prices for things we purchased in India. So when Mountbatten walked into the briefing room, he was met quietly and with no outburst of emotion.

"Gentlemen," he said, "you are leaving soon to carry on the war in other parts, to bring the war home to the Japanese people. As you know, you have been under my command during the past few months. I wish to extend to each and every one of you the thanks and appreciation of all of us in India for your valiant efforts on our behalf in this theater of war.

At the Quebec Conference, General Arnold told me that he had a new bomber, which was to be used solely against the Japanese mainland. He asked for bases in India, and even though we were sorely pressed for men and materials ourselves, I agreed to help him in any way possible. "You must understand that the large camps and the extra-long runways, which you required, placed a great burden on our strained resources. But you have made excellent use of the facilities, and we are deeply grateful. And now goodbye to you all, and may you have even greater success over Tokyo than you have had out of India and China."

At the end of this speech, his frank, convincing manner completely captivated us. When he left the briefing room, cheers and hand clapping followed.

Those who expected a dramatic turn around with LeMay in command of the 21st Bomber Command in the Marianas were disappointed. Aircraft losses rose to 5.7 percent of all B-29s dispatched on 22 missions during January 1945. They resulted from a concentration of Japanese fighter forces and the long flights over water. They took their toll on planes when mechanical troubles developed or they tried to return after being badly shot up.

After the war we learned that Prince Higashikuni, commander-in-chief of Japan's Home-Defense Headquarters, told his superiors that he knew "nothing in Japan that we can use against such a weapon." He admitted that from the point of view of his Home Defense command, he felt that the war was lost. He made it clear to all who would listen that the ability of the B-29s to fly over Japan left them no options for success.

LeMay continued to run the type of operations during February that Hansell had initiated, while he concentrated on training inexperienced crews. He set up the same kind of lead-crew training that he had initiated in England and later in India for the 20th Bomber Command.

Five weeks after LeMay assumed command of the 20th Bomber Command, he was a troubled man. He sat at his cluttered desk in a corner of the Quonset hut that served as his office in Guam. He stared straight ahead while he puffed reflectively on his pipe. His face was rigid, and there was no movement of his facial muscles as he faced his operations officers. Colonel Montgomery strode up to his desk. There was no formality between them. They had known each other for years. Montgomery didn't speak, unwilling to break into LeMay's spell.

Finally LeMay looked up, and his face grew even more serious as he waved Montgomery to a seat.

"I've been studying the intelligent reports for the last two months of 1944, and January and February of this year." He put his pipe down and idly flipped through a report. "I haven't done any better than 'Possum' Hansell, who preceded me. Our number one target, Musashino-Tama on the outskirts of Tokyo, has suffered only four percent damage despite 835 B-29 attacks during a series of missions. I hate to admit it, but Navy planes did more damage with a single strike." He picked up his pipe, noting it had gone out, and scratched a match to light it. His face was wreathed in a cloud of smoke. "During January of 1945 only half of all planes on each of the missions were able to bomb their primary targets."

Montgomery nodded in agreement. "I've gone on a number of missions lately. Our poor showing is due to inexperience, particularly poorly trained mechanics on the ground, and shortages of almost everything. These problems will take time to resolve."

LeMay's eyes became alive and his voice rose. "Arnold isn't interested in problems. I've seen him cashier generals in the European theater for far less reason. He's a 'now' man. He hates excuses." He paused in deep thought. "I don't intend to make excuses. I'm too old to adapt to such bad habits."

Montgomery smiled. "Old at 39?"

LeMay ignored the attempt at humor. "With those jet-stream winds at high altitudes over Japan, we could go on forever trying to get up to a target. General Arnold crawled out on a dozen limbs a thousand times to get the funding and resources to build those Superfortresses and get them into combat. Now he finds that they're not doing well. But he is determined to get results. The turkey is around my neck. I've got to deliver."

Montgomery signified that he agreed with each of LeMay's statements.

LeMay continued. "Our losses during the early part of February are still too high. We've already sent 360 B-29s on missions this month, but we've achieved little. Bombing results are poor because the weight of bombs has to be reduced from 10 to three tons for the extra fuel required to climb above 25,000 feet." He knocked the ashes out of his pipe into an ashtray, and continued to tap while he spoke. Unintentionally, the action served to emphasize his words. "Using 22 tons of fuel to drop three tons of bombs, often less, doesn't make sense. Even worse, only the best crews seem able to make a round trip to Japan with a safe fuel reserve." He stopped tapping his pipe and reloaded it from a pouch. He started to put the pipe in his mouth but dropped his hand instead to his desk. "Those who can't make it back end up in the ocean, particularly if they've lost an engine. Reports of shot-up airplanes with half a tail gone, or part of a wing shot away, are common after such missions. Such damage was not unusual in Europe, but here a return flight of 1,500 miles under those conditions is too often fatal."

"With our mounting losses," Montgomery said, "perhaps we should switch to less heavily defended targets than those at Nagoya and Tokyo."

LeMay looked thoughtfully at Montgomery. Then he stood up and walked over to a large map in the center of the Quonset. Montgomery turned in his chair so that he could view the map.

"That's not the answer to our basic problem, but it will have to suffice for the time being." He pointed to Iwo Jima on the map. "The island of Iwo Jima was invaded January 19, as you know. It will give us an emergency landing field for shot-up airplanes and those low on fuel. But Iwo won't solve our major problem." He walked slowly back to his desk and sat down. "I've studied weather patterns over Japan and even in the best weather month, only one to seven days are clear enough for visual bombing. The rest of the time the weather is 'stinkin.' You have to forecast those good days accurately, and make sure that you are over those targets on those specific days." He leaned back and lit the pipe. There was a long pause while he stared at the ceiling. "There has to be a better way to destroy Japan's capacity to wage war. Chief of Staff Norstad keeps insisting that we firebomb Kobe. Sure, it's an important port city, with concentrations of shipbuilding yards and plants for marine engines. But he doesn't understand that high-altitude incendiary bombing does not work. The British found that out over Germany. General Hansell tried before I took over. You remember; you were with 'Possum.'"

Montgomery nodded soberly in recollection. "We found it impossible to get a concentration of fire bombs on the ground after releasing them from such high altitudes."

"That's right. Fire raids against major cities do not pay off unless the force is larger than we have now. We'd need at least 400 bombers."

"Our whole campaign will fail," Montgomery said. "Unless something is done to get a better delivery of bombs on targets. We can bomb secondary targets forever by radar and it will have little significant impact on Japan."

LeMay leaned back in his chair, his face set in grim lines. He remained quiet for so long that Montgomery stirred restlessly in his chair. When LeMay spoke, his voice was low but vibrant with pent-up emotion. "I'm considering the plan to reduce bombing altitudes from 30,000 to 5,000 feet, and using incendiaries to attack urban areas."

Montgomery was startled by LeMay's words and he looked up to see if he was serious. He couldn't believe that he had heard LeMay correctly. "Five thousand, General?"

LeMay nodded. "Tom Power and Colonel Whelass have suggested a plan for a low level attack that would use radar to direct planes along the east side of Tokyo Bay, and then on to Tokyo. Each plane would have its own heading, fly at a predetermined speed and altitude, and bomb at a specified time. I like the idea, and I've asked them for an overall plan within 24 hours." He leaned forward and stared intently at Montgomery. "What do you think Monty?"

Montgomery carefully chose his words. Some of LeMay's thoughts were familiar and matched his own, others were so radical that he was not sure. "It has great advantages of going against high flammable urban areas at low altitudes that will assure vast destruction, particularly now that Brigadier General John Davie's 313th Wing is trained and Brigadier General Thomas S. Power can commit his 314th Wing, but several points concern me. Are you serious about 5,000 feet?"

"I am! That would be the base altitude. For separation, some of the others would be thousand or so feet higher."

Montgomery's mind was in a whirl, and he spoke slowly, trying to collect his thoughts about LeMay's startling proposal. "Bomb loads would increase by a factor of three because we won't have to lift each B-29 to altitude, thereby saving fuel." He stood up, and began to pace back and forth. "The natural dispersion of bombs by radar would give us good coverage if the aiming points are selected properly. Further, the increase in bomb loads will give us a new approach to the whole thing." He stopped his pacing and stared at LeMay. "I'm not so sure about the availability of incendiary bombs. They are in short supply." He looked frankly at LeMay, and returned to his seat. "I admit I'm concerned about losses."

"The Japs won't be ready for this kind of attack." He picked up his pipe, relit it, and sat back in his chair, puffing thoughtfully. "Drastic action is needed, otherwise this whole B-29 program will fall apart. The Navy is upset about hauling all our tonnage to the islands. Admiral Nimitz says the Twentieth is dropping everything the theater has on nothing while the Navy is expected to drop nothing on everything. He demands some changes. So is Arnold. I am well aware that some general had to come out there and face the Air Force doctrine of bombing selected targets at high altitudes. If he fails — whoever the man is — and comes up with nothing else to get on with the job, he's expendable. At the moment that general is me. If I fail, I have no doubt what action General Arnold will take."

"Surely Arnold will understand," Montgomery said. "He's given us an underdeveloped airplane with engines prone to catch fire, and inexperienced crews. I can't. . . ."

"You don't understand," LeMay interrupted him. "Arnold isn't interested in my problems. He's got enough of his own. I understand that." He took a long drag on his pipe and smoke billowed around his head. He stared thoughtfully at Montgomery. "It's up to me to solve our problems one way or another. If I succeed, I'll be a hero in the eyes of the American people." He paused, taking another deep drag. He looked up and there was a tight smile on his face that came and went so fleetingly that Montgomery almost didn't see it. "If I fail? You know the answer. I'll be removed and quietly forgotten. My career in the Army Air Forces will come to an end. But I am not important. Ending this war — and quickly — is my sole consideration. If I'm not up to it, then Arnold will find someone who is."

Montgomery shook his head in disagreement. His admiration for LeMay was so great that such a dire outcome was inconceivable. "Surely you're exaggerating."

LeMay banged his pipe on the ashtray and hot ashes tumbled out, creating a spiral of smoke that almost obscured his face. "Not in the least. A commander must accept the consequences of his actions." He leaned forward, focusing his eyes intently on Montgomery. "The day I become more concerned with my own career instead of the best interests of my country, and those who serve under me, is the day General Arnold should fire me. If our roles were reversed, I would not hesitate."

"I understand," Montgomery said as he stood up and started to leave.

LeMay also got up and walked over to the map, and motioned Montgomery to join him. He pointed to a small island off Saipan. "Set up a training mission to Kito Iwo — that small island of Saipan — for an attack by 12 bombers in columns of three at 50 feet with delayed action fuses."

Montgomery corrected him, assuming he had spoken in error. "You mean 5,000 feet."

LeMay had a slight smile on his face. "No. Fifty feet."

"But General, that's too low...."

LeMay stopped further words with a gesture. "I have my reasons." His smile broadened. "Set the mission for the first of March. Call General O'Donnell at the 73rd Wing right now, give him precise details. Here. Use my phone." He pointed to his desk, and started to make notes. Montgomery picked up the phone and placed the call. "Let me speak to General O'Donnell. Oh?" He turned to LeMay. "Rosey is on Guam. In my office." He dialed again. "Is General O'Donnell there? Okay, put him on." He waited until O'Donnell could come on the line. "Rosey, General LeMay has ordered me to set up a training mission for March 1. I'll teletype details, but here is the gist of it. Set up 12 planes to bomb Kito Iwo — you know, that small island off Saipan — at an altitude of 50 feet using delayed action fuses." Montgomery listened with a grin and moved the receiver several inches from his ear. "No, the altitude is not an error. Five zero feet." His grin got broader as he listened. "The altitude is correct — 50 feet. General LeMay's orders. What's that? You want to see General LeMay?"

LeMay's grin had grown wider as he listened to the last part of the conversation. To Montgomery's inquiring look, he nodded his head affirmatively.

"Okay, Rosey," Montgomery said. "Come right over. We'll expect you." He hung up and started to leave.

"Stay here," LeMay said. "O'Donnell needs to be brought down a peg. I've been waiting for the right opportunity for a long time." He continued to make notes while they waited and Montgomery returned to his seat.

O'Donnell hurried in, giving LeMay a quick salute.

"Well Rosey, what is it?"

There was a stubborn, almost truculent look on O'Donnell's face. "I cannot fly that mission."

There was a dead silence. LeMay slowly took his pipe from his mouth and looked directly at Rosey. His voice was soft, but the words had a cutting edge. "You will fly that mission!" Their eyes locked and there was such an implacable expression in LeMay's eyes that it was O'Donnell who finally looked down. He squirmed, first on one foot and then the other. "Anything else?" LeMay asked.

O'Donnell was furious, but he did not dare to challenge LeMay. "No," he said. He walked stiff legged out of the office as a satisfied smile momentarily highlighted LeMay's face.

"He thinks that just because he is close to General Arnold that he can throw his weight around here."

Montgomery, who had watched the scene with open-mouthed astonishment, let out a pent-up whistle. "He won't try that again."

"Don't be too sure. He thinks he is God's greatest gift to the Air Force." He paused. "He's a good man. He's just not as good as he thinks he is."

Montgomery started to leave but LeMay stopped him. "As soon as Iwo Jima is ready to receive our planes I want it used up to the hilt. We've refined our cruise control techniques to the point that crews can get to Japan and back with an adequate reserve. But flight procedures have to be properly used. I want each mission planned so that the most inefficient crews will be forced to land at Iwo because of a shortage of fuel. After a few landings on that God forsaken island, they'll get it into their thick skulls that they have to fly their airplanes the way that they were briefed; otherwise they'll run out of fuel. I want Iwo saturated with gas-shy airplanes and cripples on each mission. It was taken at awful cost, let's make it worthwhile for those who sacrificed to give it to us." He walked over to the map again. "I called in Doctor Gould, the MIT radar expert assigned to us. I asked him to go to Saipan, fly with half a dozen of the worst radar operators, and find out if they can fly over this tit of land on the northern part of Saipan at 5,000 feet." He put his finger on the point. "Gould confirmed my worst misgivings. He told me that he had not realized how bad the operators really were."

"I know," Montgomery agreed. "But they received very limited training in the States because their sets hardly ever worked properly."

"I'm not blaming the operators," LeMay said. He pointed again to the tip of land. "With additional training, I believe most operators will be able to identify that tit of land on their radar sets. Gould agrees with me. If they can, then all radar operators will be able to locate a similar tip that sticks out into Tokyo Bay. From that point we can start a run into the target areas on prescribed courses and drop bombs after a precalculated number of seconds. Like me, you're a qualified bombardier and navigator. Do you foresee any particular problems?"

"It should work."

LeMay returned to his chair and sat down. "I've reached the point of no return. Further procrastination is useless. I've weighed the alternatives and now is the time for action, not further words. The Air Force doctrine of high altitude, precision bombing isn't working in the Pacific theater. There is nothing wrong with the doctrine. The problem is due, in large part, to the B-29's limitations. With this new strategy we have a better chance of defeating Japan without an invasion — and with far fewer American casualties. What MacArthur doesn't understand is that the Japanese home army has two million men, each of whom will fight with incredible ferocity to preserve his homeland. Then there are millions of civilian men and women — including children — who can serve as partially trained irregulars. An Allied invasion force would have to dig them out of every cave from Xyushu in the south to Hokkaido in the north." Stubborn lines formed on his face. "If I fail, Arnold will replace me until he finds someone who can do the job. But I don't intend to fail. Basically success or failure of our strategic bombing campaign lies with the thousand or so crews who will be out here by summer. With proper leadership, they will perform miracles. I have an enormous faith in America's youth. They have never failed us in the past, and they won't this time."

Loberg's Pathfinder Crew

Standing, from left, Lieutenant Robert C. Albert, Lieutenant Robert G. Fessler, Lieutenant James White, Major Edwin A. Loberg, Captain Richard Renz, and Lieutenant Wilbur H. Morrison. Kneeling, Technical Sergeant Clayton K. Knight, Staff Sergeant James O. Bush, Technical Sergeant Guido J. Bianchi, Staff Sergeant Isidore Scheinman, and Staff Sergeant Norman C. McLeod. (Author's collection)

All the Way

Captain George Hadley's crew, kneeling second from left, was one of the crews that went overseas with the 462nd Group to India, China, and then the Marianas and completed their 35 missions. Others, from left, front row, Sergeant Wilbur W. Cipperly, radio operator; Sergeant John R. Evans, flight engineer; Sergeant Kenneth Crowell, right gunner; and Sergeant Francis J. Boyer, radar operator. Standing, from left, Sergeant Thomas F. Walsh, left gunner; Lieutenant William W. Meader, co-pilot; Lieutenant James C. Whitehurst, bombardier; Technical Sergeant John Karl Dates, central fire control gunner; Lieutenant William J. Meuwissen, navigator; and Sergeant Stanley K. Lewison, tail gunner. Hadley was killed later while flying on a combat mission during the Korean War. (Author's collection)

Lead Crew

Captain Wilbur H. Morrison, lead bombardier, stands in foreground. Others, from left, Staff Sergeant James O. Bush, Major Thomas R. Vaucher, Technical Sergeant Guido J. Bianchi, Lieutenant Ralph Todd, Staff Sergeant Isidore Scheinman, Lieutenant James White, Technical Sergeant Albert I. Carmona, Captain Michael V. Egan, Staff Sergeant Norman C. McLeod, and Lieutenant Robert C. Albert. (Author's collection)

Chaotic Conditions

Early operations by the 73rd Wing at Saipan's Isley Field were aggravated by the limited time available for Army engineers to complete the first runway. (Courtesy of U.S. Air Force)

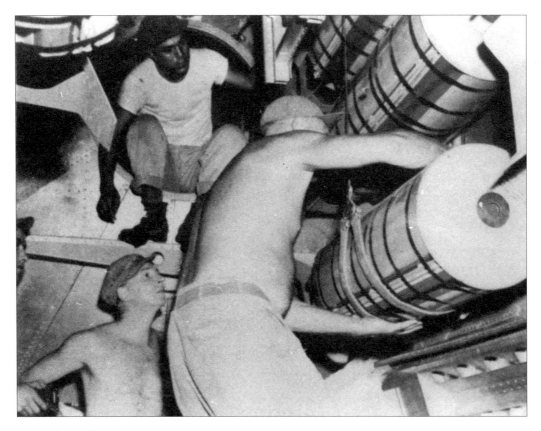

Incendiaries for Japan

These bombs are loaded by armament men on Tinian prior to a mission in 1945. Names of men are unknown. (Courtesy of Frank Rosenberger)

Characteristic Pose
Major General Curtis E. LeMay briefs lead crews. (Courtesy of U.S. Air Force)

Map Check

Mapping 20th Air Force operations against the Japanese by its newly created 21st Bomber Command are three Army Air Force Generals who will play a large part in forthcoming attacks. Shown at a new Boeing B-29 Superfortress base in the Marianas are left to right, Brigadier General Emmett O'Donnell, Jr., Commanding General of a wing of the new bomber command; Lieutenant General Millard F. Harmon, Commanding General of Army Air Forces in the Pacific Ocean areas and deputy commander of the Twentieth Air Force; and Brigadier General Haywood S. Hansell, Jr., Commanding General of the 21st Bomber Command. (Courtesy of Official U.S. Air Forces)

Blood Chit

Each crew member was given a "blood chit" by the Chinese Government. This one was issued to Technical Sergeant Guido J. Bianchi. The Chinese underground frequently picked up crewmen even behind Japanese lines and returned them to their B-29 base. Airmen were warned not to exchange "chits" because if a person's "blood chit" didn't match his other identifying documents he would probably be beheaded as a spy. (Courtesy of Guido J. Bianchi)

Precision Bombing

Marshalling Yards at Rangoon, Burma, are destroyed in this pin-point bombing by the 462nd Group. (Courtesy of T. R. Vaucher)

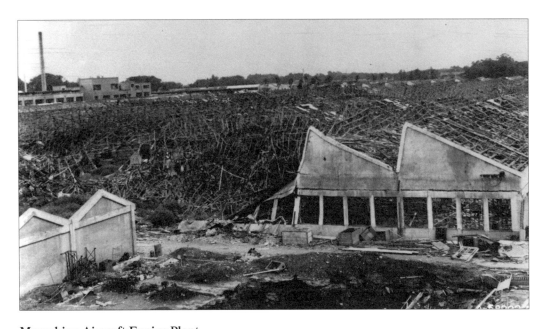

Musashino Aircraft Engine Plant

This is all that remains of the plant outside Tokyo after repeated attacks by the 20th Air Force. (Courtesy of U.S. Air Force)

The Hump
Aerial view was taken along the China-Burma border (Courtesy of U.S. Air Force)

Fourteenth and Twentieth Attack Hankow, China
The dock area, storage and supply center of Hankow, China, is seen here under attack by B-29
Superfortresses of the U.S. Army 20th Air Force. They were followed by more than 200 bombers
and fighters of the U.S. Army 14th Air Force, in China's heaviest coordinated bombing mission.
This was the first joint operation of the Fourteenth and Twentieth, planned by Major General
Albert C. Wedemeyer, commanding the China theater. (Courtesy of U.S. Army Air Forces)

Generalissimo Chiang Kai-shek and Lieutenant Joseph W. Stilwell
(Courtesy of National Archives)

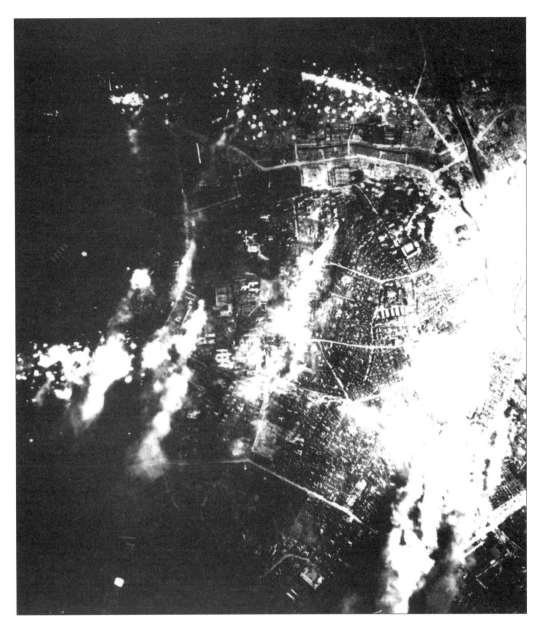

Tokyo Night Raid
Fires spread throughout the Japanese capital as B-29s poured liquid fire on the city. (Courtesy of U.S. Air Force)

Tokyo, Japan
Night raid, May 26, 1945.
(Courtesy of U.S. Army
Air Forces)

Tokyo's Devastation
This photograph was taken on August 30, 1945, during a flight to drop food and clothing to Allied prisoners in Japanese internment camps. (Courtesy of Eldridge Beck)

Japanese Phosphorous Bomb

The bomb explodes beneath B-29s of Major General Curtis E. LeMay's 21st Bomber Command during a recent mission over Kagamigahara, Japan, site of a huge air depot approximately 30 miles north of Nagoya. Two large plants of the Kawasaki and Mitsubishi aircraft companies are located here. Phosphorous bombs such as seen in this picture may be fired from ground batteries or dropped from enemy aircraft in air-to-air bombing attempts to break up B-29 formations. (Courtesy of U.S. Army Air Forces)

Tinian

High-altitude view of the island shows the location of the two bombardment wings. The base at left center housed the 58th Wing, and the upper base was home to the 313th Wing and the 509th Composite Group. (Courtesy of T. R. Vaucher)

Hiro Arsenal
Raid of May 5, 1945, Naval Aircraft Station. (Courtesy of U.S. Army Air Forces)

Kure Arsenal
Bombs smother arsenal buildings during this June 22, 1945, attack. (Courtesy of T. R. Vaucher)

Nagoya in Flames
Superfortresses caused new damage to Nagoya during this May 14, 1945, raid. (Courtesy of U.S. Air Force)

Main Street, Japan, 1945

Hiroshima, after the first atom bomb had exploded. This view from Red Cross hospital buildings about one mile from bomb burst. (Courtesy of U.S. Strategic Bombing Survey)

Main Street, Japan, 1945

A street through a formerly congested residential area of Nagasaki reduced to nothing. This was 1,000 feet northeast of atom bomb burst. (Courtesy of U.S. Strategic Bombing Survey)

Prisoners of War

Prisoners recover parcels of food and clothing dropped by B-29s shortly after war ended. This camp was at Fukuoka. (Courtesy of National Archives)

Twentieth Bomber Command Cemetery

Americans were buried at Chengtu after their deaths in B-29 crashes in China. (Courtesy of U.S. Air Force)

Chapter 11

Incendiary Attacks
Devastate Tokyo

On the morning of March 1, Montgomery came to LeMay's office before the wing commanders were scheduled to arrive. LeMay told him, "I've set March 9th as the date for the first fire bombing of Tokyo. It will be followed by 10 days of unremitting attacks against Japan's major cities." LeMay noted the concern on Montgomery's face, and he understood. "I've weighed the risks, along with the charges that such attacks are inhuman against Tokyo's civilian population. I constantly remind critics that the Japanese rape of Nanking in 1937 cost the lives of 200,000 Chinese civilians. Twenty thousand women were raped and then murdered. And, after the Doolittle raiders were forced to land in Japanese-controlled China, a quarter of a million Chinese men, women, and children were slaughtered for aiding the fliers.

In the past, natural disasters, such as those caused by earthquakes, have destroyed some of Japan's cities. But most importantly, these fire raids will save lives in the long run." He noted the questioning look on Montgomery's face. "I know it sound incongruous, but possibly millions of lives on both sides will be spared if the main islands don't have to be invaded. Failure to defeat Japan through airpower means the loss of most of our crews, and hundreds of millions of dollars worth of airplanes. But, if we succeed, and I believe we will, the destruction of Japan's war industries will shorten the war. Not only will these fire raids destroy large factories, but also thousands of small industries that feed Japan's war effort will be burned out. These feeder shops could never be destroyed by conventional bombing." He took a long puff on his pipe, and his mood turned reflective. "When I headed the B-29 command in India and China, I tried to explain these things to General Stilwell, who at the time, was theater commander. I spent most of one night trying to teach him the finer points of strategic bombing." He shook his head in exasperation at the memory. "He's an excellent ground commander, but he's so incredibly old fashioned. By morning I knew I had failed completely to convince Stilwell of the importance of strategic bombing to shorten the war and make an invasion of the Japanese homeland unnecessary."

"I've heard MacArthur wants Stilwell to head the invasion of Kyushu if it is approved by the Joint Chiefs," Montgomery said.

LeMay nodded. "He's as good a man for the job as any the Army has out here. I still don't believe an invasion will be necessary." He changed the subject. "I decided several weeks ago that we had to take a whole new look at our operations. In the past six weeks we've sent crews on 16 missions and only one caused appreciable damage. That was the February 25 attack on Tokyo that burned out a square mile of the city." He banged his pipe on the ashtray for emphasis. "Not one important target has been destroyed. We still don't have enough planes, but we're not getting the maximum out of those we do have."

"Now that we have three fully trained wings, our operations should improve," Montgomery said.

LeMay's mind remained on his same line of thought. "My popularity amongst the men has gone down in direct proportion to the failure of each mission." He paused to contemplate that fact. "During the month of February, only one day was suitable for visual, high altitude bombing. My weathermen tell me that March won't be much better. As Rosey O'Donnell says, 'you can't hit 'em if you can't see 'em.' He's right. We're still going in too high, still running into those big jet stream winds upstairs, and weather is almost consistently bad." He picked up a report. "Hell, I wasn't sent out here by Arnold to win friends and influence anyone but the Japanese." His face grew grim, reflecting the gravity of the situation. "The nagging worry in the back of my mind is that such a drastic change could be suicidal. Sending bombers over Germany at five or six thousand feet would be murderous — even at this late date. But I am convinced Japan's anti-aircraft defenses are not comparable. Most importantly, I expect to surprise the Japanese by the first attacks. You never could surprise the Germans, but I believe you can surprise the Japanese. Their top leadership becomes paralyzed any time drastic changes occur. They are not very imaginative, and combat commanders must get approval to make even routine changes in tactical plans. Surprise is the keynote, despite the risks involved. I'm willing to take the risks."

"Our losses haven't been too bad — about 78 B-29s since we arrived in the Marianas," Montgomery said. "That represents a rate of four percent — far below the peak monthly loss rate of 25 percent in the European theater."

"I agree," LeMay said. "From my analysis of Japan's defenses, I am convinced they are strongest at high altitudes, but that their defenses at low and medium altitudes are almost negligible." He changed the subject, and a wry grin appeared on his face. "I wrote General Norstad in Washington that I was thinking of doing a little gambling to get something done. I said I didn't know General Arnold or his traits and characteristics. I asked him whether Arnold would go for something like this. Norstad was noncommittal. I should know better. You can't rely on a staff officer in Washington to help you make the tough decisions in the field." He straightened up and his jaw stiffened. "I have to do something, and do it quickly. If I make the wrong decision, the responsibility will be mine alone. Arnold expects results, and it is up to me to get them. Therefore, I've decided not to seek his permission to make the low level night fire raids."

Montgomery's face reflected his doubts. "Is that wise?"

"If I fail, Arnold can remove me and try someone else until a successful way is found to destroy Japan from the air. Night fire raids are unacceptably risky. Night fire raids are unacceptably risky, the loss rate will be too high." He sat down and stared defiantly at Montgomery. "This is a drastic change in the classic doctrine of daylight precision bombing. But bombing at five to six thousand feet will double the number of hits on targets and the elimination of the long climb to high altitudes will save more than 5,000 pounds of gasoline that can be traded for bombs, and the service life of the engines will be lengthened."

Montgomery had a smile on his face when he spoke. "Now I understand why you ordered Rosey to run those training missions at 50 feet. Afterward there were wild untrue rumors that some bombs hit the grounds and almost jumped into the bomb bays of the planes following in line. One prize story was that a bomb came up even with the horizontal stabilizer and flew formation with a B-29."

LeMay grinned. "That's in utter defiance of the law of gravity."

"With the rumor widespread that you would make the crews drop bombs over Japan at 50 feet, five or six thousand feet won't seem bad at all. It's a masterful lesson in psychology."

LeMay had been only half listening to Montgomery's words, with his mind obviously on other matters. "I want every plane in commission for these raids. Inform wing commanders that I will expect a report about each plane that fails to participate."

"Will do. By the way, your information officer has been bugging me for a story for the press. What shall I tell him?"

LeMay was blunt. "This outfit has been getting a lot of publicity without accomplishing a hell of a lot in bombing results. Right now, the less said the better until we justify our existence." The phone interrupted him. LeMay picked it up. "Send them in." He turned to Montgomery. "The wing commanders are here."

Brigadier General Rosey O'Donnell strode in, followed by Brigadier General John H. Davies, and Brigadier General Thomas D. Power. They saluted LeMay and he casually returned their salutes. He motioned them to bring up chairs and they sat in a semicircle in front of his desk. "I am encouraged by the February 25 incendiary attack on Tokyo," LeMay started, "and I intend to continue such night attacks when bad weather precludes daylight strikes. Despite the low altitudes I estimate that flak losses will not exceed five percent." He noticed the skepticism on their faces. "Attacks at low altitudes will have the added advantage of surprise."

"What about Jap fighters?" Davies asked.

"There are only two units of night fighters in all the main islands. You can discount their effectiveness." He paused and then dropped a bombshell. "That's why I'm sending B-29s in without guns."

O'Donnell let out a low whistle, and Power and Davies looked at LeMay with stunned expressions.

"Frankly, I'm removing the guns because I'm afraid crews will be shooting at each other more than at Japs. And, we'll save about 3,000 pounds that will give us another ton and a half of bombs on each airplane. I have long favored night missions, although crews have not been trained for them. It is my hope that these night missions will reduce losses at sea because returning B-29s will be over Iwo Jima in daylight to make emergency landings if necessary."

Power said, "I agree with your assessment."

LeMay glanced inquiringly at O'Donnell and Davies. They nodded their agreement. LeMay walked over to the map. "Tokyo will be first, then Kobe, Nagoya, Nagasaki, and Osaka during a 10 day period." While he spoke he pointed out each city on the map. He looked at each wing commander to judge reactions. "It will be the most massive incendiary attack ever conceived. Before it is finished, these missions will use every incendiary bomb in the Marianas, with more unavailable until the first week in April." He returned to his desk with brisk strides. "I intend to get in and out of the empire before the Japs make things too costly for us. Get back to your wings and set up practice missions with maximum take-off loads. Make instrument-bombing attacks on tiny Rota Island in the Marianas chain. You might even schedule flights to Truk so crews can learn how to form a bomber stream at night. Careful preparation is the key to success. We must seek maximum compressibility to confuse and saturate Japanese defenses."

Power asked, "What does Admiral Nimitz think of your plans?"

"He's appalled. We've kept Nimitz abreast of our activities through mission reports and damage-assessment photos. He knows that Japan's industries are concentrated in her major cities when tens of thousands of household shops feed the big factories. As you know, the main industrial areas of 20 of Japan's principal manufacturing cities contain more than 16 million people, or 22 percent of all Japanese in the home islands. Fire bombing these cities, brutal as it will be for non-combatants, is the only way to destroy Japan's ability to wage war — a war her leaders provoked by their sneak attack on Pearl Harbor."

"Japan's cities are firetraps because they are made mostly of wood," Power said. "They have known conflagrations before due to earthquakes and other natural causes. Our new incendiary bombs, those filled with napalm or jellied gasoline, will be deadly against such cities."

LeMay picked up his pipe, then laid it down. There was a deep sadness in his eyes when he spoke. "I wish there were some other way to bring Japan's leaders to their senses. But an invasion of ground troops would cost at least a million Allied casualties, plus untold hundreds of thousands of Japanese civilians. An invasion should be ordered as a last resort, but only if we fail to create a hell on earth in Japan. That's the only circumstance that her fanatical leaders will understand."

LeMay watched departing B-29s on March 9, a cigar clamped tightly between his teeth while his eyes noted each airplanes take-off. Finally, still lost in his thoughts, he turned away and headed back to headquarters for a long, lonely vigil awaiting the first reports to come in.

Fifteen hundred miles away millions of Japanese went about their usual routines never suspecting that death rode on wings for thousands of them before dawn of a new day as B-29s flew parallel in three long streams en route to Tokyo. They carried an average of six tons of firebombs per airplane. Pathfinders were ahead to light up specific points in the city so those who followed would know exactly where to drop.

The commander of the 314th Wing, General Power, went in first to drop his bombs, then his plane circled Tokyo at 10,000 feet to observe the results as Superforts from three wings streamed in.

He talked to his crew as they circled. "Notice how the city is already engulfed in flames." His voice was tense, but subdued. "I'm glad the weather held. The pathfinders have no trouble marking the heart of Tokyo." He pointed out the meager anti-aircraft fire, commenting that he had seen only an occasional fighter. "I would have sworn that hundreds would come up to defend their biggest city. LeMay was right."

Power noted that the surface winds had increased and that the fires were leaping rivers and fire breaks and racing through a rectangular area three by five miles. Power glanced at his watch. He said with a touch of incredulity, "It has taken only 30 minutes for the fires to get out of control." When he spoke again, his voice reflected the shock and horror of the scene below. "What a horrible sight! God knows how many thousands are dying below us."

His flight engineer reminded him that they were getting low on fuel and so his B-29 headed for home.

On Guam, Montgomery and LeMay were both exhausted, having been up all night, as Montgomery gave LeMay the first report on the mission. "Tommy Power says the raid was highly successful. He says the early bombers encountered very little opposition, but that anti-aircraft fire increased as the raid progressed. There are losses, but not too heavy. He says you really have to see a huge city in flames to comprehend the reality of modern warfare."

LeMay nodded soberly. "I'm sure it's a terrible sight."

"I'll have a full report later," Montgomery said.

LeMay visibly relaxed. "We caught them by surprise. The next time may be different." He added hastily. "I still don't believe they had the fighters to oppose us seriously. Their good pilots have long since been killed, and their shortage of gasoline will prohibit adequate training of new ones. Was the mission flown as planned?"

"Our planes dropped 2,000 tons of fire bombs. Tommy says tremendous updrafts generated by the heat tossed B-29s violently. Some were hurled skyward hundreds of feet a minute. This could be a problem. He reports that his tail gunner could see a glow in the sky 150 miles from Tokyo."

LeMay's face registered a great sadness. "They asked for it. They can quit at any time. The sooner the better. I am determined to continue these attacks until they do quit. Arnold sent me out here to end this war without an invasion by ground troops, if that is humanly possible. I intend to do my utmost to bring that about. We didn't start this war — the Japanese did. I hope to end it with the least possible number of American casualties. The longer the Japanese government holds out, the greater the suffering of their people. The decision is in their hands." He looked directly at Montgomery. "I'll want a full written report to forward to General Arnold." His phone interrupted him. He picked it up. "LeMay. Yes he's here. I'll put him on." He turned to Montgomery. "It's for you."

Montgomery listened for a moment, jotted down some notes and said, "Good work. I'll be in touch." He hung up and turned to LeMay. "That was my office. We lost 14 B-29s with another 42 damaged. Five crews were saved by the air-sea rescue teams."

LeMay winced at the news. His voice was low, but there was a depth of feeling in it. "You pay a price for success. Thank God it's no worse."

Montgomery glanced at his notes. "The losses were due primarily to anti-aircraft fire. A number of crews reported they were bracketed by searchlights and then fired upon. Three hundred and twenty four bombers hit Tokyo."

LeMay glanced up when there was a rap on his door. "Come in."

Garcia walked in. "I have early intelligence reports, mostly from monitored radio stations in Tokyo. They don't attempt to minimize the destruction of life and property. They call the raids 'slaughter bombing.' One broadcast said that the sea of flames that enclosed the residential and commercial sections was reminiscent of the holocaust of Rome caused by the Emperor Nero."

LeMay removed his cigar from his mouth and eyed them soberly. "Unlike Nero, I'm not fiddling with joy. I see nothing to rejoice about in the suffering of hundreds of thousands of people. What is the intelligence department's estimate of the damage?"

"It's too soon to give an accurate report," Garcia said. "But the area contained 22 industrial targets and thousands of home factories. According to radio reports, there is total destruction in this part of Tokyo. Radio stations claim that people were unable to escape and their bodies were found piled up on the bridges, roads, and in the canals. I'd say at least 80,000 died, with twice that many injured. Radio Tokyo minces no words, claiming that conditions are horrifying beyond imagination."

LeMay chewed absentmindedly on his unlit cigar. His emotions were obviously under tight control. "It's a diller." He turned to Garcia. "Thank you for your prompt report." Garcia hurried away, and LeMay motioned for Montgomery to remain. "Are we all set for Nagoya?"

Montgomery nodded. "As Japan's third largest city, and the center of its aircraft industry, the results should be more important than Tokyo." He hesitantly changed the subject. "General, I've been getting complaints from some gunners who say that a number of crewmembers will finish their combat tours before the others."

LeMay was about to brush the matter aside, but he paused to think it over. He changed his mind. "They have a point. The integrity of the crew system may be at stake." He paused. "I'll permit the lower turrets to be manned, but only to shoot at searchlights. Make that emphatic. I'm still concerned that our gunners will shoot down other B-29s. "He picked up a slip of paper from his desk. "I heard from General Arnold this morning. He wires, 'The results of yesterday's missions show that your crews have the nerve for anything.' I guess that signifies his acceptance of our new strategy. This is the first time I've heard directly from him."

Montgomery started to leave, but recalled something. "One of Power's squadron maintenance officers stormed into my office last night. He was dirty, unshaved, and red-eyed from lack of sleep. He said his men had worked 36 hours straight to get an airplane in commission but that his squadron operations officer told him he was a few minutes too late to round out a crew. I ordered that a crew be put together, no matter how they got the men. This was done. The plane made the mission, although it was 45 minutes late taking off."

There was a hint of moisture in LeMay's eyes that Montgomery almost missed. His voice was soft but vibrant with emotion when he said. "That's the kind of Gung-ho spirit that will win this war. Give me a note and I'll send that maintenance officer my personal thanks and appreciation. I want a record of his dedication included in his 201 file so he won't be overlooked for promotion. We need more men like him."

In India, the 20th Bomber Command flew its last mission on March 30, after fire bombing targets near Singapore. This was the last of the worthwhile strategic targets.

We had been overseas almost a year, and now we knew how to take a mission from the planning boards and execute it with successful results. We could not help but feel that our job was finished. We had proved that Japan was vulnerable and had established the tactics for future operations. All of us were tired and we wanted to go home. After a talk with Kalberer however, it was evident that events were developing in another part of the world and that there was a vital need for us in great undertakings still to come.

A pleasant break in the monotony of waiting for the mass flight to Tinian occurred when 30 of us were granted permission to take a week off in Kashmir.

Our first attempt to reach it was unsuccessful because of complete cloud cover over the valley. We flew back to Rawalpindi to spend the night.

Kashmir was an independent state in north central India, nestled in a huge valley in the Himalayas. Our overnight stop at Rawalpindi was pleasant because it was the most beautiful city in the northern part of India.

The weather was favorable the following morning so we took off at 7 A.M. The fabulous valley ahead of us was ruled with an autocratic hand by Maharajah Sir Hari Singh. Kashmir lies between Afghanistan and Tibet. It has the same latitude as Los Angeles, but its mile-high altitude makes it a cool, verdant land of unsurpassed beauty.

"What kind of airfield is there in Kashmir?" I shouted to Buchta over the roar of the engines.

"There isn't any," Joe said with a grin. "The Maharajah has an open field for his small private planes. But they told us that if it is muddy it can be pretty bad."

When we neared the valley, the clouds had formed low and obscured the field. We made a turn above the clouds and finally found a hole, through which we caught glimpses of the valley. We dived through it, emerging into a luxurious valley of green trees, sparkling rivers, and lakes. Ahead of us we could see the city of Srinagar with its narrow streets and dirt-covered buildings along the banks of the Jhelum River. On a hill to the north a huge fortress-like structure stood on a peak.

"What a beautiful place!" Joe said ecstatically.

I nodded and gazed at the valley with eyes full of wonder and delight. Major Laidler B. Mackall, the group's air inspector, was our pilot. He located the field and our wheels touched down gently. We rolled along until all of a sudden we stopped dead and our tail rose high in the air.

"We're tipping over!" someone yelled.

Before anyone could reply the tail settled down and we looked at one another with surprise. The fear that clutched our hearts had come and gone so quickly it left us breathless.

"What happened?" someone asked.

"The wheels sank to the hub caps," another replied.

Mackall shook his head when he saw the wheels buried in deep muck. "We'll never get out of here heavily loaded," he said. "Before anyone goes to town, we'll have to dig the wheels out. There won't be a bus for a while anyway."

Later on, as we rode into the city, I said to Buchta, "I don't know how we're getting out of here but right now I don't care. The 20th Bomber Command can worry about that."

We rode straight through rows of bare poplar trees while peasants dressed in ragas plodded along the muddy road with barely a glance in our direction. Their thin shawls and straw sandals seemed totally inadequate to keep out the chill in the air. Light tongas, with their bells tinkling were quickly left behind us as we drove through small villages whose wooden houses and walled gardens gave us brief glimpses of fruit trees in blossom. I recognized the pink blossoms of almond and quince trees with little, wild, pink and white striped tulips growing in the grass alongside the road. In contrast, the homes of the wealthy had elaborately carved fronts that seemed incongruous in settings surrounded by filthy lands leading up to them.

The huge palace of the Maharaja, built of white stone, had fluted pillars, columns and long glass windows. We learned later that he spent little time here, preferring his palaces in India. During his visits to Kashmir, people floated roses down the Jhelum River to greet him.

On each side of the river were narrow, muddy paths, crowded by oxen and pack animals. In the shopping area, merchants wrapped in shawls and carpets sat among various wares of steaming food, fur hats, shoes, and embroidered felt rugs. Women shoppers, dressed in filthy cotton robes of various colors, wore white veils. Many had bunches of silver earrings hanging on each side of their faces.

I had read that Kashmir was often called the Venice of the East because of its beautiful bridges over the Jhelum, and its elaborately carved houses where balconies overhung the water of the rivers and canals. But for all its occasional richness, Srinagar was a filthy, hideous place of abject poverty.

Poets have described Kashmir as a pearl between the mountains; a pearl of water and flowers. Its abundant water comes from glaciers on the snowy peaks of the Pir Panjal Mountains, whose streams run through high alps and valleys. This water nourishes millions of acres of flowers in the spring and summer, plus forests of trees farther down the mountain slopes. Each sparkling stream ends in rapids where the water flows swiftly to the valley floor to fill Kashmir's lakes, rivers, and waterways.

Now that spring had come again to the Vale of Kashmir, the shores of the lakes were studded with willows, kingfishers flitting through their new green leaves, heralding another change of season, celebrating the end of the harsh winter. The roofs of houses, covered with sod for warmth, now were hosts to myriads of scarlet tulips and yellow mustard.

There was endless traffic on Wular Lake because most of the valley's commerce was moved by boats of various kinds. Taxi shikaras, with their embroidered canopies, curtains, and cushions were given American-style names such as "Whoopie" and "Dreamboat" to attract tourists. Three or four men using heart shaped paddles paddled each.

"Where shall we stay?" Buchta asked. "I understand there's a beautiful hotel in the city."

"How about a houseboat on Wular Lake?" I suggested eagerly. "Four of us can share the expenses, and it would be fun."

"Sounds good to me," Joe said. He leaned forward in the seat and talked to Eldridge "Al" Beck and Captain Paul D. "Zim" Zimmerman. "How would you like to join us in a houseboat instead of putting up at the hotel?"

They agreed and it was all set.

After lunch at the hotel we went to inspect the houseboats. They were lined up for half a mile, and were moored permanently on the lake. Their bottoms were built like barges with a long rectangular house on top.

"We'll need a four bedroom boat," I said. "How about that one over there?"

"It's a beauty," Joe said. "Hey boy!" Joe yelled across the water. "Bring your boat!"

A shikara paddled by three natives rushed toward us. We gave directions and headed for the houseboat. It was furnished simply but adequately. The shikara went with the houseboat and would be at our disposal night and day for a nominal sum. The shikara was long and canopied over the middle in bright colored tapestries. It was shaped much like a canoe but larger.

That night I said to the others, "Why don't we inspect the city. I'm anxious to see it."

"You go along," Zim said. "I'm going to the hotel for awhile."

"I'll go," Joe said. "You coming Al?"

"I'll go with Zim. We've got plenty of time to see the city."

Joe and I inspected Srinagar for several hours and found it in sharp contrast to the glorious green amphitheater that surrounded it. Rickety houses were perched precariously on their foundations, every line at a different angle. Their roofs were covered with earth and grass, and flowers grew on them despite the steep pitch. Overhanging balconies, supported by pillars, hung over the narrow dirty streets.

"I hate the Far East most because of its smells," Joe said.

"What can you expect?" I said, pointing to the sewage running beside us in the gutter.

Only an unappeasable curiosity carried us through this ancient city they called the "City of the Sun." Its name was hardly in keeping with the looks of its dilapidated structures amidst this beautiful valley.

The congested metropolis was four miles long and two miles wide. The river Jhelum divided it into two parts but the numerous canals with their earth encrusted bridges built centuries earlier by the grand moguls provided the quickest means of transportation for the people.

"The people seem sullen and reserved," Joe said.

"There's a lot of hatred in this country," I said. "The Moslems are in the majority but the Hindus run the government."

Writers for generations have written glowing accounts of this paradise nestled in the Himalayas. Our first day was enough to make us appreciate their enthusiasm. The towering peaks surrounding the valley, 84 miles long and 30 miles wide, were indescribably magnificent. Their snow-capped crowns glistened brightly in the sun and their green-forested slopes were covered with virgin timber.

The next morning I said to Joe. "How about going to the pleasure gardens today? We can get another shikara for a few hours and let Al and Zim do what they want."

Joe's eyes brightened. "I particularly want to see the Shalimar Bagh."

I did too. Kashmir is justly famous for its pleasure gardens. Lawrence Hope's "Kashmir Song" tells of the most famous of these gardens, the Shalimar Bagh, or "Abode of Love."

While we cruised the lake, lolling on brightly colored cushions, we felt we were in paradise. After we stepped out of our shikara and gazed up at the gently rising terraces, our eyes sparkled. There, in groups of carefully tended gardens were wild roses, jasmine, clematis, iris, phlox, larkspur, snapdragons, lilies, and poppies. Not all were in bloom but they were easily recognized plants, similar to those at home.

The Mogul emperors loved Kashmir; especially Jehanghir and his Queen, Nur Jehan, or "Light of the World." Of the three gardens, the Shalimar is the most famous, although the Nishat is the most beautiful. Its wide terraces have a central water channel through the middle to fill its pools and fountains. Water runs from terrace to terrace down slopes of marble carved in intricate designs. It is all patterned to create water music that is delightful and soothing. At each slant there is a small marble dais so one can sit, listen, and contemplate.

That afternoon Joe and I sat on our front porch luxuriating in the warm sunshine and cool breezes.

"It's like springtime back home," Joe said with a dreamy look on his face.

A spell of enchantment was upon me, and I did not reply but looked at the tremendous mountains surrounding the valley with their snowcapped peaks and green slopes. After a long silence I said, "It's truly a fairyland of unbelievable beauty and magnificence."

Toward the end of the week Joe cornered Abdul, our chief cook, "What are we going to eat tonight?" he asked belligerently.

"Mutton, Sahib."

"I don't want any more mutton!" Joe shouted. "It's bad enough to have mutton for the meat course, but it's even worse to have mutton soup."

Abdul spread his arms in an attitude of resignation.

"Get us duck for tonight," Joe said.

"No Sahib, no duck."

"Abdul! We want duck tonight!" Joe shouted.

"Yes Sahib," Abdul said submissively.

"He's been feeding us the cheapest food that he can buy," Joe said. "I have never liked mutton, and after four days of this mutton diet my stomach just can't stand anymore."

That evening over dinner Beck wondered. "Do you think it's really as delicious as it tastes, or just the change in diet that makes it seem so?"

"Anything is preferable to mutton," Joe growled as he gnawed on a leg.

"Did you guys ever take a look at the kitchen boat behind us?" Zim asked.

"Please, don't bring it up while we're eating," Joe said with a groan. "You'll ruin my appetite."

"It's the dirtiest, greasiest kitchen I have ever seen," Zim added.

"Stop it!" Joe said. "My stomach has enough cramps as it is."

While we were listening to the radio one evening an announcer from the BBC gave us the news of President Roosevelt's death. We were stunned and speechless. The Persian who owned the boat happened to be visiting at the time and expressed his regret at the death of so great a man.

"Which son will take the president's place?" he asked.

"There's no such thing as succession in our country," I explained. "The vice president takes over."

He was puzzled by this remark and more confused than ever.

Every day we were besieged by countless hordes of gem merchants. Finally we succumbed to a young, well-dressed man with an ingratiating smile who worked his way into our living room. The net result was that I bought four stones for $40 and Joe bought two for $30.

Quite proud of our purchases, Joe and I went to a jewelry store in the city for an appraisal of our buys.

After looking at the stones through a magnifying glass the Hindu shrugged and said "Synthetic."

"Are you sure?" Joe exclaimed.

"All you Americans are alike," the merchant said. "Why don't you come to a reputable jeweler instead of dealing with a cheap peddler?"

I looked sheepishly at Joe. "He really took us. They are kind of pretty," I said wistfully.

"I'd like to get my hands on that peddler!" Joe said.

Our days in Kashmir came to an end all too soon. The plane took off without us so we had to hire buses to take us over the mountains to Rawalpindi. The field was still soggy and wet so a heavy take off was unthinkable. And this began the most horrible automobile ride of my life.

"I'm sick," Joe said with a wince as we started to drive out of the valley. "I must have dysentery because I'm doubled up with cramps."

"You're getting old," I said kidding him. "You can't take it anymore."

"Don't be so cocky," he said. "You may get it yourself."

"I doubt it. If I were going to come down with it, I would have had it long before this."

We drove through the outskirts of Srinagar along a dusty road lined with beautiful homes and blossoming fruit trees.

Our driver was a bearded native of Kashmir who had no concept of the meaning of the word "fear." The vehicle was a wreck, at least 20 years old, with tires worn to threads. It was not a bus in the strict sense of the word, but a converted touring car with a box-like cage bolted to the body with seats for 12 people.

The road was dirt and rutted, and we passed numerous oxcarts and other two-wheeled vehicles.

"I don't like the looks of this vehicle," I said dubiously. "The mountains are high and treacherous. I don't know how it can expect to climb over them."

"There's an 8,000 foot mountain pass ahead of us," Joe said.

The road weaved through country villages and across cultivated fields until we reached the foothills. It hadn't been bad so far, despite the dirt from the road and the hardness of the wooden seats. But this was nothing. The worst was yet to come.

Ahead we could see no signs of the road, just high towering cliffs and rushing rivers. It seemed impossible that there could be a road through all this. But it was there and wound tortuously around hairpin turns. Our driver never paused for curves but kept the ancient automobile roaring wide open with the pedal to the floorboards. We swung around one sharp curve and I looked down into a canyon thousands of feet below. I was in the rear with Joe and we swung inches from the precipice.

"Take it easy!" I yelped. "Do you want to kill us all?"

The driver uttered not a word nor gave us a backward glance. Never slackening his speed, he tore around the mountain like a demon. The higher we climbed the more precipitous the ascent became. The road got more narrow and crowded, but he never reduced his breathtaking speed.

We were nervous and angry but our shouts were useless. After five hours of this maddening speed we reached the summit of the last mountain. It was cold and windy but the view was magnificent. Roaring torrents gouged their way through the very heart of the mountains. Looking back I could see the thin, dusty line of the road over which we had come. Our faces were caked with gray dust. It powdered our hair and eyelashes and we looked unnaturally old.

"That damn fool will kill us yet," I said angrily.

"I've given up trying to change him," Joe said wearily. "My stomach really aches now."

The driver stopped the car and pulled up the hood of the vehicle.

"What's he up to now?" someone asked.

Someone else said, "He's disconnecting the carburetor."

"Do you suppose he's going to coast down the mountain?" I asked.

"I wouldn't be surprised," Joe moaned.

That's just what he did, and we cursed him all the way. Around S turns, sharp curves, and that rutted oxcart road, we tore down the mountainside twice as fast as we had come up. We were too tired and exhausted to interfere, not that it would have done any good.

At the bottom of the mountain the driver reconnected the gas line and we tried to relax in our seats for the remainder of the trip to Rawalpindi. We had left Srinagar at 9 o'clock that morning and arrived at Rawalpindi at 9 o'clock that night. After getting cleaned up and scraping some of the caked dust off, we felt better and headed for town in hopes of getting a beer.

Every bone in our bodies ached after that mad ride over the Himalayas. It felt good to relax in an armchair at the hotel.

"I'd rather go on a mission of Yawata than take that ride again," I said.

"It would be a lot safer," Joe agreed.

The next day we headed for Piardoba, with a brief stop at Agra to see the Taj Mahal. But there I headed for bed and lay down.

"Come on," Joe said. "We'll take a look at the Taj Mahal."

"You go," I said.

"What's the matter?" he said, feeling chipper again.

I clutched my stomach. "That mutton has finally caught up with me," I said with a weak grin. "I've got dysentery."

Joe laughed. "I told you"

After we arrived at Piardoba, I ran in to Ralph Todd, now an aircraft commander. "You got back just in time," he said. "Our orders to leave for Tinian are in, and you're flying with my crew on the 27th."

Part III
Tinian

Chapter 12

Medal of Honor

In the Marianas, the 21st Bomber Command's operations were diverted from the strategic bombing of Japan by an urgent call for assistance from the Navy in early April because their ship losses during the invasion of Okinawa were very heavy.

By using suicide planes, the Japanese came close to winning the Battle of Okinawa. Intelligence reports said Navy units were subjected to devastating low level suicide attacks by Japanese bombers and fighters. They claimed that the Navy was practically helpless to prevent serious losses.

LeMay ordered the bombing of airfields on Kyushu with thousands of regular and delayed action bombs and most Japanese fighters and bombers were either destroyed or unable to use the fields.

LeMay split his 21st Bomber Command on April 7 to attack the two most important precision targets. In near perfect weather, the 313th and 314th Wings dropped bombs on the Mitsubishi Engine Works at Nagoya, destroying 90 percent of the plant. The 73rd Wing attacked the Nakajima Musashino-Tama plant again on the outskirts of Tokyo, but succeeded in only causing heavy damage to the machine shops.

The 73rd did better on April 12 when it caused such severe damage in Musashino-Tama that it was removed from the top priority list.

This was the eleventh mission against this tough target and only the last two missions had been partially successful. It was learned later that Nakajima officials abandoned the plant, and engine production was stopped.

B-29s now had fighter support over the mainland. A hundred P-51s from Iwo's 7th Fighter Command escorted bombers on the April 12 mission, and despite attacks against the bombers by 100 Japanese fighters, only 36 B-29s were damaged.

In an attempt to split Japan's fighter defenses at Tokyo, LeMay sent the 313th and 314th Wings to Koriyama, a hundred miles away. The attack on two chemical plants and an aluminum factory at Koriyama was successful and all three targets were severely damaged.

Captain George A. Simeral, commander of the "City of Los Angeles" was assigned to lead a formation against one of the Koriyama targets.

Near the formation's assembly point, 175 miles from the target, Simeral called the radio operator, Sergeant Henry E. "Red" Erwin, to drop another phosphorus smoke grenade. "Some of our flight failed to spot the first colored burst to identify us as their leader," he said.

Flak was bursting around them, and bright flashes appeared with growing regularity. There was a note of urgency in Simeral's voice as he said, "We've got to form up quickly. We're under fighter attack."

"Roger," Erwin called. He picked up a small, six-inch smoke grenade, pulled the pin and quickly inserted it into the floor chute. Now that it was armed it would explode in six seconds. To his horror it exploded at the bottom of the chute and flew back into his face. A cry of pain escaped from him as flaming phosphorus covered his face. The cabin quickly filled with smoke.

Simeral was blinded by smoke and lost control of the plane. He yelled to his co-pilot, Roy Stables "Help me pull out of this dive!"

Stables caught a glimpse of Erwin as he grabbed the wheel on his side. He recoiled in horror as he saw Erwin was covered with flaming phosphorus.

Erwin, almost blinded by smoke, tried to grab the red-hot grenade as it rolled across the cockpit's floor. It finally came to rest, and started to burn the metal flooring.

Simeral's voice had a desperate note of urgency when he cried, "I can't see the instrument panel. I'm losing control."

Stables turned to look back for one quick moment to see what was happening behind him. He saw that Erwin was groping for the grenade. He noted with shock that Erwin's clothes were on fire, and that the flesh was burning off parts of his body. He yelled to Simeral, "Erwin is terribly burned. Parts of his face and body are covered with flaming phosphorus. His nose and right ear are burned off."

Simeral took a quick, stunned look at his co-pilot. "I've got to get this plane out of its dive, or we've all had it."

Stables pulled back strongly on his wheel, helping Simeral to get the nose up and the plane flying straight and level. As he strained, he called, "She's coming up." He glanced back just as Erwin's right hand picked up the flaming grenade, a grimace of pain that distorted his features as the phosphorus burned the flesh from his hand. He watched Erwin stumble across the narrow confines of the cockpit, hurrying to get to a window in the pilot's compartment. Stables watched him with fascination, quickly remembered to open his window as Erwin, the flaming grenade tucked under his arm against his burning body, rushed forward. More dead than alive, Erwin almost feel into the pilot's compartment yelling for Stables to open his window.

Stables screamed over and over. "It's open! It's open! It's open!"

Erwin spotted the open window and hurled the grenade out, then collapsed.

It had taken only 12 seconds but it seemed like a lifetime to the crew. Simeral now had the plane under control and he pulled up just 300 feet from the water and climbed to a safer altitude.

Erwin was a mass of flames, particularly his rubber life jacket, as the navigator, Gene Strouse, grabbed a fire extinguisher and put out the flames while Erwin, uncomplaining, lay in agony on the floor.

Simeral turned the plane around and raced at full power for Iwo Jima. Erwin was the only member of the crew trained to give first aid, and he had to instruct them how to give him morphine to deaden the pain, and later blood plasma.

Erwin never lost consciousness on the flight to Iwo Jima. There, Simeral was notified that the island was under Japanese attack but he landed despite the raging battle above him.

Erwin's life hung in the balance for four days as doctors sought to save him. They moved him to Guam, where the hospital was better equipped to handle his massive burns.

General Arnold sent Major General Willis Hale from Hawaii to honor Erwin five weeks later with award of the Medal of Honor. The 23-year-old Erwin was covered with bandages from head to toe and he could barely hear the general as he said, "Your gallantry and heroism, above and beyond the call of duty, saved the lives of your comrades." He pinned the nation's highest medal for valor on Erwin's chest.

He was the only member of the 20th Air Force to be so honored. General Arnold later said of Erwin's action, "The country's highest honor will still be inadequate recognition of the inspiring heroism of this man."

LeMay met with his wing commanders on April 13 while the 58th Wing was still in India. "After the April 1 invasion of Okinawa, I told Admiral Nimitz that our preinvasion strikes had flattened the air bases on Kyushu. He agreed. I said that we had been lucky in the weather and that now we ought to go back to strategic bombing. I claimed that all we could do now was put more holes in the fields, and that we could not stop an occasional airplane that the Japs had hid down the road some place, from taking off. I tried to convince him that we had done all we could. He leaned back with a slight smile on his face. He stood up, patted me on the back, and put his arm around me. He said, 'You've done a fine job, LeMay. Let's check to see what Sherman says.'"

"Who's he?" Davies asked.

"Rear Admiral Forrest P. Sherman is Nimitz's chief of operations. Well, Sherman refused to release our bombers despite my protests. He wired Admiral King in Washington that he would pull off and leave the ground troops on shore to fend for themselves if we did not continue bombing Kyushu's airfields." LeMay shook his head in angry frustration. "So, the strategic raids are on hold for awhile."

Montgomery was bitter when he said, "Just when we were hitting our stride."

"I've protested to Arnold," LeMay said. "Not that it will do any good. An amphibious operation like this one against Okinawa is the most difficult of all military operations. We've got to help. Actually, we're short of incendiary bombs, so we couldn't keep up the March pace."

He stared at the ceiling in a reflective mood. "It must be hell over there. I understand the Navy has already lost a number of ships and hundreds of men. Yesterday, the Japs sent 335 suicide planes over the invasion area, and an equal number of conventional fighters and bombers. Losses of ships and men are at the critical stage." He turned to Montgomery. "Recap our March raids."

Montgomery shuffled through a handful of notes. "B-29s gutted 32 square miles of urban areas in four key cities — Tokyo, Nagoya, Osaka, and Kobe. Many important targets were destroyed, including some listed for daylight strikes."

LeMay interrupted. There was a note of satisfaction in his voice when he said, "Tell me about our losses."

"Despite predictions by some staff members and wing commanders," Montgomery began with a glance at O'Donnell, "that our losses would be prohibitive, less than one percent of all crews on these missions were lost. That rate is far below losses on previous daylight, high altitude strikes."

Power spoke up. "My combat crews, most of whom flew all five missions are exuberant. We've had an uplift in morale that is almost incredible. Although my maintenance crews worked night and day for 10 days during March to help get each plane into commission, their morale and spirits have never been higher."

"My hats off to the maintenance crews," LeMay said. "They performed a genuine miracle by having 83 percent of all B-29s available for each mission. The previous average was 56 percent. We've found the answer to the ultimate destruction of Japan's ability to wage war." He started to light his pipe, but put it down. "Compared to day raids the bomb load per aircraft has more than doubled. B-29's can now fly twice as many missions because engines are subjected to less strain at lower altitudes. The end result is the same as if the force had been doubled."

"It's apparent that Japanese cities are now more vulnerable than we had thought," Davies said.

"Fire raids are not suitable for all targets," Montgomery reminded them.

LeMay nodded his head in agreement. "I plan to continue daylight attacks against aircraft plants whenever weather permits. But for most of the next few months, I'll send B-29s with fire bombs to destroy 33 urban areas selected by the Joint Target Group." He methodically lit his pipe and drew strongly on it. Then he glanced thoughtfully at each of them. "I told Nimitz that I'll need more supplies because I plan to fly combat crews 120 hours each month."

They were astonished, but O'Donnell voiced their concerns. "That 's impossible. No crewmember can stand that many combat hours."

LeMay slowly removed his pipe from his mouth and riveted his attention on O'Donnell. "Don't underestimate America's young men. They can stand a hell of a lot more than you realize."

"But 120 hours!" O'Donnell said. "That's 40 hours more than commercial pilots are permitted to fly. You're expecting too much. I can't go along. . . ."

LeMay dared O'Donnell with his eyes to refuse to go along. O'Donnell's mouth opened and shut but now words came forth. "We're going to do it, and that's that."

Power said, "What did Nimitz say?"

"He passed my request along to his staff," LeMay said with a grin. "They scoffed at it. Nimitz later told me his staff claimed we flew on 30 hours a month in Europe. He said they wanted to know how in hell I was going to fly 120 hours out of here. Nimitz ended the conversation by saying the Navy planned for a maximum of 60 hours. That made me mad. I wrote back that I was planning to fly 120 hours a month and that when I ran out of supplies the Navy would have to explain it to the Joint Chiefs because I was going fishing."

They all smiled.

"Do you think they'll cooperate?" Power asked.

LeMay didn't respond for a moment. "We'll get them. The Navy has already performed miracles in the Pacific. They won't let us down." His voice hardened. "Make sure that we don't! Everyone will have to pitch in to get planes loaded on the hard stands. Use Marines, Seabee, all available personnel who are not otherwise engaged." He changed the subject. "Monty, tell them about our analysis of Japanese radio broadcasts."

"After the big fire raids, we monitored Japanese radio stations to learn what they were telling their people. Broadcasts often verged on the hysterical. LeMay is convinced that our new tactics have the Japanese at a decided disadvantage."

LeMay interrupted Montgomery. "The Japs did not foresee the possibilities of strategic air attacks. We have them cold. The Koiso Cabinet has been dismissed, and a new cabinet has been formed under Admiral Suzuki, the former Navy chief of staff. I've told the Pentagon that the present stage of development in the air war against Japan presents the Army Air Forces with the opportunity of proving itself. I said that the destruction of Japan's ability to wage war lies within our capability, provided maximum capacity is exerted unstintingly during the next six months. I emphasized that the opportunity warrants extraordinary measures on our part. My greatest concern is the shortage of crews. My flight surgeon claims that crews can average a maximum of 60 combat hours a month for an extended period, but beyond that he won't be responsible for their ability to function effectively." He paused for emphasis. "As I told you, I plan to double those hours."

Davies said, "That could be the crux of the matter."

O'Donnell had been gathering courage to intervene. Now he voiced a strong protest. "One hundred and twenty hours of combat a month is impossible to achieve. Why . . ., the men will be walking zombies."

LeMay stared at O'Donnell. "I disagree. This command can end this war in a matter of months. I do not foresee losses averaging more than two percent. The present tour of duty of 35 missions is another matter. We've got to have more new crews, or extend the number of missions to complete a tour. I don't like to do that, but I won't flinch if that decision becomes necessary."

O'Donnell's voice rose sharply. "The men will blow their tops." He turned truculently, but only for a moment. "You're not keeping faith with them. They have looked forward to a maximum of 35 missions and you're...."

LeMay interrupted him as his anger boiled over. "I have no intention of breaking faith with these men. They've performed magnificently. That still does not resolve the problem faced by this command. If it comes to a question of cutting back on missions rather than extending their tours, I won't hesitate. Once the problem is explained to them, I'm sure they'll go along. They'll bitch about it, but they have a unique opportunity — seldom granted to any military organization — to end this war quickly." With biting sarcasm, he lashed out at O'Donnell. "You don't have the faith in your own men."

O'Donnell, stung by LeMay's remark, fought back. "I know my men better than you do."

LeMay responded just as sharply. "You don't talk like it."

O'Donnell subsided, realizing that he had gone too far. "I'll support whatever operations you authorize. I am only voicing my deep concern about a decision that affects my men with which I disagree."

LeMay studied O'Donnell's face, while puffing on his pipe. "I accept your right to disagree with me. But I expect my orders to be carried out to the fullest. Is that clear?"

O'Donnell's voice was tightly controlled when he replied. "It is. Your orders will be carried out to the best of my ability."

LeMay was satisfied with his response. "That's all I ask."

Montgomery spoke up. "We'll soon have the 58th Wing from India on Tinian. That will give us four wings. By July, the 315th Wing will be ready to join us."

LeMay nodded, but his concern for future operations was evident when he stubbornly reminded them that the command would still be short almost 300 crews by August. "Such a situation will drastically reduce bomb tonnages." He searched their faces for understanding. "There is only one solution. One that I don't like to take. To get the maximum number of bombers on the March fire raids it was necessary for crews to fly 80 hours. My flight surgeon has opposed because that number is greater than the 8th Air Force ever flew in one month. Unlike European operations, most of our flight hours are not over Japan but on long ocean flight to and from targets where strain is less." He was quick to note the continued doubt on their faces. "If we fly 120 hours per crew each month through the first of December — assuming that the November 1 invasion of Japan is still on — we can bring Japan to the point of total collapse; hopefully precluding an invasion."

O'Donnell again voiced his doubts. "It can't be done. I couldn't disagree with you more."

LeMay's voice was soft but underneath there was a quality as tough as steel. "It not only can be done, but it will be done! I have no illusions. By December if the Japs haven't called it quits this command will fall flat on its face. We'll be out of crews, planes, supplies, everything. But my schedule allows us 30 days after the invasion for follow-up strikes. If our efforts to destroy Japan before the invasion fail to achieve its objectives, we'll have to sharply curtail operations on December 1."[1]

"You're expecting the impossible," O'Donnell said in protest.

LeMay eyed him impatiently. "Every time we stick up copies of our reconnaissance photos, the men go wild. They're really gung-ho. Strangely enough the people who are falling by the wayside, and dropping like flies, are those in the top squadrons."

Power glanced inquiringly at LeMay. "Who?"

"Those are the men who prepared the target material." He looked from one to another, noting their serious doubts. "From now on crews will fly 120 hours per month." He searched each face, daring anyone to protest.

Montgomery tactfully changed the subject. "Did Nimitz give you an idea when he might release the command from duty to support of the Okinawa invasion?"

"Nothing definite. We'll probably be forced to support it until the middle of May. Not total support. I'm hoping to get at least 25 percent of our missions assigned to strategic targets. Nimitz has praised our efforts on behalf of the Okinawan invasion. I guess it has done some good. But no matter how we stock those airfields, we can't reduce the kamikaze threat to zero. Without our intervention Navy losses undoubtedly would have been much higher. They're not out of the woods yet."

O'Donnell refused to drop his objections, but he tread more cautiously. "Really, General LeMay, I'm still concerned about the number of combat hours you propose each month. What will I tell my men? I...."

LeMay was blunt. "The truth. If Japan can be defeated without a costly invasion of ground troops that could result in a million casualties of American troops, the risk of airmen's lives is worth it. That's the way it's going to be. This discussion is closed!"

They all stood up, and all but Montgomery departed.

LeMay continued to press General Arnold to send his command more crews, but they could not be trained fast enough in the States. This condition lasted for the rest of the war despite LeMay's offer to train B-17 and B-24 crews in the Marianas.

Once land-based airplanes began to operate off Okinawa's fields, the need for B-29 assistance lessened. On some missions over 100 B-29s were dispatched to bomb Kyushu's airfields. Although there was little fighter opposition, 24 Superfortresses

---

[1] During my last interview with LeMay I pressed him to explain his meaning more fully. "This statement implies that you were willing to sacrifice ten or eleven thousand airmen to save possibly a million American's deaths or maiming in the invasion. Am I correct?"

"You must realize that all my instincts told me our losses would not be that high. This was a worst case scenario."

"I understand, Curt. But if it did happen, were you willing to accept such a loss?"

He paused only a moment. "Yes, I would. But again, I must stress that...."

"I'm not being critical, but merely trying to understand what must have been an agonizing decision."

He nodded. "I don't fault your reasoning because that's how wars are won. I'm glad we didn't know at the time that we were being considered as sacrificial lambs, so to speak. Fortunately, it didn't work out that way."

were lost to all causes and another 233 damaged. There were more than 2,000 separate B-29 attacks against 17 air bases on Kyushu and Shikoku from April 17 to May 11, when Nimitz released LeMay's command with warm words of praise for their efforts. These missions amounted to 75 percent of LeMay's total effort. Japanese forces on Okinawa finally capitulated on June 21, after 12,500 Americans were killed and 160,000 Japanese died in the island's defense.

I did not leave Piardoba for Tinian with Ralph Todd until the 29th of April because of a bad engine on his B-29. The first leg of our 18-hour flight took us to Luliang, China. We refueled and took off for the long flight to the Marianas. After the China take-off, I crawled into the tunnel and promptly fell asleep. Several hours later the violent pitching of the airplane interrupted my peaceful slumber.

"What's going on?" I called over the interphone to Todd.

"We're in some bad weather. My arms ache from trying to hold this beast straight and level."

"I'll have to strap myself in," I said.

The plane rolled and pitched and shot up like an express elevator as we flew over the Philippines, then plummeted thousands of feet a minute. The storm lasted an hour and then the plane roared smoothly toward the east.

Just after sunrise the outlines of three islands came into view and we gathered at the nose to see our new home. Tinian was in the middle of the three. It was a small, low, green-covered island just above the ocean's surface.

Todd made a straight-in approach and landed nicely. The "Follow me" waved to us and we lumbered behind the jeep to the parking area.

The fresh sea breeze was intoxicating as we climbed out of the plane. The hot sun, reflected off the coral, stabbed blindingly at our eyes. Master Sergeant James L. Alexander, one of our crew chiefs, came up to me with a big grin on his face. "What do you think of the beautiful isle of Tinian, Captain?"

"From what I've seen so far," I said appreciatively, "it's a big improvement over India."

He shook his head in a knowing way and said, "You can say that again!"

During the 58th Wing's transfer by air to Tinian not one life was lost or B-29 destroyed during the 18 hour flights. We had been tested in the most grueling theater of all, and our experience level had reached such a peak that few if any organizations in the United States Army Air Forces could match us. But we had paid a high price.

Of the original 160 B-29s the 20th Bomber Command had sent to India, we had lost 147 in 1944 alone, and 30 percent of the crews. There were additional losses due to operations out of India in 1945 but at a much smaller scale. The command had dropped 11,477 tons of bombs, including a few mines, on 49 missions. Superbly trained, and forged in the crucible of experience, we were as tough and reliable as any fighting organization the United States had ever produced. Proud, but not boastful, we were ready to take on any task LeMay assigned to us.

Chapter 13

A Proud Beginning

After our first day on Tinian it was evident that all that had gone before had been just a prelude, or dress rehearsal, for the events to come. The war in Europe was drawing to a close and the eyes of the world were turned to the Pacific with a questioning look. How long will it take to conquer Japan?

Four of us shared a tent in the area set aside for the 462nd Group's officer personnel. Captain Richard H. Goddard, group radar officer; Captain Oprzendek; Joe Buchta, and myself had a tent on a promontory with a view of the Pacific and green clad Aguijan Island to the south. A fresh sea breeze made the warm days pleasant.

The Seabees had done a remarkable job of creating a base for us out of acres of sugar canes and blasted dugouts. In constructing the base, they had moved enough coral in construction of two airstrips to build three Boulder Dams. Our 8,000-foot runways crossed a valley that had to be filled in.

Almost 90 miles of hard surfaced roads connected all parts of the island and we even had a harbor for several merchant ships to dock.

Colonel Kalberer had sent shudders down our spines when he said there were at least a thousand Japanese soldiers hiding out in caves along the coast. They often came out at night and attempted to kill our men. A doctor and a nurse who went exploring were never seen again, although their jeep was found.

Air traffic control now was a problem with our 58th Wing sharing the island with the 313th at North Field.

I carefully studied the reports about operations before our 58th Wing came to the Marianas. I grasped at highlights, noting that the March 9 raid against Tokyo had gutted 16 square miles of the city. I marveled at the extent of LeMay's courage and vision. If he had planned wrong, hundreds of men's lives would have been lost as well as most of the bombers they flew in. His foresight, I realized, proved him to be a man of great vision. I noted that the March 11 raid on Nagoya, and those against other major cities were part of a pattern.

I noted with interest that none of the 11 high priority targets such as aircraft factories and aircraft engine plants had been totally destroyed. Production had been interrupted from time to time, but most plants remained in operation.

The report dealing with mining operations by the 313th Wing was especially interesting. March 17, the wing's B-29s started mining the Inland Sea. This wing carried out the only mining operations of the command through the rest of the war, and caused tremendous damage to the Japanese Merchant Marine.

Buchta stopped at my desk. "Time for our meeting with Kalberer."

The staff met in Vaucher's office while Kalberer leafed through his notes. We were anxious to hear what the future had in store for us.

"I have just come from a conference of group and wing commanders at LeMay's headquarters," Kalberer said. "First off, let me say, we'll run our first mission in a couple of days."

"We can't fly a mission that soon," Vaucher said. "Our planes haven't all arrived. And most of them need a good checkup."

"I know," Kalberer said, "but LeMay wants us to get going so that's all there is to it. Eight missions are planned this month, and we are to schedule every plane in commission. It won't be easy, but we've worked under difficulties before.

So much for this month, now about the future. The day the war in Europe ends, a three-month blitz will be inaugurated to attempt to destroy the will and resources of the Japanese people to continue the war. By August he expects to be able to muster 1,000 B-29s over Japan on any one mission. As I see it, the Air Force, for the first time, has a chance to prove that a nation can be made to surrender by air power alone without a costly invasion of its homeland. I believe it can be done."

"Oh, come now, Kal," Vaucher said with a laugh. "Surely you don't believe Japan can be knocked out of the war just by air raids?"

"It certainly can!" Kalberer said emphatically. "The same signs are showing here as were evident in Germany during the last six months. General LeMay believes that we will be out of targets by October 1, and that Japan will have nothing left with which to continue the fighting."

"I don't believe it," Vaucher said.

"I'll make a prediction," Kalberer said. "By the first of August the Japs will have asked for a negotiated peace, but it will be unacceptable to us and the war will continue. By October 1 they will have had enough and they'll quit."

We all laughed. "LeMay has really sold you a bill of goods," Vaucher said. "The Japanese have hardly felt the effects of the war yet."

"Talk is cheap," Kalberer said. "I'll tell you what I'll do. I have a thousand dollars that says the war will be over by October 1. Let me see the color of your money."

"I'll take five hundred of that!" Vaucher said.

"Good! I only wish I had more to put up. I'd come out of this war a rich man. Anyone else want to try their luck?"

Although we found it difficult to believe the war would be over in five months, we did not follow Vaucher's example. Colonel Kalberer's prediction had proven correct too often for the rest of us to risk our money.

"I wish I could go on this first mission," Zimmerman said to me.

"Why can't you?" I asked.

"I haven't been able to get a new bombardier since Thurman Sallade went home."

"I'll go with you."

"Would you?" he asked eagerly.

"Why not? I'm anxious to see for myself what we have to face over Japan from this side."

The briefing was held the night of May 4. On our way to the line Zim said, "We've done pretty well to get 12 planes together so soon. With Childress's crew leading us, we should give a good account of ourselves."

"We'd better," I said. "We've got quite a reputation to uphold."

Our planes were loaded with eight 1,000-pound demolition bombs. The target was in the well-defended Kure area of Japan on the main island of Honshu.

The mission against the Hiro Aircraft Factory was my first since February so I painstakingly checked my equipment.

"I'm going to take all 8,000 feet of runway for take-off," Zim said. "We weigh 137,000 pounds."

"Those extra 2,000 pounds increase the 'sweat output' considerably," I said with a not very convincing laugh.

Zim made a smooth take-off and we started the trip around the south end of the island following the pattern and then headed for Iwo Jima.

The night was clear and beautiful and the plane rode smoothly and effortlessly. The stars were bright and sparkling and I relaxed in contentment.

"You know," I said to Zim, "a year ago we were just arriving in India. I never thought I'd be flying missions 12 months later."

"Those 35 missions will take a lot more time to accumulate," Zim said. "I'll be the happiest man in Tinian when I complete them."

We arrived at Iwo in daylight, but only patches of the small island could be seen because of the layers of fluffy clouds above it. Mount Suribachi was clearly visible but not much else. The planes turned and headed for the assembly point near the island of Honshu.

As we headed for the Empire, B-29s were visible here and there.

"I can't get over seeing so many planes in the air at one time," I said to Zimmerman. "It's a striking contrast to the old days. We used to think we were doing well to get 75 B-29s out, but over here hundreds go on every mission."

At the assembly point only six planes were lined up behind Childress's plane and the rest of the formation was nowhere to be seen. Zim and I exchanged worried glances.

"I don't like it," I said. "This is no place to bomb without a full 12-plane formation."

Zim nodded soberly but turned with the formation in the IP. On our way into the target I had fleeting glimpses of the rolling countryside, now green, now brown, but beautifully picturesque. We weaved back and forth as the lead plane's radar operator directed the formation to the target. Clouds billowed around us and I appreciated their protective covering because Japanese fighters would have a tough time attacking us.

I opened the bomb bay doors and waited for suspenseful minutes. The whole area ahead of us presented itself to our view as the clouds parted. Ahead lay the Kure Naval Base with all kinds of ships in the harbor. Installations were everywhere we looked. Below, and just ahead, the naval aircraft factory lay exposed to view, still untouched.

It had been months since my last mission and I felt the tension renew itself in my throat and stomach. It was an eerie feeling to be riding high above one of the strongholds of the Japanese Empire without being shot at. But soon all doubts about our arriving unexpectedly were dispelled as the sky filled with various colored puffs of ack ack.

My eyes were narrowed in tense sockets as I peered at the lead plane. The intensity of fire increased and we were completely surrounded by bursts that echoed loudly throughout the airplane. The bombs of the lead plane started slowly downward toward their final resting place and I salvoed. The formation dived away to the left.

"Pinky put them right on the old button!" I cried exultantly, with a feeling of enormous relief.

I had watched for the bursts to see where Lieutenant Marvin E. Ballard had placed the formations' bombs, and it was an inspiring sight to see them blanket the aiming point and blow one of Japan's fighter factories into fragments.

Back at the base it was learned that the deputy leader assigned to our formation had led a formation of four planes over the target but the bombardier had an early release and none of the bombs hit the plant. However, Ballard had placed 100 percent of his bombs within the thousand-foot circle. Every group from the 58th Wing hit the plant and it was completely destroyed. It was a proud beginning for us out of the Marianas.

That night on Tinian Joe asked me, "Did you see any Superdumbos on the mission?"

"There was one orbiting an area not far from the mainland."

"What in the world is a Superdumbos?" Murph asked.

"It's a B-29 equipped with emergency sustenance kits and extra life rafts," Joe said. "They go out on every mission and circle the area near the target. The pilot and radio operators monitor emergency frequencies. If a plane is in trouble, the pilot calls the Superdumbos and gives his position, time, heading, and altitude. The Superdumbos then calls all emergency rescue planes and ships to the spot where the B-29 is ditching in the ocean."

"I understand there have been cases where crewmembers have been picked up by our submarines within sight of the Japanese coast line," I said. "I have a profound respect and admiration for the men in the 'subs.' The rescue service is doing a bang-up job here. It gives me a good feeling to know there's a friend to watch over me in time of trouble. The Superdumbos have cut the casualty list considerably."

The Japanese were running low on oil and gasoline because of the naval blockade, so it was decided to run a full effort against storage areas to destroy what remaining reserve they had left.

The 58th Wing attacked the Oshima Oil Storage area on the southern part of Honshu on May 10. The wing sent up every available plane and helped to destroy the numerous tanks of the storage depot.

Lieutenant Leonard A. Lampert, the lead bombardier of the first formation from the wing to hit the target, dropped his bombs and was rewarded by tremendous explosions of oil and gasoline. By the time the last plane left the area, southern Honshu was under a pall of smoke that rose to 40,000 feet. Damage assessment later proved that the area had been totally destroyed.

The other wings of the 21st Bomber Command had heard a great deal about us before we arrived in the Marianas. As a matter of fact, they had heard too much and were sick and tired of having their own shortcomings pointed out and hearing our men say. "In the 58th we did it this way."

We had come to the Marianas with two strikes against us. We had to make good on the first mission or we would never have lived it down. That was all past history. The 58th Wing had made good, and the others grudgingly admitted we were a pretty good outfit, after all.

The German war was over. The blitz against Japan was unleashed. Nagoya was picked as the city to be fire blitzed first. May 14, in a high altitude daylight raid, 3.15 square miles were burned out. The highly important surface wind was not in our favor so it was only a moderately successful mission.

One day of hurried preparations elapsed before the second mission against Nagoya was set up. I had gone on the first two missions, skipped the first Nagoya, and assigned myself to the second mission. Our co-pilot from India days, Ralph Todd, now had a crew of his own. He needed a bombardier so I attached myself to his crew.

"The bombs all okay?" Todd asked, as I crawled out of the bomb bay.

"I checked every cluster carefully," I said. "We won't have any trouble."

"Those fire bombs worry me," Todd said. "There are so many things that can go wrong with them."

"Not really," I replied. "As long as the arming wires are secured."

"How many bombs do we have?" he asked.

"Thirty-seven 500-pound clusters."

"I never did understand how they work," one of the gunners said.

"Quite simple in operation," I said. "Each cluster has 38 individual fire bombs, weighing six pounds apiece. There's a time fuse in the nose of each cluster that works on the principle of the actual time of fall of the bomb. You set a clocklike mechanism on the fuse so that the prima cord will explode and break open the cluster 5,000 feet above the target. The smaller bombs tumble down and explode on contact and spread the fire jelly in all directions."

"I've heard of some crews having had trouble with the clusters," Todd said.

"The clusters are dangerous to use," I said. "Don't get me wrong. I'm not minimizing the danger. That's why I spend so much time before a mission checking each bomb and each fuse. Some of the bombardiers take the cotter pins out of the fuses before a mission. I leave mine in until we get past Iwo. It's not fun crawling in the bomb bay removing pins in the air, but it's a lot safer than on take-off."

"Can you really set those fuses accurately?" a crewmember asked me.

"They function expertly. As I said before, the only real danger in the air is if the arming wire, which holds the vane in place, is pulled out. An explosion might result in the bomb bay if the vane spins off."

"Has that ever happened?" one of the men asked, bug-eyed.

"No," I said with a grin. "One of the bombardiers added a few gray hairs when one of the fuses started to tick in the bomb bay."

"Why didn't the bombs go off?" Todd asked.

"It couldn't as long as the arming wire was in place. Still, the mechanism should not have ticked off the seconds and he feared the worse. Aren't we about ready for take-off?"

"We're number 12," Todd said.

"How's the beast. Is she ready to go?"

"I hope so. I'm worried about number-two engine. The prop governor isn't working properly. They are checking it now."

The first planes of the wing were taking off and we watched them as they rolled down the long runway, their lights poking at the blackness ahead of them, and at last searching eagerly for the sky east of the island.

"Lieutenant Todd!" the crew chief called.

"Yes."

"We'll have to install a new prop governor."

"How long will that take?"

"Not long."

"We won't be able to take off on time," Todd said ruefully.

"Oh my God! Look!" a gunner cried.

I jumped nervously at the sound of his fright filled voice.

"Look up there," he said in a hoarse whisper.

"It's on fire!" Todd said.

High above us in the night sky a B-29 poured long streams of fire from its number-four engine. We watched in horrified silence as the fire flared out, died down, and flared again.

"He's got another extinguisher," Todd said in a choked voice. "I don't think it's going to do any good. That fire has too much headway."

The fire gained in intensity so we knew the CO_2 had failed to put it out. The plane swung in wide circles and we watched parachutes blossom out below. The plane constantly lost altitude until it circled in tight sweeps, ever lower, toward the ground.

"Whoever is piloting that plane sure has guts," I said. "He's been getting lower and lower and fighting it all the way down to give his crew a chance to get out. I've counted 10 chutes. Hope the pilot makes it."

The aircraft hit the ground with a tremendous explosion. Flames shot high into the night sky and silhouetted our taut faces.

"I guess he didn't make it," I said.

"I'm going to call the tower and find out who it was," Todd said.

He went into the cockpit and called while we waited dispiritedly.

"Who was it?" Lieutenant Marvin H. McAdams, our navigator asked.

"Albert Abronovic," Todd said. "And he got out just in time. They told me he stayed with the plane until all were out and then, with only a few hundred feet left, he bailed out."

"That's what I call guts in any man's language," I said emphatically.

"Aren't we ready to go Ralph?" McAdams asked.

"Not yet. Say! What's that?"

A flash of light and a dull roar split the sky followed by thick black clouds.

"There goes another one," I said tensely. "A B-29 must have crashed at the end of the runway at North Field."

"How are you coming with that prop governor?" Todd yelled to the crew chief.

"It won't be long. We're about done."

"I can't stand much more of this waiting," I said. "I'm getting the jitters."

"You're not the only one," Todd said.

"Oh no! Not another one!" McAdams cried.

My heart seemed to stop beating and my expression froze into grim rigidity. I looked down to the end of our runway and saw many small fires spreading beyond the end of the strip of coral. My whole body trembled with horror.

"The plane got off alright," Todd explained. "They lost an engine right after take-off and jettisoned their bombs."

"One more incident and I'm taking off for the hills," I said. "My nerves are shot to pieces."

Another half hour passed while we paced back and forth restlessly. Two planes had landed, each with a feathered engine.

"I don't like it," I said to McAdams. "This is one of those nights when everything goes wrong."

"Board up!" Todd yelled.

I breathed a sigh of relief and headed for the nose compartment.

"Here's hoping ...," Ralph said.

After take-off we relaxed and our nervousness began to abate. The dull, tiresome monotony of flying hour after hour took its place. Iwo appeared ahead of us, alight with thousands of tiny lights in the living quarters and on the runway.

"I'm going back and take the pins out of the fuses," I said to Todd. "Don't bounce me around too much. With all those bombs there's little enough room as it is."

I crawled into the bomb bays, checked the fuses and removed the pins. They seemed in order. I took a last look around before leaving and came back to the nose compartment satisfied there would be no malfunctioning bombs.

We had taken off about 10 o'clock at night. Thinking it over I realized we were in the unenviable position of bombing Nagoya in daylight, all by ourselves, at only 8,000 feet.

I called the navigator, "Mac, I've been figuring our approximate time over the target. It seems to me we'll hit the coast of Japan in daylight."

"You're right. We took off too late, there's no doubt but that we'll be over Japan after the sun rises. Some fun, huh?"

"I am not amused," I said tightly. "After all the other B-29s get over the city and start fires they'll be hopping mad and pounce on any late stragglers."

We reached the coast of Japan just as the darkness began to fade away and the first light shades of dawn appeared.

"There's a complete cloud cover over the mainland," I called to the radar operator.

"I'll set up a radar run," he said.

Todd headed towards the city and we apprehensively scanned the sky for enemy fighters.

"I don't get it," I called to Todd. "There isn't a plane visible. We are completely alone."

"This is too good to last," he said. "Keep a sharp lookout."

We turned on the IP and headed for the southern part of the city as it showed up on the radarscope. The dock area was our aiming point. As we neared the bomb release line, a few bursts of flak appeared but it was widely scattered. Thirty seconds to go and then we would high-tail it for home. Unexpectedly, a large hole appeared in the clouds and I could see the dock area of the city.

"I've got it," I called to the radar operator.

Our track was bringing us too far to the right so I made a 40-degree correction, which was barely completed when the bombs started to drop.

When the bays were empty I leaned over the sight and looked down through a hole in the clouds at the raging fires below. It was an awesome picture of burning homes, warehouses, and factories. It was like looking through the keyhole of the gates of hell. All over the lower half of the city, bright red flames ate their voracious way through the great metropolis of Nagoya. There seemed to be nothing left standing in the lower part of the huge city. I had a sickening feeling in the pit of my stomach. All the horrible awfulness of a tremendous conflagration roared unchecked through the city.

"Fighter at three o'clock!" the right gunner called.

A solitary fighter gave us a cursory glance and then took off in the opposite direction. We headed back.

Major Fawcett, the group intelligence officer, approached me in the briefing room. "How did it look?" he asked.

"It was awful," I said in a hoarse voice still choked by emotion. "You can't imagine anything like it."

"Would you say the city was destroyed?"

"It's completely burned out. There's nothing left."

He raised his eyebrows. I noted the doubt in his eyes. "How about the Mitsubishi Aircraft Plant?"

"It was burning from one end to the other."

"Are you sure? I'm going to send in a report to headquarters on your observations. You were last over the city. I don't like to make a report like this unless you're absolutely sure."

"I'm positive about it, Joe. I tell you I saw it with my own eyes."

Nagoya was not completely destroyed, nor was the Mitsubishi Aircraft Plant. However, 3.81 square miles of the city were burned out and half of the Mitsubishi plant, the largest in the world, was destroyed. This all added up to better than nine square miles of Nagoya that was gutted.

Fawcett mildly chastised me later. "How could you have been so wrong about your observations?"

"I don't know Joe. Its' proof again that a combat crewmember's observations can't be completely relied upon. A plane is over a target such a short time that it's impossible to accurately assess damage."

May 19 was the date we participated in a raid on Hamamatsu, dropping hundreds of tons of demolition bombs on the heart of the city.

As Joe Buchta and I headed for operations May 23, he asked me, "What's the target tomorrow?"

"Tokyo," I said in a lifeless tone.

"Whew!" Joe said. "That'll be a tough one."

"LeMay wants four missions in succession to burn down Tokyo. He says it must be completely destroyed."

The first mission bombed Tokyo in the early morning hours of May 24. Five hundred and twenty B-29s dropped 3,700 tons of firebombs while they braved the withering fire of a thousand heavy guns, scores of searchlights, night fighters, and Japan's latest suicide craft — the Baka.

The protective darkness disappeared as brilliant beams of light roamed the skies on the night of May 26, when Captain Bruce Whitfield's plane passed over the coast of Japan at 8,400 feet and headed for its initial point at Mount Fujiyama en route to strike Tokyo in the second all-out fire raid.

Then the searchlights focused on them with blinding intensity. Whitfield's voice was tense but under control as he turned to his co-pilot, Lieutenant Ned Payne. "Radar controlled," he said, pointing at the searchlight beams, as his plane headed inland. When they passed out of range of one battery of lights, another took over, and Whitfield knew that they were in for it. Now Japanese fighters could more easily follow their path in the sky. Meanwhile, anti-aircraft fire concentrated on their plane. It was heavy at first, and then it ceased. "This is it," Whitfield told the crew. "Prepare for fighters." They continued on, one of a long stream of Superfortresses flying in trail with B-29s ahead and behind them.

Unknown to Whitfield's crew, Captain Richard S. DeWitt's B-29 was behind and slightly above Whitfield's level. His plane was not visible because it was out of the lights.

The intercom crackled and Sergeant William Doakes, the tail gunner, warned the crew. "Sixteen Jap fighters at 6 o'clock high." The searchlights outlined them against the sky as they roared in and the Superfort's turrets filled the cabin with the acrid smell of gunpowder. Doakes, a Cheyenne Indian, who had been a rodeo rider before the war, aimed his guns carefully as each fighter swept in. Three or four fighters broke away without hitting the B-29 but more followed as Sergeant Wendell W. Sheffield, at central fire control, brought the two top turrets to bear on the attacking fighters. The attackers were persistent, coming in close in desperate attempts to knock down their Superfortress.

Whitfield glanced at his co-pilot with dismay as the tail gunner reported. "Captain, I'm out of ammunition, but I'm chewing tobacco and if one of those guys gets close enough I'll shoot him down with a squirt of tobacco juice."

DeWitt, still above and behind, and out of the searchlights ordered his crew to come to Whitfield's assistance. The fighters were caught by surprise at this rear attack and DeWitt's gunners claimed that they shot down a couple.

Now, one after another of Whitfield's gunners reported they were out of ammunition with only a few rounds remaining in the lower turrets. And, they still hadn't reached their initial point! Whitfield breathed a momentary sigh of relief when he spotted Fujiyama ahead of them. He turned quickly to the right. Ahead he could see the bright glow of hundreds of fires in Tokyo. They seemed to erupt continually and then spread throughout large sections of the city. They finally merged into one large mass of flames capped by massive smoke clouds filled with debris boiling up from the ground in the superheated air above the city.

Whitfield called, "Pilot to crew. I want everybody to adjust your safety belts as tight as you can because I feel sure I can fly through these smoke clouds, although we've been warned not to."[1] It's our only chance because we're out of ammunition — and these guys out there know that — they are going to meet us on the other side and we're not going to have a prayer of surviving. Our only chance is to fly through the smoke clouds."

After they dropped their bombs, Whitfield turned his B-29 deliberately into the huge smoke clouds above the city, rearing threateningly like giant anvils. He was momentarily disconcerted when the B-29 began to act like a runaway express elevator. It was hurled upward with the altimeter needle windup up so fast that he could barely read it. After peaking out, Whitfield fought the controls as the Superfortress tipped up on its left wing. He cranked the controls far over in the opposite direction to level the

---

[1] Prior to the mission, all crews were warned never to fly though these smoke clouds because experience had demonstrated it was almost impossible to survive the tremendous thermal effects.

plane. Instead, it tipped over to the right, sliding into a vertical position. He pulled back on the throttles for numbers three and four engines and advanced one and two throttles to offset this new condition. He knew that if the plane flipped over on its back, it would not recover. In the midst of this boiling air mass, sweat poured off them because the cabin was like a cauldron. Now the B-29 alternately tipped from one side to another; first the right wing went down, and then the left. The altimeter needle seemed to go crazy, whirling madly in one direction, and then reversing itself. On downdrafts the airplane was buffeted as violently as on the updrafts. Incredibly, they went through four smoke clouds, although they seemed to be one huge smoke cloud, as Whitfield fought to keep the airplane from hurling itself into the ground. When it dropped thousands of feet in seconds, the airplane shuddered sickeningly, and for a time they feared it would tear itself apart. Whitfield's feet beat a nervous tattoo on the rudder panels, but his mind remained alert and instinctively he did everything correctly.

During the terrifying drop Whitfield noted that the B-29 bottomed out at 2,400 feet. Another time they broke out of the smoke and found themselves at 32,000 feet. A gunner called. "Six Jap fighters circling to our left."

Whitfield glanced that way, noting they were far below them, highlighted by their own searchlights.

Whitfield called to his navigator, John Mack. "Give me a course to the bay." To his engineer, he said, "Give me full rpm."

He shoved the nose down at a 35-degree angle and pushed the throttles almost to their stops. He nervously reminded himself that his Superfort redlined at 300 miles an hour; and indicated airspeed that must never be exceeded. The air speed indicators touched 300 and quick went to 352 mph. He pulled back the throttles to keep the air speed four or five miles and hour below 300.

They roared across the middle of Tokyo Bay, ships below firing constantly at them, but the Japanese fighters were left far behind. Now Whitfield felt sure that they were safe. He slowly throttled back the engines to a normal 200 mph as he leveled off outside of the bay.

He marveled that the Superfortress had held together in its mad plunge and decided it would be wise to land at Iwo Jima because he was fearful it had suffered serious structural damage.

After landing at Iwo Jima the crew inspected their scorched B-29. It had a few holes in it, but none were in vital areas. Whitfield decided to spend the night there to give the ground crew a chance to go over the structure more thoroughly.

They were assigned to two tents near the airplane and Whitfield gathered his crew in his tent. Although it was "against regulations" he always carried two bottles of liquor on a mission, so each member of the crew could have a drink or two after they landed. This time, following their wild ride of Tokyo, and their close encounter with death, they finished the bottles.

Whitfield told his crew, "There had to be a 12th person up there with us, and watching over us. The good Lord had to be with us, or we would not have survived."

There were nods of agreement from all present.

While they prepared for take-off the next day, Whitfield watched F-51 fighters land at Iwo Jima after their long flights from Japan during a daylight mission. They had returned after providing protection for another bombing strike. He was shocked to see ambulances heading out to each fighter, assuming that all the pilots had been wounded because none had exited his cockpit. With mounting concern he watched as each pilot was lifted out of his cockpit. He learned later that none had been injured but that the pilots were so stiff and sore after five or six hours in their cramped cockpits that they couldn't get out on their own and had to be assisted. Unable to walk, they were placed on litters and taken away in ambulances.

The first fire raid against Tokyo had caused considerable damage, but it was nothing compared to the second raid on the 26th.

This time 564 B-29s were over the city. All returning crewmembers were shaken and appalled by what they had seen. The night sky above Tokyo had been a maelstrom of bursting flak, the red ball of fire denoting the paths of the Baka and the suicide dives of the night fighters. The latter had tried desperately to beat off the waves of Superfortresses that were pouring liquid fire on their capital.

The city became a sea of flames as the strike progressed. Small fires started by each B-29 were whirled into a raging inferno by surface winds that reached hurricane velocity. Here and there a Superfortress was hit and crashed into the city. That night over Tokyo was one that the crewmembers would never forget. I had planned to go on the third mission so I had not made either of the first two. The preparations and briefings for the missions had kept me hopping, and my mission reports had to be completed eight hours after the last plane landed.

The bombardiers reported to me for interrogation after the second mission. It was evident that the experience had shaken them to the core. They were pale, sunken-eyed, with hands that visibly shook as they handed me their reports.

"Don't you wish you had been along?" Lieutenant Joseph E. Flaherty asked with a tired grin.

"If it was as bad as you guys say, I'm content to hear about it second hand."

"Are we going back to Tokyo?" he asked anxiously.

"I'm afraid so."

Another Tokyo mission was not necessary because the first two had accomplished the astounding job of burning out 22.1 square miles of the city.

That night as I relaxed with Joe and Murph in our tent, I told them about the raid. "The destruction was appalling. It makes me sick to look at the pictures."

"How much of the city is destroyed?" Joe asked soberly.

"Fifty-one percent of the total area is burned out. That does not tell the whole story because the total area includes the fringes of the city that are sparsely populated. For all practical purposes Tokyo has ceased to exist."

Whole neighborhoods had been incinerated in Tokyo. We learned later that four million people had fled the city, although three million remained throughout the raids.

At least 300,000 of these people were homeless. Large animals in the city's zoos were put to death so they couldn't run wild in the streets if they got free.

"It cost our group two experimental crews," Joe said.

"Who went down?" I asked.

I was shocked to learn that Major William H. Ellerbe and Lieutenant Seldon G. Mouser and their crews were among the 26 B-29s that had gone down. They were two of our oldest crews and reports indicated they had crashed in the city. "That makes 43 B-29s lost on the Tokyo missions," Buchta reminded me.

"Why don't they give up?" I cried. "Surely by now they must have realized that the war is lost. There won't be anything left of Japan if this keeps up for another six months."

"LeMay and Kalberer were right," Joe said. "I didn't believe them at the time but I'm beginning to think the Japanese will quit by October 1, if not before."

"It's a horrible thing to do to a nation," I said quietly. "But they started it and they can stop it any time they want to."

Tokyo was removed from LeMay's target list, but he was so concerned by the night losses over Tokyo that he scheduled the next mission on May 29 to Yokohama in daytime, and sought fighter support from the VII Fighter Command on Iwo Jima.

After the Tokyo missions we felt more confident about the possibility of an early end to the war. It was evident, even to the most pessimistic, that if we could keep up our fire raids against Japanese cities, plus occasional daylight attacks against industrial plants when weather permitted, that no nation could stand the pressure. Japan's squeals of fright and anger had a different ring to them now. She was a cornered nation, fighting for her very existence. We had her right where we wanted her and the pressure increased instead of letting up.

When we got word about the Yokohama mission, I told Vaucher, "I've got to go on this one."

"You've got too much work," Vaucher said stubbornly. "You're a staff officer, not a combat crew member."

"I want to go," I said. "Besides Bruce Whitfield needs a bombardier. Several crews are bombardiers."

Buchta asked, "Where's it going to?"

"Yokohama," Vaucher said.

"We're using Fujiyama as an IP," I said. "What a sight that will be."

"All right," Vaucher said. "If you are determined to go. Get one of the squadron bombardiers to do the interrogation when the crews return."

"This is going to be quite a mission," I told Buchta. "I've been studying the target charts. Look here," I said, pointing to the mosaic. "It's perfect for a high-altitude daylight mission."

"I'd say it will present quite a bombing problem," Joe said.

"It will. We're using 12 plane formations and dropping thermite clusters. The city is more modern than others in Japan so we're using thermite. It generates tremendous heat and is the only kind of firebomb than can be used against heavy installations or well built up areas. Yokohama is quite a seaport and the northern part of the city rests on Tokyo Bay."

"You'll get a good look at Tokyo," Joe said.

"We'll swing to the right after the bombs are dropped to miss it. I won't relish those hundreds of heavy guns. I imagine, though, that the defenses of Yokohama are good."

Bruce Whitfield swung our B-29 in wide circles above several small Japanese-held islands as we joined our formation. The coast of Honshu could be seen clearly as we headed in. Hundreds of B-29s in loose formation were ahead and behind us.

"The Japs are in for it today," I said to Whit. "I never thought I'd see so many B-29s on one mission. This is what the strategists mean when they speak about air power."

"We're going to have fighter cover from Iwo," Bruce said.

"I don't think it's going to be too bad," I said optimistically. "The Japs would have to throw up a thousand fighters to give us any trouble. I don't think they have them to spare. There's Fujiyama," I cried.

I gazed in wonder at this famous volcanic mountain. It rose before us and glistened in the bright morning sun. There was a ring of white above the snow line. Below the snow the contrast was striking as a beautiful greenness covered the slopes. It was impressive and magnificent.

"Take a look at Fuji," I called to navigator Johnny Mack.

"I've seen it before. Beautiful, isn't it?"

The formation turned and we rode above the snow-filled crater. I looked directly into it and forgot everything else. "What an inspiring sight," I said with awe.

"Will, look dead ahead," Bruce said. "There's quite a sight. The Japanese flak was so thick that I believe we could get out and walk on it if we had to."

The flak was frightening to behold. The sky was black with puffs as the formations ahead bored through to the target.

"Fighters at three o'clock!" cried the right gunner.

I was shocked back to reality and grabbed my gun sight.

A quick glance to the right revealed three fighters. After closer inspection I could see two P-51's hot on the tail of a Jap. I warned the crew not to fire for fear of hitting our own fighters.

"The sons of Nippon are not having it so good today," I said with a smile.

"I don't know how these fighters flew through the bad weather from Iwo," Bruce said. "I wouldn't want to do it."

The flak was thick and wicked looking as it reached us. The life-raft packs were pressed against the seats in our anxiety. I took fleeting glimpses of the city below and ahead of us and could see fires beginning to break out along the streets of the long, narrow city. I released my bombs and we made a gradual turn to the right over Tokyo Bay. There was a pall of smoke over Tokyo and I could see very little evidence of the two-day blitz of that city several days before. The city of Yokohama, as I looked back, was burning vigorously, and the fires were spreading, aided by a strong wind off the bay.

Back over the Pacific one of the gunners called, "We've got a P-51 with us."

"We're supposed to navigate for them," Bruce said. "He'll stay with us to Iwo. I'll see if I can get him on the radio."

"Big brother from little brother. Can't you get more speed out of that tub? I can't fly 200 miles an hour all the way to Iwo."

"Sorry, little brother," Bruce replied. "That's the best we can do."

"Suppose I get in back and push, big brother? Will that help?"

"I'm afraid not," Bruce said, with a chuckle.

The fighter snuggled under our right wing and we waved back and forth.

The P-51s had served us well because 150 Japanese fighters had tried to attack our B-29 formations but were unable to break through because of the Mustangs.

After the mission I filed my report and dragged myself down to my tent. I was completely exhausted and ready to turn in.

"Is the city destroyed?" Murph asked.

I dropped down on my cot and stretched out. "I saw the final report. It's fantastic and horrible what 450 B-29s can do. Eighty percent of the city has been gutted."

"That much?" Murph said with surprise. "There can't be much left of Yokohama."

"There isn't. Almost seven square miles of it has been destroyed. About all that's left standing are the outer fringes. Why can't the Japanese see that it's hopeless to continue? Even part of Kawasaki caught the fury of our firebombs and a good part of it is in ruins. No nation has ever been so completely blitzed as Japan. And the horrible thing about it is that every day the war continues, the more we destroy. It's senseless for the Japanese to hope for victory at this late date."

"I'll bet they really don't believe they'll win anymore," Goddard said.

"Reports are coming out of Japan that they would like to quit if they could get terms."

"They won't get them," Murph said.

"No," I said with a sigh. "It's unconditional surrender or more war."

This had been an incredible month of accomplishment but the command lost 88 B-29s — its highest monthly total. May proved to be the 20th Air Force's worst month for losses.

I was waiting for Joe to go to the briefing room on June 4 and reading reports of the last few days. Osaka had taken a terrible drumming on June 1, with the warehouse area near the harbor bearing the brunt of the attack. Three square miles of the city had been leveled.

"Let's go," Joe said.

"I'm glad I'm not going to Kobe today," I said.

"The bad feature about Kobe and Osaka is there's only one approach and that's right up the bay. The formations catch it from all sides. It's bad enough to go in at 20,000 feet but wait until the crews learn the bombing altitude for this mission."

Osaka was at the head of the bay and Kobe sprawled along its south side. It was a hot corner, as I knew from personal experience.

"The Seabees have been invited to attend the briefing," Joe said.

"They've done such a fine job for us, I'm glad they have been given a chance to hear how we do things."

Buchta ascended the platform to give the navigation briefing and looked down upon the serious, upturned faces of the crewmembers. "Take-off time is 3 A.M. tomorrow," he began. "Kobe is your target. Here's your assembly point." He pointed to a bay near Shikoku on the large map. "Your bombing altitude is 15,000 feet."

A roar of protest broke out and Joe stood there, saying nothing, until it subsided.

"That's suicide," someone yelled.

"That's one of the hottest targets in Japan," another said angrily.

"I know," Joe said. "But there's an overcast at 17,000 feet and the bombing altitude had to be set below it."

Vaucher, now a Lieutenant Colonel, as well as the group's operations officer, tried to quell the protesters, reminding them that he was going along as 58th Wing Commander. "I didn't set the altitude. LeMay did. As flight commander I have no authority to cancel the mission. When I hear from weather planes en route, I'll determine the actual bombing altitude."

Whitfield's crew was assigned to the Kobe mission on June 5 and they were all disturbed by the bombing altitude, so it was a sober looking crew that met at their airplane after the briefing.

Whitfield inspected his aircraft with the crew chief, Master Sergeant Jack A. Smith, and everything looked fine. He thanked him and walked over to the wheel well, which provided entrance to the cockpit. Of medium stature, Whitfield had to jump up a foot to reach the first rung of the ladder to haul himself into the forward section. This had never been a problem but this time he could not seem to reach it despite his best efforts. He tried again and again, getting more red in the face, but there seemed to be no strength in his body.

Smith hurried over, deep concern in his eyes. "Captain, are you okay?"

"Yeah, Jack. I'm just tired. If you'd give me a hand so I can reach that first rung, I'd appreciate it."

Smith hoisted him up and Whitfield settled in the left hand pilot's seat with a deep sigh.

Before the engines were started, Smith called to Whitfield who was leaning out of his window. "Are you sure you're all right, Captain?"

Whitfield waved, "I'm fine."

He knew he was not. He felt rung out, but he had a mission to fly with 10 men counting on him. As he went through the routine checklist, his momentary concern about his condition faded away.

The concern that crews expressed at the briefing proved valid. Eleven Superfortresses were lost. One formation had a particularly rough time and lost two of its 12 planes over the target. One of those shot down was flown by Major Carl T. "Shorty" Hull, who had already completed his 35th mission and was grounded until LeMay made a decision about increasing the number of combat missions to complete a tour. He had begged to go on the mission, but Vaucher had refused. Hull was persistent, however, saying they would all have to fly more than 35 missions and he might as well keep flying. Vaucher finally relented and he was assigned as deputy leader of a formation.

We did not learn until after the war that eight of Hull's crew bailed out and landed close to a military compound. They were taken before the ground commander who immediately held a court martial and sentenced them to death the same day for their so-called war crimes. Hull and the others were taken outside and beheaded.

Vaucher was heartsick about Hull's loss because LeMay later set the number of missions at 35 to complete a tour and "Shorty" Hull need not have flown his 36th mission.

But the mission objective was achieved. Several square miles of Kobe were burned and the city was chalked off the list.

Iwo Jima proved a godsend for crews on this mission as hundreds of B-29s radioed for emergency landings and the control tower was so swamped it could not help every one. Some planes were in such bad shape — like the one Vaucher was in — that they had to land immediately or ditch. Planes broke into the pattern and landed against instructions. They could not help it. Several crews bailed out over the island and their planes crashed into the sea.

As the gathering darkness settled over our tent that night and we lay exhausted on our cots, I could see the beginning of the end. "Japan is doomed," I said. "After this destructive month — long blitz of her principal cities it is more apparent she stands no chance of winning or even stopping our steady march to victory. Damage assessment reports only approximate the havoc. Can you imagine the suffering and deprivation that millions of Japanese are enduring?"

"The morale of the Japanese people must be at a low ebb," Joe admitted.

"I don't see how it can be otherwise," I said. "I can't understand one thing. We have orders not to bomb Nagasaki, Hiroshima, and Kyoto. I wonder why?"

"Kyoto is a sacred city," Goddard said.

"That may explain why we are leaving Kyoto alone. Why don't we attack Hiroshima and Nagasaki? Those are the only large cities left."

"What's the new plan Vaucher mentioned today?" Joe asked.

"The planners on Guam are lining up all cities of 100,000 population. Each will be destroyed in turn," I said.

"Are they going to be night attacks?" Joe asked.

"Yes, when the weather is good over Japan, we'll go on high-altitude, daylight precision strikes against the airplane factories, aircraft engine plants, and arsenals."

"Why are they trying to destroy all the cities?" Goddard said. "I would think it would make the Japs that much madder and more inclined to fight to the bitter end."

"The idea is not just to destroy cities for the sake of destruction," I said. "You see, Japan is a combination of backwardness and modern ingenuity. Actually much of her war machine is manufactured in tiny shops in the homes of the people. This is total war. Japan could fight on even though her factories were destroyed because of this home industry. It's a brutal business, but there seems to be no other way than to invade her home islands. A ground invasion would be terribly costly. I hear estimates that we would suffer a million casualties among ground troops in a land invasion of the main islands."

"It's sickening to burn out their cities," Joe said.

"I agree, but the pressure must be steady and constant until the Japanese can't take it any more and sue for peace. It's cruel, inhumane work, but they went to war against us and now must pay the penalty. The lives of hundreds of thousands of our troops will be saved if we succeed. It's well worth the attempt."

Chapter 14

When Is This War Going to Be Over?

Despite his misgivings, Bruce Whitfield completed the mission to Kobe without incident, and the following day he was called into Colonel Kalberer's office. The group commander told him that he needed a pilot to fly a B-24 to Hawaii to pick up some parts, and also to get several cases of liquor for the new non-commissioned officers club. "You've been checked out on the B-24 so I've assigned you to the job. You'll be gone for 10 days, and I'll see that it does not reduce your terminal leave."

Whitfield was surprised. He suspected that someone had reported that he needed a rest from combat operations. Regardless of the reason, he eagerly agreed to go.

The crew enjoyed their days in Hawaii and then headed back. Whitfield decided to by-pass Kwajalein — their regular stop — and land at a nearby island where a friend from his hometown was assigned. He figured he had an extra day and he did not want to return early.

He never did locate his friend and they returned to Tinian. On the ramp Whitfield noticed a jeep coming towards their plane with a general's flag. He called his crew to attention as the jeep drew up. It was Wing Commander Brigadier General Roger Ramey. He strode up to Whitfield and said, "Captain, do you realize that you have cost the United States Government at least $430,000 by your late arrival?"

"Late, sir?"

"That's right. You're a day late, and when you did not report at Kwajalein, we've had the Air Force and Navy searching the Central Pacific for you."

After Ramey explained, Whitfield realized that he had completely forgotten about the International Date Line and his westward return flight had added a day's time to his trip. He admitted his error. Ramey said he could not let him get off without some kind of punishment.

The B-24's cargo was plainly visible to Ramey with the bomb bay doors up and he obviously could see the cases of liquor, two of which Whitfield had purchased with his own money for himself and his crew — one of scotch and the other of bourbon.

Ramey said he wanted to think about a suitable punishment for Whitfield, saying he was aware of his outstanding record. "I'm going to go through your airplane," he told Whitfield, "starting in the cockpit, while I decide what punishment to order." He walked away.

Whitfield knew Ramey liked scotch so he quickly signaled to one of his men. "Take my case of scotch and put it in the general's jeep. Quick now, before he returns."

This was accomplished and when the general came back to confront Whitfield, he noted the case on the rear seat of the jeep. "Well, Captain," he said. "I've decided to confine you to the base for a couple of days as punishment. Of course, you'll have to fly a mission if it occurs during that time."

"Yes sir," Whitfield said. "Thank you, sir." There was no place to go on Tinian so confinement was a nothing punishment.

Five years after the war Whitfield was in San Francisco and noticed Ramey and his staff get on the elevator he was riding. It was crowded as he rode to the lobby with them. Ramey, surrounded by his officers, started to move away. He spotted Whitfield, and came over with a grin. "I know you!"

"I remember you, sir. I'm...."

"Don't tell me." Then his eyes lit up. "You're Captain ... Scotch."

"General, that's close enough," Whitfield grinned. "It's good to see you again."

General Arnold visited LeMay on June 6 at Guam. His first words were, "I've been following your operations closely. You're doing a great job."

LeMay was pleased and waved Arnold to a seat. "Thank you, sir."

Arnold came right to the point. "We must capitalize on the present critical situation in Japan."

"That's why we're concentrating on urban areas. I've just scratched Nagoya off our list — along with the city of Kobe — except for a few precision targets that must await clear weather. The command has recently burned out 12 square miles of Nagoya, and most of its industry is either damaged or destroyed."

Arnold's eyebrows rose with surprise. He looked inquisitively at LeMay. "As you know, I'm touring the Pacific bases. George Marshall wanted me to get out of Washington after my heart attack. He thought it might improve my health. Out here, where the action is, I feel better already." He laughed and his humor was infectious, bringing a smile to LeMay's face. "I didn't realize you were this far along in your campaign. I've sort of been out of touch with things lately."

LeMay nodded. "We could do more if we could get an increase in new crews. I've made a number of requests...."

"I know, we can't seem to train new B-29 crews fast enough in the States. I foresee no early change in that situation."

LeMay pressed his case. "I'll take B-17 and B-24 crews and complete their training out here, if that would expedite matters."

"A good point. I'll see what I can do when I return to Washington." He changed the subject. "Your decision to drastically reduce bombing altitudes appears to be paying off. How are your losses?"

"Our losses since March 24 are minimal, considering the extent of our operations. The B-29 loss rate due to all causes, and not just to Japanese defenses, is 1.3 percent. Of late, Japan's defenses have stiffened and losses have gone up. But they still are within the tolerance level. May was our worst month with 88 B-29s lost but we flew more than 3,000 sorties against the most heavily defended targets."

Arnold was pleased by the news, and somewhat surprised. "Is that right? I had heard otherwise."

LeMay smiled slightly. "Those who resisted my decision, claiming that losses would be prohibitive, have been effectively silenced by the actual figures."

"What about the next few months?"

"I've approved what I call the 'Empire Plan.' It goes into effect June 9 — three days from now. It will govern operations until the war's end."

"Are you changing the tactical doctrine?"

"Not at all," LeMay replied. "During clear days we'll attack the aircraft industry. When weather is bad, and radar runs are necessary, we'll drop incendiary bombs at night on urban areas. It is no longer necessary to send a maximum effort to one target so I'm dividing the command to hit separate targets."

"I'd appreciate a thorough briefing before I leave."

"How about right now?" LeMay said. "I have Colonel Montgomery standing by."

Arnold nodded his acquiescence. "I'll be returning to Washington soon and I want to give the Joint Chiefs a briefing about your activities. I don't believe they fully appreciate what you are doing out here."

LeMay picked up his telephone. "Ask Colonel Montgomery to join us."

Montgomery walked in and looked inquiringly at LeMay.

LeMay said to Arnold, "You remember Monty, don't you?"

"Of course. Good to see you Monty. I haven't seen you since our Langley Field days." He pointed to the roll of butcher paper Monty was carrying. "What do you have there?"

"That's my 'flip board,'" Montgomery said. "For want of anything better, we use butcher paper for graphs and diagrams." He set it up on the map easel.

Arnold walked over and studied the charts. "I'm impressed. Particularly by your loss rate. The doomsayers can't argue with those figures." He turned to LeMay. "I talked to Nimitz this morning. He agreed to my suggestion that a strategic air command headquarters be established on Guam. I'm recommending 'Tooey' Spaatz to command it now that the European war has ended. I'm sure you know him."

"Not well," LeMay said. "But I had some contact with him in England. You can't do better than General Spaatz."

Arnold looked approvingly at LeMay. "Nimitz speaks highly of you. You evidently have established a good relationship with him. He says he doesn't always agree with your operations, but that's par for the course with the Navy." He chuckled. "He says the few problems that have developed were magnified out of all proportion by junior officers on both sides. He has promised to talk to his own people about common problems, and I suggest you do likewise with your staff. We'll get nowhere perpetuating the old rivalry with the Navy. Ernie King has been most supportive of me in Washington."

"Nimitz is a grand old man," LeMay said. "I like him."

"Old?" Arnold said. "Nimitz is 60. I'm a year older, and I don't consider myself old."

LeMay spoke quickly to rectify his error. "Just a figure of speech, sir."

Arnold roared with laughter. "That's all right, LeMay. You young fellows are all alike. Anyone past 50 has one foot in the grave." A thought occurred to him. "I met MacArthur in Manila. He's against setting up a strategic air command out here, saying it would be a mistake, particularly in Tooey's hands. They have fought for years. He said he would not object if I kept command with Barney Giles as my deputy, but he's dead set against Spaatz. I tried to explain our plans for destroying Japanese cities and industrial targets, but he didn't understand. He's no different than he ever was. I've fought his outmoded ideas of airpower all my life. He concedes that bombing will be helpful in winning the war, but primarily in support of his ground troops. He says the doughboys will have to march on Tokyo."

"He's wrong!" LeMay said forcefully. "He doesn't understand. I tried to teach General Stilwell the facts of life about airpower in China, but he didn't understand either, what I was talking about."

"They both have closed minds," Arnold said. "We'll just have to prove our theories. You've got a good start."

"They are too rigid in their thinking," LeMay said.

"They don't want to understand," Arnold said. "It would upset all their cherished ideas that only the Army can win wars. I've fought this theory since World War I." He shook his head in exasperation. "MacArthur was surprised at the size of the B-29 effort." There was a touch of bitterness in his voice. "I've never understood the man, and I've known him for years. He is incapable of understanding our plans to reduce Japan to impotence through air power. Oh, hell, he'll never change." He paused. "I'm asking this question of everyone I see out here. When is this war going to be over?"

"We've been too busy fighting to figure out a date," LeMay replied, "but if you will give me a few minutes I'll provide an estimate." Arnold nodded. LeMay turned to Montgomery. "Find out when we're going to run out of industrial areas as targets." Montgomery hurried out of the office as LeMay turned back to Arnold. "In the past, when the concentration was on visual bombing, planes had to be assembled, fueled, bombed up, crews briefed, and then they all had to wait until the weather was clear for bombing. Sometimes that took days. Now that the command is trained for radar bombing, once we're ready we take off regardless of the weather because we can hit industrial areas without seeing them."

Arnold nodded. "I'm sending General Marshall a message that I will support the November 1 invasion of Kyushu and I've requested bases for 40 more groups of heavy bombers. I'm also recommending an all-out bombing offensive to complete Japan's destruction. I'm still convinced that your command will force Japan to surrender without an invasion, but there is too much opposition in the other services to support such a theory. They just don't believe me."

LeMay spoke with assurance. "Japan will quit before the invasion."

"I agree," Arnold said. "But we are alone in our conviction. That's why I'm telling Marshall to stress to the Joint Chiefs that emphasis should be placed on a continued strategic air offensive with a naval and air blockade. The air war should be stepped up so that conditions will be favorable for the invasion with a minimum loss of life. I estimate that it will take a million and a half tons of bombs to destroy Japan's industry and to paralyze her economic life."

"Sir, that figure is much too high," LeMay protested. "I doubt it will take a tenth of that tonnage to bring Japan to the point of surrender."

Arnold's eyebrows rose expressively. "Oh, come now, LeMay. The Strategic Bombing Survey has just released a preliminary evaluation of the bombing of Germany. We dropped more than 550,000 tons of bombs on Germany and that figure doesn't include bombs dropped by the Royal Air Force. Actually, in the entire European theater the Army Air Forces released 1.4 million tons of bombs."

LeMay refused to accept this thesis saying, "Operations here are different. Japanese opposition is a lot less than it was over Germany, and Japan's targets and cities are more vulnerable. Then, too, we've learned a lot in the last two years about strategic bombing."

Montgomery hurried in and handed LeMay a slip of paper. "This will tell you what you want to know."

LeMay glanced quickly through the report. "We'll run out of strategic cities and targets by October 1. I don't see the war going much beyond that date."

Arnold was astonished, and he uttered a low whistle of incredulity. "I want you to go back to Washington and give the briefing you've given me, to the Joint Chiefs."

"Yes, sir."

"The Joint Chiefs are meeting with President Truman on June 18 to discuss invasion plans and to brief the president for his mid-July Potsdam Conference with Churchill and Stalin. I've always believed that Japan could be defeated by air power. We could have done so in Europe, but they didn't have the planes and the men. After your briefing, I'm more convinced than ever. I hope you may convince the Joint Chiefs to call off the coming invasion, or at least delay preparations for it."

"I've never doubted that once this command demonstrated its abilities that Japan would be forced to surrender through the proper use of strategic air power," LeMay said. "At first, it was a matter of timing because we could not get the airplanes, and early operations at high altitudes were losing B-29s faster than they were being delivered."

Arnold studied LeMay's face thoughtfully. "President Truman has repeatedly expressed his deep concern about the heavy casualties predicted for the invasion. He's had estimates that range as high as one million. He's also concerned about the length of time it may take to defeat Japan through a blockade with sea and air strikes."

"He should be concerned," LeMay said. "I believe casualties could be much higher. The Japanese Army is undefeated in the home islands, and there are two million men ready to resist an invasion. Along with millions of irregulars, their Army will fight savagely for their homeland. Look what happened at Iwo Jima. We'll have to dig them out of every cave from Kyushu to Hokkaido. They are a fanatical race, and the only thing that will force their surrender is brute force. I'm concerned about saving American lives. If we can force Japan to end this war, we'll save hundreds of thousands of American servicemen from maiming and death. Personally, I've long been convinced that it was a mistake to announce publicly that we would invade Japan. If the president had announced instead that we had no intention of invading but would continue our air attacks on an ever increasing scale, while blocking her main islands, we would have cut the ground right out from under her militarists." He looked at Arnold almost pleadingly. "Give me a chance to prove what this command can accomplish. I ask only five more months."

"You've got it," Arnold said. "Meanwhile, try to convince the Joint Chiefs in Washington."

"I'll do my best sir."

On Guam's Northwest Field, Arnold and Nimitz later witnessed the christening of a 315th Wing's new B-29 as the "Fleet Admiral Nimitz." Wing Commander, Brigadier General Frank Armstrong, told the gathering that the airplane was dedicated in honor of Nimitz for his marvelous logistics support even though the 20th Air Force was not under his command.

This new wing had B-29's with no gun turrets other than the one in the tail. Its electronic radar equipment was unique because it had the 18-foot airfoil Eagle Antenna System, which permitted greater target identification and made these B-29s look somewhat like biplanes. The "Eagle" system was conceived by Professor Luis Alvarez, and developed by M.I.T.'s radiation laboratory and Bell Telephone Laboratories. It was being used for the first time in the Pacific.

Arnold addressed a large number of officers and men at the ceremony. He expressed the congratulations of the Joint Chiefs of Staff for Nimitz's outstanding use of minimal forces in achieving a continuing advance against Japan, and in securing the Marianas. In praising Nimitz for his command of United States forces in the Central Pacific since the Pearl Harbor attack, he said they were now in a position for the final assault by whichever means was necessary to achieve surrender of the Japanese.

Nimitz said, "The B-29s have had tremendous success in bringing Japan closer to surrender." He conceded that he had had misgivings when the first eight groups were sent to the islands because they were not part of his command, although their logistics support would have to be assumed by his forces. "Their success has been so great that I'm welcoming 12 more groups."

Nimitz and Arnold inspected the new B-29 after the ceremony, and were particularly interested in the APQ-7 radar and the new navigational aids. Colonel Boyd Hubbard, commanding officer of the 501st Group, answered their questions. When Nimitz asked him what more assistance he could provide, Hubbard said the establishment of a loran site would improve navigation facilities on an island near Japan. He said his earlier request had been pigeonholed. Nimitz made a note and the site was operational two weeks later.

Arnold visited each of the islands before he departed. Most of the 462nd crews were on a mission so the remaining personnel were turned out at the last minute and told to come as they were dressed at the time. They arrived in greasy coveralls, t-shirts, cook's whites and every possible clothing combination.

Arnold approached them with a half smile on his face, oblivious to the disheveled men, but an immaculately dressed brigadier general in Arnold's party took one horrified look as he stared at the gathering with disbelief. Arnold told the group, "I've wanted to see and talk to you for some time and felt it appropriate to use the anniversary of the first big raid on Yawata to do it." He was warm in his praise of their efforts. "In Washington there are two groups of opinion," he said, "about the end of the war without an invasion." He added that he was not sure about those who believed an invasion would not be necessary, but he hoped that they were right.

He reminded them that a year had passed since the first raid of Japan. "I'm pleased to award the 58th Wing a Presidential Unit Citation for that historic mission." (It was the first of three that the wing was eventually awarded, along with five battle stars.)

Thirty-three urban areas had been selected for attack by the Joint Target Group in Washington, concentrated in eight of Japan's largest cities. Yawata was the only one that hadn't been destroyed by June.

LeMay's intelligence officer, Colonel James D. Garcia, now recommended attacks against smaller cities, as the larger ones had been leveled. His list — included cities like Hachioji with over 60,000 people and Fukuoka with more than 320,000. They were all highly flammable, contained war or transportation facilities, and were highly congested. Garcia told LeMay their destruction would break Japan's will to continue the war and through their cumulative effect force her leaders to sue for peace. LeMay agreed, but he had to finish off precision targets in the larger cities before he could turn his attention to the smaller ones.

Six targets were hit in the Tokyo area June 10 and heavy damage was caused to the Hitachi Engineering Works at Kaigan and to a seaplane base.

The constant strain of two missions a week began to take its toll and we were all in a state of exhaustion.

"I wish I had not assigned myself to this one," I said to Buchta on June 18.

"Why don't you just forget about flying missions?" Joe said.

"I want to get my 35 missions chalked up and then I'm going to try to get back to the States."

"The colonel will never let you go," Joe said. "You know that. He told me he wants to keep the same staff until the end of the war."

"It will be a talking point," I said stubbornly.

"I saw the strike photos of Amagasaki," Murph said. "Our men really clobbered the Kawanishi Aircraft Factory."

"Fifteen planes did it," I said. I was still amazed by the perfection of the bombing. Captain Dock O. Waller and Captain Ralph T. Holland led two small formations. The area was socked in and they had to rely on radar to bring them up to target. Then, with only seconds remaining, their bombardiers synchronized on the plant and completely destroyed it.

"I don't see how the Japanese can take much more," Murph said.

"I went on one mission to Amagasaki but we had to bomb by radar and only started a few fires," I said.

"Where are you going tonight?" Buchta asked.

"Toyohashi. This is Bobby Roth's 35th mission, and he is anxious to complete his tour. His bombardier has already finished up, so I agreed to fly with him."

"How many missions do you have?" Joe asked as we headed for the briefing room.

"Twenty-three. They are adding up slowly but surely."

"Toyohashi shouldn't be too bad," he said.

"I hope so. It should be a relatively easy plum to pluck from Japan's family tree. I think it will be a milk run."

All our hopes for an easy mission seemed to be coming true. We had flown to Japan without incident and as we approached the target it was evident that we would have a protective screen of clouds above and below us.

The night was pitch dark, without even the pale glow of the moon as we roared through the clouds. Layer after layer of light fluffy clouds obscured the ground and the sky. We flew across the coast of Honshu and headed inland. Soon a dull red glow pierced the clouds ahead and to the right of us.

I reported to the crew, "The city is already in flames."

A tense stillness permeated the airplane with only the dull roar of the four engines adding reality to the scene. Closer and closer, the distance from the city grew less and less, until the clouds parted and we were looking into a glowing read sea of flames that was once the city of Toyohashi.

Over the city long strings of fire floated down. Clusters, set to burst at 5,000 feet, looked like roman candles as the prima cord exploded, and each cluster tore apart and descended as liquid fire.

The city was aflame from one end to the other so there was no choice but to add my load of incendiaries to the inferno below. The tens of thousands of fires in the city were sufficient to destroy it, but I heaped mine on top for good measure.

After we landed on Tinian I shook hands with my old friend Bobby Roth and congratulated him on completing his tour. "It won't be long before I'll be taking that one way trip to San Francisco and Uncle Sugar," he said happily.

I lagged behind when we entered the briefing room because I knew what was awaiting Bobby and his crew. Above the stage was a 10 foot long banner, two feet high, saying, "Our Bobby Never Aborts the Primary Target. He Always Hits It. Welcome Home on Completion of Your 35th Mission." He was stunned by the reception as everyone broke into cheers. He was not only one of our best pilots, but a marvelous human being.

I later flew with another crew to Omuta but for some reason not a single plane hit the city with its firebombs. It had been raining heavily for several days and perhaps the firebombs were put out. But this failure was rare as one city after another succumbed as flames and smoke boiled up through the clouds.

LeMay walked into his office on Guam, June 26, with a grim look on his face. He was so exhausted that he removed his jacket with an effort.

Montgomery hurried in. "How'd it go in Washington?"

LeMay dropped wearily into his chair. "I was all fired up to tell the Joint Chiefs a convincing story about our operations, but they weren't interested. My presentation was about the most frustrating I've ever given. The chiefs sat there in disbelieving silence, and General Marshall slept through the entire briefing. I'm disgusted. What a waste of time."

Montgomery was shocked. "What went wrong?"

I learned afterward that the president had already approved the invasion. I didn't stand a chance to change their minds at this late date. Now we'll have to prove by actions what they refused to believe in words. How have things been going here?"

"Couldn't be better."

Garcia stood at the door and LeMay motioned for him to come in.

"Japan is already defeated," LeMay said. "It's merely a matter of time until her leadership finds a way to capitulate with some semblance of honor." His voice rose. "She must surrender or face total destruction. Her very survival as a nation is now threatened."

"Even Nimitz agrees," Montgomery said.

LeMay's spirits revived. "He's tough to convince, but he's honest enough to admit it when he's wrong. More than I can say for MacArthur and some others." He paused deep in thought. "In a few days we'll be up to full strength with a thousand Superfortresses. I intend to throw the full weight of this command against Japan." He asked Montgomery. "Is opposition increasing?"

"If anything it's less. Their air-raid system is so primitive that it collapses soon after an attack begins. Japan's air defenses are completely ineffective. Our crews meet little opposition."

"That's what I believed would happen." LeMay thought for a moment. "It's comforting to have my views vindicated." He searched Montgomery's face for reaction when he said, "I've decided to try psychological warfare." He had Montgomery's full attention. "With opposition ineffective, I want you to prepare leaflets to drop on Japanese cities during July to warn them in advance that they will be firebombed."

Montgomery and Garcia stared at LeMay with astonishment. Garcia's doubt was mirrored on his face. "Are you sure that's wise? If...."

"I won't be specific," LeMay said. "Just warn a dozen at a time of an impending attack and then hit four of them." He spoke directly to Garcia. "Do you have anyone who can write the leaflets in Japanese?"

Garcia thought for a moment, still shocked by LeMay's proposal. "We have three Japanese officers in custody as war prisoners who have been cooperative. They might volunteer. We can't force them."

"I know that," LeMay said impatiently. "Ask them if they will cooperate. I want the message to be simple but blunt. It should say something about America's well-known humanitarian principles, and that this action is taken to spare innocent people. And warn them to evacuate their cities."

Montgomery also had his doubts. "I'm fearful of the adverse impact on our crews."

"They'll get used to the idea," LeMay said. "Once they see that opposition does not increase — and it won't — they'll like the idea."

"This will create panic in Japan," Garcia said. "Discipline is already a serious problem. Such warnings will cause the Japanese militarists to sue for a negotiated peace."

"That's the whole idea," LeMay said. "The ultimate fate of hundreds of thousands of Allied soldiers lies in our hands. We must not fail." He looked up and there was an implacable look of determination in his eyes. "We will not fail!"

On June 29, I went with a crew to Okayama, with a repetition of the holocaust that had engulfed Toyohashi. But it was one of the most hair-raising missions because the crew panicked when they thought a Baka was on its tail. Afterwards I was inclined to believe it was the planet Venus that had been mistaken for one of these suicide craft. If you stared long enough at it, you'd swear it was moving toward you. As far as we knew the Baka had never knocked down a B-29, but their presence always made us uneasy. There had been too many B-29s that failed to return from night missions for unknown causes. These suicide crafts, with a thousand pound warhead in the nose, tried to ram a B-29. The pilot was killed regardless so he set out to ram a plane with a deadly seriousness. They were rocket propelled and at night appeared as a "ball of fire" in the sky.

That night a B-29 got hit just ahead of us over the city. Cold sweat trickled down my face as I watched with a creeping sense of horror. The plane soon became a flaming torch and my insides were tied in knots of fear as I watched for parachutes. There were none. The huge plane, flames licking through its wings and fuselage, fluttered down like a falling leaf. It was impossible to comprehend the tragedy before our eyes. Eleven men's lives were being snuffed out in an unreal, savage death. It sent shivers down my spine.

I told Joe Buchta about my experience after the mission.

"That's odd," he said. "The other crewmembers reported no opposition over the target. One of the other wings lost a plane but that was all."

"That's the way it goes," I said wearily.

"You'd better get some sleep," Joe said. "You'll have to brief the bombardiers for a mission to the city of Kure tomorrow."

"I'm glad I'm not on that one," I said. "It will be rough."

"Let's get some coffee before we turn in."

"You know, Joe, the worst thing about these missions is that you never can tell when you're sticking your neck out. The mission that you think will be bad turns out easy. The one that should be easy turns out to be awful. That's what makes the life of a combat crewmember so nerve wracking."

The 58th Wing Commander, Brigadier General Roger E. Ramey, called a meeting of all personnel amid rumors that LeMay had decided to ask the crews for more than 35 missions.

We stood up as he walked in. Few of us liked this hard-drinking, martinet of the Army's old school, but he had a reputation as a good tactician, although his actual combat record amounted to very little.

"I know you have heard rumors that your tour may be extended. I am not here to verify that rumor or discount it. At the present time nothing has been decided. Perhaps I can clarify the situation and explain it fully."

His words were met with stony silence and defiant stares. "It is not my intention, nor is it that of General LeMay, to demand that you do more than your share. You have already done enough, but that does not answer the problem the 20th Air Force faces.

General LeMay is doing everything possible to speed up the flow of replacements from the States and he hopes he will be successful. If we do have to ask you to fly more missions there is a definite, compelling reason behind it.

If we allow our organization to be stripped of crews, without replacements coming in, we will have to postpone our blitz against Japan at a time when it is becoming clear that Japan is cracking under the strain. She must not have a chance to recover. General LeMay is convinced that Japan will surrender providing we can keep up the pace we have set. Don't feel we are being unnecessarily hard on you, or that we are not concerned about your welfare. We are making the best of a bad situation.

You must realize that crews are being used up at a very rapid rate. Sooner or later General MacArthur plans to land on the islands of Japan. If Japan can be compelled to quit through our efforts, hundred of thousands of men's lives will be spared. Think of it in that light and bear with us in the weeks to come."

We listened to the general in silence, knowing he was right, but still not believing in the necessity for such drastic action, inasmuch as it was our hides we were risking. Fortunately, replacements did arrive from the States. Although we were short of individual crewmembers from time to time, by using staff personnel like myself, we were able to keep every plane we had in commission and flying on missions. It was a painful period for all. Tempers were on edge and words were voiced that were best left unsaid, even between friends. Despite some hard feelings our efficiency as a fighting organization never was impaired, thanks to the fighting spirit of the members of the whole command. Aircraft that were supposed to fly 60 hours a month on combat missions were flown twice that much. And, to the undying credit of the mechanics on the line in my own 462nd Group, no planes ever had to ditch at sea.

LeMay was carefully studying a report in his Quonset office, July 2, when Montgomery walked in. He waved the report at him. "This is impressive. I agree that completion of Phase One of the urban area program has achieved our initial objectives.

Since the first of March we've destroyed 105 square miles — roughly 40 percent — of Japan's six largest cities.

These cities have experienced incredible destruction." Montgomery continued, "with great factories destroyed or damaged, and tens of thousands of small household plants wiped out."

LeMay said that he agreed. There was a touch of sadness in his voice, when he said, "No modern nation has ever endured such havoc. Millions of Japanese are without homes and places to work. Garcia tells me that most Japanese have fled their cities and that industry is practically wiped out." He glanced again at the report. "On 17 maximum effort incendiary raids involving 6,960 sorties, we've lost 136 B-29s." He paused to scrutinize the report more carefully. "You say our loss rate is 1.9 percent?"

"That's right. About what you predicted. Not all are combat losses. Quite a few are due to operational accidents. The B-29 is still an unforgiving airplane."

"The loss of even one crew is regrettable," LeMay said, "but this is a dangerous business. In comparison to the gains we are achieving, our losses are acceptable."

Montgomery pointed out, "Note that I have compared our present losses to previous missions at high altitudes. They are far less — a third of January's losses."

LeMay turned reflective as he gazed off to the right, slowly puffing on a cigar. He put the cigar down. "I'm smoking too much. My wife keeps writing to me to cut down. She claims my pipes and cigars are merely pacifiers — like those that mothers give babies to suck on. She's probably right. But you need something in this business to keep from going bananas."

The Philippines finally fell to American forces on July 5, after 10 months of hard fighting and the loss of 12,000 American lives.

Meanwhile, the fire blitz rolled on. July 7, four more cities fell to the crushing blows of firebombs and were left blackened ruins.

Missions were run off on a production line basis. There was no time for careful, detailed work because crewmembers knew their job and often started out on missions that had been hurriedly prepared.

On July 10, a rain of fire deluged Sendai, Sakai, Wakamutsu, and Gifu.

General Arnold issued orders on July 10 to deactivate the 20th and 21st Bomber Commands during a reorganization. General Nathan F. Twining was named to head the 20th Air Force, and personnel of the 20th Bomber Command, formerly in India, were transferred to the 8th Air Force on Okinawa. Spaatz was assigned to head the new Strategic Air Forces based on Guam. He was told to report to the Joint Chiefs or to Arnold as its executive agent.

As he entered his office, July 11, LeMay called back over his shoulder, "Get me Colonel Garcia."

He sat down with a tired sigh and picked up a report. He studied it intently while he waited for his intelligence officer. When there was a knock on the door, he called, "Come in."

Garcia walked in and stood before LeMay's desk. "You wanted to see me?"

LeMay waved him to a seat. "I've been re-reading your April report about Japan's petroleum industry. Now that we have the 315th Wing operations, with their advanced radar, I want them to concentrate during July on oil facilities and storage depots."

"We've already hit some of those targets," Garcia said, "and right now the petroleum industry is in a critical stage. Its destruction will have an immediate impact on Japan's ability to wage war."

"I agree. Japan has always been dependent upon imported oil. Her need for oil precipitated her drive southward at the start of the war."

"That's right. But her shipping lanes from the south have been under increased attack by airplanes, ships, and submarines since mid-1943. As a result, all shipments have declined drastically in that period while expenditures of petroleum products have skyrocketed. Actually, oil shipments have ceased and Japan must rely upon her limited supplies in storage."

"Japan's available oil supplies have done more to reduce air opposition than any other factor. Most of her combat aircraft are grounded for lack of fuel," LeMay said.

"There are at least 8,000 combat and training planes on the main islands," Garcia said. "They are still a serious target."

LeMay looked up, surprised by the disclosure. "That many? You'd never know it from the opposition we are getting."

"Normally I would not consider training planes a threat but after the kamikaze raids against our ships around Okinawa, they must be considered more seriously. I'm sure they'll be used against us." He changed the subject. "Oddly, for a nation so dependent upon oil, Japan never developed much of a synthetic oil industry."

LeMay was only half listening, with his thoughts on something else. "I've decided to use the 315th Wing to destroy Japan's oil industry because their crews have had special training. Their June 26 mission against the Utsube Oil Refinery in Kokkaichi destroyed about 30 percent of the plant. These refineries are located on or near the coast where the new Eagle radar can effectively pick them up."

Garcia handed LeMay another report. "This report reviews the success of our mine warfare activities. I remember how hard you fought for it last winter."

LeMay flipped idly through the report. It was quite voluminous. "I don't have time to read all this. Give me the gist of it."

"Arnold initially recommended that only one bomber group be allocated to mine laying. He. . . ."

LeMay interrupted. "It wasn't enough. I wrote Arnold of my opposition, saying that if my command was to take on the job, I wanted it done right. That meant a larger force than one group. I insisted that 1,5000 mines be laid by an entire wing — but that such a wing must be available for other operations. Arnold agreed and I selected the 313th and set up a training program for them."

"The five-day mining of the key Shimonoseki Strait in late March has paid huge dividends," Garcia said. He walked over to the map and LeMay focused his attention on it. Garcia pointed to the various routes to Japan as he spoke. "Japan has now withdrawn her two million remaining tons of shipping to her inner zone. Ships have been diverted through the narrow Shimonoseki Strait, dividing the islands of Kyushu and Honshu, for entrance into the Inland Sea. This limited tonnage cannot provide the Kobe-Osaka industrial area with the raw materials that are the lifeblood of their existence."

"I agree," LeMay said. "Japan's population is more than half as large as the United States, but her arable land amounts to only three percent. Shipping is vital to bring in the food and raw materials for her survival and to prosecute the war."

"Mining the eastern narrows of the Shimonoseki Strait served two purposes," Garcia said. "It stopped troop reinforcements to Okinawa, and restricted movement of the remaining elements of the Japanese Navy."

"We caught the Japanese by surprise with our mine-laying," LeMay said. "I knew eventually they'd sweep the mines. That's why I sent two wings in April to lay 2,000 more mines, including smaller mine fields in the harbors of Tokyo, Yokohama, and Nagoya."

"These mine operations have helped to keep much of Japan's shipping in her harbors. Small suicide vessels are being used to clear channels but the variety and complexity of our mines make effective sweeps almost impossible."

"What's the food situation in Japan?" LeMay asked.

"Fire raids have destroyed 25 percent of her rice stocks. It is considered suicidal to send ships through the mined areas; therefore, Japanese shipping is practically immobilized, with her Pacific ports closed down, and the Inland Sea bottled up. Major ports that depend upon water transportation for 75 percent of their requirements are at a standstill as the crescendo of our operations rises daily."

"I want Shimonoseki Strait kept mined on a regular basis with new pressure mines. They are almost impossible to sweep. Use them in addition to the types that have ship-counting mechanisms and delay features. Some of these devices are so ingenious that they defy imagination. An area can be swept time and time again before the delay mechanisms cause the mines to explode." He stared thoughtfully at the map. "The Japanese people soon will be existing at or below the starvation level." He turned again to Garcia. "Let us not forget that the mining campaign is an important complement to our bombing. Hopefully, our operations will reduce Japan's essential supplies and hasten her surrender."

Garcia returned to his seat. "Mine laying, on the scale we are using, is unique."

"Most military leaders failed to understand its potential. MacArthur has only authorized one mining mission during the war. Except for General Arnold, the Joint Chiefs regard blockade and serial bombing only as contributing to victory, but not as war-winning strategies. They specifically are not regarded as a substitute for invasion."

Garcia asked a question that had long intrigued him. "Why have we been ordered not to bomb Kyoto, Hiroshima, Nigata, and Kokura? I understand Kyoto because it's a religious center. But the others don't make sense."

LeMay was evasive. "I know why, but I can't talk about it." He quickly changed the subject. "What about the political situation in Japan?"

"The Supreme War Council is divided. Half believe Japan should seek peace under any conditions, and evidently they have the concurrence of the Emperor and Premier

Suzuki. The opposition is strong, including the war minister and two chiefs of staff. There is some indication they have broken American security and know about the November 1 invasion of Kyushu. The Army is confident the invasion can be defeated by moving the mass of its troops to this area."

"There is no way such a massive build-up can be hidden." LeMay lit his pipe and puffed on it. "I believe if we made an announcement that the invasion was indefinitely postponed, and that Japan would be subjected to ever increasing air attacks, we'd pull the rug out from under the militarists. By talking of invasion we're playing right into their hands."

LeMay's phone rang and he picked it up.

"Yes, send him in."

He turned to Garcia. "Colonel Tibbets wants to talk to me. I'll have to run you out."

"Is he the commander of the new 509th Composite Group on Tinian?"

"Yes," LeMay said.

Garcia was intrigued, hoping to learn more, but LeMay did not cooperate. "I'll talk to you later. Close the door when you go out."

"Of course."

He passed Tibbets on his way out.

LeMay returned Tibbets' salute and motioned him into a seat in front of his desk.

"I understand that you have been briefed about the 509th."

"Yes, some time ago."

"Colonel Montgomery insists that we go through a training program, just like other crews. I must protest. We've been training for more than a year."

LeMay removed his pipe and put it in an ashtray. But his eyes never wavered from Tibbets' face. "He's acting under my orders."

"But...."

"It has been my experience that every new outfit in a combat theater, although they have been exposed to intensive training in the States, 'screws up' its first mission. I am not about to let that happen to the 509th."

"But we're so special...."

LeMay was blunt. "To me, you're just another group. Sure, the weapon you will use is vastly different, but it will be delivered like any other bomb."

"But it isn't like just any other...."

"It's been a long time since I've studied college physics so what I know about the atomic bomb has not made much of an impression upon me. Obviously, it will be far more powerful than anything we've ever seen in warfare. But I do know something about bombing, and I do not foresee that an atomic bomb will be much different to drop than a conventional bomb. Perhaps I am mistaken in how big a bang it will make, but that has little to do with its delivery to a target."

Tibbets looked at LeMay with frustration, believing that he did not understand the problem. "I can't emphasize too strongly that the dropping of an atomic bomb poses difficulties. You have to release the bomb and pull sharply away because of the anticipated blast."

"So, you'll practice quick getaways. But you will also undergo routine training just like any other group coming out here for combat operations!"

Tibbets got the message, and he backed off. "Yes, sir."

"I want your group to make practice runs on nearby Japanese held islands. Then take our usual new-combat-crew runs to Truk and Marcus with regular bombs. When is the Alamogordo test firing scheduled?"

"Five days from now. July 16."

LeMay digested this thought. "I want your group to be prepared to drop conventional bombs on Japan. Do you have large casings of similar type bombs but filled with TNT?"

"Yes sir. We plan to drop them on actual targets. They are pumpkin shaped and weigh approximately 10,000 pounds."

LeMay's eyebrows rose in surprise. "That much? When these casings are filled with atomic material — I gather just a few pounds — what will their equivalent blast effect be, compared to TNT?"

"We won't know for sure until after the Alamogordo test. The scientists predict 20,000 tons of TNT."

LeMay was surprised and somewhat shocked. "It will be a big bang."

"That's what I'm trying to tell you."

LeMay's voice sharpened. "It's still a bomb, and will be dropped like one!" He mulled over Tibbets' revelation for a moment or two. "That's equivalent to 1,000 B-29s with a conventional bomb load." His face turned grave. "The future of bombardment aviation will never be the same with the dawn of the atomic age." There was a touch of sadness in his eyes when he said, "The world better learn to live in peace. This war has been deadly to the people of Europe and Asia where at least 50 million people have already died. God knows what an atomic war would be like. The casualties would run into the billions."

"I agree," Tibbets said.

LeMay brushed aside such dire thoughts and turned to more practical matters. "You'll get your orders from me through Colonel Montgomery." He studied Tibbets' face thoughtfully. "There is no better man in my command. You may not know it, but Montgomery was Arnold's first choice to command the 509th. My predecessor, General Hansell, refused to release him because he was too vital as his operations officer. At the time, Hansell did not know what the job entailed. So, what Monty says must be carried out to the letter. Do you understand?"

"I do," Tibbets quietly replied.

"I want you to make 12 strikes against Japan in small formations at high altitude. I doubt if you'll encounter any opposition." His voice turned bitter. "Japan is licked, but our Joint Chiefs in Washington haven't found out about it yet."

Chapter 15

Tick, Tick, Tick

Although the weather grew progressively worse, adding to the 20th Air Force's difficulties, missions continued with Utsonomiya, Taurago, and Uwajima smothered under thousands of bombs.

The days rolled by in endless succession. A mission was set up, planned and executed. We were running out of cities and only a few remained. Numazu, Kuwana, Hiratsuke, and Gita were destroyed by July 17.

Reports kept coming in that the Japanese were serious about ending the war if they could save face by doing so. Although we did not put too much stock in these rumors, we were exceedingly bolstered by the fact that the Japanese were getting more concentrated hell than it was possible for any nation to endure. It began to look like the beginning of the end.

On July 19, Buchta asked me, "Are you going on the mission tomorrow?"

"Yes," I said wearily. "I don't have any enthusiasm for the trip but Maraist needs a bombardier."

"It will be a long haul," Joe said. "All the missions from now on will be long. The cities on the east coast of Honshu and Kyushu have been destroyed so we've got to go to the other side."

"Fukui will be a tough target to find," I said. "The other targets are no better."

"Where are the other wings going?" Joe asked.

"Hitachi, Chosi, and Okazaki."

After briefing, Joe and I returned to our tent and I lay back and tried to relax. I felt weary and near the exhaustion point but I couldn't sleep. I had a bad case of the jitters, not because of the mission, but because of the accumulation of months of overwork and combat fatigue.

"These missions are getting me down," I said.

"I feel the same way," Joe said. "Trying to fly them and do staff work is taking 10 years off my life."

One of our problems was the continuing shortage of bombardiers and navigators. Two bombardiers had broken under the strain and had to be sent home before completing their required number of missions. One had tried to force his pilot to turn around en route to a target by grabbing the wheel, screaming, "Turn around! We'll all be killed." The other suddenly developed an internal illness that he said prevented him from flying. Much to my disgust these two men were immediately sent home, although I was convinced that both were faking their symptoms. My strong protest to Colonel Kalberer was turned down. He said placatingly, "We're a fine outfit. We don't want those kind of people."

"They'll get home and be promoted," I said.

Kalberer smiled. "No, they won't. I'll see to that."

I had flown with a crew on a night mission that had panicked before we reached the target, and the pilot had turned around, screaming at me to drop my bombs. I refused at first but when he continued on the route back I had to salvo them. After we left the target my accusing eyes made him wince, knowing that I could get him court martialed for such cowardice. All the way to Tinian I refused to talk to him and left him fearful of what I might do. This was the crew's 33rd mission, and I reluctantly decided not to report the matter. It was a judgmental decision made at the time because I believed my condemning eyes would haunt him forever after.

Prior to the Fukui mission, I rested for a couple of hours and then, in a gloomy mood, headed for the line. The usual bantering of the crewmembers rubbed me the wrong way and I sat by myself without engaging in their repartee.

In my present frame of mind I expected all sorts of trouble, before and after take-off, but fortunately nothing out of the ordinary occurred and we headed for Japan. Lieutenant James E. "Frenchy" Maraist was an old friend from the earliest days and I had faith in his ability as a pilot.

My spirits lifted as we flew quietly through the night, passing Iwo after a few hours, and then heading for the coast of Japan.

"I'm going to pull the pins," I said to Maraist.

I crawled through the crowded compartment and entered the front bay. I went to work on the clusters and I was sweating prodigiously in no time. Soon the front bay was completed and I crawled through the narrow space of the center wing section and entered the rear bay. It took an hour to finish the job.

I started to walk along the narrow catwalk in the front bay towards the nose section. I stopped dead in my tracks. Was I hearing things? I listened fearfully. Unmistakably there was a tick, tick, tick at regular intervals. I was frozen on my perch but only for an instant. I realized one of the fuses must have malfunctioned. Any moment there might be an explosion. I hastily swung my flashlight at each fuse to check that the arming wires were inserted.

Tick, tick, tick. On and on it ticked of the seconds. My body shook, and I thought frantically of something to do. It was futile. The bad fuse could not be located. It's not supposed to go off, I thought hopefully. Tick, tick, tick. And then, an awful silence. I stopped breathing for a moment and stood rigidly erect in the bomb bay waiting for I knew not what. After what seemed like an eternity, I breathed easier and headed out of the bay.

A fuse was not supposed to go off if the arming wires were still in place but — that was just it — the but. I decided not to alarm the others now that I was sure nothing could happen.

The clouds were thick and "Frenchy" Maraist flashed the landing lights on and off to warn other B-29s of our presence. The even roar of the engines, blending with the friendly voices of the crew, made my earlier fears seem ridiculous.

The land was just a faint dab of blackness in between holes in the clouds as we started across Honshu, but with the clouds around us we felt secure against attacks by enemy fighters. It was the kind of cover we liked best because it afforded us maximum protection.

"Did you see that tremendous explosion off to our left?" I said to Frenchy. "I wonder what could have caused it?" A new feeling of apprehension gripped me.

"I saw it," he said. "Beats me what it can be."

"There it goes again," I said.

The flashes occurred at irregular intervals. Brilliant jabs of light that stabbed at the darkness like lightening in mid-summer back home. Suddenly it dawned on me what it was.

"That's the 315th Wing bombing the oil refinery at Nagoya," I told the crew.

It seemed ages until the navigator told us we were coming up on the IP. A dull red glow on the clouds gave evidence that the city of Fukui was doomed. The clouds were thick as we headed in. Twenty miles from the city the clouds parted and all the horrible awfulness of a large city in flames lay before us. The terrible destructiveness of our firebombs was awesome to behold. The city was the bed for a funnel — like mass of smoke and flames that narrowed at the top and then spread anvil fashion around 10,000 feet with smoke rising as far as the eyes could see. It was like looking into a furnace of glowing coals, with nothing resembling human habitation visible. The mass of flames covered the city.

"I can see to bomb visually," I called to the radar operator in choked voice.

It was impossible to pick out the aiming point so I synchronized on the center of the city and let them go. After bombs away we turned quickly to the right and were swallowed by clouds. There was no doubt about it. Fukui had ceased to exist.

When I returned to Tinian there were a number of new majors among the pilots, but promotions for Buchta and I had not come through. We had both completed the time in grade for promotion and I was furious, believing that Kalberer had broken his promise.

I went to see the colonel. He took one look at my red face and angry eyes, but before he could make a comment, I said, "Colonel Kalberer, you are not a man of your word."

He flushed, started to make some angry retort, but I didn't let him get the words out.

"I took this group bombardier's job nine months ago despite the fact that I didn't want it. You insisted despite the fact that I had only a short time in grade as a captain and it would take nine months to qualify for the rank specified by the position." He tried to intervene but I was too mad. "I've put in the time required for the promotion, but you passed me over, giving my majority to some pilot who has never had a responsible position. Personally, I think you ought to be ashamed of yourself. You're a great one for praise, and I've received my share, but you only pay off for pilots."

His face was red, and he tried again to intervene but I had not finished. "You can take this group job and shove it. I want out. I won't be part of a staff whose commander only uses people for his own ends. I want a transfer to one of the squadrons where I can finish my missions and go home."

Kalberer fought to keep his emotions under control as I started to walk out. He stood up. "Wilbur, come back here. I promised you a promotion and you are going to get it."

My words were biting. "I'll never again believe anything you tell me. I want a transfer. Immediately." I stormed out of his office.

He called me back in 15 minutes and his face was crestfallen. "I've just checked. General Arnold has cancelled all officer promotions because he believes the war will soon be over."

I was tightlipped. "I expected that. Just get me transferred out of here. I don't want to work for you anymore."

Kalberer looked at me, and he was truly unhappy. But I had had enough. I turned on my heel and started to walk away.

"Wait a minute, Wilbur. I'll call LeMay."

I had no hope that LeMay could help, even assuming that he would want to, with the promotion ban coming from General Arnold.

I only half listened as Kalberer got LeMay on the line. "General LeMay, I've done a disservice to one of my finest officers," and he explained the situation. Kalberer's face lit up and he said, "Thank you sir. I appreciate it."

There was a relieved look on Kalberer's face as he said, "LeMay told me to submit your promotion and pre-date the orders prior to General Arnold's order."

I was disbelieving. "You've got a week. Meanwhile I'll withdraw my request for re-assignment." I turned on my heel and walked out.

A few days later I received my promotion, and so did Joe Buchta, but I was still bitter that I had been forced to push the issue.

Multiple incendiary attacks were made on an average of two nights a week, and in general, four cities went up in flames each time. The 315th Wing often integrated its night attacks against the oil industry, while crews from other wings gazed in awe as a huge refinery exploded near them en route to their target cities.

These fire raids were carried out over Japan with little opposition as Japan's air defenses proved totally ineffective. The Japanese had never developed a first rate night fighter, and those they had were controlled from the ground. As a result, only one B-29 was known to have been lost to a fighter.

On July 24, I met Captain Miles B. Thomas and his crew for a daylight strike against the Takarazuka plant between Kobe and Osaka. It was another aircraft plant and it had a high priority on our list.

"It's good to be flying with you and the crew again, Mike," I said as we prepared to take off.

"Nice to have you along."

"Flying with a strange crew is often unpleasant. With you guys I feel at home after so many missions. Sometimes I have the feeling I'm an outcast in an otherwise happy family."

Mike nodded understandingly. "Board up!" he yelled.

We circled our assembly point near the coast of Shikoku. We were the last plane to sight Captain Raymond K. Childress's B-29, so we lost no time in getting to him. The lead plane was supposed to use its small smoke grenades to identify itself but we had not yet noticed the yellow phosphorus bursts. However, Childo's plane bore distinctive markings and we had no trouble identifying it. As we came in close, I noticed a grenade swinging back and forth beneath the plane with the cord still attached. I realized that the cotter pin had not jerked free. I turned to Mike with a warning. "Don't get behind Childo. He's having trouble releasing a grenade."

Childress circled to the left, but inasmuch as we were on the inside of the circle, it was difficult to keep from falling behind and trailing the lead plane. During one turn a puff of phosphorous smoke appeared right in front of our number-two engine as the grenade burst close to our airplane.

"Did you see that?" I said excitedly. "Back off a bit or we'll get the next one in the engine nacelle."

"I'm trying to," Mike said grimly, as he labored at the wheel.

There had been much bad weather on the route from Iwo so our formation's planes were off on their assembly timing. We circled for 40 minutes before we had a large enough formation to enter the target area. Even then we only had seven planes.

The northern half of Shikoku was a beautiful land of green hills and sparkling rivers. This peaceful scene made our whole mission incongruous. It seemed impossible that any people who lived in such magnificent surroundings could have carried out the brutality and lust for power that characterized the Japanese.

Tokushima was visible below, or what used to be Tokushima. Only a few houses on the outskirts were left standing. Where the town had been was just a brown patch of burned rubble surrounded by green luxuriant hills.

The IP was a small island between Honshu and Shikoku and as we made our turn I could see what used to be the city of Wakayama. It was now a mass of burned out houses and factories. Those two cities symbolized the prostrate form of the Japanese Empire. What had happened here was happening all over Japan.

The morning sun was bright, and the whole bay was open with only one ship on the water. This once great shipping center was dead. It was a fitting tribute to the effectiveness of the mine warfare carried out by the 313th Wing.

"No fighter planes waiting for us," I said happily.

Osaka and Kobe were in plain view as we neared Amagasaki. Just below and slightly ahead, a ship rode at anchor in the bay.

"I wonder what that ship is doing down there?" I wondered aloud.

The words were barely out before our plane was rocked as if by a violent wind and gray puffs appeared all around us. We looked at them with shocked surprise. Wicked red flashes surrounded us and we bounced like a toy airplane.

"It's a flak ship!" Mike called.

I looked at that seemingly harmless vessel loaded with heavy caliber, anti-aircraft guns and felt a surge of impotent rage. A formation led by Captain Karl L. Briel was just ahead and below us, and we received the full brunt of fire directed at his formation and at our own.

The bomb bay doors were open and only seconds remained before bombs away. A steady hail of fire still came from the ground after we were out of range of the flak ship. The target was exposed to view, not having been hit as yet, and sprawled at the crook of two small rivers. It looked larger than I had envisioned after seeing it on the mosaic back on Tinian.

The formation in front of ours was just a few hundred feet away at a lower elevation. I watched their bombs fall away and ours followed a few seconds later. Quickly closing the doors, I peered down through the Plexiglas at the target below us. The first bombs hit to the left of the aiming point, tearing great gaps in the engine run-up sheds.

A few seconds later, our bombs hit, completely blanketing the aiming point. The bombs from the two formations caused a tremendous upheaval, and the whole plant seemed to rise and then fall back. Gray, debris-strewn rubbish mingled with smoke and rapidly ascended to our altitude as we pulled away.

"They won't make anymore fighters in that plant," I said with savage delight.

"Hey!" Mike yelled. "What's going on?"

I looked back. "What's the matter?"

"Child slowed down so much I almost overran him."

I looked at the lead plane and my heart stopped beating. Number-two engine was puffing out clouds of black smoke and the prop slowed to windmilling speed.

"He's lost number two," I said. "Why, he's feathering number one also."

An impending tragedy began before our eyes but was quickly overcome. The number-two engine had been hit and Childo had pulled back the throttle and called for feathering of the prop. The co-pilot, who thought he had said number one, started to feather the wrong engine. The error was quickly corrected and the plane gained speed.

The countryside west of Osaka unfolded before us. As we turned to the right we could see Japan's sacred city of Kyoto beneath us, surrounded by shimmering blue lakes. Another tight turn to the right and we were headed back for the coast, arriving there without having spotted a single Japanese fighter.

"It's unbelievable," I said to Mike. "Today we penetrated the Jap's most powerful defense zone and they didn't even challenge us."

"They've about had it," Mike said.

"I think you're right."

The tally board in the briefing room on Tinian gave us the full information on the missions. Five hundred and ninety nine B-29s had been over Japan striking at four large aircraft factories, the Osaka Arsenal, and a textile mill in the Osaka sector. The results were good to excellent on all targets.

"I don't see how the Japanese can continue to fight," I told Joe that evening. "Today, not a single fighter opposed us. They must be on their last legs."

"They can quit any time," he said. "I've had a bellyful of war. Enough to last a life-time."

"Me, too," I agreed.

As President Truman prepared for the July 17 Potsdam Conference, he and high officials of the government studied their options to bring the war against Japan to an early conclusion.

General MacArthur had written Marshall on April 20, recommending an early invasion of Kyushu because, he said, such a course would bring the full power of ground, naval, and air forces to bear on Japan. A year's delay, he claimed, would make Japan more difficult to invade. He called for a continuation of offensive methods, which had proved so successful in the Pacific campaigns. "Reliance upon bombing alone is still an unproved formula for success." He reminded the Army Chief of Staff that the bomber offensive against Germany had not forced the Nazis to capitulate without a ground invasion. He said that a ring of bases around Japan to intensify air attacks would disperse Allied forces even more, and that seizure of bases on the China coast would only escalate operations on the Asiatic mainland without any military benefits.

Marshall agreed with MacArthur's views. President Truman's final decision to approve an invasion was based upon his strong reliance on Marshall's views and the fact that the Joint Chiefs had voted unanimously that an invasion of the home islands was necessary.

General Arnold was visiting Pacific bases while this decision was made but he told Lieutenant General Ira D. Ekker, who was representing him, not to oppose the position taken by Marshall because he had been such a firm supporter of the Army Air Forces and he did not want to risk alienation on such a vital matter.

Marshall had told Arnold that he would support an independent air force following the war, and the Air Forces chief did not want to lose his support by proclaiming that airpower alone could win the war against Japan.

After explosion of the atomic bomb at Alamogordo's test site, which proved it to be as powerful as the scientists had predicted and a practical weapon that could be carried by a B-29, Truman asked each of his advisors about it's use. Arnold advised against it on the grounds that Japan was already just a hollow shell and could be brought down by continued conventional bombing.

Marshall still disagreed.

In Japan, the Supreme War Council was still divided with half believing Japan should seek peace under any conditions. This group had the support of the Emperor and Premier Suzuki. But the war minister and the two chiefs of staff in the Japanese government were overwhelmingly against a peace initiative. By now, they were aware of the projected invasion of Japan and the Army and Navy had asserted that Japan's armed forces could defeat the invasion. Top Army officials pointed out that the Japanese Army in the main island was undefeated and still strong.

President Truman's decision to use the atomic bomb against Japan was influenced by General Marshall's conviction that the invasion of Honshu on the Tokyo plain, scheduled for March, 1946, would cost at least a quarter of a million American casualties, and probably even more Japanese. These losses would be in addition to those incurred during the Kyushu invasion. Truman's ultimate decision to use atomic weapons was motivated by his sincere belief that they would save lives in the long run. But he was adamant that Japan must agree to Allied peace terms.

Acting Secretary of State Joseph C. Grew told the president that he disagreed, although he would not vote against the decision. He said the Japanese might surrender if the Allies made it clear that they had no intention of destroying Japan or insist upon the removal of its Emperor. Secretary of War Stimson and Secretary of Navy James Forrestal agreed with Grew, so Stimson was ordered by Truman to draft a proposal on July 2. It offered hope to Japan if she surrendered but promised total destruction if she continued to resist.

A draft of the proposal was prepared at the Potsdam Conference. It stated the American position that if Japan refused to heed the warning, the air and sea war would be stepped up.

The British agreed to use the atomic bomb against Japan. The Combined Chiefs of Staff approved an intensification of the war while preparations were made for a Kyushu landing, now scheduled for November 15.

Japan's civilian leaders were convinced by now that they had lost the war. Her industries had been crippled by air attacks, the sea blockades had brought the nation to the brink of starvation, and Japan's overseas possessions and conquered territories were isolated from the homeland. Japanese military leaders continued to disagree. They urged the Emperor and Premier Suzuki to fight on until more acceptable peace terms could be achieved.

Emperor Hirohito had indicated as early as April of 1945 that he wanted the war to end as quickly as possible. The Suzuki Cabinet, which had just come into power succeeding that of Premier Tojo, was convinced after the fall of the Marianas, that peace must be achieved. This viewpoint was strengthened when the Soviet Union announced it would not renew their neutrality pact. The German surrender in May precipitated a peace move to the Soviet Union in which the Japanese sought its intercession with the United States. The suggestion was passed along to Moscow, June 3, but was never acted upon. The Russians never did entertain any thought of acting as a mediator.

The Potsdam Conference reviewed plans already made and approved them. For planning purposes, the conferees agreed on November 15, 1946, as the date when the war was expected to end.

Stalin told Winston Churchill that the Russians would attack Japan soon after August 8. At previous conferences he had agreed to such participation.

Truman did not tell Stalin about the explosion of the atomic bomb at Alamogordo, but on July 24 he said casually that the United States had a new weapon of unusual destructiveness. Stalin showed no special interest, saying merely that he was glad to hear it and hoped the United States would make good use of it against the Japanese. Years later it was revealed that Russian spies had obtained atomic bomb secrets and that Stalin knew all about the bomb.

Allied leaders signed what was called the "Potsdam Declaration" on July 26. It was approved by Truman, Churchill, Stalin, and Chiang Kai-shek, and was based on Stimson's July 2 memorandum to the president, although there was no reference about the Japanese keeping their Emperor. Secretary of State Cordell Hull had objected to any such reference because he believed it indicated the Allies condoned appeasement. There was no mention either of the atomic bomb, although the Japanese were warned that continued resistance would result in Japan's prompt and utter destruction.

General Arnold received authorization for General Spaatz to be given responsibility for delivering the atomic weapons once the president reached an irrevocable decision. His plea that Spaatz be given as much latitude as possible as to choice of target was approved without argument.

The Potsdam Declaration caused consternation in Japan. Military leaders demanded that the government denounce it, and Suzuki did so publicly the following day.

Allied leaders considered Suzuki's denunciation as a complete rejection of their peace terms and they were convinced that the military continued to dominate the Japanese government.

Most of the 462nd Group's older crews were nearing the end of their combat tours and there were many frayed nerves at the July 28 briefing. I grinned to myself as I saw Colonel Kalberer making notes while Captain Seward B. Oleson completed the briefing of the mission to Aomori on the northern tip of Honshu. I knew what was coming.

"Do you have anything to add?" Oleson asked the colonel.

This was a formality at the end of all briefings and usually there was nothing to say beyond what had already been covered. But tonight he nodded and got up from the front bench to address us.

"You old-timers will remember our India missions when we had to make too heavy take-offs for a mission to Japan. That's the reason we have been chosen for this assignment because we are experienced in this type of operation. It just proves what I have always said, that we are the best group in the Army Air Forces."

There were a few wisecracks but I noticed fleeting smiles beginning to form. This was the old routine, which hardly ever varied, and always met with the same response from the crews.

"You can laugh if you want to," Kalberer said. "But I can prove what I say. Everyone knows that the 20th Air Force is the finest in the world. And isn't the 58th Wing the best in the Twentieth? All right, you know as well as I that the 462nd is the best group in the wing. So, you see, that makes us the finest group in the whole Air Force. There's nothing complicated about that, is there?"

I enjoyed these sessions when the colonel talked in his solemn sincere way. I looked around the room and observed the tired, drawn faces of men who had already endured too much, and watched them change, as broad, youthful grins creased their weary faces. I felt with them, the same stirrings of pride that would never be eradicated. Perhaps we weren't the best group in the Army Air Forces, but we thought we were.

The mission was a night fire raid. Aomori, a city of 99,000 people in an area of 71 square miles, was 3,780 statute miles from the Marianas. The Japanese had considered northern Hokkaido safe because of the distance. They had not counted on Iwo Jima. Fires had often swept the city, and because of its vulnerability it had the highest insurance rates in Japan. It had the largest, most highly developed ferry terminal and it was the terminus of two railroad lines. Its great marshalling yards, shipbuilding facilities and coal distribution yards made it a perfect target. The plan was to take off early from Tinian, proceed to Iwo Jima, rest there for several hours, and then fly on to Aomori. The return trip would be flown directly back to Tinian.

I had often seen Iwo Jima from the air as we flew on our way to Japan, but this was my first view of it from the ground. The vestiges of the bloody battle were still in evidence. Stubby trees were torn and blasted, and the volcanic soil was filled with cartridges and shell cases. There was still a smell of death and destruction.

The Seabees had transformed Iwo into an air base that was beyond description. Hard surfaced runways, taxiways, and ramps took up most of the island. I appreciated more and more the comment of a Japanese officer who had been hiding in a cave on Iwo Jima for several months before he was captured from his place of concealment, near the top of Mount Suribachi. After being removed from his hiding place, he was led away to be placed in the prison stockade.

He blinked his eyes in the glare of the unaccustomed sunlight and looking over the tiny expanse of the island, exclaimed, "Impossible!" That's the way we felt about it.

Iwo Jima was our only refuge coming back from Japan. Our feelings toward the Marines who had taken the island could never be expressed in words. The V Amphibious Corps suffered 4,590 dead, 301 missing, and 16,000 wounded. The Japanese losses were 21,000 dead and 212 captured. At this staggering cost to the landing forces, they saved hundreds of flier's lives that otherwise would have been sacrificed. We hoped to repay them by knocking Japan out of the war so they would not have to repeat the performance on the shores of Honshu and Kyushu.

We were alone as we headed for Japan because of a late take-off. It was getting dark so I made myself comfortable and switched the communication's box from interphone to radio. Radio Saipan came in clearly. An announcer was reading what sounded like a news program in Japanese.

Just as I was about to turn back to interphone, I heard, "Ichinomiya, Uwajima, Ogaki, Usi-Yumada, Tsu" repeated over and over, and then several other Japanese cities were mentioned, including our own target city, Aomori.

I turned to our pilot, Lieutenant Marvin E. Paty, "Have you been listening to the radio?"

"Yes. I don't get it."

"I'm puzzled. Some of those cities are our targets for tonight."

"Do you suppose the Japanese know that we are coming?"

"I hope not," I said. "I wish this gibberish would end and they would announce it in English."

Later on a newscast was read in English. "Major General Curtis E. LeMay announced tonight that 12 cites have been warned in advance that they are to be fire-bombed," the announcer said.

My pipe fell out of my mouth and crashed on the floor. "Did you hear that!"

Paty nodded and the lines around his eyes grew tighter.

"Six thousand pamphlets were dropped on 12 cities," the announcer continued. "Warning the populace of their cities' impending doom. General LeMay said that four of these cities will be destroyed tonight by Superfortresses based in the Marianas."

"That's nice of the old boy to warn those poor, defenseless Japanese!" I said with biting sarcasm. "Why doesn't he tell them the time we'll be over the target? I hate to think of those Jap pilots spending hours waiting for us."

"If the night fighters meet us over the target and we get shot up, I'll go back and wring LeMay's neck," one gunner said angrily.

"What in the world did he do that for?" Paty said.

"For propaganda purposes, I suppose. He's said for some time the Japanese don't have the fuel to send fighters up. I hope he's right."

At Chosi Point, near Tokyo Bay, we turned north following the coast of Honshu. Several fires were beginning to blaze up in two small cities. Those were not targets but evidently some planes had aborted and bombed them as targets of opportunity. Bombs were never wasted if it could be helped. North of Sendai we turned inland and headed for the other side of Honshu. Clouds now obscured the countryside. It looked like another radar job.

The glow of the burning city of Aomori was visible, reflected off the clouds to the right of us, as we neared the west coast. Our track to the target was almost a complete circle from the coast. Numerous bays and islands made radar navigation possible. Otherwise, we would have had great difficulty keeping on course.

We turned on the IP and I searched the sky ahead anxiously for the telltale red exhausts of night fighters. The redness shining through the clouds up ahead indicated where the city lay. No flak or fighters challenged us as we headed for the city. Just before bombs away I caught a glimpse of the city and saw that we were going to hit over, so I twirled the telescope up half an inch. Away went the clusters.

I warned Paty, "Don't fly into the smoke cloud!"

He tried to avoid it, but we were bucking a head wind and the cloud was on our side of the city. The full brunt of it shook our plane and we rocked and slid off one wing as we tossed in the hot, boiling air mass. Then we were away.

Halfway across Honshu I fell asleep, waking hours later with the morning sun shining in my face. The five hours of sleep that I had accumulated in the past 48 hours had not been sufficient to keep my eyes open another five minutes. My back and neck ached from the uncomfortable position I had slept in and cramps developed in all parts of my body.

At the briefing I met Lieutenant Robert C. Gibson and his bombardier Lieutenant Clyde P. Norwood. "You look as tired as I feel," I said.

Gibson gave me a tired grin. "Anyone get hurt on your plane?"

"No."

"We were bounced around like a yo-yo, but no one got hurt. From what I hear, we were lucky. The turbulence over Aomori was terrible. Several pilots have reported injuries among their crews."

I headed for my tent, with only one thought in mind — stretching out. My six-foot frame was never comfortable in a bombardier's compartment, and 18 hours in one position had almost crippled me.

Goddard was already in the sack. "General LeMay's warning to the cities that would be attacked didn't make any difference," he said, as I flung myself flat.

"No," I replied. "As usual, he knows what he was doing. I imagine those warnings threw the people in those cities into panic. It's good psychological warfare."

Murph walked in. "How about the other cities? Were they destroyed?"

"Uwa Jima, Ogaki, and Usi-Yamada were leveled," I said. "The Twentieth had 562 B-29s out. The 315th Wing knocked out the Shimotsu Oil Refinery at Wakayama."

Buchta joined us. "I think the Japanese have adopted a new policy. Lately we never run into fighters on our missions."

"LeMay thinks they don't have the gas and oil," Goddard said.

"I believe both answers are true," I said. "I'll see you guys in the morning. I have got to get some sleep."

There was a serious look on Montgomery's face when he walked into LeMay's office as he was conversing with Garcia.

"I've talked with quite a number of crews lately. Many of them are close to the end of their tours."

LeMay looked at Montgomery with concern. "Do we have a problem with them?"

"I don't think so. Each has said the same thing." Montgomery noted that LeMay was looking at him with intent eyes as he paused. "They all say they will keep on flying as long as you need them."

LeMay relaxed, but he was visibly moved by Montgomery's words. "Hopefully we won't have to extend their tours. Send out word that no one is to be assigned to fly missions after he has completed 35. I don't want them sent home yet. We may still need them. But I want them grounded."

"The men will appreciate that news," Montgomery replied.

"We are getting more crews from the States. As you know, I appealed to General Arnold when he was out here in June, and he has come through. Continue to use staff personnel whenever necessary to fill out crews for B-29s in commission." He sat back and there was a softening of the usual stern lines on his face. "I'm proud of these men. They have fought so hard to end this war without an invasion. Of the more than two million men and women in the Air Force, I'd say less than 10 percent have experienced extensive combat. That's unfair to those who have had to do more than their share, but that's always been the case in war. The American people may never appreciate what these men have done, but I'll never forget them." He turned to Garcia. "What's the latest word about our advanced warnings to cities that they will be attacked?"

"The leaflets were dropped on schedule. Apparently the warnings did not increase opposition. Last night's missions were routine. There is no evidence that the warnings have increased the incidence of fighter attacks. And, there is no report yet of any losses. But those who flew to Aomori had a rough time."

LeMay glanced quickly at Garcia, alert for bad news. "Oh?"

"Smoke turbulence over some sections of Aomori was extremely bad. Some crews reported injuries. Nothing serious. Evidently B-29s were tossed violently in the hot, boiling air masses over the city."

LeMay nodded in understanding. He changed the subject. "General Spaatz will take over the Strategic Air Forces on July 29, with General Twining as our direct boss over the 20th Air Force. No restrictions have been placed upon us, and MacArthur and Nimitz have been told to keep hands off our operations. After what happened in Europe with Eisenhower gaining control of strategic air power, this is a big victory."

Montgomery brought up the problem uppermost in his mind. "I'm still concerned about having sufficient crews for operation these next few months."

LeMay replied. "I've reminded Arnold again of our situation, and I've explained to him and Spaatz that replacement crews are the major limiting factor for continued, high-level operations. I've asked that the principle of two crews per aircraft, such as we had initially in India and China be reinstated."

"Colonel Irvine has performed miracles to keep airplanes in commission," Montgomery said. "Flight crews don't realize it takes 12 officers and 73 enlisted men on the ground to keep one B-29 flying."

"Colonel Bill is one of our unsung heroes. He's a doer. When we needed a steady flow of parts, Irvine set up his own 'airline' to and from California. He didn't ask me for authorization, or seek approval from the Air Transport Command." He grinned with delight. "It's a wonder the Army bureaucracy didn't chop him off at the knees. As long as the job is done I never question how he does it. All I know is that a transport plane arrives from Sacramento every day loaded with spare parts. It's an under-the-table operation, but I wisely ask no questions."

Montgomery voiced his own admiration of Colonel Irvine. "Each morning at 5 A.M. there are an average of 50 B-29s out of commission because of parts shortages. About ten o'clock an airplane lands with a load of stuff and Irvine's people are all set to disperse the materials to the fields that need them so their airplanes can take off on a mission that night."

LeMay spoke with some bitterness. "I have to supply 500 men every day to the Guam depot, but I get no results. They haven't fixed a plane the whole damn time we've been out here. They are worthless. I wish I could solve that problem, but, hell, the war will be over before I can find the time."

LeMay's phone rang and he picked it up. He listened for a moment. "By all means, send him in." He turned to Garcia and Montgomery. "General Leslie Groves is coming in. I'll have to run you out."

Chapter 16

"My God!"

They exited reluctantly as Groves entered and LeMay stood to greet him. "I had hoped to get out here sooner," Groves said, "but I stayed behind to witness the firing of the first atomic bomb at Alamogordo."

LeMay motioned Groves to a seat. "That must have been an incredible experience."

"It proved to be as powerful as the scientists in my Manhattan Project had hoped. Moreover, it's a practical weapon that can be delivered in a B-29."

"So I understand."

"Some scientists are opposed to its use. President Truman set up a special civilian committee to set guidelines for use of atomic bombs. The committee has advised the president that the atomic bomb should be used as soon as possible and against a military target without prior warning. Those who are opposed believe the United States will alienate many peoples of the world. They recommend that the bomb should not be used until it has been demonstrated to members of the Allied nations on a desert or barren island."

"Which is it to be?"

"The president's advisory board disagrees with their colleagues. They claim they can foresee no alternative to military use because of the danger that the bomb might be a dud if dropped before officials of the Allied nations. Such an occurrence, they claimed, might stiffen Japan's resistance."

LeMay nodded. "That might well happen. In my opinion, Japan is already defeated. She...."

Groves obviously wasn't listening as he continued his train of thought. "The president's civilian advisers were virtually unanimous in June that an announced test in the New Mexico desert should be held in July, with the first bomb released on a Japanese target in August."

"I see," LeMay said. "Well, the 509th has completed its training. You give me the word, and we'll deliver the bomb to whatever target is recommended."

"Admiral Leahy, who served Roosevelt as chief of staff, and who now performs the same function for Truman, has been opposed to the program from the start. Before our successful test he called it a 'professor's dream.' He told Truman that this was the biggest fool thing ever done. He claimed the bomb would never go off, and that he was speaking as an ordnance expert."

LeMay grinned. "Sounds like he boxed himself into a corner."

"He's been rather quiet since the bomb was tested on July 16. All along Leahy has believed that an air and sea blockade, and air attacks against the home islands would end the war against Japan without an invasion."

"I agree with him," LeMay said.

"He has repeatedly said that an invasion cannot be justified because Japan is already defeated. I gather that is your viewpoint."

"It is."

"Arnold does too. But Japanese troops have often demonstrated their tenacity in battle and the two-million-man Japanese Army is still a military force to be reckoned with. That's what MacArthur tells Marshall, and he's got his ear. He says the November 1 invasion of Kyushu will bring the full power of ground, naval, and air forces to bear on Japan but that a year's delay will make Japan more difficult to invade. He claimed that reliance upon bombing alone is still an unproved formula for success. He cites the failure of the bomber offensive against Germany which did not force the Nazis to capitulate without a ground invasion."

LeMay's temper had been held in check with difficulty. "But we didn't have the planes! Germany could have been defeated by air power if our leaders had waited until our strategic air power was built up."

"I don't know, LeMay, but it's all academic now. I personally believe that the shock value of dropping a couple of atomic bombs on key Japanese targets will be sufficient to force Japan's surrender."

"I wish the Joint Chiefs and the president would listen to Arnold," LeMay said with exasperation.

"General Arnold has always advised against use of the atomic bomb because he believes Japan is already just a hollow shell and could be brought down by continued conventional bombing. Marshall disagrees with him."

"Japan's Supreme War council is divided, according to our intelligence reports. Half believe that Japan should seek peace under any conditions. It appears that the Emperor and Premier Suzuki are in agreement about peace now."

"When Marshall told the president that the invasion of Honshu on the Tokyo Plain, scheduled for March of next year, would cost at least a quarter of a million American casualties, and probably far more Japanese, Truman decided to authorize the dropping of atomic bombs to save lives unless Japan agrees to peace terms. The British agree and the Combined Chiefs of Staff have called for an intensification of the air and sea war while preparations are made for a Kyushu landing now scheduled for November 15.

For planning purposes, they agreed at Potsdam on November 15, 1946, as the date when the war is expected to end."

A look of incredulity appeared on LeMay's face when he heard these words. "Doesn't anybody in Washington look at the damage assessment picture I sent to Arnold or the reports that describe in detail Japan's true status?"

"I don't know," Groves said. "I have never seen them." He turned his thoughts to more practical matters. "General Spaatz has been given responsibility to deliver the two atomic weapons that are now available, after the president has reached an irrevocable decision to go ahead with their use. Spaatz has been given as much latitude as possible as to which targets. Personally, I am anxious to drop the first bomb. We've proved it at enormous cost and I believe it is a legitimate weapon that can very quickly end this war."

"I understand," LeMay said.

"I insist that once the decision is made by the president that every B-29 in the Marianas should surround that 509th plane with its atomic bomb load and escort it to Japan."

LeMay looked at Grove with total disbelief. "That's not the way to do it. We're running individual planes up there all the time and nobody pays much attention to them. We'll run yours up there like any other and all will be well."

"I disagree!" Groves said. "If I must, I'll go over your head." He looked at LeMay with stubborn resolve.

With equal stubbornness LeMay replied. "I'm in charge of B-29 operations, and we're going to do it my way." He softened his tone, but remained adamant. "I have great respect for the job you have done with the Manhattan Project. But you have little experience in combat operations, and I insist on carrying out the mission my way. If you go over my head I will fight anyone who opposes me." He paused to let his words sink in. "Do you understand my position?"

They glared at each other unwaveringly. It was a test of wills pitting two strong-minded officers against each other. Groves decided to give in. "You're right, LeMay. My combat experience can't match yours. I'll go along with your operational plan."

"Good," LeMay said. "You've done your part well. I'll do the same here. When will the first atomic bomb be available?"

"The cruiser *Indianapolis* delivered the bomb's components to Tinian in May."

LeMay was surprised. "I wasn't aware of it."

"Few were. Security has been very tight. The fissionable material is on its way. General Spaatz has been given standby authority to select the target, and the actual time and date, but final approval must come from the president. Truman has told Secretary of War Stimson that the order to drop the first atomic bomb will stand unless he notifies that the Japanese have changed their minds on the Potsdam Declaration calling for unconditional surrender."

The 462nd Group staff was gathered in Vaucher's office on July 31 for a meeting, to discuss the next mission.

"August 1 is Air Force Day," Vaucher said. "We have been instructed to send out every B-29 we have in commission. That were a show of strength over Japan."

"What cities are we going after?" I asked.

"The 58th Wing is going to bomb Hachioji, near Tokyo," he said.

"The whole wing is going after one city?" Joe said.

"Yes," Vaucher affirmed.

"That's wasteful," I said. "Why send the whole wing? Only a formal effort has been needed to wipe out a city that size in the past!"

"There just aren't enough cities left," Vaucher said. "As I said before, the Air Force wants to put on a show of strength."

"I am not impressed by such logic," I said. "It's ridiculous to send men and planes over Japan when they are not needed."

"We're not making the decisions," Vaucher said wearily. "I hear LeMay protested to General Arnold but was told to follow orders."

Crewmembers heard about the mission at the briefing and voiced their own complaints.

"Are we going to announce the targets in advance?" one pilot asked.

Colonel Kalberer turned to the questioner. "Yes, they will be announced. As a matter of fact, they have been broadcasting the news to the Japanese people all day."

A loud uproar broke out.

"There's nothing to worry about," Kalberer shouted. "The Japs don't have the fuel to send fighters up against us."

The crews were not convinced, and they shook their heads in disagreement, but kept silent.

I started out with Lieutenant Paty's crew. Just as our B-29's wheels lifted off the runway, our number one engine failed and the prop was quickly feathered.

"Salvo the bombs!" Paty yelled.

I looked down, noting we were flying over a huge bomb dump, and delayed my release until we reached to coastline, much to Paty's concern until I explained the reason. At the water's edge, I opened the bomb bay doors, salvoed the entire load of firebombs, and quickly closed the doors all in a matter of seconds.

We were badly shaken as we were ordered to circle near the island until all planes were off. Paty handled the situation superbly and we were relieved to land safely an hour later. It took a couple of stiff jolts of rye liquor in the briefing room to calm us down.

The wing put up 180 planes over Hachioji and thoroughly burned out the city. Our group lost one plane but they reported by radio they were bailing out over land, and we were hopeful they were prisoners of war. The mission was a success, and very little opposition was met by any of the crews.

Besides Hachioji, incendiaries were dropped on Nagasaki, Toyama, and Nito. A demolition attack destroyed the Kawasaki Petroleum Center. It was a display of power that left the Japanese reeling with shock and dismay. Even their propaganda broadcasts made no attempt to minimize the destructive power of the B-29s.

A long, uneventful mission to Saga on Kyushu was run on August 5. I went along with Marist's crew and except for the long flight it was the most uneventful mission in which I had ever participated. The city was inland and small, and consequently a poor radar target. Later, reconnaissance photos showed we had failed to drop a single incendiary on the city. It was still very much in existence.

It was apparent that the actual damage to vital installations in Japan exceeded the most optimistic reports, and that Japan was defeated, although as yet, she refused to concede. Much of her homeland was a vast wasteland and certainly one of the primary reasons was the increase in numbers of B-29s over her main islands, and the greatly increased bomb tonnage dropped on each mission. With lower altitudes, LeMay had been able to increase the 2.6-ton load of each Superfortress in November of 1944 to 7.4 tons.

To the delight of the officers on Tinian, 500 nurses arrived to help run a huge hospital to take care of the thousands of wounded who were expected following the invasion of Japan.

By August 1, the suffering of the Japanese people reached the limits of human endurance as more than 43 percent of the built-up area of Japan's smaller cities was destroyed and production was reduced by 33 percent. Toyama was engulfed in a firestorm that left crews shaken as 99.5 percent of the city was destroyed. On these missions, bomb bays trapped the smell of burning flesh and carried the sickening stench back to the Marianas. In all, 58 of Japan's small-to-medium cities succumbed and 23 major aircraft factories, six major army and navy arsenals, and numerous steel, petroleum, and gas plants went with them.

B-29s had dropped 147,000 tons of bombs, but now that the command was up to full strength with 1,000 B-29s and 83,000 men, LeMay was prepared to drop an equal amount in the next three months.

Most of Japan's refineries were now inoperable due to the concerted efforts of the 315th Wing. Their Eagle radar bombing equipment proved 98 percent as good as visual bombing. Through no fault of its own, the wing's effectiveness was reduced because many storage tanks were empty due to the oil shortage, and refinery production had dropped to four percent of capacity.

United States Navy submarines sank 54.7 percent of all Japanese shipping during the war, but the 20th Air Force accounted for 9.3 percent in just four and a half months. In that time span, B-29s dropped over 12,000 mines. There were 16 B-29s lost, with only nine of those losses due to enemy action.

The 21st Bomber Command's work in plugging Japan's arterial waterway through the Inland Sea, and closing the Shimonoseki Strait at the sea's northwest entrance, along with bottling up the other two entrances on the east and south — the Kii and Bungo Channels — cost Japan her last vital lines of communication with the outside world.

Prince Konoye after the war indicated that Japan's economy was strangled and in such dire straits toward the end, that all food supplies and critical materials were prevented from reaching the home islands.

Mining had always had a low priority among America's pre-war military services, and in some theaters during the war. Except for General Arnold, the Joint Chiefs regarded blockade and aerial bombing only as contributing to victory, but not as war winning strategies. They should have been considered substitutes for invasion. If a large mine laying program had been established earlier in the war, it is possible the Joint Chiefs would have concluded that a massive invasion of Japan's home island was unnecessary. Billions of dollars of excess military supplies and equipment could have been saved, and quite possibly thousands of lives.

Garcia briefed LeMay, August 2, about Japan's reaction to the Potsdam Declaration after it was released to the press on July 26.

"It caused near panic in Premier Suzuki's cabinet. The military insisted that the government denounce the declaration. Suzuki did so publicly the following day."

LeMay sat back and puffed more rapidly on his pipe as his emotions rose. "This is rejection, at least for the time being. I thought Japan's leaders had more sense."

"Our government leaders are convinced that the military continues to dominate the Japanese government."

"Japan's militarists had hoped for a quick victory over the United States and its allies because Japan's industrial and military power was inadequate to sustain a long war. I've always said that once American industry, with ten times Japan's production capacity, was geared up for war, the end was inevitable."

"Japanese radio stations do not play down the havoc we've inflicted. Evidently production of civilian goods is below the level of subsistence. Munitions output has been curtailed to a level that cannot sustain military operations. In effect, the economic basis of Japanese resistance has been destroyed. This economic decay is the direct result of the sea-air blockade of the Japanese home islands, and the direct bombing attacks against industrial and urban area targets. With Japan's militarists bent on continuing the war, I see no other alternative than to reduce civilian morale and their will to continue fighting by destroying urban areas."

"I wish our nation had not pressed Stalin to join in the war against Japan," Garcia said. "The Russians aren't needed, and they will gain an easy foothold in Asia that they could not have won otherwise."

LeMay thought for a moment, and then took a more practical point of view. "The Communists would have taken advantage of the situation without our prodding."

"I suppose so," Garcia said somewhat wistfully. "I wish the Joint Chiefs had realized earlier what our operations were achieving. There is no justifiable reason to drop atomic bombs at this late date. Arnold knows that, but his protests have been ignored."

LeMay's reply reflected his inner bitterness. "How well I know. I tried to tell them when Arnold sent me back to Washington in June, but they had their minds set in concrete. I don't blame Truman. Except for Arnold, the Joint Chiefs and MacArthur are advising him that without the atomic bombs we'll have to invade Japan. He has little choice but to authorize their use."

"If he only knew what we know," Garcia said.

LeMay shrugged and his gesture was indicative of his own feelings of helplessness. "The atomic bomb will precipitate Japan's earlier surrender by a month or two." He put down his pipe and stared at Garcia. "Few people understand that air power could not demonstrate its potential early in the Pacific war because we were constantly short of planes and trained men. Now, more and more damage is done because of the increase in the size of our forces and the increased efficiency of our operations." He paused, his eyes dwelling on the past. "Think what the early missions would have been like if they had operated as efficiently as they do now. We can thank people like Colonel Joseph Preston, whose land-crew school turns out professionals. Then, there is the reorganization of the maintenance system that kept an under-developed airplane flying. Thanks to Preston, crews can now hit an inland target by radar with no land-water contrast in the middle of a thunderstorm." He knocked out his pipe in an ashtray. "No other command during the war has even approached our flying time per airplane."

"Thanks to you," said Garcia.

"I had a helluva lot of help. I merely provided some of the guidance; things I learned the hard way in Europe after seeing an awful lot of men killed because our nation was not prepared to fight a war. It takes years to assemble and train people to form a combat outfit."

Garcia nodded in sober agreement. "I hope the American people will never forget."

LeMay tried unsuccessfully to keep the bitterness out of his voice. "Don't count on it. Most people have short memories. That's why history so often repeats itself." LeMay glanced up as a discreet knock sounded on his door. "Come in."

Montgomery hurried in. "Hope I'm not disturbing anything important."

"No," LeMay said. "We were just yakking."

"Some group commanders have voiced concern about the start of the typhoon season. I tried to disillusion them that typhoons will reduce our operations."

"Bad weather will not be considered an excuse for canceling a mission. Route the planes around typhoons."

"I hope the weathermen can spot them accurately."

"I foresee no particular problems," LeMay said. "This is no time to reduce the pressure on Japan. What about yesterday's big effort?"

"We had 762 B-29s over Japan on August 1. We're practically out of targets."

"I know," LeMay said. "How about losses."

"That's the good part. Only one plane was lost and the crew was seen to bail out over Japan."

LeMay picked up his pipe, started to fill it, but then put it down. "That's a welcome change since the early days, I noted the other day that the command has lost over 500 B-29s — most due to operational accidents while we were flying at high altitudes. Now its more dangerous to fly back home in the training command." He noted their skeptical looks. "I mean it. Training losses in the States have exceeded 250 planes. Right now their monthly loss rate is higher than ours." His telephone rang and LeMay picked it up.

"LeMay," he listened for a moment. "Send him in." He hung up and turned to Garcia and Montgomery. They both rose, expecting to be asked to leave. "Tibbets is coming in. You'd better hear what he has to say."

Tibbets strode in, saluting LeMay, and remained standing. "The 509th is ready for its first atomic mission."

LeMay turned to Montgomery. There was a note of inquiry in his voice. "Agree?"

"They have completed their training. They're ready to go."

LeMay studied Tibbets' face. "I believe everything has been done to prepare your organization for its big mission." For Garcia and Montgomery's benefit, he said, "Hiroshima is the target city for the first atomic bomb. We could have destroyed it months ago but it was spared for this operation. How about the weather?"

"A clear day is mandatory so there will be no mistake. The weathermen tells me Hiroshima will be clear August 6. With your concurrence, that date is my recommendation."

"I've been delegated by Spaatz to pick the date for the first atomic mission. Let's shoot for the 6th. When will you take off?"

"At 2:45 A.M. This will get us over Hiroshima at 9:15."

"How many B-29s are involved?"

"Seven. One will be a spare airplane stationed at Iwo Jima in case my 'Enola Gay' gets into trouble. Three Superforts will take off first to serve as weather planes, and the other two will fly with me as observation planes. Both will be filled with cameras and scientific instruments plus military and civilian observers."

LeMay digested these details. "I'll order all other B-29s to fly at least 50 miles from Hiroshima four hours before your scheduled release and six hours after." He turned to Montgomery. "Schedule two photo reconnaissance planes to get post-strike photographs of the city."

Montgomery looked thoughtfully at Garcia. "Hiroshima is a big city, but is it worth an atomic bomb strike? I mean as a strictly military target?"

"It is Japan's sixth largest city, and the headquarters for the Second Army," Garcia replied.

"I have long recommended it for firebombing," LeMay said. "Now I understand why it was always rejected as a target in Washington."

"The city is an important port and it contains many vital industries," Garcia said.

Montgomery, who had been making notes throughout this exchange, turned to LeMay. "What if Hiroshima is cloud covered? Will the bomb still be dropped?"

LeMay turned to Tibbets. "Tell him."

"Kokura and Nagasaki have been selected as second and third alternates."

Garcia voiced a mutual concern. "Suppose you crash on take-off? Is there a danger of a premature explosion? In that event, I'm sure the whole island of Tinian would be destroyed."

"Good point," LeMay said. "We'd better have a disaster plan."

Tibbets sought to calm their fears. "I have been advised there is little danger. For one thing, Navy Captain W. S. Parsons and his assistant will assemble the atomic bomb after take-off. The scientists claim atomic material will not explode unless the triggering mechanism is attached."

"What about intense heat?" Garcia asked. "B-29s usually blow up on take-off in the event of a crash. It's a nasty sight and few survive."

"I can only tell you what the scientists have advised me. There is little risk due to fire or heat."

"How about radiation?" Montgomery said. "Even if the bomb does not explode during a take-off crash, will there be any residual radio activity?"

"Possibly," Tibbets conceded. "You must realize we are all new at this atomic business. Even the scientists don't know all the answers."

Garcia shuddered. "They have created a monster for the future."

LeMay turned to Montgomery. "We'd better be prepared for any eventuality. We have a responsibility to more than 80,000 members of the 20th Air Force plus thousands of men and women from the other services."

"Will do."

Garcia looked at Tibbets solemnly. "I don't envy you. I for one, will be happy when you are off the ground safely and on your way."

LeMay and Montgomery nodded that they agreed.

LeMay faced Tibbets. "The risks are great. But don't take any unnecessary chances. I'll take the heat if you have to abort. There is always another day."

Those of us still involved in the conventional bombing of Japan had no inkling of what was going on in secret in LeMay's headquarters on Guam, or at North Field, just a couple of miles from the 58th Wing's operational base. We had heard rumors that the 509th had some big bombs — like those the British used against Germany — but the truth would never have occurred to us. Even Tibbets' crew was not told of the true nature of the weapon they would soon carry to Hiroshima. They were merely told they would drop a new bomb that would shorten the war by at least six months.

Chaplain William Downey stood before the crews of the 509th Composite Group in the early morning hours of August 6. "We pray thee that the end of the war may come soon, and that once more we may know peace on earth. May the men who fly this night be kept safe in thy care, and may they be returned safely to us. We shall go forward trusting in thee, knowing that we are in thy hands now and forever. In the name of the Lord Jesus Christ, Amen."

The take-off at 2:45 A.M. went smoothly and so did the flight to Japan. An hour from Hiroshima, Tibbets received a report from a weather plane over the city at 8:15 A.M. that there was only scattered clouds, so, if the weather held for another hour, he knew they would hit the primary target at Hiroshima, and not have to go to Kokura or Nagasaki, which had been selected as second and third alternates.

Navy Captain W. S. Parsons and his assistant, Lieutenant Morris B. Jeppson, had assembled the atomic bomb after take-off. "Little Boy" weighed 9,700 pounds. An armored cylinder, dull black in color, it had a slightly rounded nose. A triple-fusing system had been designed to arm it. The mechanism's main component was a radar unit adapted from a tail-warning system developed to alert combat pilots when an enemy aircraft approached from behind. At a predetermined altitude above the target, this radar device would close a switch. When two of four similar units sent a firing signal into the next stage, a bank of clock-operated switches would start the sequence to detonate the bomb. Arming wires, similar to those used to "safety" a conventional bomb, were attached to the airplane and threaded through these switches. These switches were activated when the arming wires were pulled out of the bomb as it began its free fall. An added safety precaution prevented the clock switches from closing, or activating themselves, until 15 seconds after the bomb was released. This precaution was taken to prevent detonation of the bomb in case the switches were prematurely fired by signals reflected off the B-29. The second arming devise was a barometric pressure switch that did not activate itself until the bomb reached an altitude of 7,000 feet. If the clocks and the barometric arming devises functioned properly, a firing signal would be sent directly to the primers to light the cordite charges and fire the gun to set off the nuclear explosion.

Captain Parsons advised Tibbets that all was in readiness once "Little Boy" was fully assembled and ready for its historic release.

Three Superfortresses had taken off first to serve as weather planes, and the others flew with the "Enola Gay" as observer planes. Major General Charles W. Sweeney piloted "The Great Artiste," and Captain George W. Marquardt flew the other Superfortress. Both planes were filled with cameras and scientific instruments, plus military and civilian observers.

The "Enola Gay" reached the initial point at 9:11 A.M. and Tibbets turned the airplane over to bombardier Major Thomas W. Ferebee, navigator Captain Theodore J. Van Kirk, and radar operator Sergeant Joe A. Stiborik. After a smooth, tense run at 31,600 feet, "Little Boy" dropped at 9:15.

Set to go off at 2,000 feet, it exploded at 9:17.02 Hiroshima time, 43 seconds after it left the airplane. Crewmembers felt two distinct shock waves seven seconds later as they were pulling away from the city. Then a huge mushrooming cloud erupted above the city and rose quickly to 50,000 feet as the crews stared in awe.

"Tibbets to crew. Fellows, you have just dropped the first atomic bomb in history."

Observers on the ground first saw a huge pinkish glare in the sky, followed by a wave of intense heat and wind that withered everything in its path. Seventy one thousand, three hundred and seventy nine Japanese died instantly, and 68,023 others were horribly burned or seriously injured and suffering from the effects of intense radiation, writhed in agony on the scarred ground.

Debris whirled into the sky as a massive cloud of smoke, fire, and pulverized matter ascended thousands of feet in seconds. Fires quickly burned what was left of the city and only devastated land remained. Here and there on a pavement was the outline of what had once been a human being, now completely disintegrated and only a shadow to testify that the person had ever existed.

Tibbets sent a radio message to the Marianas. "Mission successful. No hostile fighters, few flak bursts."

As "Enola Gay" headed back toward Tinian, the co-pilot wrote only two words in his diary. "My God!"

About noon that day I went to the 768th Squadron's operations office. I needed some extra bombing tables for the next mission. The sun was hot and bright, and after the recent heavy rains, everything was green and glistening. Lovely morning glories climbed up the tent that the '68th Operations occupied. I stopped for a moment to admire them. Tinian had been devastated when it was captured from the Japanese, and it had been sprayed with insecticides to kill the swarms of mosquitoes that had infested it. As a result, bird life had disappeared and only now, more than a year later, could one occasionally hear the cheerful sound of a bird as they started to return to the islands. Years later, when I read Rachel Carson's "Silent Spring," I recalled how weird it was living in a world without insects or birds.

I walked into Operations and spoke to Captain Karl Briel, the squadron's operations officer. "Is Flowers around?" Lieutenant Harold D. Flowers was squadron bombardier.

"I haven't seen him all morning. Did you hear the news?"

"What news?" I said without interest.

"President Truman just announced that an atomic bomb was dropped on Hiroshima this morning."

"An atomic bomb?" I laughed. "Karl, you're ready for rotation."

"I'm serious. The president said it wiped out the entire city of Hiroshima and killed everybody for miles around."

"It's probably some propaganda we're using to scare the Japs."

"I don't think so," he said excitedly. "It must be something special because Truman announced it himself."

"I don't believe it. Who ever heard of an atomic bomb outside of a comic strip?"

I walked back to group operations and chuckled to myself.

"Hey skipper," I said to Vaucher. "They dropped an atomic bomb on Hiroshima today."

I laughed, and he laughed with me. "What next?" he said. "There are more fantastic stories around here than in any outfit I have ever been in. Who's spreading the rumors now?"

"Karl Briel said President Truman announced it awhile ago."

"That new group on the north end of Tinian may have some new kind of blockbuster. I've heard hints about it. It's certainly no atomic bomb."

Colonel Kalberer hustled in. He was so excited he could hardly talk.

"Did you hear about Hiroshima?" he said. "An atomic bomb was dropped by the 509th Group this morning and the whole city was wiped out."

I felt a surge of excitement sweep through me as I stood gaping at the colonel. Vaucher was speechless. We knew Kalberer was not the kind to be taken in by idle rumor.

"So its true?" I shouted. "That should make the Japs change their minds about fighting to the last man!"

Kalberer had a wide grin on his red face as he said to Vaucher, "Might as well pay me that $500 now. The war won't last long."

"It isn't over yet," Vaucher said stubbornly. "I've still got until October 1."

Turning to me, Kalberer said, "He's a hard man to convince. I can wait a few more days."

I felt no elation, just a tremendous feeling of relief that the "bomb" might hasten the end of the war.

B-29 photo reconnaissance planes took pictures five hours after the bomb exploded. Although smoke and dust were so heavy over the city that an accurate damage assessment could not immediately be made, it appeared the 4.8 square miles of Hiroshima had been destroyed. Later it was determined that the number of dead was lower than after the March 9 fire raid on Tokyo, but the number of injured was higher.

After Truman was informed of the successful mission, he authorized the release of a statement to the press. We listened to it that night.

"The world will note that the first atomic bomb was dropped on Hiroshima, a military base. We won the race of discovery against the German. We have used it in order to shorten the agony of war, in order to save lives of thousands and thousands of young Americans. We shall continue to use it until we completely destroy Japan's power to make war." The president warned the Japanese that if they did not surrender they could expect "a rain of ruin from the air, the like of which has never been seen on this earth."

Premier Suzuki again advised the Emperor that Japan should accept the Potsdam formula for ending the war, but the Army stubbornly resisted such a move.

After General LeMay studied post-strike photographs of Hiroshima, he called Garcia and Montgomery into his office on August 9. They looked at the photographs with awe. LeMay said, "To think that one bomb caused all that destruction. It's mind boggling."

"Not that it matters, but their bombing accuracy was terrible. They missed the aiming point by 800 feet."

"The bomb's wide area of destruction makes the error relatively unimportant. Still, you'd think after all their training they could have done better than that."

"It's a horrible weapon," Montgomery said.

LeMay leaned back. "Evidently we're going to have a few more days of good weather. He addressed Montgomery. "I heard the flash reports about the daylight strikes against the Nakajima Aircraft Plant and the Toyokawa arsenal near Tokyo. I understand both were knocked out."

"They were flattened," Montgomery said, "and the 58th Wing firebombed Yawata."

"Keep up the pace. Schedule daylight strikes at high altitudes whenever targets are clear and night bombing raids when clouds cover them. We've got the Japs cornered and squealing for their lives. Despite the atomic bomb, we must not relax our operations. Sooner or later the Japanese will be unable to take anymore and they'll quit. I don't believe we have long to wait."

Garcia addressed LeMay. "I sent you a note that Russia has declared war on Japan. Did you see it?"

"Yes, I did. Some Japanese leaders have been searching for a way to end the war for months. Perhaps this will clinch the deal."

"Emperor Hirohito is opposed to the war," Garcia said, "and wants it stopped. But he has little authority — except in a moral sense. The cabinet has sent messages to the United States and its allies that Japan will accept the Potsdam terms if they don't threaten the prerogatives of the Emperor. The United States received the word through Switzerland, and the British and the Russians through Stockholm."

"And?" LeMay said.

"Our State Department believes any Japanese qualifications might be construed as a lessening of the terms agreed to at Potsdam."

"Truman and his cabinet have never insisted that the office of the Emperor should be abolished," LeMay said.

"That's right. The whole issue is under high-level review. By the way, your propaganda campaign is paying off. The latest leaflets dropped over Tokyo gave details of the Potsdam Declaration, and described what atomic bombs can do to Japan. We've also included the fact that the Russians have joined the war. The Japanese government has withheld this information from its people."

LeMay asked Montgomery. "Any word about the bombing of Kokura with the second atom bomb?"

"Major Sweeney ran into foul weather over Kokura," Montgomery said. He walked over to the map, and LeMay joined him. "Sweeney made three separate runs looking for a hole in the clouds over Kokura. He had to admit failure. With his fuel running low, he headed for Nagasaki."

"Nagasaki has been bombed several times," LeMay said, "but it has not been appreciably damaged. The huge Mitsubishi plants have been barely touched."

While they continued to study the map, Montgomery said, "It's not a good target because the city's valleys are deep within the hills across and up-and-down terrain."

LeMay nodded. "Sweeney had no choice with Kokura under cloud cover. Any word of the bombing of Nagasaki?"

Montgomery looked at his watch. "They should have dropped by now. Let me check my office." He placed a call on LeMay's phone. "What's the word on Nagasaki?" He hung up and turned to LeMay with a troubled look. LeMay's face turned rigid with worry. Montgomery shook his head. "No word. That's strange." He glanced nervously at his watch again. "They should have bombed a half hour ago."

LeMay sat down heavily, deeply troubled. He picked up his pipe, lit it and forced himself to relax. "It could be a failure in communications, or it could be...." He didn't finish the sentence and his face showed the strain of not knowing what had happened to Sweeney's crew. "Everything has been going along too smoothly. I've been afraid of this."

Montgomery spoke up. "I've left word at operations that they were to notify us as soon as word is received. I'm sure we're borrowing trouble."

"Trouble is this business's middle name," LeMay said. "But you're right. No sense worrying about something that hasn't happened."

Montgomery tried to dispel LeMay's gloomy mood. "I've never seen crews so charged up. I heard a story yesterday that one of the 73rd's pilots on Saipan got up in the mess hall saying he had just heard the Premier Suzuki had asked you to provide him with air transportation to Washington to try to end the war."

LeMay looked up and a smile appeared around the corners of his mouth. "What will these guys think of next?"

"That got their attention. But, when the pilot just stood there without saying a word, finally someone yelled, 'What happened?' When the pilot reported that you had refused to provide a plane, there was an anguished chorus of protests. He continued to stand there, saying nothing more and someone asked why you had said no. That pilot must be a real ham. He said that you had refused because Suzuki hadn't finished his 35 missions."

LeMay broke up with laughter. "I needed that. I guess we all badly need a good joke." He quickly turned serious. "I've heard indirectly from General Arnold through Spaatz. He has recommended that the Tokyo area be hit by a thousand B-29s to prod the Japanese militarists into an early surrender."

Montgomery looked at LeMay with growing concern. "We can do it, but there is no justifiable reason for such a strike. I'm not concerned about Japanese defenses but 1,000 B-29s over Tokyo would pose operational problems of separation that are well-nigh impossible to resolve."

"I know," LeMay said. "I'm against terror for the sake of terror. Instead I've recommended that we bomb the Hikari Naval arsenal on the Inland Sea. I've so informed General Spaatz. He agrees and he has sent word to Arnold. I believe in keeping up the pressure on the Japanese — and I intend to do so — but at the least risk to our crews. We've only lost four crews to all causes in the past month of combat operations. It would be tragic to unnecessarily expose men on a mission with such high operational risks." He got that stubborn look on his face that Montgomery knew so well. "I won't do it!"

Chapter 17

"The War is Over!"

After the atomic bombing of Hiroshima a great surge of excitement swept the Marianas. We were all convinced that the war was about over. When another mission was announced it was greeted with howls of anger.

Colonel Kalberer spoke in the briefing room to quell the tumult. "The war is not over yet," he said. "I believe it will be very soon. We cannot expect the Japs to quit suddenly. Such things take time. Meanwhile, we've got to keep hitting them so they won't have a moment's peace. Go out and let them see that the 462nd is still pitching."

Our long practiced firebombing technique finished off another city in the early morning hours of August 9, meeting no opposition even though the target was announced in advance. Fukuyama, in the middle of Honshu, was rocked by a tremendous rain of fire and fiercely destroyed as the huge dye works exploded, adding its horror to that of our own bombs.

The 20th Air Force was split up so that B-29s were over the Japanese homeland almost constantly day and night. We were exhausted because of the constant pressure of briefings, interrogations, mission reports, and the many details that must be handled whenever a mission is flown. The war could not end too soon for us. Despite our weariness we were buoyed up by a great hope — a hope that the war might be over tomorrow, or the day after tomorrow.

I was working late at Operations the night of the ninth of August, preparing my report on the mission to Fukuyama. Several of our planes had been late in returning so I had held up the report until they arrived. I was just getting started when Lee Wieschaus, our group flight engineer, burst into the room.

"It won't be long now," he shouted. "They just dropped another atomic bomb!"

"Where?" I asked excitedly.

"Nagasaki. It dropped this morning."

My report was finished in a hurry and I rushed to join the crowd at the radio. Nothing new was added to what we already knew, so I returned to my tent. Oprzendek, Goddard, and Joe Buchta were as excited as I was about the latest turn of events. Oprzendek was talking in a rush of words as I entered the tent.

"They'll quit now! They can't hang on any longer. Why, if they do, we'll drop atomic bombs all over the country!"

"Provided we have any more atomic bombs," Joe said. "I wouldn't be surprised to find that's all we have. It may take time to manufacture more of them."

"I agree with you," I said. "I doubt if we have any more. (Kalberer had hinted privately to me that such was the case.) I've felt for some time that they were ready to quit and just needed a good excuse. This should give it to them. I'm keeping my fingers crossed until they have signed on the dotted line."

"Same here," Joe said.

Goddard had been quiet until now, and as he rolled over on his cot he added his two cents worth. "Oh, cut it out. Let's get some sleep."

Murph was still excited, and he had to have the last word. "Oh, Goddard. All you ever think about is sleep!"

The tent was silent after this but I knew that no one was asleep. They were tormented by the same thought: If this war would only end — and quickly!

LeMay hung up his phone with a stricken look. He motioned to Montgomery at the door to come in. "Garcia was just killed in an airplane accident."

Montgomery's face was drawn and there was a deep sadness mirrored in his eyes. "I was coming to tell you. He was on a routine inter-island transport flight. It's tragic that he didn't at least see the war's end. He certainly made a major contribution to our operations."

LeMay nodded. "I've read Major Sweeney's report on the bombing of Nagasaki. He was surprised to learn that we did not receive his bombs away report. Oh, well, at least he and his crew are safe. I note that his report says the explosion was worse than at Hiroshima, and his plane was rocked by the shock waves."

"Intelligence estimates predict that 35,000 Japanese are dead, and almost twice that many injured," Montgomery said. "Forty-three percent of the city was obliterated, including more than two thirds of the industrial section. Due to the hilly terrain, destruction spread laterally through the valleys. Surprisingly, the destruction was less than a normal air raid with incendiaries."

"Those are the last two atomic bombs available for the present," LeMay said. "So we'll have to continue our operations to keep up the pressure."

"After the second bomb was dropped August 9, I went to see General Twining, telling him I thought it was foolish to send any more missions out because Japan was trying to end the war," Montgomery said. "I said it would simply play into the hands of the militarists who keep telling their people that we're trying to destroy them and not defeat them."

"Oh?" LeMay said.

"He was impressed by my arguments and stood the command down for maintenance. Then he received word from General Marshall through Spaatz's office ripping him to pieces for such an act. He was badly shaken by Marshall's denunciation." He grinned sheepishly. "So was I."

LeMay grinned tiredly. "I was also bluntly reminded that the war is not yet over."

Since the summer of 1944 the Japanese Imperial General Headquarters had been drawing units back to the main islands of Japan to make a final stand in the homeland. These units had extensive infantry and armor battalions.

In early August of 1944 the Japanese Navy had 1,030 fighters, 330 ground attack planes, and 3,725 other aircraft including kamikazes. Japan's First Army had 600 kamikazes and 500 other aircraft. The Sixth Air Army had 1,000 kamikazes and 500 other aircraft. It is possible that Japan had 10,000 in all but two thirds of them were designed only for suicide missions. In addition, suicide boats were available and large numbers of men had volunteered to become human torpedoes.

The Japanese were aware of the possible landing zones on Kyushu and Honshu to be used by Allied invasion forces. They assigned strategic positions to the home army to overwhelm the Allied invaders with a three-to-one advantage of manpower. Civilians were being trained as guerrillas and to strap explosives to their bodies and throw themselves under tanks. Construction battalions had completed tunnels, bunkers, and installed barbed wire barriers on the anticipated landing zones along the shores of Kyushu and Honshu.

On August 9, General Korechicka Anami, Japan's war minister, reviewed Japan's "Ketsu Go" operational plan for defense of the Empire at a meeting of the supreme Council for the Direction of the War. He advised them that the military planned to commit 2,300,000 troops to repel the invasion and call up four million civil servants. He said the draft for men had been extended to include those 15 to 60 years of age, and for women 17 to 45 to provide a total defense force of 28 million people.

Army Chief of Staff Yoshijiro Umezu told Foreign Minister Shigenori Togo that, "With luck, we will repulse the invaders before they land. At any rate, I can say with confidence that we will be able to destroy the major part of an invading force."

The American Joint Chiefs of Staff had approved a two-stage invasion force of five million troops, most of who would be American. They gave an estimate on June 18 that casualties in the first 30 days of the Kyushu landings would be 31,000. Admiral King raised the toll to 41,000 and Admiral Nimitz said 49,000 while General MacArthur said 50,000. The Joint Chiefs agreed that the final total for both invasions would be in the range of 250,000 to 500,000 casualties.

General Marshall gave a more reliable estimate to President Truman. "In my opinion, such an invasion will cost at minimum a quarter of a million casualties, and might cost as much as a million on the American side alone, with an equal number of the enemy. Other army and navy officials agreed. They had not forgotten the 26,000 men killed and wounded on Iwo Jima, or the 48,000 during the invasion of Okinawa."

By August 9, the split between the peace faction led by Prime Minister Kantaro Suzuki and the war faction composed of Anami and the army chiefs had deepened. Emperor Hirohito had aligned himself with the peace faction June 22, when he criticized the Supreme War Council for the first time. "We have heard enough of the determination of yours to fight to the last soldiers. We wish that you, leaders of Japan, will now strive to study the ways and means to conclude the war. In so doing, try not to be bound by decisions you have made in the past."

Japan's leaders deliberated all day August 9 and into the night. At a cabinet meeting that began at 2:30 P.M. — hours after the atomic bomb had been dropped — Anami said, "We cannot pretend to claim that victory is certain, but it is far too early to say the war is lost. That we will inflict severe losses on the enemy when he invades Japan is certain, and it is by no means impossible that we may be able to reverse the situation in our favor, pulling victory out of defeat."

At 2 A.M. on August 10, the Emperor told the "Big Six" meeting of the Supreme War Council that the time had come to "bear the unbearable" and to "suffer the insufferable." I give my action to the proposal to accept the Allied Proclamation on the basis outlined by the Foreign Minister.

The cabinet adopted a message for radio transmission to the Allied powers, saying in part, "The Japanese government is ready to accept the terms enumerated in the joint declaration, which was issued at Potsdam on July 26, 1945, by the heads of the governments of the United States, Great Britain, and China, and later subscribed to by the Soviet government, with the understanding that the said declaration does not comprise any demand which prejudices the prerogatives of His Majesty as a Sovereign Ruler."

The Allied response on August 11 said that the "authority of the Emperor and the Japanese government to rule the state shall be subject to the supreme command of the Allied Powers." And that the "Emperor shall authorize and ensure the signature of the government of Japan and the Japanese General Headquarters of the surrender terms."

Anami fought every attempt to surrender but at noon on August 14, the Emperor asked the cabinet to prepare an Imperial Prescript of Surrender. He said that "a peaceful end to the war is preferable to seeing Japan annihilated." The Anami faction attempted to disrupt such action but at 11:30 P.M. the Emperor recorded his radio message for broadcast the following day.

Anami committed suicide at 5:00 P.M. on August 15.

LeMay informed his command on August 10 that there would be another mission the following day. It was set up with heavy hearts. The radio was full of news that the Japanese had accepted the Potsdam ultimatum and we thought our last mission had already been flown. The 462nd Group's target was the Hikari Naval Arsenal on Honshu's Inland Sea.

A few hours later Sergeant Botkin met Joe Buchta and I at Operations with a happy grin on his face. "The mission is cancelled. I just got the call from wing."

"The war is over!" Joe shouted hysterically, and banged me on the back so hard I almost toppled over.

We grinned at each other and the tired lines slowly began to erase. It was difficult to grasp the idea that there would be no more missions to the Empire. No more screaming Japanese fighters, and no more bursts of ack ack. We had seen so much of it that the prospect of peace somehow didn't seem real.

Our enthusiasm knew no bounds. At the radio shack we listened as a news announcer from San Francisco said that "the Allied governments had acknowledged, officially, receipt of a Japanese offer to accept the terms of the Potsdam Declaration provided it did not include any demand that prejudiced the prerogatives of Emperor Hirohito."

"They can keep their Emperor," Joe said. "They're licked and they know it."

We were too tired for any kind of celebration and the whole area was quiet. Later on, a few men staged a party in the briefing room, but most of us were happy just to lie down and sleep.

The following day promised to be an historic one so we spent most of it listening to the radio. According to news reports, a segment of the American people were against letting the Japanese retain their emperor.

The reaction to this news was violent. One air crewmember put it bluntly, "Would you listen to those phonies back home? If they're so eager to carry on the war, why don't they come over here and fly some missions to Japan?"

This feeling was almost unanimous; with just a few like myself who voiced thoughts that we should not compromise the peace in any way.

August 12 found us in a state of high tension, worrying about the outcome of negotiations. Our planes were still loaded for a mission and there was talk at wing headquarters that we might still go out again, after all.

"There's going to be another delay," Joe said as we entered our tent. "Secretary of State Byrnes has announced that the Big Four have agreed on the Japanese surrender offer, subject to the condition that the Emperor will carry out the orders of the Supreme Allied Commander."

"More uncertainty," I said wearily. "Now the Japanese will have to make another decision whether to accept these new terms."

The night of August 13 we were informed that we would carry out our original plans of bombing the Hikari Naval Arsenal. The crews were assembled, a hasty briefing was given, because it had all been done before, and they were given the take-off time.

"I don't think the mission will be run," I told Buchta. "If the planes do get off, they'll be told to jettison their bombs and return to base."

I stayed at Operations until take-off time, hoping that the mission would be canceled, but no call came through. The men were grumpy and in no mood to go on another strike.

Joe and I watched the planes circling the island as they followed the familiar pattern and headed for Japan.

"It will be tragic if some of them don't get back," I said. "I sure hope they receive orders to return before they reach Japan."

"I doubt they'll complete the mission," Joe said.

We returned to our tent and spent a fitful night. I got up at nine the next morning and leisurely showered and shaved before returning to Operations. Loud voices could be heard as we entered the building and found ourselves in the middle of a happy shouting throng.

"What are you guys so happy about?" I shouted.

I almost collapsed as a large hand pounded me on the back. "The war is finally over. The war is over!" Wieschaus shouted close to my ear in a tone that made me wince.

"That's what you told me before," I said with disbelief. After all our disappointments, I was afraid it was just another false alarm.

"It came over the radio," Goddard said. "The Japs have accepted the peace terms."

I was too dazed to think clearly. After the last few months it seemed impossible that the long struggle had ended so dramatically.

But we listened to the radio, and the story was confirmed. The war was really at an end.

Three hours before the first planes arrived back from the mission the announcement was made in Washington. It would be a gross understatement to say we were happy. We were delirious and numb with excitement and relief.

No sooner had the crews landed than the word spread like wildfire. When they came to Operations, they quickly turned in their reports and headed for their quarters to celebrate. Lieutenant Marvin E. "Pinky" Ballard, old pickle barrel himself, had led one of the formations. He was all excited as he handed me his report.

"I got another arsenal," he said with a wide grin on his freckled face.

"Really smacked it, eh?" I said. "That's the last one you'll have to lead."

"That was my 35th," he said. "I was finished no matter what happened."

What we thought would be a period of wild revelry turned out to be a quiet night. We were all sobered by the peace that had descended upon the Far East. A few flares were shot up but that was all. We were much too exhausted from the past strenuous months for any kind of brawl.

At LeMay's headquarters, he told Montgomery, "I want the command kept on maximum alert. I don't trust the Japs. We may have to give them a clincher to end further resistance." His phone rang as Montgomery scribbled notes to himself. "LeMay." He listened carefully, and made a few notes. Then he hung up with a look of disgust on his face. "Guess who has been appointed Supreme Allied Commander?"

Montgomery replied without hesitation. "Admiral Nimitz."

LeMay slowly shook his head. "He should have gotten the job. He deserves it." He paused and there was a frustrated look on his face as Montgomery expectantly awaited the word. LeMay looked up. "MacArthur!"

Montgomery's face registered his shocked incredulity. "You're kidding. You have to be kidding."

"I wish I were but Truman just made the announcement. There will be a surrender ceremony aboard the battleship *Missouri* on September 2 in Tokyo Bay."

"Will you be there?"

"I've been invited to attend the ceremony."

"I'm glad to hear that. Your contribution to victory deserves at least as much recognition."

"It's no big deal," LeMay said. He paused deep in thought and his voice reflected his deep sense of pride. "For the first time in history a nation has been defeated through the effective application of air power, although air power was not the sole reason. Certainly Admiral Nimitz's long and costly drive across the Central Pacific to secure the Marianas as airbase sites were a prerequisite for the final strategic air offensive against Japan."

Montgomery nodded in agreement. "I brought my records up to date this morning. Sixty-six cities, virtually all of those of economic significance, suffered destruction ranging from 25 to 90 percent."

"All we'll hear in the future is how those two atomic bombs forced Japan to surrender," LeMay said bitterly. "In reality, Japan was defeated by the end of July. You and I know that, but will anyone else believe it?" He shook his head in exasperation. "The sea-air blockade of the Japanese home islands and the bombing attacks against industrial and urban targets had Japan on the ropes. I told Arnold in June that I did not believe the war would last beyond October 1. I wasn't far off — just a month." His phone rang again. "LeMay." Montgomery started to walk out but LeMay stopped him. He quickly made notes. "Yes sir. We'll take on the job, and glad to do so." Montgomery who had followed LeMay's comments, looked at him questioningly. "That was General Spaatz. Arnold has accepted responsibility to deliver food and clothing supplies by air to prisoner of war camps."

"Air drops?"

"That's right. It may take weeks to rescue some of these men who have been prisoners for years. I've heard that most prisoners are in pitiful condition because of the starvation diet they have been subjected to, and the rough treatment meted out by the Japs."

"I'll give each group a number of camps and make them responsible for delivering supplies with as little contact from us as possible. We'll need an accurate list of camps."

"MacArthur has demanded that the Japanese furnish such a list immediately." There was a troubled look on his face. "I'm fearful that we won't get many of our own prisoners back. Intelligence sources claim the Japanese murdered most of the B-29 crews." He shook off such thoughts. "We'll see. Meanwhile, make certain that all crews are on the alert during these supply missions. It will be some time before American troops are in Japan in sufficient numbers to control the situation. Remind group commanders that these missions are combat missions, and they should be treated as such."

"It would be tragic to lose even one crew now that the war is over. I'll stress caution."

"If a crew has any doubt, tell them to shoot first and ask questions later. This is no time to relax our vigilance."

"When will Allied fleet units enter Japan's coastal waters?"

"Plans call for their entry on August 27 with hundreds of planes above them for protection. Major occupation forces won't land until August 30. MacArthur and Nimitz will fly to Atsugi Airfield the day before." He glanced at his notes. "Let me reiterate. This is no time to relax. General Arnold has advised that the 20th Air Force will be kept on alert until Japan is fully occupied."

"The crews aren't going to like that," Montgomery said.

"I know, but we'll have to educate them. I agree with Arnold. We've got to be on the spot to lash back with full force if some of Japan's militarists get the upper hand and decide they want one final battle to assuage their so called honor. His face had a look of grim determination. "If they do, they'll never know what hit them. We've got more than a thousand B-29s just waiting for them to make one false mover. I hope they have more sense."

The following day none of us was interested in the results of the last mission. But I had a report to get out so I inspected the photographs and listened to Al Beck as he explained the percentage of bombs within the target area. The bombing results by our three formations were excellent. The 58th Wing had put up 155 Superforts and 95.6 percent of their bombs had fallen within the 2,000-foot circle.

Colonel Kalberer had led one of the formations on the last mission. There had been 829 B-29s and 186 fighters over Japan for a total of 1,014 to set a new high for one day's activities. Most important of all, not one plane was lost.

At any other time this feat would have been something to brag about for weeks. The production capacity of the arsenal was reduced to zero by our strike. General LeMay cited the results as the best on any mission performed by the 58th Wing and without a doubt, among the best turned in during the war by any heavy bomber outfit. To those of us still in the group who remembered the early days, it was a satisfying climax to our accomplishments.

"We've finished our job," Joe said. "I want to go home."

"It shouldn't be long now," I replied. "I can see no point in keeping the 20th Air Force overseas any longer."

However, there was still work to be done, as we learned the next day. The Air Forces was to be kept on a war footing until Japan was occupied. Then if she decided to change her mind, we could pounce on her prostrate form and pummel her some more. This was all well and good and reasonable, but we were not in a reasonable mood. We still wanted to go home!

Buchta and I were sitting in Vaucher's office toward the end of August when he received a telephone call from wing.

"We've got to prepare for a long flight," he said with a grin on his face. "Fifteen planes per squadron."

"Where are we going?" Joe and I chorused.

"I don't know. We'll have to wait and find out."

"What do you think?" I said to Joe, as we left Vaucher's office.

"Beats me. We can't be going back to Japan. I think we're going to fly home as a unit." (General Arnold had proposed that the 20th Air Force return to the United States and take part in mass aerial demonstrations over America's major cities. We learned later that the Joint Chiefs rejected his idea.)

The next day we learned that the long flight was to be to Japan and not to San Francisco. When we learned why, we felt better about it, and we're eager to be doing something again.

After General MacArthur was given a list of the camps, each group was assigned a certain number. Our group was given seven of them, and we divided our planes so that a two-week's supply of food could be dropped at each camp.

The staff at Operations was eager to go, so we persuaded Vaucher to make up a crew. The day before we were scheduled to head for Japan again we gathered in Vaucher's office.

"I've asked you to come here to find out which camp you would prefer to go to. We will have enough gas to take a tour of the countryside after we drop our supplies. Pick a camp near enough to the place you most want to see."

"How about the Hiroshima camps?" Wieschaus said. "I'd like to see what the atomic bomb did to the city."

"I'd rather see Tokyo," Buchta said.

We argued back and forth until finally a vote was taken. Most of us wanted to see Tokyo.

Vaucher looked again at the list. "Fukashima Prison Camp seems to be closest," he said. "It's north of Tokyo but we can fly across the city and have a good look at it."

"What kind of camp is it?" Joe asked.

"A civilian internment camp."

After briefing at wing I returned to group intelligence and worked with Lieutenant Jack Laberee, plotting the different camps.

"Not much to go on," I said.

"Our information is very limited," Jack said. "But I think I've got them pinpointed fairly well."

The crews were briefed and told where to drop their supplies. We hoped to see some kind of signal from the prisoners to aid in identifying the camps.

I went into the bomb bays prior to take-off and checked the wrappings of each group of parcels. Difficulty had been experienced in dropping these makeshift bundles by parachute. They were to be released from 500 feet and I wanted to make sure the shroud lines did not get caught on the airplane. Everything seemed in order, so I rejoined the crew.

With only six tons of supplies in the bays, we were light compared to a combat mission, and with Vaucher in the pilot's seat there was no sweat job involved as we headed for Japan. Iwo Jima appeared ahead after a couple of hours. Then we left it behind and headed for Tokyo Bay.

There were only a relatively small number of American troops in Japan even though this was the 30th of August. Therefore, we entered Tokyo Bay on the alert, ready for action, as I turned on my turrets and warned the gunners to do likewise.

Our group executive officer, Major Norman, was leaning between the pilots. When he noted my action, he said. "I see you still don't trust the Japs."

"I want to be prepared in case some kamikaze decides he wants to be a hero," I said.

At 5,000 feet the whole countryside was clearly visible. Advance units of the America Pacific Fleet rode at anchor in the bay and Mount Fuji was visible between layers of clouds on our left.

It was an odd feeling to be flying in the middle of Tokyo Bay at this altitude, all by ourselves, because this area had been a fearsome hell hole of flak and fighters during the war. Now all was quiet and peaceful, and nothing rose to challenge us.

Photographs of the blackened ruins of Tokyo had given us some idea of what we had done, but the effect of seeing it just below was appalling. Everywhere we looked there were blackened ruins of what had been one of the world's great cities. Now it was a city of the dead. A few people were visible on the broad streets, and occasionally an automobile or a truck moved along the street. Otherwise there was the emptiness of almost complete ruin. We quickly flew the length of the city and headed up through the green valleys and hills toward Fukushima.

The country was wondrously beautiful with its clear, shining rivers, its green wooded hills, and the glossy greenness of the fertile valleys. Here and there we spotted what had once been a thriving city, now reduced to ashes. These smaller cities were just scars on the countryside, nothing resembling a populous city remained.

Buchta leaned over my shoulder as we neared Fukashima, studying the map. He nudged me as a large river came into view.

"See that fork in the river?" he said, "Fukashima should be at the apex."

"There's the race track," I said. Laberee had said the camp's most visible landmark was a circular racetrack.

Our camp was reported to be in the racetrack's grounds. The prisoners, according to reports, were quartered in stables and other track buildings. We flew directly over the buildings but there was no sign of prisoners. We were sure that this was the right place so we circled over the city and prepared to drop our first supplies.

By the time we arrived back over the camp, I could see a swarm of figures running about excitedly. I dropped the first bay of parcels and noticed a gang of men running to retrieve them. The supplies dropped perfectly and the chutes opened.

On our second turn a large body of men were visible on a sand bar near the river. They were formed to make the two letters PW. This was reassuring so I dropped the next load. After watching the PW's pick up the supplies we headed back for Tokyo. Our mission was accomplished.

"Circle Tokyo and Yokohama at a lower altitude this time," Buchta said to Vaucher. "If you get down to a thousand feet we'll see a lot more."

"How much gas do we have, Wiesch?" Vaucher asked.

"We can spend an hour over Tokyo and still have a good reserve," he said.

Clouds were forming above Tokyo but we flew underneath until we reached the outskirts of the city. On the fringes patches of dwellings still stood but the greater portion of the city lay in ruins. Reinforced concrete buildings were still standing but many of them were gutted by fire. We could see the Emperor's palace area, with its moats and bridges, and even parts of this area were burned. The afternoon sun streaked across the desolate city and certain areas sparkled as the sun hit them. I was puzzled at first but soon surmised it must be melted glass from the factories and homes that was reflecting the sunlight.

The city was unbelievably deserted except for an occasional train running across it. We learned later that four million people had fled Tokyo while three million remained, although at least 300,000 were homeless. Large animals in the city's zoos had been put to death to prevent them from running wild in case they got free. Already the streets appeared neat and clean swept of the debris that must have accumulated during the fire raids.

Down by the harbor areas, which we thought had gone untouched, we could plainly see twisted cranes and burnt out factories and warehouses. Circling Tokyo, the scene of destruction was appalling. It was too much to observe and absorb at one time. It was clear why the Japanese had quit. We had never realized that such destruction had been wrought. No atomic bomb could have done a more thorough job on Tokyo than we had accomplished with our firebombs.

In Kawasaki and Yokohama the same scenes of destruction and desolation were evident. In Yokohama it was even more complete, if that could be possible, than in Tokyo.

I was saddened when I thought of those who had suffered from our blitz. I knew the millions of Japanese who suffered from this wholesale destruction were not to blame. It was the work of their fanatical leaders and not those who followed them blindly in World War II. Such was the price of peace in our time, I thought helplessly.

I hoped that future generations would understand what total war meant and strive mightily for peace.

The coast of Japan disappeared behind us as we headed home to Tinian. Behind us we left the wreckage of an empire. It was an empire that we, in a large part, had destroyed in a few months, almost as the result of strategic air power alone.

After two B-29s dropped supplies on a prisoner of war camp at Mukden, Manchuria, on September 2, the prisoners made a huge white sign of rocks that read "3885 kilocycles!" Radio operators in the Superfortresses tuned in on these kilocycles and established contact with a prisoner on the ground using a walkie-talkie. He identified himself as Lieutenant Matthews.

"Thank God you've come," he said. "We'll see you in the States by Christmas." He asked the crewmen to relay a message to the 20th Air Force that "Captain Campbell and nine members of his crew are in a prisoner of war camp at Mukden."

Another B-29 crew talked with the men later and learned there were 1,700 prisoners there, including 17 SOS cases.

Captain Sam A. Roberts, pilot of the B-29, said the prisoners appeared to have the run of the camp, which he said was "looking pretty good."

The B-29 suppliers watched as the prisoners danced and cheered as they gathered up the supplies.

The message from Campbell was sent to Guam, but never forwarded to the 462nd Group.

One hundred and fifty four camps were supplied by late August and September but the 20th Air Force paid a heavy price. Eight bombers were lost and 77 men died in operational accidents. These mercy missions proved more deadly than most combat missions.

General LeMay flew to an airfield near Yokohama to attend the surrender ceremony on board the battleship *Missouri* anchored off Yokohama. He was assigned a seat in one of the 200 automobiles the Japanese had been ordered to furnish for the Americans.

After they started driving for Yokohama, he was surprised to find at least half of the automobiles abandoned alongside the road. They were so decrepit that they could not make those few miles into town, although the Japanese assured the Americans that they were the best available.

He couldn't help but think about the mountains of supplies piled up on Guam and other Pacific islands awaiting an invasion that was no longer needed. To himself, he wondered how much money and resources the United States could have saved if it had recognized earlier that an invasion was not necessary because the Japanese could be defeated by sea and air power. These wrecks of automobiles epitomized for LeMay the fact that the Japanese had run out of everything.

LeMay stood on the deck of *Missouri* and stared at the Japanese delegation when it arrived at 8:56 A.M. on September 2. It was headed by Foreign Minister Mamour Shigemitsu and General Yoshijiro Umezu, Chief of the General Staff, who had been ordered by Emperor Hirohito to sign on behalf of the Imperial General Headquarters despite his bitter protests. He and Navy Chief of Staff Soemu Toyoda had argued unsuccessfully for one final battle to preserve the nation's honor. The eleven-man delegation included representatives from the Japanese Army, Navy, and Foreign Office.

LeMay noted the frigid atmosphere among the Allied leaders as the Japanese were piped on board. Shigemitsu, who had lost a leg to a terrorist's bomb in China, was in pain as he limped across the deck. It was obvious that the wooden stump that had replaced his leg fit poorly. To LeMay, Shigemitsu's helplessness seemed to symbolize his nation's dire straits. He was dressed formally in top hat, cutaway coat, and striped trousers. In contrast, LeMay noted Umezu strode on board with a blank stare, dressed in the live drab of a general officer with cavalry boots and sword.

The Japanese were arranged in three rows on *Missouri*'s deck facing a table covered by a green cloth. Military men from all nations at war with Japan stood across from it. The Americans wore khaki "suntan" uniforms without ties, in contrast to the other more formal attire. The British delegation wore shorts and white knee stockings, while the

Russians were dressed in red epauletted uniforms. Representatives from Australia, Canada, France, New Zealand, and the Netherlands were in more traditional uniforms.

General MacArthur had flown to Atsugi Airfield on August 29, and Admiral Nimitz arrived the next day. While the gathering awaited MacArthur's appearance, the Japanese tried to retain their dignity but they were obviously uncomfortable.

At 9 A.M. MacArthur came on deck followed by Nimitz and Halsey and strode to the table facing the Japanese. He picked up a piece of paper and, in an emotional voice, said, "We are gathered here, representatives of the major warring powers, to conclude a solemn agreement whereby peace may be restored. The issues, involving divergent ideas and ideologies, have been determined on the battlefields of the world and hence are not for our discussion or debate."

LeMay eyed the proceedings with excitement, fully appreciating the historic significance of the events unfolding before him.

MacArthur's emotion made his hands shake as he continued to read from his prepared text. "The terms and conditions upon which the surrender of the Japanese Imperial Force is here to be given and accepted are contained in the instrument of surrender now before you.

As Supreme Commander of the Allied Powers, it is my firm purpose, in the tradition of countries I represent, to proceed in the discharge of my responsibilities with justice and tolerance, while taking all necessary dispositions to insure that the terms of the surrender are fully, promptly, and faithfully complied with."

He stepped back and motioned for the Japanese to sign. Shigemitsu stumbled forward, his wooden leg almost tripping him while the wind whipped at his hat. He sat down, placed his silk hat on the table, and with trembling fingers removed his yellow gloves and placed them on top of his hat. He picked up a pen, but it remained poised uncertainly above the document.

MacArthur spoke sharply. "Sutherland! Show him where to sign." His Chief of Staff, Lieutenant Richard K. Sutherland, showed the embarrassed foreign minister where to sign, and then stepped back. Shigemitsu signed at 9:04 A.M.

General Umezu followed him to the table and scrawled his name underneath Shigemitsu's without an expression, the general marched stiffly back to his delegation, some of whom had tears in their eyes.

MacArthur stepped forward. "Will Generals Wainwright and Percival accompany me as I sign?"

They moved up behind him. They had recently been released from Japanese internment in Manchuria. Both were haggard and distraught after more than three years in Japanese prison camps.

MacArthur sat down to sign the surrender documents on behalf of all Allied powers. He used six pens, signing his name in segments, using a different pen for each. He gave the first to Wainwright, and the second to Percival. The third pen he later gave to West Point for the American archives, and the fifth was given to his aide, General Courtney Whitney. He finished his signature with a red-barreled pen that he placed in his shirt pocket to give later to his wife Jean and their son, Arthur in Manila.

Admiral Chester Nimitz signed for the United States, and Sir Bruce Fraser for Great Britain. Representatives of the other Allied nations completed the process with their signatures.

MacArthur went before the microphones for the last time. "It is my earnest hope — indeed the hope of all mankind — that from this solemn occasion a better world shall emerge out of the blood and carnage of the past; a world founded upon faith and understanding, a world dedicated to the dignity of man and the fulfillment of his most cherished wish for freedom, tolerance, and justice."

For the first time that morning the sun broke through as MacArthur said, "Let us pray that peace be now restored to the world and the God will preserve it always. These proceedings are closed."

Overhead 450 carrier planes and a large fleet of land based bombers swept majestically over *Missouri* in a triumphant climax to the end of the hostilities. Our group's Lieutenant Colonel Vaucher had been assigned to control the massive formation as it flew over *Missouri*. LeMay looked up in pride as tight formations of B-29 Superfortresses roared overhead, fully appreciating as no other man, how much they had done to bring about the events of this day.

Japan's top military leaders were willing to sacrifice everyone but themselves while they and the Emperor remained safely in a mountain sanctuary built to assure their survival. For months, top priority was given to the construction of eight miles of tunnels, 10 feet high, 13 to 23 feet wide, and cut from solid rock, 100 feet beneath the surface in the mountains near Matsushiro. Approximately 8,000 Koreans were assigned to the project. They suffered a high loss of life and countless injuries as they were urged to expedite the project.

The move to transfer Emperor Hirohito and the seat of government from Tokyo to this sanctuary was made in late July. The atomic bombing of Hiroshima and Nagasaki convinced the Emperor that the war should be ended despite protestations from some of Japan's military chiefs.

The idea behind the sanctuary was to assure the survival of the Emperor and Japan's military leaders until a peace agreement could be negotiated on more satisfactory terms than the allies had previously offered. It was apparent that there was little or no concern for the fate or well being of the Japanese people who were urged to die for their country.

Chapter 18

Mission Accomplished

LeMay entered his office on September 3, calling over his shoulder, "Tell Colonel Montgomery I want to see him right away."

He had flown back to Guam after the ceremony and he sat back in his chair with a sigh. He was close to the point of exhaustion. While he waited for Montgomery, he glanced through his mail. When Montgomery knocked, he called, "Come in."

In contrast, Montgomery was relaxed. "How'd the surrender ceremony go?"

"Impressive. In more ways than one." He motioned to Montgomery to sit. "Photographs of Tokyo's blackened ruins give only a small idea of what our bombing did to the city. We circled the city when we flew back." He slowly picked up his pipe and lit it. He grinned at Montgomery. "I'll cut down when I get home." He took a deep pug and exhaled the smoke in obvious pleasure. His body was tense and seemed to shrink as the full awfulness of what he had seen returned to him. His tenseness was reflected in his voice, which he had difficulty in controlling. "Tokyo is a dead city. A few people are visible on the streets, but there is an emptiness of almost complete ruin. Yokohama is no different."

"It must be an awful sight," Montgomery said.

"It is. You have to see it to fully appreciate what they have gone through. I'm surprised that the Japanese held on this long."

"It's regrettable that so many millions had to suffer the consequences of following their fanatical leaders. There's a lesson to be learned for future generations. I hope they take heed."

"This has been total war. It is estimated that half as many civilians died compared to those in military services."

"Any word on the B-29 prisoners?"

"Of the 2,400 crewmembers missing in action, a great many of those who bailed out over Japan was killed. B-29 fliers were singled out. If they fell into the hands of the civilians, they were often brutally murdered. Some were also killed by the military."

They remained silent for a moment. "What were you thinking when those formations of B-29s flew over *Missouri*?" Montgomery asked.

LeMay took so long to reply that Montgomery thought he had not heard him, but then he broke the silence in a quiet but firm voice. "Just an enormous feeling of pride." He knocked out his pipe in his ashtray. "How we ever managed to train tens of thousands of men who had hardly ever been in an airplane before the war, let alone to have flown one, and made them into the world's finest air force, staggers the imagination. I still don't believe it, but it happened."

"Thanks to professionals like yourself, and a few thousand others."

"Yes, you and I made a contribution because we were trained for this business. That still does not explain something that is inherently American; the will to achieve despite impossible odds."

Montgomery nodded. "I know what you mean. These young men — and most are in their early twenties — have performed miracles."

LeMay turned thoughtful and sat back in reflection. "I hate war. It's a stupid way to settle differences between nations. George Washington's advice that the United States should be prepared for war if it hoped to maintain the peace is the best advice he ever gave the American people. But we've never paid any attention to his words. We've never been prepared for any of the wars this nation has fought. As a result, we have suffered heavy casualties. From now on, particularly with the advent of the Atomic Age, everyone will be involved in modern war. World War II demonstrated how devastating and bloody such a war can be. I believe, as Washington said, that we should maintain our strength and make it too costly for any enemy to attack us."

"Hopefully, the American people have learned their lesson this time," Montgomery said.

LeMay didn't respond at first and Montgomery noted that he had become uncharacteristically tense. "Don't count on it," LeMay said. "But we live in an imperfect world and everybody doesn't believe that. Future wars may be difficult to avoid. But once civilian authorities in the United States government make the decision to use military force, the nation's armed forces should be permitted to hit with all their strength. Then, if we are successful, we'll win the war quickly and save American lives. If we go in timidly — too little, too late — the results will be disastrous."

LeMay's phone rang and he picked it up. A look of surprise came over his face. "Of course I can see him. Please ask him to come in." He turned to Montgomery with a look of incredulity, and some concern. "General Stilwell is coming in. He asked to see me. Wonder what he wants?" His tenseness increased to the point where he was almost jittery. "Probably going to chastise me for bombing Japan's cities. Some of these Army types seem to believe that it is dishonorable to bomb the enemy. As if there were anything honorable about war."

"I'll be back later," Montgomery said. "There are plans that need your approval for rotating crews back to the States."

LeMay nodded. He was still astonished — and increasingly apprehensive — because Stilwell had asked to see him. He stood up as Stilwell strode in with a big smile on his face and his right hand outstretched.

"I'm on my way home after attending the ceremony on board *Missouri*."

"Won't you sit down?" LeMay said.

"I can only stay for a minute, but I just had to see you before I boarded my plane for California."

LeMay looked at Stilwell in wonder and despite his visitor's warmth LeMay couldn't help but be nervous and somewhat stiff.

"I'm honored sir, that you should take the time to stop by my office."

"I just wanted to stop to tell you that, when I went through Yokohama for the ceremony, I realized for the first time what you were trying to tell me in the Chengtu Valley. I knew Yokohama well because I was a language student there when I was a second lieutenant. I remember its size and what it was like. When I saw what is there now — nothing but ashes and rubble — I understood what you were trying to tell me about strategic bombing."

LeMay looked at Stilwell with utter astonishment. For the first time in hours his body relaxed. As Stilwell waved goodbye, a broad smile of satisfaction wreathed LeMay's face and he sat back and lit his pipe with growing satisfaction.

For those of us on Tinian, Guam, and Saipan, sweating out missions had been hard enough during the war, but now the greatest sweat job of all faced us. We were impatiently awaiting our orders to go home.

Colonel Kalberer brought back good news after a personal visit to Tokyo. He reported that our first commander, Colonel Carmichael, had been found alive although he was a gaunt caricature of his former self, weighing only 140 pounds. Major Perry, former group navigator, and Major Mann, former wing bombardier, were alive but in poor physical condition.

I had been waiting for a consolidated report about our missions from the group statistician, Allan Parker. When it arrived I was astonished by the destruction that the 20th Air Force had caused. It was unbelievable! However, facts do not lie and they were presented before me in black and white. I brought the report back to my tent and studied it page by page.

The 20th Air Force had flown more than 100 million miles on 380 combat missions, released 91 percent of all bombs dropped on Japan's home islands for a total of 147,000 tons plus 6,000 tons of mines, or a count of 12,049. Nine times as many tons of bombs had been dropped on Germany with approximately the same total damage. In Japan, 40 percent of the built-up area of 66 principal cities, and 602 major war factories had been destroyed.

During the war there were 3,628 B-29s produced, 512 were lost overseas, and 576 crewmembers were killed. Our 58th Wing lost 125 B-29s, and our 462nd Group lost

38 Superfortresses. A normal group complement was 45 (180 for the wing) so these losses were heavy. But this was not the total picture. 2,406 men were listed as missing and presumed dead, and 433 were evacuated from prison camps at war's end. Training losses in the States were high, claiming another 260 B-29s.

Iwo Jima, taken at such high cost, was a safe haven for 2,396 emergency landings, including 524 B-29s who required major maintenance there. The P-51s stationed there and who had served as our escorts over Japan, lost 91 pilots.

The report stated that fire raids destroyed 2.3 million homes and 672,000 civilians were killed while another 476,000 were injured. In addition to those killed and injured, 8.5 million civilians were left homeless while 21 million were displaced. Japanese military deaths were estimated at 1.3 million men.

Our attacks against the aircraft industry were not evaluated until after the Strategic Bombing Survey completed its post-war assessment. They reported that 7,200 combat aircrafts were denied to the Japanese when their aircraft and engine factories lost 75 and 80 percent respectively of their production capacity. Approximately 83 percent of oil refinery production was destroyed. Crews reported that they destroyed 714 Japanese aircraft in combat but this figure was undoubtedly too high. The true figure will never be known.

Two days after the surrender ceremony, Prince Haukiku Higashi-Kune told the Japanese Diet that the general conditions of the country began to show marked signs of impoverishment and exhaustion. "So much so," he said, "that in the days just prior to the end of the war it seemed almost impossible to carry on modern warfare for any extended period of time."

"The production methods such as we had adopted before would shortly have to face insurmountable difficulties as a result of the destruction of transportation and communications facilities caused by air strikes. Our losses in naval and aerial strength were so enormous as to obstruct seriously the prosecution of the war. Moreover, various industries suffered directly from air raids which caused huge damage to plants and lowered the efficiency of the workmen."

He blamed air raids for the loss of railroad equipment, which created a tendency to lose unified control of the nation. "Despite the exertion of all possible efforts, the carrying capacity of railways would have had to be reduced to less than one half as compared to last year."

Prince Konoyo, who had helped to bring down the Tojo government in 1944, said, "Fundamentally the thing that brought about the determination to make peace was the prolonged bombing of the B-29s."

Premiere Suzuki was even more specific. "It seemed to me unavoidable that, in the long run, Japan would be almost destroyed by air attack so that merely on the basis of the B-29s alone, I was convinced that Japan should sue for peace."

I put down the report, and stared off to the west where the Pacific Ocean pounded against our rocky shoreline. I thought about those two atomic bombs that undoubtedly triggered an earlier end to the war, and I had no regrets about their use. But I could see in the future how they could be used, by Japanese militarists, to justify their surrender despite the fact that they had been soundly defeated before the first atomic bomb had dropped. Conventional bombing, I firmly believe, would have forced them to the same conclusion in a few weeks or a month at the most. But there was a danger that in the future years, many Japanese — particularly those in power — would become convinced that they were only defeated by an overwhelming power for which there was no defense; ignoring the fact that they had been decisively defeated on land, sea, and air throughout their vast empire.

General Arnold, in a statement after the ceremony, made it clear that in his opinion the atomic bombs did not bring about Japan's defeat, although they had created a situation in Japan where officials of the Japanese government could accept surrender. Arnold claimed that the 20th Air Force had been directed to defeat Japan, and make an invasion of the home islands unnecessary, and that this objective had been achieved.

Months later, when the Strategic Bombing Survey completed its work, they reported that Japan would have surrendered before the end of the year regardless of the atomic bomb and without an invasion. In all probability, the survey concluded, Japan would have surrendered by November 1.

It was disclosed by the report that the food situation in 1945 had become so desperate that Korean rice was loaded into 55-gallon containers and dropped into the Sea of Japan where, hopefully, the tides would drift it to the shores of Honshu. The Japanese told interrogators that if the war had continued for another year, seven million Japanese would have died of starvation. When this figure is compared with the actual civilian casualties it almost pales into insignificance.

It was clear to me that air power, as a primary war-winning force had come of age in 1945. Japan's ability to sustain her armed forces, particularly those abroad, were undermined by the war at sea. The flow of raw materials from Southeast Asia had been cut off early in the war, but the flow from China and Korea continued until the 12,000 mines dropped by Superfortresses eliminated Japan's last commercial contact with the outside world.

After putting the report aside, I hoped in my heart that people throughout the world would realize there was no longer any frontlines. We had engaged in total war that no longer discriminated between soldiers and women and children.

I had never hated the Japanese, but their brutality against helpless civilians and prisoners of war in China, Korea, Guam — where 684 Chamorros were executed — in every place that they occupied by military force, was incomprehensible to me. Most nations, including the United States, have been guilty of isolated acts of military atrocities, but only Germany and the Soviet Union were involved on the same scale as the Japanese. It must never be forgotten that Japan's atrocities were not committed by a few vicious leaders, but willingly and consciously by millions of Japanese soldiers who formed a cross section of their nation.

It took the Japanese government more than 50 years to reverse decades of denials that they had used thousands of "sex-slaves" during World War II. In mid-1993, a government spokesman finally admitted that thousands of unwilling Asian and European women were forced to become prostitutes. Many of these women who survived this enforced slavery, as "comfort women" for Japan's armed forces have long demanded an apology and compensation. A government spokesman finally apologized for the "immeasurable pain and incurable physical and psychological wounds inflicted upon these women." Nothing was said about compensation, nor did he acknowledge that these were war crimes. Japan only promised never to do it again. Survivors now live in Korea, China, Japan, Taiwan, the Philippines, Indochina, and the Netherlands.

The Korean Comfort Women Committee called the apology a "Whitewash," and demanded an accounting of the number of women involved. The committee claims that women were kidnapped and shipped to the front lines. Some were tortured with hot irons when they tried to escape. Many of these young women — some in their teens — were reportedly murdered or left to die when Japan's armed forces retreated.

The Japanese government has always maintained that it was not responsible for these acts of barbarism because the brothels were privately owned. But a Japanese scholar in the 1990s unearthed evidence that the military was involved. Government officials have consistently claimed that the compensatory claims were waived by the peace treaty that ended World War II, and by subsequent agreements. Perhaps so, but Japan has a moral obligation to make financial restitution to these women.

I went to war, as most Americans did, because the country had been attacked. There were no heroics involved. War is a dirty, brutish business and this one had not ended too soon for me.

The 20th Air Force had helped to win the greatest war in history. It was now up to the statesmen to win the peace or an even greater tragedy faced the world in the new age of atomic weapons.

Under normal conditions, a few weeks in a man's life are of little consequence but it had been a year and a half since we had left the United States, so the days dragged endlessly as we awaited our departure from Tinian.

Higher authorities grew concerned that the thousands of us, who were just waiting to go home, needed something to occupy our days. Major B. K. Thurston was assigned to fly a B-29 to the States in September to bring back athletic equipment on the theory that busy people stay out of mischief. They failed to understand that Tinian and the other islands, allowed for few opportunities. Authority was granted for crewmen who had completed their 35 missions to return to the States. There were 35 on board Thurston's plane — mostly pilots — who happily embarked with him. We were stunned a few days later to learn that Thurston's plane had taken off from Kwajalein and crashed into the ocean, killing all on board. The disaster shook us as nothing ever had before. It seemed so unfair that men who had endured so much should die on a routine flight home.

Vaucher, Buchta, and I went to Guam one day after word came from Johnny Campbell, that he and those of his crew, who had survived their bailout near Mukden, would like to see us before we flew home. It was a warm, tearful reunion that had us all emotionally aroused as they told their tales of incarceration in a filthy, unheated cell so narrow that they could not stretch out during their confinement. Johnny told us that they were given rice balls to eat three times a day, which would be rolled, across the floor of their cell through their own body wastes.

Before they were freed by Russian troops, their Japanese captors tried to make amends by giving them a party with the first decent food they had eaten during their incarceration, but it was too late for that. When the Russians occupied the camp they lined up the Japanese outside and handed a rifle to one of the former prisoners, indicating that he should use it on the Japanese guards. The Russians were contemptuous when not one American, despite their inhumane treatment, would commit the act of murder. The Russians had no such inhibitions.

After we received our orders to return to the United States, I cleaned out my desk. In one secret compartment I gathered up the bombing tables for chemical weapons. Not many people knew I had them but I had been given them in case the Japanese used chemical weapons against our bases in the Marianas, which they had privately threatened to do. Through third parties, not involved in the war, the Japanese had bluntly been informed that if they ever dropped gas bombs on us, we would retaliate immediately. They had used chemical weapons in China prior to American's entry into the war, and we knew that they had the capability. All of us had been indoctrinated in recognizing deadly chemicals and gas masks were always at hand even when we slept. The bombing tables covered the old familiar gases of World War I, such as mustard gas and phosgene, plus some of the newer ones. I shuddered just looking at these tables, thankful that I had never had to use them. I returned them to the ordnance section with relief. I wondered what would happen to the bombs in storage — there were thousands of them — after we left. I was glad that I didn't have that responsibility. (Years later I learned that their disposal became a problem. They were still stacked in the Marianas, and once the cases started to disintegrate, it became imperative to dispose of them. One suggestion was to drop them into the ocean near the islands where the Pacific drops off to one of its deepest depths. A scientist pointed out that the cases would rupture possibly releasing enormous gas bubbles to the surface and into the atmosphere. So this possibility was rejected. They were finally destroyed in a specially constructed incinerator ship where the gases could be neutralized without harm to the atmosphere.

We were given orders to fly home as a group on October 4. Even the elements were still against us because a hurricane swept the islands, sending 40-foot waves over the shoreline during the night. Our tent, and everything except the wooden mess hall, was swept away by huge gusts of wind that reached a velocity of 175 miles an hour, while driving sheets of rain pelted us. It was a wild melee of flying debris that frequently caused injuries. We had left a half full bottle of whiskey by the ridgepole and incredibly it had survived the onslaught. It didn't last long that morning, but it temporarily boosted our spirits as we huddled cold and wet in the mess hall. Our greatest fear was that our B-29s on the flight line would be damaged. But they were securely tied down in time, and were still in flyable condition when the storm subsided the following day.

It was with a vast relief that we took off October 6 for the long flight back to the States via Kwajalein and Hawaii. Vaucher was our pilot and Buchta and I agreed to share the navigation responsibilities. He agreed to chart our course to Kwajalein while I would take over the navigator's job from there to Hawaii.

It was an uneventful flight until we approached Hickam Field in Hawaii. Then, as Vaucher entered the prescribed pattern I looked down in horror as another B-29 swept beneath us at the wrong heading, missing us by only a few feet. I spotted the tail markings.

"Damn!" I yelled. "That was Kalberer's plane."

It was a badly shaken crew who landed smoothly at Hickam, where we were peremptorily ordered out of our aircraft without our luggage so that the airplane could be searched for drugs. Although we realized that drugs had long been smuggled to the mainland from Asia, their actions caused tempers to rise. No drugs were found, and we were trucked to a barrack for the night.

That night, after our first meal in a civilized American restaurant in 18 months, Cecil Durbin showed us Honolulu. He had served at Hickam before the war, and had been on the field when it was attacked December 7, 1941. He recalled his experience with a wry sense of humor. "I was playing tennis when the first bombs began to fall. I raced toward the field, and when a Japanese bomber came over, I dived under the nearest place that seemed to offer shelter. When the bomber departed I learned to my horror that I was under a gasoline refueling truck!"

The beach at Waikiki, with its palms and glistening sands, and a bright moon silvering the gently rolling waves, seemed so unreal that it was hard to believe. Only the large number of men in uniform gave any indication that a long and savage war had just ended. We were shocked by the sudden change, and became silent. It dawned on us that we who had fought in the world's war theaters were suddenly strangers returning home with experiences fundamentally different from those who had remained behind. It was an unsettling feeling and one we were not sure we knew how to handle.

By sea or air the first sight of the Golden Gate bridge at San Francisco is a phenomenal experience, and its magnificent arches beckoned with a positive reminder that at last we were home.

We landed at Mather Field near Sacramento and began the process of going our separate ways. At the time Vaucher planned to remain in the post-war Air Force — a decision he later changed — while I was destined for separation to return to civilian life. I was ordered to nearby McClelland Field for separation along with Buchta and several others.

I walked up to Vaucher and bid him goodbye. We had gone through so much together, and in the past, there had never been a problem of communication. But now, wondering whether we would ever see one another again, we shook hands, uttered some inconsequential words, and parted. This scene was repeated between others with whom I had shared so many anxious days. We had lived and worked closely for almost two and a half years, and now we parted with typical masculine reticence. I knew I would never see most of them again. This saddened me but it proved to be all too true. Except for Vaucher and Loberg and a few of the original crewmembers with whom I had flown in combat, we never saw one another again.

During processing at McClellan, my right leg became swollen, and I hobbled around with difficulty. I finally went to the base hospital where a doctor took one look at the blue-black streaks and consigned me to the hospital. I was furious, because I wanted to go home.

He was just as mad. "Major, you have blood poisoning in that leg. Unless it is arrested by penicillin, you'll lose it!"

I calmed down. The culprit, it was clear from what the doctor said, were the new socks I had bought at Hickam Field. I had a severe case of athlete's foot — an open sore the size of a silver dollar — and the unwashed new socks had caused an infection.

Buchta and I planned a final get together in Kansas City before we went home, but now I could not take part. He came to say goodbye as I lay on my hospital bed, and his chiding remarks died on his lips when he saw the acute state of depression I was in.

Epilogue

After five days in the hospital I was on a train heading home. I bought several newspapers and perused them eagerly, but there were several stories that raised my blood pressure. The sudden end of the war was largely attributed to the atomic bombs, and almost nothing had been written about the activities of the 20th Air Force.

One story told how Secretary of War, Stimson had confided in General Dwight D. Eisenhower about the atomic bomb after its successful test at Alamogordo, New Mexico. Stimson was reported to have been upset by the general's reaction, because Eisenhower said the news depressed him. When his opinion was sought about its use, Eisenhower had said that he was against it on two counts. "First," he said, "the Japanese are ready to surrender and thought it was unnecessary to hit them with that awful thing. Second, he hated to see the United States be 'the first to use such a weapon.'"

Stimson, who had fought for years to continue development of the atomic bomb, was reported to be furious. Eisenhower understood his feelings after his long support of the project.

Eisenhower was correct about Japan's condition. She was a defeated nation with her mighty navy destroyed by the United States Navy and the ships of America's allies in the Pacific. Her merchant ships were either sunk or confined to harbors after extensive mining around her home islands, and most of her cities and factories were in ruins following massive bombing attacks by B-29s of the 20th Air Force. By August 1, her destruction was almost total as B-29s roamed at will over her main islands.

The development of the atomic bomb was an unmatched scientific achievement, but some scientists were appalled by its inherent potential for abuse by any nation in possession of such a powerful weapon. Others were against atomic bombs for moral reasons. But they overlooked the most important point. This was a historic breakthrough that would have come sooner or later because scientists in several nations were exploring the development of atomic weapons. As President Truman said, "We won the race of discovery against the Germans."

If all people could have seen what I have seen from my bombardier's seat — the utter horror of watching a great nation disintegrate before my eyes — I am sure that the world today would be a more peaceful place for all mankind.

Now that the atomic "genie" has been released, all the scientists in the world cannot put it back in the bottle. Therefore, it is now imperative that the world's statesmen resolve issues dividing their nations without resort to war. I firmly believe that then the war just ended — tragic as it had been — would be insignificant compared to a nuclear holocaust that could devastate vast areas of the earth and return mankind to the Stone Age. All that has occurred since 1945 only serves to reinforce my earlier views.

I had been given a unique preview of what such a world would look like in my 30 missions over Japan. That nation had experienced a hell on earth that could be duplicated throughout most of the civilized world in the event of another global war with nuclear weapons. It is a prospect almost too horrible to contemplate, but one that must be faced if it is to be avoided.

Since the end of World War II the possibility of a global nuclear war has horrified millions of people throughout the world, and rightly so. But the perspective President Truman faced in 1945 was far different. He said then, and his words are still valid, "I regarded the bomb as a military weapon and never had any doubt but that it would be used."

It must not be forgotten that the attack on Tokyo the night of March 9, 1945, killed more people than either the Hiroshima or Nagasaki atomic bombs.

Attitudes in Japan about responsibility for World War II may hopefully be undergoing a change. Comments made by Emperor Hirohito's younger brother Prince Mikasa in 1944, suppressed for 50 years by Japanese Army officials, were finally released July 6, 1994. Fifty years before, he spoke to Japanese troops in China and condemned their atrocities and Army policies in general. The 78-year-old prince granted an interview with the *Yomiuri Shimbum* in which he acknowledged that he had spoken out but that copies of his speech were destroyed by military authorities. One copy survived and was discovered in the Library of Parliament by a Kobe university professor.

Prince Mikasa said he had written and delivered the speech "out of a desperate desire to bring the war to a close." At the time he was a staff officer assigned to Japanese expeditionary forces in the eastern Chinese city of Nanking (Nanjing). He told the newspaper that he was revolted when he discovered that military officers were using Chinese prisoners of war for bayonet practice to instill "guts" in the Japanese soldiers. He said he learned that Japanese soldiers gassed and shot Chinese soldiers after tying them to posts. Prince Mikasa declared that he was shocked by these horrible scenes that he called "massacres." He said military officers were acting against the Emperor's strong desire for peace, although he admitted that he only gave "bits and pieces" of the story to his brother, the Emperor.

He said his remarks were considered dangerous and that the army demanded that all copies be destroyed. Prince Mikasa said he was spared charges of treason because he was a member of the royal family.

The prince's comments take on special significance because the Japanese military has long claimed that their behavior was sanctioned in the name of the Emperor.

The present Emperor, Akihito, has expressed "deep sorrow" for the "severe suffering" the Japanese inflicted upon the Chinese during the war. Japan will never resolve its moral dilemma about the war until its rulers stop ignoring facts that have long been a matter of record in the western world. Prince Mikasa did not evade the issue, saying, "if you kill prisoners in an atrocious manner, that is a massacre." There is no doubt that Japanese soldiers committed many barbarous acts such as the slaughter of possibly 300,000 Chinese men, women, and children during the "Rape of Nanking." Regrettably this is just one of many substantiated cases that lies heavily on the conscience of the Japanese people. Their acts were similar to those the Germans inflicted upon six million Jews in their notorious death camps. The unnecessary brutality is the same in both cases, although the methods to accomplish it were different.

Despite fears that those exposed to heavy doses of radiation during the bombing of Hiroshima and Nagasaki would pass on genetic defects to their children, this has not proven to be the case. Comprehensive studies in Japan since the war indicate that survivors had a 12 percent additional risk of cancer than those who were not exposed. Their children, however, are at no greater risk than healthy individuals. For example, the number of stillbirths among them is approximately the same as in the general population.

The dangers of radiation sickness should not be discounted, but most Japanese died of massive burns and injuries due to explosions whether they were subjected to atomic bombing or other types of bombs.

Some misguided Americans today believe that Japan was a victim of World War II instead of an aggressor. The atomic bombing of Hiroshima and Nagasaki had done much to foster such an incredibly naive belief. The facts deny such a characterization. Unfortunately, such beliefs play into the hands of older Japanese who have never come to terms with their defeat. It is to be hoped that the people of Japan born after the war will be more inclined to seek the truth.

The End.

Bibliography

Arnold, H. H. *Global Missions.* New York: Harper & Bros., 1949.

Baxter, James Phinney, III. *Scientists Against Time.* Boston: Little, Brown and Company, 1945.

Collision, Thomas. *The Superfortress is Born.* New York: Duell, Sloan and Pierce, 1945.

Craven, W. F., and Cate, J. L. *The Army Air Forces in World War II, Vol. 5, The Pacific—Matterhorn to Nagasaki.* Chicago: University of Chicago Press, 1945.

Grew, Joseph. *Turbulent Era: A Diplomatic Record of Forty Years, 1904–1945, Volume I and II.* Edited by Walter Johnson. Boston: Houghton Mifflin, 1952.

Hansell, Major General (Retired), Haywood S. *The Air Plan That Defeated Hitler.* Atlanta: Higgins-McArthur Longino and Porter, Inc., 1972.

MacArthur, Douglas. *Reminiscences.* New York: McGraw-Hill, 1964.

Mansfield, Harold. *Vision—A Saga of the Sky.* New York: Duell, Sloan and Pierce, 1956.

Marshall, General of the Army, George C., Arnold, General of the Army, H. H., and King, Fleet Admiral, Ernest J. *War Reports.* Philadelphia and New York: J. B. Lippincott, 1947.

Morrison, Wilbur H. *Hellbirds: The Story of the B-29s in Combat.* New York: Duell, Sloan and Pearce, 1960.

—— *The Incredible 305th: The "Can Do" Bombers of World War II.* New York: Duell, Sloan and Pearce, 1962.

—— *Wings Over the Seven Seas: U.S. Naval Aviation's Fight for Survival.* Cranbury, New Jersey: A. S. Barnes, 1974.

—— *Above and Beyond: 1941–1945.* New York: St. Martin's, 1983.

Pogue, Forrest C. *Organizer of Victory. 1943–1945, George C. Marshall.* New York: The Viking Press, 1973.

Potter, E. B. *Nimitz.* Annapolis, Maryland: Naval Institute Press, 1976.

Rhodes, Richard. *The Making of the Atomic Bomb.* New York: Simon and Schuster, 1986.

Sallagar, F. M. *Lessons From an Aerial Mining Campaign.* Rand Corporation Report No. R-1322PR, Santa Monica, California: 1974.

Smith, Robert R. *Command Decisions.* New York: Harcourt, Brace and Company, 1959.

Sallagar, F. M. *Lessons From an Aerial Mining Campaign.* Rand Corporation Report No. R-1322PR, Santa Monica, California: 1974.

Truman, President Harry S. *Years of Decision.* New York: Doubleday & Company. 1955.

Truman, Margaret. *Harry S. Truman.* New York: William Morrow, 1972.

United States Strategic Bombing Survey, U.S. Government Printing Office. Washington, D.C.: 1946–1947.

WELCOME TO
HELLGATE PRESS

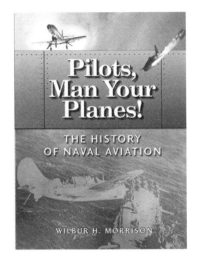

PILOTS, MAN YOUR PLANES!
A History of Naval Aviation
by Wilbur H. Morrison

An account of naval aviation from Kitty Hawk to the Gulf War, *Pilots, Man Your Planes!* tells the story of naval air growth from a time when planes were launched from battleships to the major strategic element of naval warfare it is today. This book is filled with rare photographs, detailed maps, and accurate accounts that can be found nowhere else. Ideal for anyone interested in aviation.

ISBN: 1-55571-466-8   474 pages, Hardcover $33.95

LOST BLACK SHEEP
The Story of the Unaccounted Member of the Black Sheep Squadron
Robert T. Reed

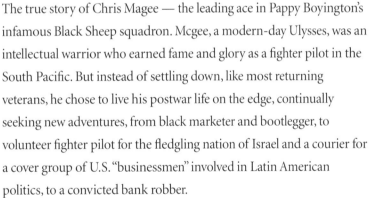

The true story of Chris Magee — the leading ace in Pappy Boyington's infamous Black Sheep squadron. Mcgee, a modern-day Ulysses, was an intellectual warrior who earned fame and glory as a fighter pilot in the South Pacific. But instead of settling down, like most returning veterans, he chose to live his postwar life on the edge, continually seeking new adventures, from black marketer and bootlegger, to volunteer fighter pilot for the fledgling nation of Israel and a courier for a cover group of U.S. "businessmen" involved in Latin American politics, to a convicted bank robber.

ISBN 1-55571-549-4   230 pages, Hardcover $24.95

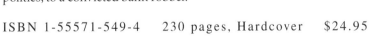

TO ORDER OR FOR MORE INFORMATION
1-800-228-2275 (*telephone*)
info@psi-research.com (*email*)
www.psi-research.com (*Website*)

A DYING BREED
The Courage of the Mighty Eighth Air Force
by Neal B. Dillon

"… the true story of a WWII air combat crew's amazing courage, touching camaraderie, uplifting faith and indomitable spirit … I applaud *A Dying Breed* for preserving the lore. What had to be told has now been told."

– Lt. Gen. Stephen B. Croker, USAF, retired
Former Commander of the Eighth Air Force

"Neal Dillon is a brilliant writer who puts you into that sturdy B-17 at 28,000 feet and takes you where the flak is intense and seventy-five Luftwaffe fighter aircraft are attacking from all directions. Even before you finish reading, you will be recommending it to your friends and family."

– Major General Perry M. Smith, USAF, retired
Author, *A Hero Among Heroes* and *Rules and Tools for Leaders*

ISBN: 1-55571-529-X   225 pages, Paperback $15.95

MY CARRIER WAR
A Naval Aviator in WWII
by Norman Berg

From his days as a Naval aviation cadet learning his trade aboard the "Yellow Peril" biplane trainers in 1942, to his first bombing runs on Guadalcanal, to life aboard an aircraft carrier in the South Pacific, Norman Berg offers a fast-paced narrative filled with humor and meticulous attention to detail. Much more than a simple WWII memoir, this story goes beyond the action of battle to explore one young, wartime couple's struggle to balance love, duty, and their commitment to each other.

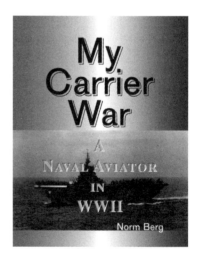

ISBN 1-55571-619-9   250 pages, Paperback $17.95